Beyond Domestication in Prehistoric Europe

Investigations in Subsistence Archaeology
and Social Complexity

Eric Higgs (1908–1976)

Beyond Domestication in Prehistoric Europe

Investigations in Subsistence Archaeology and Social Complexity

EDITED BY

GRAEME BARKER

Department of Archaeology and Prehistory
Sheffield University
Sheffield
 and
British School at Rome

CLIVE GAMBLE

Department of Archaeology
Southampton University
Southampton

1985

ACADEMIC PRESS

(Harcourt Brace Jovanovich, Publishers)

London   Orlando   San Diego   New York
Toronto   Montreal   Sydney   Tokyo

This is a volume in *Studies in Archaeology*

A complete list of titles in this series appears at the end of this volume.

ACADEMIC PRESS INC. (LONDON) LTD.
24–28 Oval Road
LONDON NW1 7DX

United States Edition published by
ACADEMIC PRESS, INC.
Orlando, Florida 32887

LIBRARY OF CONGRESS CATALOGING IN PUBLICATION DATA

Main entry under title:

Beyond domestication in prehistoric Europe.

Includes index.
1. Economics, Prehistoric—Europe—Addresses,
essays, lectures.   2. Agriculture, Prehistoric—
Europe—Addresses, essays, lectures.   3. Archaeology—
Methodology—Addresses, essays, lectures.   4. Europe—
Antiquities—Addresses, essays, lectures.   I. Barker,
Graeme.   II. Gamble, Clive.
GN799.E4B49   1985   930.1'028   84-24498
ISBN 0-12-078840-3 (alk. paper)

PRINTED IN THE UNITED STATES OF AMERICA

85 86 87 88   9 8 7 6 5 4 3 2 1

This volume is dedicated to the memory of
ERIC HIGGS

An unintentioned but quite uncanny likeness of Eric Higgs, from Brian Wild-smith's edition of the Aesop fable The Rich Man and the Shoemaker. *(Re-produced by kind permission of Oxford University Press)*

Contents

1   **Beyond Domestication: A Strategy for Investigating the Process and Consequence of Social Complexity**

Graeme Barker and Clive Gamble

2   **Patterns in Faunal Assemblage Variability**

J. M. Maltby

7   Regional Survey and Settlement Trends: Studies from Prehistoric France

Nigel Mills

8   Social Factors and Economic Change in Balearic Prehistory, 3000–1000 b.c.

James Lewthwaite

9   Subsistence and Settlement in Northern Temperate Europe in the First Millennium A.D.

Klavs Randsborg

List of Figures

List of Tables

Contributors

Numbers in parentheses indicate the pages on which the authors' contributions begin.

Graeme Barker[1] (1), Department of Archaeology and Prehistory, Sheffield University, Sheffield S10 2TN, England

Roger Cribb (75), Department of Anthropology and Sociology, University of Queensland, St. Lucia, Queensland 4067, Australia

Andrew Fleming (129), Department of Archaeology and Prehistory, Sheffield University, Sheffield S10 2TN, England

Clive Gamble (1), Department of Archaeology, Southampton University, Southampton S09 5NH, England

Martin Jones (107), Department of Archaeology, Durham University, 46 Saddler Street, Durham DH1 3NU, England

James Lewthwaite (205), Undergraduate School of Studies in Archaeological Sciences, University of Bradford, Bradford BD7 1DP, England

J. M. Maltby (33), Department of Archaeology, Southampton University, Southampton S09 5NH, England

Nigel Mills (181), Department of Archaeology and Prehistory, Sheffield University, Sheffield S10 2TN, England

Klavs Randsborg (233), Institute of Prehistoric Archaeology, University of Copenhagen, Vandkunsten 5, DK-1467 Copenhagen K, Denmark

Marek Zvelebil (147), Department of Archaeology and Prehistory, Sheffield University, Sheffield S10 2TN, England

[1] Present address: British School at Rome, Via Gramsci 61, 00197 Rome, Italy.

Preface

The development of subsistence theories and techniques in prehistoric archaeology has been primarily in the context of studying the earlier periods of prehistory (up to the first farmers), which are characterised by societies regarded rightly or wrongly as more or less self-sufficient in their food base and certainly less complex than the hierarchical societies of later prehistory. Our concern in this book is to address the question whether this kind of archaeology—such as the study of animal bones, plant remains, and site catchments—is relevant to the study of complex societies in prehistory (that is, societies without documentary evidence with which theories of economic complexity can be tested). We find that the answer is emphatically yes, but only if we integrate this approach properly with other studies of the archaeological record and also face up to major problems in the theory and practice of subsistence archaeology. Whilst the approach has often been termed *palaeoeconomy* or *economic archaeology,* our starting point is to recognise that subsistence and economy are not the same: *subsistence* refers to what people live on, whereas *economy* deals with the management and mobilisation of resources. 'Subsistence data', such as bones and grains, can be used to study both.

Following our introductory statement (Chapter 1), Chapters 2–5 deal with the methodological advances that are necessary for the proper study of subsistence and economy using these and related data. Chapters 6–9 present case studies, both of selected regions (and a regional approach has to be the framework for any realistic enquiry into prehistoric economy), integrating a variety of subsistence and nonsubsistence data in a consideration of long-term trends in resource exploitation, and of the models available to explain them. These case studies are drawn from a transect of European environments: Mediterranean island, littoral, temperate forest, and boreal. At the same time, however, a strict dichotomy is deliberately not made between discussions of theory and method and discussions of their application. What links all the contributions is a concern with the complexity of the database available to us, the need for theories and methods appropriate to such data, and the potential impact on prehistoric archaeology as a whole once such an approach becomes commonplace. As we conclude in our first chapter, "[Subsistence] data, so often ignored or poorly used in past studies, have the capability to be the critical foundation of an integrated archaeological approach to the investigation of social and economic complexity in the future."

Dates in calendar years are indicated by b.c. and a.d., while uncalibrated radiocarbon dates are indicated by b.c.

Individual acknowledgements are given at the end of the chapters, and specific acknowledgements for illustrations are given in the captions. However, the editors would like to make two principal acknowledgements: first, to Barry Vincent for preparing all the line drawings and, second, to our contributors for their patience and good humour during the process of editing.

Finally, both of us take great pleasure in dedicating this book to the memory of Eric Higgs, our mentor as undergraduates and Ph.D. students at Cambridge. As director of the British Academy Major Research Project on the Early History of Agriculture (from 1968 until his death in 1976), he made a profound contribution to the development of subsistence studies in prehistory, confronting (and often confounding) the rest of the archaeological world with his insistence on their centrality for saying anything that really mattered about the past. As a teacher he was astonishingly gifted, at once inspiring and maddening, but always committed above all to make his students think, and expecting from them his own unswerving commitment to his kind of archaeology. His personal legacy is an archaeological generation from Cambridge now scattered all over the globe, all armed with outrageous 'travellers' tales' from fieldwork with him and a string of impersonations of his delphic mannerisms and utterances. The publication in 1982 of the third and final volume of his project (*Early European Agriculture*, edited by M. R. Jarman, G. N. Bailey, and H. N. Jarman) was in one sense a fitting memorial to him, as it represents very much the kind of book he would have written at the time of his death. We hope there is room for another, though it is very difficult: addressing issues of current relevance about later prehistory that Eric either never did, or did only half-heartedly and with none of the impact he had on earlier prehistory. The editors certainly have a profound debt of gratitude to his teachings; he also taught several of the other contributors, and all of them have been greatly affected by the direct or indirect stimulus he gave to their research. Apart from our frontispiece portrait of him, we also include opposite our contents page a drawing from a children's book that, quite by chance, captures much of Eric's presence exactly: sitting in his dark and subterranean study at home in Cambridge, casting a quizzical and no doubt jaundiced eye on our efforts on his behalf. *Beyond Domestication in Prehistoric Europe* could not have happened without him, and it is dedicated to his memory with great affection.

1

Beyond Domestication: A Strategy for Investigating the Process and Consequence of Social Complexity

GRAEME BARKER

CLIVE GAMBLE

Living conditions are among the consequences of domestication, not the mark of it.

Pierre Ducos 1978

Introduction

It is an archaeological truism that the Neolithic revolution—whatever its precise definition—formed a great watershed in the organisation of Old World societies, with food production and village life being the two critical advances in the journey from Palaeolithic hunting and gathering to late prehistoric statehood. As a consequence, the investigation of the beginnings of agriculture in the Near East and Europe has for 30 years been a major focus of activity for archaeologists and natural scientists interested in the subsistence data of the archaeological record, such as the animal bones and plant remains that make up the food refuse of ancient settlements. Inevitably, far less attention has been paid to the study of the production base upon which subsequent developments in prehistoric agriculture were built, yet there has been a growing realisation that the plants and animals of the farmyard community are likely to have been critical resources in the construction, transformation, and reproduction of the social formations and

BEYOND DOMESTICATION
IN PREHISTORIC EUROPE

1

institutions of later prehistory (Barker in press a; Gamble 1982; Gilman 1981; Renfrew 1972; Renfrew and Shennan 1982; Sheridan and Bailey 1981). Except for one or two societies such as those of the Aegean Bronze Age, we cannot call upon archival or documentary evidence to test theories of economic complexity; rather, we must rely wholly on archaeological techniques. The purpose of this book is to investigate how subsistence theories and techniques that were developed primarily for the earlier periods of prehistory, up to the first farmers, can be applied to more complex societies in later prehistoric Europe.

Most subsistence studies in prehistoric archaeology have been associated with a relatively restricted range of questions and problems: diet, crop and animal management strategies, butchery systems, and, more recently, disposal patterns. The data consist of animal bones and plant remains, items of subsistence technology, information on settlement locations and distributions, the battery of environmental techniques for reconstructing land use and potential at a variety of spatial scales, and, occasionally, landscape features such as field systems. Because research development has generally depended on input from the natural rather than the social sciences, Clark (1972) proposes the term *bioarchaeology* for this kind of enquiry.

Although pioneering work in archaeozoology (the study of animal bones) and archaeobotany (the study of plant remains) began in the last century, for example with analyses of the food residues of alpine lake villages, the major stimulus in the emergence of these disciplines has been the postwar investigation of the origins of farming and of domestic species. Archaeozoologists and archaeobotanists were key members of the international teams that excavated a series of early agricultural settlements in the Near East and southeastern Europe, the predicted 'hearths of domestication' on the basis of the modern distribution of wild species of cereals, sheep, and goats (Braidwood and Howe 1960; Hole and Flannery 1967; Hole et al. 1969; J. Renfrew 1973; Zohary 1969). However, the problem of recognising domestication in bones and grains has proved far more intractable than suspected at the time of the main excavation projects in the 1950s and 1960s. For example, there is little convincing evidence that the zoologist can distinguish from faunal residues alone either feral, tamed, domestic, or wild representatives of the same species, despite persistent and increasingly ingenious attempts to find precise criteria (Drew et al. 1971; *Masca Newsletter* 1970, 1973; McConnell and Foreman 1971; Østergård 1980; Watson 1975; Zeder 1978). The cereals present comparable difficulties (H. N. Jarman 1972).

This same point was implicit in a reconsideration of the likely process of domestication that stressed the behavioural relations between people and animals rather than the osteological differences in the animals (Higgs and Jarman 1969). More recently, these associations have been explicitly recast as part of the social relations of production, with concepts of ownership, inheritance, and protection seen as the critical features distinguishing between opposed categories of animal management (Ingold 1980). Ducos (1978:54) states the problem very clearly: "All those features which distinguish the domestic animal from the wild one (whether biological or behavioural) stem not from the evolutionary dynamics of the animal but from those of human society. Therefore, that which is characteristic of domestication must be defined with reference to human society." Thus the debate on domestication and the origins of agriculture has moved from the realm of the natural sciences to that of archaeology, as the discipline concerned with questions of long-term change in human society. Further progress will depend on the full integration of the study of biological data with that of all the other components of the archaeological record.

Subsistence studies in Europe have been shaped fundamentally by Grahame Clark's remarkable synthesis, *Prehistoric Europe: The Economic Basis* (1952). In his preface, Clark invited a broad spectrum of academic interests to explore this 'great new field of knowledge', which he approached from the perspective of the natural scientist and historian (1952:vii). His material was organised into several themes (hunting and gathering, farming, houses and settlement, technology, travel, and transport), with a timescale from the end of the last ice age to the threshold of urban civilisation. The economic behaviour of prehistoric man was assessed against an ecological background (the vegetational zones of contemporary Europe), an approach that was very much at variance with the cultural–historical goals of many of his contemporaries but that Clark had already introduced in the first edition of *Archaeology and Society* (1939). A distinction was drawn between the *biome,* or ecosystem, which embraced the whole complex of living organisms, and the *habitat,* which described the critical factors of soil and climate. Interacting between these two environmental aspects were some 13 cultural aspects ranging from science and cosmology to shelter and clothing (Clark 1957:Figure 25). We would probably now refer to these as a set of interlocking subsystems. Vocabularies have changed, but not the model:

> In interpreting the evidence surviving from prehistoric societies, it is useful to construct a model of the various aspects of social life, show how these are interrelated, and consider how a study of each may contribute to an understanding of the whole. (Clark 1957:174)

> A human society is conveniently regarded as a system, whose components are the human individuals within that society, the artefacts which they use, and those elements of the environment with which the men and artefacts interact. (Renfrew 1977:108)

The growth of the palaeoeconomy school some 20 years after the economic basis had been laid provided further theoretical input to Clark's approach (Davidson 1981; Harris 1977). The new approach stemmed from the work of Eric Higgs and the associated staff and postgraduates at Cambridge, where Higgs directed the British Academy Major Research Project on the Early History of Agriculture from 1968 until his death in 1976 (Higgs 1972, 1975; Jarman et al. 1982). In this approach, the study of subsistence was equated with the study of economy. As a result of the "commitment of palaeoeconomy to the search for trends of long-term significance" (Higgs 1975:4), subsistence studies were used to investigate the interplay between population and resources. It was proposed that the residues that had accumulated on an archaeological site could be analysed in terms of the catchments from which they were derived. In this way it was hoped that an interpretative link between archaeological *contents* and environmental *context* could be established as a step towards unlocking the processes involved in subsistence decisions.

Management leading to equilibrium formed the cornerstone behind the working definition of economy (Higgs 1975:4). An efficient solution was judged in terms of conserving calories and reducing effort. Hence, optimising strategies were invariably preferred: The best soils would be settled first, populations would be maintained at the highest safe levels (M. R. Jarman 1972:140), and the best mix of animal species would be kept to maximise the available grazing resources. Contradictory behaviour could be put to one side as the idiosyncracies of the short term, contrasting with the economic imperatives of long-term processes—"the constraints, rather than . . . the noise of choice which tends in any case to operate upon the short term trivia, on the economic fat rather than on the basic necessities" (Higgs 1975:5).

Palaeoeconomic analysis came to consist of discovering the solutions to problems caused by changes in the two variables of population and resources, an approach that the editors of this volume have followed in attempts to explain patterns in archaeological materials from Palaeolithic and other early prehistoric periods (Barker 1975; Gamble 1978a). Any critique of this approach is probably best left to those who did not share the same paradigmatic orbit and the same remarkable teacher, but with hindsight it is clear that much palaeoeconomic theory was in reality the application of post hoc accommodative models (Binford 1981). Patterns were observed in subsistence data (for the most part greatly neglected hitherto), optimiser models arranged alongside those patterns, and explanation claimed (Jarman et al. 1982). However, the positive contributions of palaeoeconomy that we would like to stress, and that have shaped the production of this book, consist above all of its insistence on a regional approach to the analysis of past human behaviour, its commitment to a case-study approach analysing changes in common adaptive processes, and its demonstration that biological data potentially provide a powerful means for organising, integrating, and understanding a great amount of archaeological material.

The main reason for planning this volume was our concern at the apparent failure of the palaeoeconomic approach to say anything of *economic* interest about later prehistory. With the development of ranking and state formation in prehistoric Europe, there is still an undoubted interest in questions about subsistence using palaeobiological data. Yet the simple identification of crop and animal species at late prehistoric sites—still a depressingly common level of 'subsistence analysis'—must provoke an entirely justified reaction in the disinterested observer: ''So they ate bread and meat; now tell me something I didn't know already''. Are the assumptions, models, and techniques of analysis pioneered by the palaeoeconomic approach better suited after all to the investigation of only those prehistoric societies that, we believe, lay beneath a critical threshold of social complexity? In many parts of Europe this threshold would have to coincide with the Late Neolithic and Early Bronze Age, and with the appearance of differentiated burials, monuments acting as a collective ideological focus, and societies that were quite clearly ranked (Champion et al. 1984).

We take the view that subsistence techniques can in fact be applied successfully and fruitfully to such societies, but only if we face up to major problems of theory, methodology, and explanation. Concepts of consumption, production, labour organisation, and so on have to be very different from those used in the past for subsistence studies of earlier prehistory. In turn, more complex theories demand changes in methodology, with analysis invariably required beyond the level of the single site. However, it is clearly undesirable to subscribe to the view that a completely different set of models is required on either side of the 'Neolithic divide' (e.g., Dennell 1983), with the ecological archaeology of the hunters and earliest farmers retreating before the social archaeology of later prehistory. While the 'isms' continue to clash, the investigation of a seamless historical process is the ultimate casualty. We would rather take the view that neither approach is exclusive to any particular period or database. Together, they provide alternative ways of lifting the lid on Pandora's box to gain a proper understanding of complete social and economic systems in antiquity.

Our starting point is to recognise that subsistence and economy are not synonyms. Subsistence refers to what people live on; economy deals with the management and mobilisation of resources. This is true, of course, for all societies at whatever level of organisational complexity and indicates that if we use only palaeoeconomic data to talk of calories and nutrients, an enormous amount of potential information is being ignored. The questions that any research design should address deal with the links between the management of basic resources (plants, animals, raw materials) and people, and with the transformation and maintenance of institutions within the process of social change and reproduction.

Research Objectives

Environmental archaeology—including archaeozoology and archaeobotany as subdisciplines—has made great advances in developing analytical techniques to answer questions about diet and subsistence on the basis of fragmentary remains (Dennell 1980). Our concern here is with questions not only about subsistence, but also about economy. There has been little attempt before now to establish a methodology that would allow a comparative approach to the study of the economic management of past societies and the role of basic subsistence resources in processes of social change. Too often, the comparative approach has consisted largely of contrasting the relative proportions of plant or animal species from different sites or assemblages. The research design we favour holds as axiomatic that palaeoeconomic data can serve as instruments of measurement both within and between archaeological records that may, when judged by their material culture, appear so different as to invite partitioning rather than comparative analysis.

The reason for this is that many of the attributes of such data are biologically rather than culturally determined, so that basic patterns of human behaviour can be studied using materials with very clear and fixed ground rules, such as the organisation of the skeleton, the shape and number of anatomical elements, and the mechanics that these unchanging factors impose on dismemberment. This may sound as though we are getting dangerously close to that familiar "So what?" question mentioned earlier, but if we can establish some of the basic properties of the archaeological record, it would then be possible to tackle the investigation of process in past systems. In this sense, questions of behaviour and formation precede those of process and change.

Archaeologists now regard prehistoric Europe—especially in its later phases—in terms of a complex social and political geography. A number of ways of studying synchronic and diachronic variation have been devised, including establishing the correlates of ranked societies, calculating 'wealth' scores from cemetery data as a guide to differentiation, and examining distribution patterns of what are assumed to be prestige goods. However, it is all too easy to explain observed variations in terms of particularly obvious features of the archaeological record, with no way of measuring their general applicability. Thus, whilst intuitively it makes sense to equate Stonehenge with a more complex social unit in its locality than existed in other parts of England lacking such a monument, this is clearly not a very secure or rigorous way of identifying units of measurement for comparative analysis. Such an approach does not deal with the problem of equivalence: How many bronze rapiers signify the same level of social complexity as one Stonehenge, or how many ceremonial functions leaving no trace in the archaeological record add up to one long barrow?

In our view, palaeoeconomic data can play an essential role in providing a means of establishing comparative measurements of past systems at a variety of spatial scales, from the individual site to major environmental zones. Unlike Stonehenge, or bronze rapiers, or long barrows, they have the advantage of being present in virtually all periods and regions. (Even if the plant remains and animal bones do not survive, there is the evidence of settlements, sometimes field systems, and the relative location of both to resources.) Although very different institutions and social formations may arise from the use of the same set of animal and plant resources, agricultural organisation provides a comparative yardstick with which to measure variations in the socioeconomic systems of prehistoric Europe.

Of course, the use of subsistence data as an instrument for measuring cultural processes begs the question of whether we know what we are comparing (a problem to which we return later). The concepts that have been employed in the past to organise the archaeological record include cultures, culture groups, societies, folk movements, and levels of exchange. The approach to research that we favour here is one that has been widely utilised in prehistoric studies. It deals with a nested hierarchy of units starting with the assemblages, household cluster, and the site and proceeding through various regional scales to a world-system perspective (Barker, in press a, b; Clarke 1972; Flannery 1976; Renfrew and Wagstaff 1982). Only at the regional scale can we come to terms with the interplay between local decisions and the wider network of social and ecological constraints that structure them and so proceed to patterning in the archaeological record.

The chapters that follow deal with analysis at all these scales. Moreover, they have been chosen to illustrate an additional facet of the regional approach, namely that environment provides a further yardstick against which systemic variation, as revealed by subsistence data, can be measured. The environment may impose constraints on subsistence and limit the production of economic resources, but it is never dominant in imposing limits to growth in nascent formations. Although they differ considerably, environments never assume an active role in determining what sort of societies will inhabit them. Instead, the social system is dominant over the ecological system: the set of social relations constituted in the institutions, roles, and organisation of a society determines how any landscape is going to be exploited (Ingold 1981). The ecological system imposes constraints on the types of resources that can be utilised, but does not determine the level of appropriation of resources from the environment or what is done with them. To illustrate this point, we have selected a series of regional case studies on a highly varied environmental transect across western Europe. The coverage is not continuous along the transect but does include such conditions as Mediterranean islands (Chapter 8), Mediterranean littoral (Chapter 7), temperate forest (Chapters 7 and 9), and boreal (Chapter 6).

A further interest in the case studies is that most of the societies they consider, although teetering on the edge of statehood, never quite took the plunge in a manner that is regarded as archaeologically convincing and uncontentious. While the monuments and architecture of the western Mediterranean littoral and islands are certainly impressive (Evans 1973), there is no evidence for the kind of fundamental change that took place in the eastern basin with the rise of the Egyptian, Hittite, Minoan, Cypriot, and Mycenaean states. All too frequently the discussion of the rise of civilisation has been limited to these examples, with great weight placed on the advantages of the Mediterranean polyculture as a basis for growth (Childe 1959; Renfrew 1972). The case studies dealing with the western Mediterranean (Chapters 7 and 8) balance this view and emphasise the importance of developing common instruments of measurement for investigating such processes. The diversity of the transect also raises many questions on reading the contributions that follow. At the first level, these involve asking what ecological constraints were present and what strategies—social, technological, and physical—were required to overcome them. At the second level, there are further questions concerning the pathways to complexity via strategies of intensification. We return to these questions in our concluding section.

Methodological Lessons and Analytical Advances

Previous studies of prehistoric farming in Europe have resulted in a model of two distinct systems, one in the Mediterranean and the other in the temperate zone, differing in environmental constraints, subsistence resources, technology, and, most critically, in their respective capacities for intensification. Several aspects of these generalisations can be criticised.

In the Mediterranean zone, the argument runs, prehistoric agriculture was dominated from a comparatively early stage by the triad of olives, vines, and cereals constituting a system of crop polyculture that still exists today. To this were added the products of stock, principally the meat, milk, wool, hair, and blood of sheep and goats. It was relatively easy to use this package to produce an agricultural surplus, in turn creating wealth to expand the system and so effect change. Renfrew (1972), in particular, has argued that the development of a Mediterranean polyculture was a fundamental part of the process of intensification in the Aegean in the third millennium b.c. that laid the foundations for the Minoan–Mycenaean civilisation of the second millennium b.c. Discussing the same phenomenon, Halstead (1981) suggests that this agricultural system was a response to uncertainty and risk in the Greek environment, factors increased by population pressure on resources. Intensification took the form of bringing together a winning combination of subsistence elements that were collectively much stronger than any one of the constituent parts. This thesis helps to explain the development of such a distinctive system but not the ever-increasing level of the mobilisation of surpluses. The most pertinent question, however, is how a surplus could have had any significant impact on Mediterranean farming, with most communities able to grow the triad of crops and herd sheep. Every prehistoric community had the option of creating a surplus and transforming society, yet this occurred only in localised pockets such as Greece, Cyprus, and Egypt.

The second system that has been intensively studied is that of northern Europe, primarily Britain, the Netherlands, northern Germany, and southern Scandinavia. The main emphasis of previous research has been on the investigation of an assumed process of neolithic colonisation and on the relationships of early farming communities to distinctive soil types and systems of forest clearance (Clason 1967; Murray 1970; Waterbolk 1971), although both the colonisation model and the system of initial farming traditionally linked with it (swiddening) now seem increasingly discredited (Barker, in press a; Barker and Webley 1978; Dennell 1983; Rowley-Conwy 1981). There have been few convincing attempts to reconstruct regional agricultural systems for later prehistory, and in particular to investigate the possibility of surplus production in subsistence resources. Large prehistoric earthworks covering several hectares have been explained as redistribution centres for agricultural produce, but with little of the conviction with which the same arguments have been put forward for parts of the Mediterranean. Concepts of equilibrium and stability, rather than risk, have most commonly been employed to characterise prehistoric farming in this region. It is not until the arrival of the Romans that farming is generally admitted to have included the production of an agricultural surplus by most communities to feed the army and pay taxes.

The difference between the two systems is often ascribed to technology. In the Mediterranean the use of only a minimal technology—hand tools and the scratch ard—could yield a rich if sometimes uncertain harvest. By contrast, the northern European system of cultivation needed the development of a capital-intensive technology (the horse-drawn mouldboard plough, in particular) to realise the full potential of the land. (The object of Mediterranean ploughing has always been to conserve the moisture content of the soil by scuffling the surface, whereas in northern Europe heavy equipment is needed to break up the thick mass of roots in order to release the soil nutrients from lower depths; Forbes 1976a.) Given such generalisations about technological constraints and opportunities for surplus production, the inferences drawn from the archaeological record about the complexity of prehistoric societies and economies in these two areas have, inevitably, differed markedly. The analysis of the early history of agriculture in particular, and of the productive economy in general, in the two areas has been characterised by a definite sense of entrepreneurial risk takers in the Mediterranean contrasting with their honest but stolid contemporaries in the north, rather like the familiar contrast between the respective football teams of southern and northern European countries today. As we argue in the following section, however, and as the case studies later in this volume confirm, there is abundant evidence for substantial advances in agricultural intensification in both areas. We would maintain that it is high time that the traditional sketches be subjected to critical examination, not only of the general processes invoked but also, and more fundamentally, of the specific interpretations linking different categories of data (such as palaces and carbonised grape pips) that have been individual 'proofs' of the general processes.

Probably the most important analytical advance in palaeoeconomic studies in the last decade or so has been the development of methodologies to recognise the natural and cultural biases that can affect our database. These methodologies are part of the general awareness by archaeologists of the need to disentangle how the archaeological record has been formed before tackling the processes of human behaviour incorporated within it (Dennell 1972, 1978; Gamble 1978b; Gifford 1981; Meadow 1975, 1976). At the forefront of this research has been the investigation of taphonomic questions, resulting in observations on the attrition of biological materials that have had major implications for studies of early hominids and later prehistoric hunter–gatherers (Behrensmeyer and Hill 1980; Binford 1981; Brain 1981). The impact of such work on many traditional assumptions about prehistoric man was aptly conveyed by Binford's book, *Bones: Ancient Men and Modern Myths*.

Comparable developments have yet to be made in other branches of environmental archaeology. For example, many of the intricate studies of pollen and nonmarine mollusca that form such an important part of palaeoenvironmental reconstruction are still largely descriptive rather than interpretative in nature. We do not yet have a reliable route to follow from counts of pollen grains to statements about plant biomass, primary productivity, or other ecological measures that provide an essential basis for assessing past human adaptations to the environment. Second, taphonomic and contextual studies of biological data have concentrated on the earlier periods of prehistory characterised by mobile systems of human behaviour, whilst comparable methodologies for the sedentary communities of later prehistory are far less developed (Mounteney 1981). Such methodologies, however, are critical for the investigation of the subsistence and economies of these communities.

A good illustration of this point is presented by the problems of analysing palaeoeconomic data from a Roman villa. This well-known class of monument is rightly considered a key element in the structure of agricultural economies in many parts of proto-historic Europe. For the most part, however, the recovery of subsistence data has not been a priority of excavation; samples of animal bones and plant remains are often rather poor, and interpretation tends to be overly optimistic. All too fragmentary samples of animal bones become evidence for a meat economy, wool production, or dairying; a corn drier built into a mosaic floor and containing a few charred grains of barley becomes evidence for surplus grain production, an arable-based system of farming, or even an infield–outfield system of land management. Little or no attention has been paid in most investigations to the primary behaviour represented by such data—consumption and discard activities rather than agricultural practices (still less, strategies). In fact, many such activities were not related to the villa in its principal phases as the centre of an agricultural estate, but often to final episodes of abandonment—the roof caved in, and the half-standing walls were used as a temporary shelter out in the fields to house a corn drier. The residues discarded in the villa at the end of its life may thus offer little evidence of earlier functions, with the decaying building now the midden of another agricultural unit.

The bones of red deer reported from many villas have often been used as an argument for the high status of the occupants. This may be so, or they may be residues left by hunting parties using a ruined building as a temporary hunting stand whilst operating some distance away from their customary base. Rigorous contextual analysis and adequate sampling are clearly essential prerequisites for any realistic assessment of the likely relationship between residues from complex sites and the behaviour of the inhabitants, yet discussions of villa economies have tended to use the existing database as a straightforward guide to complex agricultural strategies (King 1978). The critical point here is that an understanding of *formation* must precede an investigation of *process*.

On the basis of the closer understanding of our data that such an approach would achieve, we suggest three initial strategies for the further analysis of their content. The first is illustrated in Chapter 3, in which Cribb uses simulation as a device for exploring patterning in faunal residues. This approach can be compared with earlier work by Payne (1973), which made many challenging suggestions about the reconstruction of herding strategies on the basis of age–wear studies. The refinement proposed by Cribb is to allow for greater flexibility in both subsistence and economic strategies, with simulation allowing us to see how a patterned sample of animal bones is created; the resulting model can then be applied to archaeological data. The study is preliminary and has not yet come to grips with the various factors of lateral variation and differential preservation known to bias faunal samples (Barker 1978; Gamble, in press; Halstead et al. 1978; Meadow 1975; Peck 1980). Nevertheless, it is sufficient to indicate the potential of this approach.

A second approach is more observational. One strand is provided by work now available from experimental farms, which is beginning to define some of the parameters involved in low-energy farming systems in the European environment, although there will always be the problem of deciding on the initial values at which the system should be set, such as the labour input and the level of surplus required beyond the subsistence quota. Another strand consists of observations of traditional farming systems, practised most effectively to date around the Mediterranean (Cribb 1982; Dimen and Friedl 1976; Forbes 1976b; Hillman 1973; Wagstaff and Auguston 1982). Fleming (Chapter 5) develops a concept of rural sociology in which the rich oral and literary traditions of northern Europe are employed to provide meanings for patterns in the archaeological record.

We reproduce here as Figure 1.1 the remarkable photograph of the St. Kilda 'parliament', taken in 1890, to demonstrate the richness of this resource, which is still largely untapped. This remote island, the westernmost part of the British Isles, was the home of some 100 people at the turn of the last century (Steel

Figure 1.1 The St. Kilda parliament.

1975). Subsistence was based on the flesh, oil, and eggs of immense colonies of nesting sea birds. Even in such a remote region, rent had to be paid to an absentee landlord, and it was paid in oil. The photograph shows us part of this system in operation; it suggests an image of a group of hunters and gatherers deciding on their tasks for the day. Clearly, this is not a prehistoric analogue, but there are principles concerning work organisation, decision making, the division of labour, and group size relative to resources that are of considerable interest from the palaeoeconomic perspective. Following Fleming, we predict a major role for a European ethnography developed from such sources as one important foundation of archaeological methodology (Colley 1983).

The third strategy draws on a wider framework of reference in investigating the consequences of complexity. As Maltby (Chapter 2) and Jones (Chapter 4) emphasise in their studies of animal and plant remains from later British prehistory, previous analysis has consistently simplified the archaeological record. The invisible exports of prehistory—subsistence resources—have often been suspected, but like the higher forms of ritual life, they have been regarded as too difficult to recognise from prehistoric data. These two chapters provide a starting point for redressing the imbalance: By determining the formation of their samples, these authors show that it is possible to demonstrate complexity, with clear production and consumption differences at the regional scale. Zvelebil (Chapter 6) also has clear evidence for the impact of new economic goals (the fur trade in particular) on subsistence systems in his study of northern Russia.

A salutary lesson in the complexities of discard behaviour is provided by Binford (1978) in his study of the Nunamiut reindeer hunters of Alaska, an ostensibly simple society that revealed an extraordinarily complex kaleidoscope of patterning in bone assemblages generated by carcase dismemberment, butchery, storage, consumption, and discard. We are only at the preliminary stage of developing taphonomic methodologies to deal with the food residues of later prehistoric Europe, but these approaches provide the essential foundation for further analysis. At the most basic level, it is still unclear how we are to interpret biological data from the pits and ditches of occupation sites and to determine precisely what they represent in terms of the typical consumption diet of the inhabitants and the catchments from which that diet was derived.

The consequences of social and economic complexity can also be investigated through the study of settlement patterns, which make up the regional framework that is the essential counterpart to effective contextual analysis at the level of the individual site. On the island of Melos in Greece, for example, changes in the frequencies of animal species during the Bronze Age coincided with a shift from a dispersed to a nucleated settlement pattern (Gamble 1982), which resulted in a single, more elaborate settlement on the island. The aggregated population set up constraints of time and distance for the farmers, who now had to travel out to their fields from the town. The situation was exacerbated by the fact that half the catchment area of the town was marine, yet no resources were apparently taken from the sea (Gamble 1979). The change in the faunal sample therefore indicates not so much a major advance in agricultural intensification, but rather a strategic adjustment to nucleation in order to maintain agricultural output at previous levels. Another example is Berenice (modern Benghazi) in Libya, where changes in the faunal sample from a Roman town coincided with and were related to settlement changes at the regional scale (Barker 1982).

In the first and second centuries A.D., intensive farms were established in the hills of the Gebel Akhdar, south of the coastal cities, producing a surplus of foodstuffs for export. The farms gradually encroached on the traditional grazing and watering zones of the existing pastoralist population, resulting in a catastrophic breakdown in relations between the two systems in the third century A.D. The Berenice faunal sample (in terms of changes in species frequencies, anatomical composition, and mortality data) reveals the collapse of the livestock trade and a switch to local resources. The integration between subsistence data and settlement trends is a fundamental part of several of the following case studies.

Finally, site catchment analysis needs to be further developed to be effective in the study of economic complexity. The productive capacity of the catchment has to be compared with the material evidence of the site for social and economic strategies, and with the relative site size in regional terms (Brumfiel 1976; Flannery 1976; Peebles and Kus 1977). Methodologies in this area have yet to receive the same attention as those for faunal and botanical analysis, but the authors have found site catchment analysis to be very helpful when it was integrated into an economic study, combined with the analysis of biological, artifactual, and structural data from the excavated site and other sites in the region (Barker 1978, 1982; Gamble 1982).

Systems of Production and Strategies of Intensification

Subsistence production provides one strategy of intensification. Although it is closely linked with other strategies, there are features that require special mention and merit a separate approach.

The most common approach to the study of subsistence change has been to model the process in terms of cost, efficiency, and production (Earle and Christenson 1980). In this view the primitive community is regarded as the functional equivalent of what economists term the 'diversified firm' (Earle 1980:14). Decisions are evaluated on the basis of cost minimisation, with reasons given for selecting one subsistence strategy from amongst several. The model developed by Earle draws marginal cost curves whose shape is held to point to the direction in which change has proceeded. These cost curves are affected by three main parameters (environment, technology, and social organisation), with population density taken as the main variable determining output, and hence both subsistence mix and change.

The main problem in using cost as the sole means of measuring change is that a primitive economy is not geared to be very successful and is in fact well adapted to being under-productive (Dalton 1977; Sahlins 1972). Intensification and moves to more productive subsistence strategies are by and large a process of taking up slack in the system. Labour input can be increased by working longer hours; new combinations of resources can be managed, either to satisfy the demands of local self-sufficiency or to provide a surplus at the expense of local subsistence security. The slack in the system is always there to be taken up and may precede technological change or territorial expansion. As archaeologists, therefore, we have to be aware of forms of intensification that may be less visible to us than changes in technology or settlement distribution that involve the social mobilisation of the production of resources.

This 'slack in the system' became a potential resource for intensification in prehistoric economies with the first regular use of what have been termed '*r*' rather than 'K' strategy resources (Hayden 1981). The former are those resources such as fish, shellfish, and plant foods, especially grasses, that are short-lived, usually small in size, and with tremendous powers of increase since their strategy is to produce a great many offspring, few of which normally survive. K strategy species are large-bodied mammals that are slow to mature, have low reproductive rates, and for whom considerable investment is required to protect the offspring and ensure a reasonable chance of survival to maturity. The use of K strategy resources was characteristic of many Pleistocene hunter–gatherers in northern Europe and elsewhere. Shellfish were used on a small scale at an early date by some communities (for example, in southern Africa in the Middle Stone Age), but the evidence suggests that the first sustained use of r strategy resources occurred during the glacial phases of the upper Pleistocene (Gamble 1984).

One explanation for the incorporation of these foods into the human diet at such a late stage in our history has been put forward by O'Connell and Hawkes (1981). According to optimal foraging theory, available resources are ranked according to the relative cost of exploitation. r strategy resources are always abundant in the environment but are distributed in small package sizes, making them expensive to process for consumption. A great deal of time has to be spent opening up every limpet, or processing a collection of seeds. The high costs of exploiting such resources were one reason for the minimal use of interglacial forest environments in northern Europe, even though they contained a wealth of usable energy (Gamble 1984).

The great wealth of forest foods was first harvested systematically by Mesolithic populations in the present interglacial (Clarke 1976). Significantly, the abundant evidence for Mesolithic settlement sustained by a mixture of hunting, fishing, and gathering contrasts sharply with the lack of Palaeolithic material from the similar environments of earlier interglacials in the same region. Clearly, what was needed for the exploitation of the new resources was not so much an advance in technology to lower the costs of extraction, but rather a new structure in social relations to make the cost tariffs acceptable. Here, as elsewhere in the world, intensification of the subsistence quest in the Upper Pleistocene correlated with new institutions and status positions in Palaeolithic society (Bender 1978). Previously, cost thresholds had imposed restraints, and alternatives such as out-migrations and local extinctions happened instead.

Once the cost threshold had been overcome by rearrangements in the network of social relations and the demand for resources in the process of social reproduction, one facet of the later agricultural revolution was accomplished. Further shifts were still needed, in particular the transition to a mode of production based on the ownership of resources (Meillassoux 1972, 1973). What occurred at the Mesolithic–Neolithic divide was the development of a package of resources that permitted the consistent reproduction of the institutions of society on the basis of the products that these resources made available. Ingold (1980:227) has shown

Table 1.1

Attributes Required in Resources for a Pastoral Economy[a]

Attributes	Available choice
Convertible into basic raw materials for domestic consumption	Edible plants and animals
Capable of self-reproduction	Edible plants and animals
Identifiable with forebears and progeny	Animals only
Of relatively low reproductive potential	Animals only
Tolerant of crowding (excludes carnivorous predators and herbivorous species with innate mechanisms for dispersal)	Most ungulates
Capable of supporting itself in nature (ungulates that cannot be confined in a sedentary regime and that would require a proportion of food to be produced by human labour)	Gregarious ungulates

[a]These attributes are inherent in a comparatively small number of mammal species; after Ingold 1980:227.

that a pastoral resource requires a number of attributes to fit into our socioeconomic framework (Table 1.1), and that these attributes are inherent in only a small number of mammal species. The domestication of only a few grass species from among the many thousands available is harder to explain, although clearly the capability of these r selected resources to grow in dense stands that could be managed, defended, and owned must have been fundamental to their selection by man.

At the same time, however, the natural properties of the resources could not predict the whole outcome; the social context was also essential. Amongst traditional African societies, for example, the dominant factor in agricultural organisation is control of the labour force, whereas Eurasian societies are characterised by ownership of the means of production—technology and land (Goody 1976). These contrasted strategies are defined through systems of marriage and inheritance. Polygamy in the former societies provides a means of enhancing the labour force, whilst land is retained through inheritance in the small, closed breeding groups (family units) of Eurasia. Both systems can be regarded as social strategies for the retention of power within restricted interest groups through control of the means of production.

The importance of social strategies for such control is stressed by Gilman (1981) in his discussion of the emergence of stratified societies in Bronze Age Europe. Although he ignores the concept of ranking and directs his models to rather exaggerated social goals, his emphasis on the role of production and resources is an approach we support. Addressing the question of how more durable social units could have been maintained despite their inherent segmentation, Gilman concludes that new systems of exploitation (plough agriculture, Mediterranean polyculture, irrigation, and offshore fishing) required increased labour inputs that militated against the traditional option of group fission. Thus, changes in subsistence production—in effect, new insurance policies that were impossible to cash in—led to greater control by emergent elites over the surrounding population.

This model has been examined for the Bronze Age Aegean in some detail, producing at least two different views. The first sees the environment as a constraint on the development of more complex polities dependent on population growth (Halstead 1981; Halstead and O'Shea 1982). In this view, the unpredictability of crop yields in the Aegean environment would have been a critical constraint given the inflexibility of human subsistence requirements, especially under conditions of population growth. Hence, emerging elites acted as brokers for the wider system that they came to symbolise through their offices and institutions, a system that would be producing a surplus in one area but a shortfall elsewhere. They acted as redistributive agents to ensure that the population as a whole had sufficient subsistence goods by redistributing the surplus through the storage facilities of the palaces. Their activities thus attempted to stabilise an inherently unstable resource base, providing a buffer for any local population against crop failure. At the same time, the conversion of surplus into tokens stimulated a prestige good system and the further entrenchment of the elites.

This model of social storage presupposes that people were destined to live at the kind of population levels that require servicing by an elite to survive. An alternative view characterises the Aegean Bronze Age economy not as a game that everybody has to play against the environment (and that the elites just happen to win), but rather as the exploitation of production by elites to suit their own ends, thereby controlling a subject population by destabilising local subsistence systems that are inherently self-sufficient (Gamble 1981, 1982). The territories of the Aegean palaces were small, like the early state modules described by Renfrew (1975), averaging 1200 km^2. The production of a surplus helped to unbalance local subsistence by getting people to specialise in particular crops and animals to an extent where they could no longer satisfy all their subsistence needs because their labour was committed elsewhere. The elites stored the surplus wool, olive oil, wine, and wheat in the palaces. They redistributed some of it back, but without their initial demands on the productive system, there would have been less risk of the shortfalls in food and other goods that would have needed a system of social storage.

The system of storage and redistribution prevented goods (and hence, power) from accumulating on the periphery of the palace territory, beyond the control of the elites. A general concern of elites is to focus their political adherents on the centre of a control system and on their own accumulation of wealth (Diener and Robkin 1979). The two models therefore differ in the extent to which intensification is regarded as dependent on the good offices or on the ambitions of the elites—on beneficent rulers or on a mafia. In the first model, social storage is an

adaptive response to a maladaptive environment; in the second, the same imbalance is a circumstance to be exploited, with differences in rank and ultimately
in society based on the monopolistic control of socially created shortages and
risks.

Regarding the traditional generalisations about Mediterranean and temperate
farming described in the previous section, there has been far less discussion of
the role of subsistence production and the manipulation of resources in the
process of intensification in temperate Europe. However, there is now abundant
evidence that the processes of agricultural intensification and their links with
social control amongst the prehistoric societies north of the Alps were just as
complex as those—albeit more spectacular archaeologically—in the Mediterranean. With the reevaluation of initial farming systems, for example, has come
the recognition of an element of social control from the very beginning, as in
Legge's study of Neolithic animal husbandry in Britain (Legge 1981), or
Madsen's of settlement distributions in Neolithic Denmark (Madsen, in press).
These findings echo recent studies of the final systems of hunting and gathering
that preceded and overlapped them (Paludan-Müller 1978; Rowley-Conwy 1983;
Zvelebil 1981).

By the later third millennium b.c., the evidence is unmistakable, as Sherratt's
study of what he termed the Secondary Products Revolution has made clear
(Sherratt 1981). Whilst the origins of dairying, cattle traction, and ard technology are all probably earlier than Sherratt envisaged (Barker, in press a), it
remains true that this period witnessed the first consistent and widespread use of
the secondary products of domestic animals—milk, blood, hair, wool, transport,
haulage, and their live maintenance for prestige—and that the agricultural intensification that this represented was an essential component in the development of
social ranks and classes. A current reevaluation of faunal and botanical data from
henge monuments of this period in Britain has provided considerable cor-
roborative detail on the complex relationship between social control and subsistence production (Thomas, personal communication). The field systems of later
prehistory provide indisputable evidence of the same relationship (Bowen and
Fowler 1978; Fleming 1978, 1983; Spratt 1981), as does the clear relationship
between wealth and agriculture in the funerary record of Bronze Age Denmark
(Kristiansen 1978; Randsborg 1974). The evidence for the link between agricultural intensification and social complexity across Europe as a whole is summarised by Barker (in press a), and the detailed case studies in this volume all
make exactly the same point from different perspectives and using different
databases.

A further strategy for intensification relevant to subsistence–economic studies
is the importance of food as a cultural value. At the moment, this area of
investigation is very neglected by archaeologists, but its potential is illustrated by
Goody's (1982) analysis of the correlations between cuisine differentiation and

social organisation in modern communities. One goal of future research must be an archaeology of table manners and cooking, because the use of material culture associated with food, and of food itself, represents a systematic transformation of the structuring principles of society. One example of this is the development in the depiction of the Last Supper during the crucial period when Europe changed from a traditional to an industrial society: the development of place settings, the use of individual rather than communal drinking vessels, the variety of courses eaten, and the geographical catchments from which the ingredients were derived are all subtle indicators of complex social change. Similar trends can be seen in other secular contexts over the same period.

Of course, the contexts of consumption will be difficult to reconstruct by prehistorians unaided by such pictorial information, but there is surely an un-tapped wealth of information coded onto ceramic and metal vessels having a variety of shapes, sizes, and types of decoration (or the lack of it), particularly in assemblages clearly associated with individuals in burials. We believe that a symbolist paradigm (Hodder 1982) is not essential to the investigation of mate-rial culture for information about food as a cultural value. We would rather see the incorporation of this neglected area of research into a methodology that can encompass the entire socioeconomic system under consideration and so yield an understanding of how past societies ordered the world and its essential resources at every stage in a continuum of production, consumption, and discard (see also Maltby, this volume).

Interregional Patterns

Much European prehistory has often been considered in terms of core–periph-ery models, with southeast Europe or the Near East regarded as the core area that stimulates change elsewhere. This relationship was first advocated by archae-ologists before the advent of radiocarbon dating, when diffusion theories—in many ways the inevitable by-product of the system of cross-dating that had to be used then—held sway. More recently it has been greatly minimised, as local radiocarbon chronologies persuaded many archaeologists into a rather isola-tionist perspective of their regional or national prehistory. However, no part of Europe was entirely untouched by the emergence of civilisation and the apparat-us of the state in the Near East and the eastern Mediterranean during the second millennium b.c., and the trading relationships between the Mediterranean and temperate Europe in the first millennium b.c. have long been recognised as a fundamental stimulus to social complexity in the latter region. In both these and earlier periods of European prehistory, a full investigation of economic systems must take account of large-scale interregional patterns—the 'world view'.

The impact of world systems on local adaptations is well understood in hunter–gatherer studies (Leacock 1954; Leacock and Lee 1982; Marks 1976; Murphy and Steward 1956). Whilst some observers have been tempted to cast contemporary hunters and gatherers in the role of untouched economic savants, the reality is that their economies have been systematically transformed by their relationships to world systems, albeit at a great spatial remove. This is particularly evident among groups such as the Hadza, Valley Bisa, and Montagnis, who have altered their territorial and hunting decisions in order to acquire exchange commodities (such as ivory and furs) needed to facilitate the process of social reproduction. A clear example of this phenomenon in prehistoric Europe is described by Zvelebil (Chapter 6, this volume).

For later European prehistory in general, it is difficult to measure such interactions in the archaeological record, even though we may suspect that they existed. It is unlikely that the large-scale movement of subsistence products characterised later European prehistory, although as Maltby convincingly shows (Chapter 2, this volume), this phenomenon can be detected on a local and (by implication) on a wider scale in the Roman period in northern Europe. A considerable body of research has dealt with trade between southern and northern Europe prior to the expansion of the Roman Empire, but little of this work has considered the wider implications of such a process in areas where obvious material imports such as amphorae, bronze drinking vessels, or coral jewelery do not occur. Yet Jones (Chapter 4, this volume) has clear evidence for the intraregional exchange of grain during the British Iron Age, with grain export from the Danebury hillfort also implied. Hedeager (1978) has also shown how Danish societies were transformed by their exchange relationships across the Roman frontier, and Randsborg (Chapter 9) argues that differences in subsistence data across northern Europe in part reflect the differing extent to which societies were producing foodstuffs for Roman markets.

Clearly, models of local self-determination in subsistence decisions are likely to be a simplification of much more complex relations for many societies in prehistoric Europe. At present, studies of economic complexity are largely dependent on finding prestige items that can be used to define the scale of interregional patterns. The circulation patterns of such objects are inevitably taken to reflect how prehistoric societies were managed by their recipients. Thus, big men and elites become the focus for investigating change. Such a perspective ignores many of the questions discussed in the previous section concerning how local leaders maintained control over their subjects and the extent to which control was related to the subsistence activities that were the major work input of the vast majority of prehistoric people. Certainly the prestige good model of social complexity correlates well with the spectacular grave goods of late prehistoric Europe (Frankenstein and Rowlands 1978). However, without adequate settlement data and associated agricultural evidence, competitive models of elite exchange have to be accepted without any knowledge of the internal organisation of the social units over which the elites exerted variable degrees of control. An otherwise appealing model would in our view be greatly strengthened, and tested, by an examination of the subsistence economy. As Maltby (Chapter 2) and Jones (Chapter 4) demonstrate, the methodologies are available to do this.

Conclusion

It is commonly assumed that cereal yields in prehistoric Europe were as low as those of Roman and Medieval times or of subsistence farming in Mediterranean and Middle Eastern countries earlier in this century—that is, between 3 and 5 to 1, compared with 25–30 to 1 in western Europe today (Dennell 1978:220–221). It is true that yields comparable to modern yields of wheat were obtained between 1973 and 1980 on experimental plots of emmer and spelt wheat at the Butser Ancient Farm project in Hampshire (southern England) without fallow or fertiliser (Reynolds 1981). However, the land used had previously been permanent pasture with high organic levels, and it is very unlikely—on the evidence of the 100-year experiments at Rothamsted (Rothamsted Experimental Station 1970)—that comparable yields would continue for decades to come if the original fertility were not replaced. For prehistoric Europe there is in fact widespread evidence that farmers developed a range of methods for renewing the fertility of their fields, including the use of legumes, other break crops, fallowing, household refuse, and animal manure (Barker, in press a).

The field systems of northern Europe indicate that many farmers preferred small, intensively managed fields to the more extensive systems of medieval farming, so that yields from individual plots may sometimes have been as high as those of today. Given the low technology available, however, the total yields produced by a family's labour would still have been low. Prehistoric farmers had to contend with the same vicious circle that constrained the medieval farmer, one of low yields and low rates of manure: "The evil of small harvests due to insufficient manuring, the lack of manure being in turn the result of small agricultural production making it impossible to keep more cattle" (Slicher van Bath 1963:10). "How narrow were the boundaries that restricted the practice of farming. The opportunities in ancient farming were very limited" (1963:23).

Yet both the prehistory and history of European farming show that, despite the innate conservatism of the subsistence farmer, the circle was broken repeatedly. In Medieval times, for example, the creation of extra pasture allowed livestock numbers to rise, new combinations of systems of nutrient renewal were developed, and new technology enabled the cultivation of more land. So too in prehistoric Europe, the regional case studies in this volume demonstrate how initial agricultural systems were transformed in later prehistory by major changes in technology, production, and organisation, a thesis further developed in the survey of prehistoric farming in Europe by Barker (in press a).

In his study of medieval and early modern farming, Grigg (1982) discusses four major stimuli of agricultural change: climate–environment, technology, population pressure, and social complexity. His principal argument is that they rarely if ever operated in isolation from one another. Farming was often very resilient to gradual climatic change, but a succession of catastrophic harvests could result from small annual fluctuations in temperature and rainfall. New technologies enabled the cultivation of heavier soils, and improved transport facilities were fundamental to the growth of regional agricultural markets supplying towns. Main periods of agricultural intensification correlated broadly with periods of population increase, providing in several instances persuasive support for Boserup's (1965) thesis that population pressure is the key stimulus of agricultural intensification. Boserup herself argues in a study of Medieval Europe that a population increase in the later first millennium A.D. led to the adoption of the mouldboard horse-drawn plough and then to the development of three-course rotation systems in the twelfth and thirteenth centuries A.D. (Boserup 1981). However, Grigg also argues: "Whilst population growth was unquestionably a potent factor in causing agricultural change, there are too many alternative explanations of the events associated with periods of population growth for it to be the only cause" (Grigg 1982:43). Social factors such as differences in systems of land tenure were also clearly associated with the different reactions to population and income changes in different parts of Europe.

Without developing on the theme of what can precipitate the wider process of sociocultural intensification in prehistory (Friedman 1982; Friedman and Rowlands, 1977), we note that archaeologists have favoured three resulting strategies for later European prehistory: ideology (Fleming 1971; Shennan 1982), the circulation of goods (Renfrew 1972), and subsistence production (Gilman 1981; Kristiansen 1982; Sherratt 1981). A major interest for us in the preparation of this volume has been the variety of processes of economic change discussed by the contributors. Most of the authors identify the importance of several factors including demographic stress, environmental change, social competition and stratification, exchange markets, and technological innovation. Mills (Chapter 7) argues for the importance of population pressure over social competition in Languedoc in the third millennium b.c., whereas Lewthwaite (Chapter 8) emphasises social competition over population pressure for contemporary events in the Balearic islands. Yet both are agreed that the manipulation of subsistence production by the emergent elites was fundamental to intensification and that the climatic fluctuations of the third millennium b.c. have long been recognised as a further critical component of social and economic change in the Mediterranean as a whole. Randsborg (Chapter 9) points to the complex interplay between the ecological constraints and opportunities of different regions in northern Europe, the effects on these of climatic change, and the further effects on the resulting agricultural systems of changing market demands. In northern Russia, one factor in the process of social and economic intensification in A.D. 400–800, according to Zvelebil (Chapter 6), was contact with Viking Scandinavia and Kievian Russia, but more critical factors were social competition as stratification developed, changes in farming methods in response to a decline in the resource base and/or population pressure, and the introduction of an iron technology that made these changes possible.

The strengths and weaknesses of their respective databases lead these authors to prefer some factors over others, but the complexity of the interrelationships of different stimuli is stressed above all. Whilst the potential importance of population stress is recognised in all the case studies, it is also clear that the increasing complexity of social organisation in prehistoric Europe meant that most communities were increasingly capable of manipulating their technological and economic as well as social environments, and so of setting in train the kind of relationships between technology, food supply, and population that are the reverse of the Boserup model.

At the end of his study of the dynamics of agricultural change in historical times, Grigg concludes as follows:

> The search for a prime mover to explain agrarian change is to pursue a chimera. The same force will work its way out in different ways in different regions. Indeed, perhaps it can be argued that the way ahead lies in the application of specific models not simply to one area but to several regions. Comparative studies may give the agricultural historian comparative advantages. (Grigg 1982:229)

Prehistorians interested in the same issues are clearly faced with major problems in identifying and above all in explaining agricultural intensification given our timescales and database, with factors such as population increase hard enough to document satisfactorily, let alone population pressure (whether perceived or actual). However, the complexities and difficulties of our data should not dissuade us from the kind of investigations of subsistence data for economic goals advocated here. In particular, the prehistoric archaeologist has the long-term perspective of the events we are studying, a perspective employed in all the case studies presented here. This timescale distinguishes us from historical geographers and from economic historians in that we are concerned with the long-term exploitation of regional landscapes and the long-term development of increasingly complex social geographies, a perspective that gives prehistoric archaeology a powerful 'comparative advantage' in the study of agrarian change. We hope that the papers we selected for this volume demonstrate how, for all its difficulties, the database of prehistoric archaeology can be tackled effectively in pursuit of these goals.

The purpose of *Beyond Domestication,* therefore, is to discuss both why and how we should investigate subsistence behaviour in prehistoric societies that are judged by their material culture to be complex. We have emphasised that subsistence or palaeoeconomic data can be used to establish a framework for comparing the regional prehistories of Europe as their ecological potential came to be used more intensively. Such data, so often ignored or poorly used in past studies, have the capability to be the critical foundation of an integrated archaeological approach to the investigation of social and economic complexity in the future.

References

Barker, G.
    1975 Prehistoric territories and economies in central Italy. In *Palaeoeconomy,* edited by E. S. Higgs, pp. 111–175. Cambridge University Press, Cambridge, England.
Barker, G.
    1978 Economic models for the Manekweni *zimbabwe,* Mozambique. *Azania* 13:71–97.
Barker, G.
    1982 Economic life at Berenice: the animal and fish bones, molluscs and plant remains. In *Excavations at Sidi Khrebish, Benghazi (Berenice)* (Vol. II), edited by J. A. Lloyd, pp. 1–45. Libya Antiqua, Supplements V, II.
Barker, G.
    in press a *Prehistoric farming in Europe.* Cambridge University Press, Cambridge, England.
Barker, G.
    in press b *Archaeology and history in a Mediterranean valley.* Cambridge University Press, Cambridge, England.
Barker, G., and D. Webley
    1978 Causewayed camps and early neolithic land use in central and southern England. *Proceedings of the Prehistoric Society* 44:161–186.
Behrensmeyer, A. K., and A. P. Hill
    1980 *Fossils in the making.* University of Chicago Press, Chicago.
Bender, B.
    1978 Gatherer–hunter to farmer: a social perspective. *World Archaeology* 10:204–222.
Binford, L. R.
    1978 *Nunamiut ethnoarchaeology.* Academic Press, New York.
Binford, L. R.
    1981 *Bones: ancient men and modern myths.* Academic Press, New York.
Boserup, E.
    1965 *The conditions of agricultural growth.* Allen and Unwin, London.
Boserup, E.
    1981 *Population and technology.* Clarendon Press, Oxford, England.
Bowen, H. C., and P. J. Fowler (editors)
    1978 *Early land allotment.* British Archaeological Reports, British Series 48, Oxford, England.
Braidwood, R. J., and B. Howe
    1960 *Prehistoric investigations in Iraqi Kurdistan.* University of Chicago Press, Chicago.
Brain, C. K.
    1981 *The hunters and the hunted.* University of Chicago Press, Chicago.

Brumfiel, E.
1976 Regional growth in the eastern valley of Mexico: a test of the 'population pressure' hypothesis. In *The early mesoamerican village,* edited by K. V. Flannery, pp. 234–249. Academic Press, New York.

Champion, T. C., C. S. Gamble, S. J. Shennan, and A. W. Whittle
1984 *Prehistoric Europe.* Academic Press, London.

Childe, V. G.
1959 *Social evolution.* Watts, London.

Clark, J. G. D.
1939 *Archaeology and society.* Methuen, London.

Clark, J. G. D.
1952 *Prehistoric Europe: the economic basis.* Methuen, London.

Clark, J. G. D.
1957 *Archaeology and society* (third ed.). Methuen, London.

Clark, J. G. D.
1972 *Star Carr: a case study in bioarchaeology.* Addison-Wesley, Reading, Massachusetts.

Clarke, D. L.
1972 A provisional model of an iron age society and its settlement system. In *Models in archaeology,* edited by D. L. Clarke, pp. 801–870. Methuen, London.

Clarke, D. L.
1976 Mesolithic Europe: the economic basis. In *Problems in economic and social Archaeology,* edited by G. de G. Sieveking et al., pp. 449–481. Duckworth, London.

Clason, A. T.
1967 *Animal and man in Holland's past.* Walters, Groningen.

Colley, S. M.
1983 *The role of fish bone studies in economic archaeology: with special reference to the Orkney Isles.* Unpublished Ph.D. dissertation, Southampton University.

Cribb, R. L. D.
1982 *The archaeological dimensions of near eastern nomadic pastoralism.* Unpublished Ph.D. dissertation, Southampton University.

Dalton, G.
1977 Aboriginal economies in stateless societies. In *Exchange systems in prehistory,* edited by T. K. Earle and J. E. Ericson, pp. 191–222. Academic Press, New York.

Davidson, I.
1981 Can we study prehistoric economy for fisher–gatherer–hunters? An historical approach to Cambridge 'palaeoeconomy'. In *Economic archaeology,* edited by A. Sheridan and G. N. Bailey, pp. 17–34. British Archaeological Reports, International Series 96, Oxford, England.

Dennell, R. W.
1972 The interpretation of plant remains. In *Papers in economic prehistory,* edited by E. S. Higgs, pp. 149–160. Cambridge University Press, Cambridge, England.

Dennell, R. W.
1978 *Early farming in south Bulgaria from the VIth to the IIIrd millenia b.c.* British Archaeological Reports, International Series 45, Oxford, England.

Dennell, R. W.
1980 Prehistoric diet and nutrition: some food for thought. *World Archaeology* 11:121–135.

Dennell, R. W,
1983 *European economic prehistory.* Academic Press, London.

Diener, P., and E. E. Robkin
1979 Ecology, evolution and the search for cultural origins: the question of Islamic pig prohibitions. *Current Anthropology* 19:493–540.

Dimen, M., and E. Friedl (editors)
  1976 *Regional variations in modern Greece and Cyprus.* New York Academy of Science, Annals 268.
Drew, I. M., D. Perkins, and P. Daly
  1971 Prehistoric domestication of animals: effects on bone structure. *Science* 171:280–282.
Ducos, P.
  1978 'Domestication' defined and methodological approaches to its recognition in faunal assemblages. In *Approaches to faunal analysis in the Middle East,* edited by R. H. Meadow and M. A. Zeder, pp. 53–56. Harvard University, Peabody Museum Bulletin 2.
Earle, T. K.
  1980 A model of subsistence change. In *Modelling change in prehistoric subsistence economies,* edited by T. K. Earle and A. L. Christenson, pp. 1–29. Academic Press, New York.
Earle, T. K., and A. L. Christenson
  1980 *Modelling change in prehistoric subsistence economies.* Academic Press, New York.
Evans, J. D.
  1973 Islands as laboratories for the study of culture process. In *The explanation of culture change,* edited by C. Renfrew, pp. 517–520. Duckworth, London.
Flannery, K. V.
  1973 The origins of agriculture. *Annual Review of Anthropology* 2:271–310.
Flannery, K. V. (editor)
  1976 *The early mesoamerican village.* Academic Press, New York.
Fleming, A. M.
  1971 Territorial patterns in bronze age Wessex. *Proceedings of the Prehistoric Society* 37:138–164.
Fleming, A. M.
  1978 The prehistoric landscape of Dartmoor, part 1: south Dartmoor. *Proceedings of the Prehistoric Society* 44:97–123.
Fleming, A. M.
  1983 The prehistoric landscape of Dartmoor, part 2: north and east Dartmoor. *Proceedings of the Prehistoric Society* 49:195–241.
Forbes, H. A.
  1976a 'The thrice ploughed field': cultivation techniques in ancient and modern Greece. *Expedition* 19:5–11.
Forbes, H. A.
  1976b 'We have a little of everything': the ecological basis of some agricultural practices in Mettlana, Trinzinia. In *Regional variations in modern Greece and Cyprus,* edited by M. Dimen and E. Friedl, pp. 236–250. New York Academy of Sciences, Annals 268.
Frankenstein, S., and M. J. Rowlands
  1978 The internal structure and regional context of early iron age society in southwestern Germany. *Bulletin of the Institute of Archaeology of London* 15:73–112.
Friedman, J.
  1982 Catastrophe and continuity in social evolution. In *Theory and explanation in archaeology,* edited by C. Renfrew et al., pp. 175–196. Academic Press, New York.
Friedman, J., and M. J. Rowlands
  1977 Notes towards an epigenetic model of the evolution of "civilisation". In *The evolution of social systems,* edited by J. Friedman and M. J. Rowlands, pp. 201–276. Duckworth, London.
Gamble, C. S.
  1978a Resource exploitation and the spatial patterning of hunter–gatherers: a case study. In *Social organisation and settlement,* edited by D. Green, C. Haselgrove, and M. Spriggs, pp. 153–185. Oxford, British Archaeological Reports, International Series 47.

Gamble, C. S.
    1978b Optimising information from studies of faunal remains. In *Sampling in contemporary British archaeology*, edited by J. F. Cherry et al., pp. 321–353. British Archaeological Reports, British Series 50, Oxford, England.
Gamble, C. S.
    1979 Surplus and self sufficiency in the Cycladic subsistence economy. In *Papers in Cycladic prehistory*, edited by J. L. Davis and J. F. Cherry, pp. 122–133, UCLA Institute of Archaeology, Monograph 14.
Gamble, C. S.
    1981 Social control and the economy. In *Economic archaeology*, edited by A. Sheridan and G. N. Bailey, pp. 215–229. British Archaeological Reports, International Series 96, Oxford, England.
Gamble, C. S.
    1982 Animal husbandry, population and urbanisation. In *An island polity: the archaeology of exploitation on Melos*, edited by C. Renfrew and M. Wagstaff, pp. 161–171. Cambridge University Press, Cambridge, England.
Gamble, C. S.
    1984 Regional variation in hunter–gatherer strategy in the Upper Pleistocene of Europe. In *Hominid evolution and community ecology*, edited by R. Foley, pp. 237–260. Academic Press, London.
Gamble, C. S.
    in press Formation processes and the animal bones from the Mycenaean Sanctuary at Phylakopi. In *The Mycenaean Sanctuary at Phylakopi*, edited by C. Renfrew. British School at Athens, London.
Gifford, D. P.
    1981 Taphonomy and palaeoecology: a critical review of archaeology's sister disciplines. In *Advances in archaeological method and theory 4*, edited by M. B. Schiffer, pp. 365–438. Academic Press, New York.
Gilman, A.
    1981 The development of social stratification in bronze age Europe. *Current Anthropology* 22(1):1–8.
Goody, J.
    1976 *Production and reproduction*. Cambridge University Press, Cambridge, England.
Goody, J.
    1982 *Cooking, cuisine, and class*. Cambridge University Press, Cambridge, England.
Grigg, D. B.
    1982 *The dynamics of agricultural change*. Hutchinson, London.
Halstead, P.
    1981 From determinism to uncertainty: social storage and the rise of the Minoan palace. In *Economic archaeology*, edited by A. Sheridan and G. N. Bailey, pp. 187–213. British Archaeological Reports, International Series 96, Oxford, England.
Halstead, P., and J. O'Shea
    1982 A friend in need is a friend indeed: social storage and the origins of social ranking. In *Ranking, resource and exchange*, edited by C. Renfrew and S. J. Shennan, pp. 92–99. Cambridge University Press, Cambridge, England.
Halstead, P., I. Hodder, and G. Jones
    1978 Behavioural archaeology and refuse patterns: a case study. *Norwegian Archaeological Review* 11(2):118–131.
Harris, D. R.
    1977 Socio-economic archaeology and the Cambridge connection. *World Archaeology* 9:113–119.

Hayden, B.
   1981 Research and development in the Stone Age: technological transitions among hunter–gatherers. *Current Anthropology* 22:519–548.
Hedeager, L.
   1978 A quantitative analysis of Roman imports in Europe north of the Limes (0–400 A.D.) and the question of Roman–Germanic exchange. In *New directions in Scandinavian archaeology* (Vol. 1), edited by K. Kristiansen and C. Paludan-Müller, pp. 191–216. National Museum of Denmark, Copenhagen.
Higgs, E. S. (editor)
   1972 *Papers in economic prehistory.* Cambridge University Press, Cambridge, England.
Higgs, E. S. (editor)
   1975 *Palaeoeconomy.* Cambridge University Press, Cambridge, England.
Higgs, E. S., and M. R. Jarman
   1969 The origins of agriculture: a reconsideration. *Antiquity* 43:31–44.
Hillman, G. C.
   1973 Crop husbandry and food production: modern models for the interpretation of plant remains. *Anatolian Studies* 23:241–244.
Hodder, I. (editor)
   1982 *Symbolic and structural archaeology.* Cambridge University Press, Cambridge, England.
Hole, F., and K. V. Flannery
   1967 The prehistory of southwestern Iran: a preliminary report. *Proceedings of the Prehistoric Society* 33:147–206.
Hole, F., K. V. Flannery, and J. A. Neeley
   1969 *Prehistory and human ecology of the Deh Luran Plain.* Museum of Anthropology, University of Michigan, Memoir 1.
Ingold, T.
   1980 *Hunters, pastoralists and ranchers.* Cambridge University Press, Cambridge, England.
Ingold, T.
   1981 The hunter and his spear: notes on the cultural mediation of social and ecological systems. In *Economic archaeology,* edited by A. Sheridan and G. N. Bailey, pp. 119–130. British Archaeological Reports, International Series 96, Oxford, England.
Jarman, H. N.
   1972 The origins of wheat and barley cultivation. In *Papers in economic prehistory,* edited by E. S. Higgs, pp. 15–26. Cambridge University Press, Cambridge, England.
Jarman, M. R.
   1972 A territorial model for archaeology: a behavioural and geographical approach. In *Models in archaeology,* edited by D. L. Clarke, pp. 705–734. Methuen, London.
Jarman, M. R., G. N. Bailey, and H. N. Jarman (editors)
   1982 *Early European agriculture.* Cambridge University Press, Cambridge, England.
King, A.
   1978 A comparative survey of bone assemblages from Roman sites in Britain. *Bulletin of the Institute of Archaeology of London* 15:207–225.
Kristiansen, K.
   1978 The consumption of wealth in bronze age Denmark: a study in the dynamics of economic process in tribal societies. In *New directions in Scandinavian archaeology* (Vol. 1), edited by K. Kristiansen and C. Paludan-Müller, pp. 158–190. National Museum of Denmark, Copenhagen.
Kristiansen, K.
   1982 The formation of tribal systems in later European prehistory: northern Europe, 4000–500 b.c. in *Theory and explanation in archaeology,* edited by C. Renfrew et al., pp. 241–280. Academic Press, New York.

Leacock, E.
1954 The Montagnais 'hunting territory' and the fur trade. *Memoirs of the American Anthropological Association* 78.

Leacock, E., and R. B. Lee (editors)
1982 *Politics and history in band societies*. Cambridge University Press, Cambridge, England.

Legge, A. J.
1981 Aspects of cattle husbandry. In *Farming practice in British prehistory,* edited by R. Mercer, pp. 169–181. Edinburgh University Press, Edinburgh, Scotland.

Madsen, T.
in press The settlement system of the early agricultural societies in east Jutland, Denmark: a regional study. In *New directions in Scandinavian archaeology* (Vol. 3), edited by K. Kristiansen. National Museum of Denmark, Copenhagen.

Marks, S. A.
1976 *Large mammals and a brave people*. University of Washington Press, Seattle.

Masca Newsletter
1970 Bone from domestic and wild animals: crystallographic differences. *Masca Newsletter* 6(1):2.

Masca Newsletter
1973 Technique for determining animal domestication based on study of thin sections of bone under polarised light. *Masca Newsletter* 9(2):1.

McConnell, D., and D. W. Foreman
1971 Texture and composition of bone. *Science* 172:971–972.

Meadow, R. H.
1975 Mammal remains from Hajji-Firuz: a case study in methodology. In *Archaeozoological studies,* edited by A. T. Clason, pp. 265–283. Elsevier, Amsterdam.

Meadow, R. H.
1976 Methodological concerns in zooarchaeology. In *Thème spécialisé B: problèmes ethnographiques des vestiges osseux,* edited by F. Poplin, pp. 108–123. IX Congrès UISPP, Nice.

Meillassoux, C.
1972 From production to reproduction: a marxist approach to economic anthropology. *Economy and Society* 1:93–105.

Meillassoux, C.
1973 On the mode of production of the hunting band. In *French perspectives in African studies,* edited by P. Alexandre, pp. 187–203. Oxford University Press, Oxford, England.

Mounteney, G. A.
1981 Faunal attrition and subsistence reconstruction at Thwing. In *Prehistoric communities in northern England: essays in social and economic reconstruction,* edited by G. Barker, pp. 73–86. Sheffield University, Sheffield, England.

Murphy, R. F., and J. H. Steward
1956 Tappers and trappers: parallel processes in acculturation. *Economic Development and Culture Change* 4:335–355.

Murray, J.
1970 *The earliest European agriculture*. Edinburgh University Press, Edinburgh, Scotland.

O'Connell, J. F., and K. Hawkes
1981 Alyawara plant use and optimal foraging theory. In *Hunter–gatherer foraging strategies,* edited by B. Winterhalder and E. A. Smith, pp. 99–125. University of Chicago Press.

Østergård, M.
1980 X-ray diffractometer investigations of bones from domestic and wild animals. *American Antiquity* 45:59–63.

Paludan-Müller, C.
    1978 High Atlantic food gathering in northwestern Zealand: ecological conditions and spatial
        representation. In *New directions in Scandinavian archaeology* (Vol. 1), edited by K.
        Kristiansen and C. Paludan-Müller, pp. 120–157. National Museum of Denmark,
        Copenhagen.
Payne, S.
    1973 Kill-off patterns of sheep and goats: the mandibles from Asvan Kale. *Anatolian Studies*
        23:281–303.
Peck, R. W.
    1980 *Atworth Roman villa: a processual study.* Unpublished M.Sc. dissertation, Southampton
        University.
Peebles, C. S., and S. M. Kus
    1977 Some archaeological correlates of ranked societies. *American Antiquity* 42:421–448.
Randsborg, K.
    1974 Social stratification in early bronze age Denmark: a study in the regulation of cultural
        systems. *Prähistorische Zeitschrift* 49:38–61.
Renfrew, C.
    1972 *The emergence of civilisation.* Methuen, London.
Renfrew, C.
    1975 Trade as action at a distance: questions of integration and communication. In *Ancient
        civilisation and trade,* edited by J. A. Sabloff and C. C. Lamberg-Karlovsky, pp. 1–60.
        University of New Mexico Press, Albuquerque.
Renfrew, C.
    1977 Space, time, and polity. In *The evolution of social systems,* edited by J. Friedman and M.
        J. Rowlands, pp. 89–112. Duckworth, London.
Renfrew, C., and S. J. Shennan (editors)
    1982 *Ranking, resource and exchange.* Cambridge University Press, Cambridge, England.
Renfrew, C., and M. Wagstaff (editors)
    1982 *An island polity: the archaeology of exploitation on Melos.* Cambridge University Press,
        Cambridge, England.
Renfrew, J.
    1973 *Palaeoethnobotany.* Methuen, London.
Reynolds, P.
    1981 Deadstock or livestock. In *Farming practice in British prehistory,* edited by R. Mercer,
        pp. 97–122. Edinburgh University Press, Edinburgh, Scotland.
Rothamsted Experimental Station
    1970 *Details of the classical and long-term experiments up to 1967.* Lawes Agricultural Trust,
        Harpenden, England.
Rowley-Conwy, P.
    1981 Slash and burn in the temperate European Neolithic. In *Farming practice in British
        prehistory,* edited by R. Mercer, pp. 85–96. Edinburgh University Press, Edinburgh,
        Scotland.
Rowley-Conwy, P.
    1983 Sedentary–hunters: the Ertebølle example. In *Hunter–gatherer economy in prehistory,*
        edited by G. N. Bailey, pp. 111–126. Cambridge University Press, Cambridge, England.
Sahlins, M.
    1972 *Stone age economics.* Tavistock, London.
Shennan, S. J.
    1982 From minimal to moderate ranking. In *Ranking, resource and exchange,* edited by C.
        Renfrew and S. Shennan, pp. 27–32. Cambridge University Press, Cambridge, England.

Sheridan, A., and G. N. Bailey (editors)
    1981 *Economic archaeology.* British Archaeological Reports, International Series 96, Oxford, England.
Sherratt, A. G.
    1981 Plough and pastoralism: aspects of the Secondary Products Revolution. In *Pattern of the past: studies in honour of David Clarke,* edited by I. Hodder et al., pp. 261–305. Cambridge University Press, Cambridge, England.
Slicher van Bath, B. H.
    1963 *The agrarian history of western Europe, A.D. 500–1850.* Arnold, London.
Spratt, D. A.
    1981 Prehistoric boundaries on the North Yorkshire moors. In *Prehistoric communities in northern England: essays in social and economic reconstruction,* edited by G. Barker, pp. 87–104. Sheffield University, Sheffield, England.
Steel, T.
    1975 *The life and death of St. Kilda.* Fontana, Glasgow.
Wagstaff, M., and S. Auguston
    1982 Traditional land use. In *An island polity: the archaeology of exploitation on Melos,* edited by C. Renfrew and M. Wagstaff, pp. 106–133. Cambridge University Press, Cambridge, England.
Waterbolk, H. T.
    1971 Food production in prehistoric Europe. In *Prehistoric agriculture,* edited by S. Struever, pp. 335–358. Natural History Press, New York.
Watson, J. P. N.
    1975 Domestication and bone structure in sheep and goats. *Journal of Archaeological Science* 2:375–383.
Zeder, M. A.
    1978 Differentiation between the bones of carpines from different ecosystems in Iran by the analysis of osteological microstructure and chemical composition. In *Approaches to faunal analysis in the Middle East,* edited by R. H. Meadow and M. A. Zeder, pp. 69–84. Harvard University, Peabody Museum Bulletin 2.
Zohary, D.
    1969 The progenitors of wheat and barley in relation to domestication and dispersal in the Old World. In *The domestication and exploitation of plants and animals,* edited by P. J. Ucko and G. W. Dimbleby, pp. 47–66. Duckworth, London.
Zvelebil, M.
    1981 *From forager to farmer in the boreal zone.* British Archaeological Reports, International Series 115, Oxford, England.

2

Patterns in Faunal Assemblage Variability

J. M. MALTBY

Introduction

This chapter is concerned with the analysis of variability in archaeological animal bone assemblages. It reviews what we know of the factors that cause such variability and examines ways in which we might be able to isolate and analyse the effects of these factors. The data used to illustrate these methods are derived mainly from late prehistoric and historic sites in southern England. It is hoped that these represent a typical range of assemblages from temperate Europe and thus embrace most types of faunal sample variation likely to be encountered there.

Despite a substantial increase in the amount of time, effort, and money invested in archaeozoological research in the past decade, it is fair to say that the scope of faunal analysis has remained restricted. More often than not, animal bones seem to be studied simply to assess the contents of the meat diet and to obtain some idea of the basic subsistence patterns of the occupants of the settlement under consideration. Faunal analyses are usually published in excavation reports as a separate entity, often seeming to have only a tenuous connection with other aspects of the excavation and rarely being incorporated into general discussions about the settlements or societies involved. This is not to deny the need for the specialist's analysis; it is simply to question the approach to faunal remains of archaeologists and archaeozoologists alike.

The methodological framework underlying many attempts at subsistence reconstruction using animal bones must be called into question, since they have often ignored the complexities of how the assemblages were created. Subsistence reconstruction remains a worthwhile goal, but it must be accompanied by other questions of the data. If faunal studies have achieved nothing else during the last

33

10 years, they have at least shown how variable faunal assemblages can be. The problems of this variability have been recognised for some time. For example, Payne (1972a), Uerpmann (1973), and Meadow (1976) all gave carefully considered critiques of the difficulties of interpreting faunal data. Their concern epitomised the growing realisation that animal bones recovered from the partial excavation of a settlement need not be representative of the meat diet of its inhabitants, the relative number of animals of each species they kept, or the ages at which the stock was slaughtered. These problems are compounded if any comparisons are to be made between samples taken from different excavations and perhaps examined by different analysts. As a result, most attempts to equate regional or diachronic variations in faunal assemblages with variations in pastoral economies or strategies have proved, at best, to be highly speculative.

Given the complex processes that transform the animals kept or exploited by a community into collections of bone fragments (often deposited in a number of different locations), it is not surprising that variability in faunal samples must be the norm rather than the exception. Awareness of this fact in recent years has stimulated a considerable amount of research on the processes of faunal taphonomy. At the same time, it has been realised that variability in faunal assemblages need not necessarily be a bad thing. Provided that suitable methodologies can be developed to correlate some of the variations with past behavioural patterns, the interpretation of such variability should be of great value. Unfortunately, however, archaeozoologists are currently faced with enormous problems in trying to recognise the various processes that could have affected their material, but with very few independent means of understanding them (Binford 1978:8–10). There is indeed some justification for the view that we should suspend the analysis of more archaeological material until we have come to terms with all the causes of faunal variability:

> We have a backlog of investigations of the archaeological record that are almost certain to prove inadequate once we have developed methods for reliably giving meaning to archaeological phenomena. The facts demanded by the methods are almost certain to have been overlooked or recorded in ambiguous ways, rendering the 'data' from even our best excavations relatively useless. We need to discourage continuous exploratory excavation at the present time . . . We need a concentrated effort on middle-range research. We need to develop whole new methodologies. (Binford 1981:242)

It is important, however, that these new methodologies be applicable to all archaeozoological data. Ethnoarchaeological and experimental research can demonstrate the consequences of many taphonomic processes affecting faunal assemblages, but most of this work to date has concentrated on hunter–gatherer societies. Any methodological framework of general applicability must have the ability to isolate the processes of assemblage modification likely to be found in fully developed market economies, not just those of simpler situations. In this sense, research into the range of potential variation in the faunal residues of complex societies is not at all well developed.

Meadow (1976, 1980) has illustrated the series of transformations undergone by most of the bone populations we study. Each of these transformations results in a loss of data and information; after each stage, the surviving sample need not be a cross-section of the population from which it derived. These transformations can be broadly categorised as follows: *cultural practices* (for example, trade, redistribution, butchery, bone working, and ritual); *disposal strategies* (whether primary, secondary, or tertiary in the sense of Schiffer [1976]); *postdepositional taphonomic processes* (such as chemical actions in the soil, weathering, and scavenging); *archaeological sampling* (the choice of sites, parts of sites, or types of contexts within sites, for excavation); *recovery procedures* (whether or not sieving was carried out, and what kind of sieving); and finally *methods of analysis* (the type and detail of the information recorded, the presentation of the data, and so on). The scope for variation at any of these stages is enormous. Only if the consequences of these various transformations can be isolated can we begin to untangle the web of seemingly unrelated variability. As yet, no general methodological framework has been established. The remainder of this chapter explores some of the avenues that future developments in faunal analysis might take in search of this goal. To this end, I examine some specific causes of sample variability to see whether their effects can be isolated from other possible variables in the faunal record.

Analytical Variation

It is impossible to make use of many published faunal reports for comparative purposes because there is no indication of the methods of analysis used. Details of sample preservation, skeletal composition, fragmentation, butchery, and ageing evidence may be required to analyse specific causes of variability, but this information is rarely published in detail. Admittedly, such valuable information for faunal analysts is often deleted by the editorial pen. The information may be available in archival form, but it is usually inaccessible, if it exists at all. Even when more details are given, there is still the problem of the incompatability of methods amongst different workers. It has long been recognised that different quantification methods produce different results, and several authors have demonstrated this in detail (Bourdillon and Coy 1980; Grant 1975; Grayson 1973, 1978, 1979; King 1978; Maltby 1979a; Payne 1972b). Most of the discussion about the merits of various methodologies has been concerned with quantifying the relative importance of different species. However, similar problems exist with the methods used for quantifying the types of bone represented (for example, some workers count vertebrae whilst others do not, and some counts do not include limb bone shaft fragments or loose teeth or skull fragments); with the methods used to assess the age of animals at death (there are various systems of classifying tooth eruption, tooth wear, and epiphyseal fusion, and of interpreting combinations of these various types of data); and with the criteria used for assessing bone preservation and butchery techniques. Because of such incompatibilities in methodology, aggravated by the absence of accessible archives of raw data, detailed and useful intersite comparisons of material analysed by different workers can rarely be made—obviously a major and very regrettable failure in current techniques.

Analysis of Differential Recovery Rates

Several wet and dry sieving experiments to test the recovery rates of faunal remains have now been published (for example, Barker 1975; Clason and Prummel 1977; Levitan 1982; Payne 1972b, 1975; Thomas 1969). These experiments have all demonstrated that, to a greater or lesser extent, small bones have a better chance of being overlooked than large bones in normal excavation conditions. Variations in an individual's excavation ability, soil conditions, and the speed of excavation can also result in variability in unsieved material. Again, most of the concern has centred on the resulting biases concerning the relative number of bones of different species recovered, rather than the types of fragments represented. In the few examples where detailed results have been published, the findings have been disturbing. At Sitagroi, loose teeth found by usual trench recovery procedures contributed 26.2% of the sheep–goat sample, compared with 51.6% of the water-sieved sample using the same diagnostic elements (Payne 1975:15). Loose teeth and the small bones of all the major domestic species were grossly underrepresented in the unsieved samples from the site.

Barker (1975) argues that the biases in species representation may not be as serious on carefully trowelled sites, although "the sieved deposits at Monte Covolo produced, for example, individual teeth of smaller animals such as dog, pig, or sheep, which had been missed in trowelling" (Barker 1975:62). At West Hill, Uley, Gloucestershire, the sieving programme produced a greater percentage of vertebrae, carpals, tarsals, and phalanges of sheep–goat than the unsieved sample (Levitan 1982:28–29). The consequences of such biases for the types of analysis now considered essential in the interpretation of faunal data are fundamental. For example, the relative abundance of loose teeth in a sample can be used as a guide to the preservation of skeletal elements of a particular species (see next section). However, variations in recovery rates seriously impair such studies. Similarly, the absence or low representation of phalanges could be erroneously attributed to poor preservation conditions or to the removal of bones with the hides, rather than simply to poor recovery.

Solutions to such problems obviously lie with carefully considered sampling and sieving procedures during excavation (Gamble 1978; Payne 1975). In the meantime, faunal analysts are still faced with assessing the recovery efficiency of samples from excavations where little or no sieving has been done. Is it possible to establish a scale or ranking of recovery rates from different excavations or different parts of the same excavation? Watson (1972) suggests that measuring the size of fragments would give a good indication of recovery efficiency. However, whilst it is recognised that well-excavated samples include a large number of small, unidentifiable fragments (Payne 1975:14), the degree of fragmentation also depends on preservation conditions and butchery or marrow-processing practices. The construction of a recovery index must attempt to isolate or minimise numerous factors of variation. One way to achieve this is to compare the recovery rates of specific skeletal elements of different sizes. Each of these different elements must be of a consistent size (i.e., not regularly butchered or broken into various sizes). The elements to be compared must also have similar survival potential and should have been treated in similar ways during various disarticulation processes. Given these conditions, any discrepancy in the frequencies of these elements in a sample is most likely to be the result of differential recovery. Such elements, however, are rare.

Payne (1980:108) compared the relative abundance of different types of loose teeth in a Roman and Medieval sample from Towcester, Northamptonshire. He points out that the scarcity of the very small sheep–goat and cattle incisors in relation to the larger lower molars was the result of differential recovery. This test passes several of the conditions laid down for such comparisons: All teeth are dense elements that survive very well (Binford and Bertram 1977:109), they are obviously from adjacent parts of the body, and they are usually found intact. Although such an approach can act as a good guide to recovery rates, detailed quantification is made more complex by several factors. The first is that some teeth, particularly incisors and premolars, tend to fall out of mandibles postmortem more regularly than molars. This should result in more loose incisors than molars being recovered, but as yet we have no detailed knowledge of how differential preservation conditions release varying proportions of loose teeth into the archaeological record. In addition, the size of individual teeth varies with age. Wear on a sheep's second molar can reduce its length from approximately 35 mm to approximately 10 mm in old age (Carter 1975:232). Such factors, combined with the problems associated with the eruption ages of the teeth, may mean that different mortality patterns could produce biases in this type of detailed analysis, although these problems are not insuperable.

An alternative method is to compare the number of first and second phalanges recovered. These are small adjacent bones in the foot. The first phalanges of most species are significantly larger than the second phalanges. They usually survive complete or substantially intact, and in sheep at least, the density of the bones is similar (Binford and Bertram 1977:109). Given these factors, any discrepancy in the number of first and second phalanges is probably due to recovery biases. At the same time, however, the following factors also have to be taken into consideration: First, the bones may in some cases become separated during skinning or the removal of the hoof, although this does not seem to occur in well-documented modern observations of such procedures. Second, carnivore scavenging may destroy the bones differentially. Carnivores tend to chew away the skin and third phalanges of ungulates first and then work their way towards the distal metapodia (Binford 1981:74). There could therefore be instances where the

Table 2.1

Cattle and Sheep–Goat First and Second Phalanges Recovered in Various Excavations in Europe[a]

Site (reference)	1	2	3	4	5	6
Sitagroi—water-sieved (Payne 1975)	28	30	107.1	147	104	70.7
Cerro de la Encina (Lauk 1976)	61	50	82.0	39	24	61.5
Old Down Farm, Andover (Maltby 1981a)	42	27	64.3	127	58	45.7
Winnall Down (Maltby, n.d.a)	43	33	76.7	85	36	42.4
Bovenkarspel (Ijzereef 1981)	120	90	75.0	22	8	36.3
Groundwell Farm, Wiltshire (Coy, n.d.)	22	16	72.7	48	15	31.3
Münsterberg (Arbinger-Vogt 1978)	37	23	62.2	39	11	28.2
Twann (Becker and Johansson 1981)	719	468	65.1	123	26	21.1
Magdelensberg (Hornberger 1970)	802	413	51.5	231	48	20.8
Balksbury 1973 (Maltby, n.d.b)	28	11	39.3	69	13	18.8
Exeter Postmedieval (Maltby 1979a)	84	41	48.8	35	6	17.1
Exeter Roman (Maltby 1979a)	129	81	62.8	47	8	17.0
Cuesta del Negro (Lauk 1976)	177	67	37.9	84	13	15.5
Portchester Medieval (Grant 1977)	41	22	53.7	8	1	12.5
Kastell Vemania (Piehler 1976)	66	30	45.5	27	3	11.1
Portchester Saxon (Grant 1976)	182	61	33.5	18	2	11.1
Gloucester Eastgate (Maltby, 1983)	223	80	35.9	104	11	10.6
Exeter Medieval (Maltby 1979a)	183	98	53.6	115	12	10.4
S'Iliot (Uerpmann 1971)	49	19	38.8	194	20	10.3
Manching 1960 (Boessneck et al. 1971)	1023	146	14.3	29	3	10.3
Ulm-Weinhof (Anschutz 1966)	90	39	43.3	59	6	10.2
Eldon's Seat (Cunliffe and Philippson 1968)	33	13	39.4	10	1	10.0
Burgruine Niederrealta (Klumpp 1967)	60	36	60.0	11	1	9.1
Alcester 1976 (Maltby, n.d.c)	358	212	59.2	43	2	4.7
Manching 1955 (Boessneck et al. 1971)	1736	372	21.4	63	1	1.6
Manching 1957/8 (Boessneck et al. 1971)	2068	594	28.7	130	1	0.8
Canterbury Castle (King 1982)	44	19	43.2	8	0	0.0
Wüstung Wülfingen (Hanschke 1970)	232	76	32.8	13	0	0.0
Portchester Roman (Grant 1975)	411	126	30.7	32	0	0.0
Manching 1961 (Boessneck et al. 1971)	1305	377	28.9	70	0	0.0
Hockstetten (Arbinger-Vogt 1978)	67	18	26.9	12	0	0.0

[a]1, Cattle first phalanges; 2, cattle second phalanges; 3, cattle second phalanges as a percent of first phalanges; 4, sheep–goat first phalanges; 5, sheep–goat second phalanges; 6, sheep–goat second phalanges as a percent of first phalanges. All counts based on numbers of fragments except Portchester Castle and Canterbury Castle.

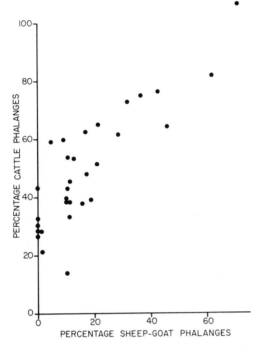

Figure 2.1 Relative percentages of cattle and sheep–goat phalanges. The samples are listed in Table 2.1.

scavenging of these bones was abandoned after the second (but before the first) phalanges had been consumed; in some cases, partial destruction by gnawing has reduced the size of these bones. Third, in assemblages derived mainly from the secondary deposition of bones, disarticulated phalanges may get separated spatially. Fourth, both bones, particularly in sheep-sized or smaller mammals, could be below the size of bones usually recovered in poor retrieval conditions. In addition, because phalanges are often removed with the hides and have poor survival qualities, their numbers in rubbish deposits tend to be low. Finally, many analyses do not differentiate between the lateral phalanges and the larger phalanges of the third and fourth digits of pigs. Given the variation in the size of these phalanges, however, such records should not be used.

The following analysis will be restricted to the phalanges of cattle and sheep–goat. Comparisons were made between the number of first and second phalanges from 31 samples (Table 2.1). Fewer second phalanges than first phalanges were recovered in all cases, apart from the cattle sample from the water-sieved material from Sitagroi. As expected, the results showed that cattle second phalanges had a better chance of recovery than those of sheep–goat. In addition, there was a strong positive correlation between the rate of recovery of second phalanges expressed as a percentage of first phalanges when the results from cattle and sheep–goat were compared (r = 0.85). This surprisingly strong linear relationship can be seen in Figure 2.1. These preliminary results are encouraging, although the index may need refinement when more samples can be included. Particularly important is the analysis of more sieved samples, since the only water-sieved sample considered here (Sitagroi) still produced fewer sheep–goat second phalanges than first phalanges, although these were much better represented than in any other sample. The reasons for this discrepancy may lie in one or more of the factors outlined above. Unfortunately, the analysis requires large samples, and it should be remembered that in poor retrieval conditions, many sheep–goat first phalanges will also have been overlooked. Further information about the sizes of bones in the sample is required, but the relevant data are usually unavailable. Nevertheless, it has been possible to compare 31 samples from 24 sites from several parts of Europe, originally analysed by 17 different workers, to produce a seemingly reliable guide to recovery rates of animal bones. If such scales are considered in conjunction with sample water-sieving experiments, it should be possible to assess the types of fragments that are likely to be slightly, moderately, or grossly underrepresented in samples collected by different systems of retrieval.

Taphonomy: Guidelines to Sample Preservation

Taphonomy may be seen as that area of paleontological research that defines, describes and systematizes the nature and effects of processes that act on organic remains after death.

(Gifford 1981:366)

This type of research on archaeozoological material is still in its infancy, but it has been the subject of several important contributions in recent years (e.g., Binford 1981; Binford and Bertram 1977; Brain 1981; Gifford 1981). The current state of research is fully discussed in these works, and their conclusions need not be repeated here. However, some points are worth bearing in mind in relation to the assemblages under study. The majority of taphonomic studies have been concerned with fossil and modern assemblages in Africa, particularly in the context of early hominid studies. Although many of the general taphonomic principles involved are relevant to samples from other periods and continents, bones deposited in late prehistoric or early historic settlements in temperate Europe may well have been subject to different sets or combinations of taphonomic processes. The possible effects of these have been given little consideration.

To date, most taphonomic studies relevant to such assemblages have been concerned with the behaviour of scavengers (Binford 1981; Binford and Bertram 1977; Brain 1967, 1969, 1976, 1981; Crader 1974; Hill 1976, 1979; Kent 1981; Klein 1975; Lyon 1970). Canid gnawing is a common feature of many late prehistoric and historic assemblages, but its effects have been given only scant attention. Brain (1976) and Binford and Bertram (1977) have established that the destruction of bone elements by dog scavenging is to some degree inversely correlated with the density of the elements. For example, the shaft fragments of limb bones have a better chance of survival than their more fragile articulator ends. In addition, since bones become denser with age, the destruction of younger bones of a particular species is likely to be greater (Behrensmeyer et al. 1979:17; Binford and Bertram 1977).

At this point, however, our knowledge of relevant taphonomic processes begins to falter. We have very limited information about the density of the bone elements of domestic animals. Binford and Bertram (1977:106–111) conducted their experiments on only a single caribou and three skeletons of sheep aged 6, 19, and 90 months, respectively. Clearly, this is not an adequate sample given the amount of variation in element densities they observed in these specimens, and the authors admit that more empirical data are required (Binford and Bertram 1977:119). For example, there are as yet no comparative data for the densities of the bones of cattle, pigs, or horses. Consequently, it is not possible to test the intuitive observation that pig bones preserve less well than those of cattle and sheep (King 1978:210–11), or conversely that some pig bones have a better chance of survival than sheep bones under certain conditions (Meadow 1978:19).

Another problem is that, in general, the effects of other taphonomic factors have not been studied in as much detail. For example, it is possible that the effects of chemical actions on bones may modify the assemblages in a different manner from dog scavenging. Although (again intuitively) we may feel that such destruction would be density-related, this has yet to be tested empirically. Some preliminary work has been done on the effects of bone-weathering (Behrensmeyer 1978; Mounteney 1981; Tappen and Peske 1970) and of trampling (Gifford 1978:81–83), but we are still at an early stage of research into all forms of taphonomic processes.

Nevertheless, it has become clear that it is essential to know how well an assemblage has been preserved in order to make any meaningful comparisons between samples. Ultimately, this requires much more rigorous and detailed recording of such variables as fragmentation, gnaw marks, and the surface condition of the bones. With such recording, it has been possible to begin to quantify the effects of differential preservation on archaeological samples. For example, in the Iron Age and Romano-British deposits from the small settlement site at Winnall Down, Hampshire (Fasham 1978:14–17), the sheep–goat samples varied enormously in content in different types of deposits. Loose teeth provided a significant proportion of each sample and were overwhelmingly dominant in some deposits (Figure 2.2). Irrespective of period, sheep–goat teeth were less dominant in pit fills than in shallow features such as quarry scoops and hut gullies. As noted earlier, teeth are the densest elements of the skeleton and can be expected to survive in conditions where other parts of the skeleton may have been destroyed by various agents of attrition. At Winnall Down there was a strong correlation between the percentage of sheep–goat loose teeth and the number of weathered or chemically eroded fragments in the assemblages as a whole (Table 2.2). In general, it seems that the better preservation of bones dumped in pits enabled a more representative range of sheep–goat elements to be recovered, although even the pits produced samples that were biased in favour of the denser elements.

Similarly, the high fragmentation of limb bones and the loss of their articulator surfaces are indicative of poor preservation. At Winnall Down it seems that the shaft fragments of the tibia, radius and metapodia survived better than other limb bones; these elements were consequently better represented in poorly preserved assemblages (Figure 2.2). Their better survival is probably related to their density and relative robusticity, although again there are as yet no empirical data to test this.

The analysis of the Winnall Down material suggests that the degree of attrition on animal bones can to some extent be monitored by studying the composition of the surviving assemblage. Given similar methods of recording, the preservation of assemblages from different sites could be compared quantitatively. However, this type of analysis assumes several factors as constant, including (1) that the carcases were brought to the settlement intact, (2) that a similar cross-section of the carcases was originally incorporated into the deposits under comparison, (3) that recovery rates were constant, and (4) that variations in butchery and marrow processing did not alter the amount of limb bone fragmentation. In other words, several other factors of variation have not been isolated.

Although in the case of Winnall Down it can be argued that these factors played only a secondary role in sample variation (Maltby, n.d.a), this need not always be the case. For example, it may be more fruitful to compare the number of loose teeth with the number of maxilla and mandible fragments; this would nullify possible biases caused by the first two factors mentioned earlier. At Winnall Down, jaw fragments were better represented in pits than in other features, and there was an encouragingly positive correlation between the percentage of loose teeth–jaw fragments and the percentage of limb bone shaft fragments–articulations (Figure 2.3). Both percentages increase in poorly preserved assemblages. However, there are still problems in making intersite comparisons. Figure 2.3 compares the Winnall Down data with a series of other samples from Exeter, Alcester (a small Romano-British town in Warwickshire), and a predominantly Iron Age assemblage from the hillfort at Balksbury, Hampshire. The results show fairly strong groupings of bones from the different sites. Most of the Winnall Down assemblages contained higher percentages of

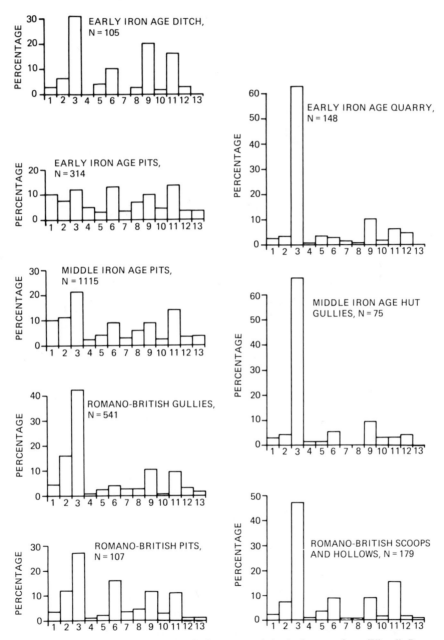

Figure 2.2 Relative percentages of sheep–goat skeletal elements from Winnall Down (Hampshire). 1. skull fragments including maxilla; 2. mandible; 3. loose teeth; 4. scapula; 5. humerus; 6. radius, ulna; 7. os coxae; 8. femur; 9. tibia; 10. carpals, tarsals; 11. metapodia (metacarpal, metatarsal); 12. phalanges; 13. others (mostly vertebrae fragments).

Table 2.2

Percentages of Loose Teeth in Sheep–Goat Samples and Percentages
of Eroded Fragments of All Species in the Deposits at Winnall Down

Phase	Context type	Loose teeth	Eroded fragments
3	Ditch	31.4	42.7
3	Pits	12.7	26.4
3	Quarry scoops	62.8	57.6
4	Hut gullies	66.7	64.4
4	Pits	21.5	18.6
6	Ditches, gullies	42.5	62.2
6	Pits	27.1	45.8
6	Scoops, hollows	46.9	62.9

loose teeth and shaft fragments, and it can be suggested that the assemblages
from Exeter, particularly the Medieval and Postmedieval samples, were better
preserved. This supports my intuitive observations about the preservation of the
samples, but since I did not record preservation data on the Exeter material in any
detail, it is only through analyses such as these that the samples can be compared. The Balksbury assemblage was fairly similar to the better-preserved Win-

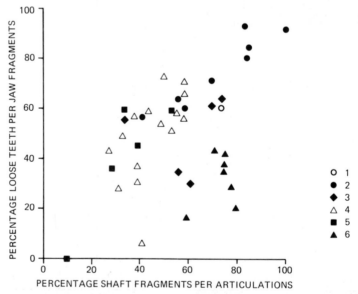

Figure 2.3 Comparison of relative percentages of loose teeth and limb bone shaft fragments of
sheep–goat from selected samples. 1, Balksbury (Iron Age): 2, Winnall Down (Iron Age and
Romano–British); 3, Exeter (Romano–British); 4, Exeter (Medieval); 5, Exeter (Postmedieval); 6,
Alcester (late Romano–British).

nall Down samples. As these assemblages were also mainly derived from pits dug in chalk, and as they belonged to a similar age range of animals (Maltby 1981b:173), similar results could perhaps be expected. The Alcester samples, on the other hand, contained markedly fewer teeth than expected from the results of the other sites. The explanation may lie partially in biases resulting from different recovery rates, as loose teeth are commonly overlooked in excavation, and it is likely that relatively more loose teeth will be overlooked than identifiable fragments of sheep–goat longbones. If so, it is perhaps significant that the sheep–goat phalanx ratio was much lower at Alcester than at Winnall Down in particular (Table 2.1).

The relationship between these two percentages may also be affected by other factors such as differential mortality patterns and variations in the preservation and fragmentation rates of the different limb bones. Obviously, more research is needed. At best, this particular technique can be used as a general guide to sample preservation, although it might facilitate comparisons with previously published data, where the discussion or description of preservation was given little consideration.

An alternative method of study applicable to large assemblages involves the analysis of the relative number of different parts of the same element. Binford (1981:217–219) suggests that the relative number of surviving proximal and distal articulations of the tibia and humerus could indicate whether an assemblage has been significantly modified by taphonomic processes. The later-fusing proximal articulations of both bones have a much lower density than their distal articulations, although both densities increase with age. Poorly preserved assemblages should therefore contain relatively fewer proximal articulations.

To test this theory on archaeological material, the data from 39 samples of sheep–goat tibia were examined (Table 2.3; Figure 2.4). Two percentages were calculated: (1) the number of proximal articulations (excluding unfused epiphyses), expressed as a percentage of the total number of proximal and distal articulations; and (2) the number of shaft fragments, expressed as a percentage of the total number of articulations plus shaft fragments. If the principal cause of fragmentation is attrition, we should expect a negative correlation between the two percentages. Fragmentation can also result from butchery and marrow processing, although in the former instance it is unlikely that an ovicaprid tibia will have been broken into more than two portions. Provided that the two portions do not regularly become separated spatially, this should not bias the results. The results of the analysis supported the hypothesis. The percentages were negatively correlated, and a fairly strong linear regression was calculated ($y = -0.74x + 73.91$; $r^2 = 0.62$). In nearly all cases, over 50% of the tibia fragments consisted of shafts only, indicating that even the best-preserved assemblages had suffered a high degree of fragmentation. The explanation for such high figures requires further analysis of the types of fragments represented. Nevertheless, the results

Table 2.3

Sheep–Goat Tibia Fragments from a Selection of British Assemblages[a]

	Site–context	Period	P	D	$\dfrac{P\%}{P+D}$	P + D	Shafts	$\dfrac{\text{Shafts}\%}{P+D+\text{shafts}}$
1	Exeter RS R2	R	1	5	16.7	6	22	78.6
2	Exeter GS R1	R	0	4	0.0	4	25	86.2
3	Exeter GS R5	R	3	16	15.8	19	49	72.1
4	Exeter GS R8	R	2	12	14.3	14	57	80.3
5	Exeter MM/CC R2 R5 R6	R	10	23	30.3	33	21	38.9
6	Exeter GS I-II Md 1	M	2	12	14.3	14	23	62.2
7	Exeter GS III Md 1	M	9	12	42.9	21	24	53.3
8	Exeter TS Md 1	M	9	11	45.0	20	23	53.5
9	Exeter GS I-II Md 2	M	18	26	40.9	44	53	54.6
10	Exeter GS III Md 2	M	32	45	41.6	77	69	47.3
11	Exeter TS Md 2	M	9	7	56.3	16	16	50.0
12	Exeter GS I-II Md 3	M	8	12	40.0	20	19	48.7
13	Exeter GS III Md 3	M	1	9	10.0	10	22	68.8
14	Exeter GS III Md 5	M	2	8	20.0	10	28	73.7
15	Exeter GS I-II Md 6	M	4	8	33.3	12	41	77.4
16	Exeter GS III Md 6	M	15	51	22.7	66	78	54.2
17	Exeter TS Md 6	M	9	23	28.1	32	31	49.2
18	Exeter GS I-II Md 9	M	3	9	25.0	12	38	76.0

		Period				P	D	
19	Exeter GS I-II Pm 1	Pm	12	28	30.0	40	33	45.2
20	Exeter GS II Pm 1	Pm	29	22	56.9	51	45	46.9
21	Exeter GS I Pm 3	Pm	7	19	26.9	26	29	52.7
22	Exeter TS F 316 Pm 3	Pm	12	6	66.7	18	3	14.3
23	Alton 1977	M,Pm	5	9	35.7	14	13	48.1
24	Silchester	R	2	12	14.3	14	39	73.6
25	Winnall Down 3, pits	I	9	13	40.9	21	13	38.2
26	Winnall Down 3, ditch	I	1	4	20.0	5	16	76.2
27	Winnall Down 3, quarry	I	0	2	0.0	2	13	86.7
28	Winnall Down 4, pits	I	14	31	31.1	45	63	58.3
29	Winnall Down 6, pits	R	1	5	16.7	6	6	50.0
30	Winnall Down 6, ditches	R	5	10	33.3	15	43	74.1
31	Groundwell Farm	I	1	16	5.9	17	132	88.6
32	Sheffield Manor	Pm	2	17	10.5	19	134	87.6
33	Gloucester Eastgate	R	2	8	20.0	10	12	54.5
34	Gloucester Eastgate 5	R	4	9	30.8	13	24	64.9
35	Gloucester Eastgate	M	9	23	28.1	32	70	68.6
36	Gloucester Eastgate	Pm	28	36	43.8	64	112	63.6
37	Alcester	R	10	73	12.0	83	314	79.1
38	Okehampton Castle	M,Pm	29	98	22.8	127	300	70.3
39	Baylham House	I/R	4	43	8.5	47	295	86.3

[a]Period: I—Iron Age; R—Roman; M—Medieval; Pm—Postmedieval. P—number of proximal articulations; D—number of distal articulations. Data for samples 1–22, 24–30, 32–39 from author's archives; data for samples 23 and 31 from archives of J. Coy; see also Figure 2.4.

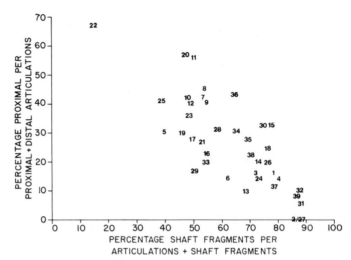

Figure 2.4 Preservation of articulations and fragmentation of sheep–goat tibiae from a selection of British archaeological assemblages. The samples are listed in Table 2.3.

appear quite encouraging, and a comparison of Figures 2.3 and 2.4 shows similar trends in the relative preservation of sheep–goat assemblages from Exeter, Winnall Down, and Alcester.

The best-preserved sample analysed (22: Exeter Pit TS F 316) contained twice as many proximal as distal articulations. It is likely that the results are biased in this instance (and perhaps in some of the other Medieval and Postmedieval samples from Exeter) by the separation of the proximal and distal halves of the bones after butchery. The assemblage in TS F 316 was dominated by good meat bones; very few bones from the skull, jaws, or limb extremities were found (Maltby 1979a:24, 148–149). The proximal half of the tibia would usually have been associated with the femur in legs of mutton, whereas the distal half was more often considered as waste and would thus be underrepresented in this particular deposit. The potential biases created by such activities may limit the scope of this type of analysis, although in this instance it can be used to support the premise that the assemblage consisted principally of bones from prime joints of meat brought to the site. Nevertheless, the method may be able to provide an indication of the survival rates of assemblages, which can be compared with other methods of analysis. Comparable results were obtained, for example, when a similar analysis was performed on the proximal and distal articulations of the humerus in the same samples.

Archaeozoologists, therefore, already have a number of methods available to them for calculating the relative state of preservation of their samples, since it is possible to separate taphonomic from other factors of variation. Nonetheless, there is obviously still a substantial amount of research to be done before we can understand in detail the survival patterns of the skeletal elements of different species. Ultimately, we have to progress much further than simple comparisons of the survival rates of different assemblages. We have to devise methods of comparing samples that have undergone substantially different degrees of destruction. Eventually, this may be achieved by employing mathematical decay models to quantify rates of bone loss (Gilbert and Singer 1982:32–37). However, we are still some way from being able to provide realistic figures to use with such formulae.

Carcase Utilisation and Disposal Strategies

Since different parts of any carcase may be valued for a variety of uses, it is logical to assume that the activities involved in butchery should produce distinct patterns in the faunal record. However, interpretation is hindered by three major problems: insufficient knowledge of the expected nature of the assemblages created by the postulated activities, admixing of bones from different activities, and biases created by other sources of sample variation. Binford (1978:7–12; 1981:88–89, 184–189) has demonstrated that many interpretations of faunal variability have not taken these problems into account. He stresses the need to obtain detailed knowledge of the effects that different processes will have on assemblages. His own ethnoarchaeological observations of Nunamiut butchery practices (Binford 1978) have helped to clarify the interpretation of many of the marks produced on bones by disarticulation, skinning, filleting, and marrow processing. He has demonstrated that, given very detailed knowledge of a society's or group's butchery practices, it is possible to make accurate interpretations of assemblage variability by comparing the relative frequencies of different skeletal elements against various predicted models. These models consist of indices derived from assessments of, for example, the relative value of meat, marrow, and bone grease associated with different elements of the skeleton, and of general utility indices in which all the different values of the element are taken into account.

Although complex in detail, the Nunamiut system of caribou carcase utilisation is relatively simple to monitor, since many of the processes took place in different locations (such as kill sites and residential sites) and thus produced discrete assemblages that closely fit the predicted models. Binford (1978:473) is probably correct in his assertion that the variability of faunal assemblages created by the Nunamiut is likely to be more complicated than that of many other groups because of their heavy dependence on large mammals for food and their consequent extensive exploitation of the carcases. He is probably overstating his case, however, when he claims: "We may anticipate that the models most likely to accommodate the vast majority of archaeological cases have already been generated'' (Binford 1978:473). In the first place, many different models of carcase utilisation are required, since the utility indices of each element will vary between different species and in different societies, depending on the methods of butchery and the importance placed on the procurement of different products.

These values may also vary both temporally and spatially. For example, it appears that the intensity of marrow extraction from cattle limb bones varied markedly in iron age and Roman settlements in southern England. Generally, the Romano-British bones seem to have been broken open for marrow, but Figure 2.5 shows that a relatively high percentage of cattle metapodia from the Iron Age deposits at Winnall Down survived intact. In addition, several other metapodia were complete except for their distal articulation. Close inspection of the bones revealed that in many instances, this more vulnerable articulation had been destroyed by weathering, or more commonly by canid gnawing. Some metapodia had been broken open, but it was by no means a consistent operation. This contrasts with an early Romano-British assemblage from the town of Silchester (Hampshire), which contained no complete metapodia at all. Contemporary assemblages from Winnall Down also revealed increased metapodial fragmentation, which cannot be fully explained by the poorer preservation of the Romano-British assemblage at that site. It seems that marrow extraction had become more important on this rural settlement as well, although its intensity was not as marked as in urban centres such as Silchester, Exeter, and London (Maltby, in press). Similar contrasts could be made for the breakage frequencies of other limb bones at these sites.

Although meat and marrow indices could be devised for cattle in a similar manner to those devised for caribou and sheep (Binford 1978:15–45), the formulation of general utility indices is much more difficult, since it appears that the relative importance of different products varied markedly. In addition to variations in butchery and marrow processing, it is possible that the use of certain elements for bone working in the periods under consideration may also have played a significant part in assemblage variation. Perhaps such general utility models, which will be extremely difficult to calculate in any case, may be less relevent to sedentary communities, since it is likely that many of their animals were killed within or close to their settlements. Decisions relating to carcase utilisation would thus be different from the extended logistical strategy of the Nunamiut, who had the problem of transporting the carcases significant distances from kill site to residential site (Binford 1978:72).

A second major problem is that in sedentary settlements, the faunal remains discarded during various activities may not be separated spatially. In addition, much archaeological animal bone must be regarded as secondary refuse (Schiffer 1976). In such circumstances, it is possible that waste bones from several activities (e.g., skinning, primary butchery, cooking, and eating) may end up in the same deposit. The problem is compounded by the timespan of archaeological

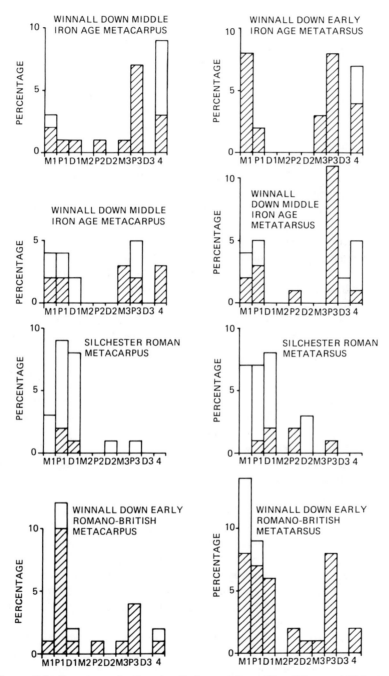

Figure 2.5 Percentages of cattle metapodia fragmentation at Winnall Down and Silchester. M, shaft; P, proximal; D, distal; 1, ¼ or less of bone present; 2, approximately ½ bone present; 3, approximately ¾ of bone present; 4, complete bone. Hatching denotes those bones recording as gnawed or eroded.

accumulations. Binford (1978:483) has pointed out that bones discarded in a location over a short period of time are more likely to display content variability than those accumulated over a long period. Given the severe limitations of archaeological dating, it cannot be assumed that different activities necessarily took place in discrete locations throughout a datable phase of occupation.

Finally, in many rural settlements in particular, relatively little bone waste would have been produced. If the inhabitants did not have spatial restrictions on bone disposal, it is likely that the disposal of bone refuse would have been fairly casual. Hence, much of it is likely to have been destroyed or modified by the actions of scavengers or weathering. It has been observed that dogs and other scavengers not only modify the assemblage by destroying bones, but they can also play a significant part in bone distribution (Brain 1981; Isaac 1967; Kent 1981; Kramer 1982:44).

Although these problems make the task of recognising clearly defined activity areas a complicated one, there are many faunal assemblages that can be shown to display significant variability due to differential usage of the carcase. The large-scale processing that took place on urban sites in Britain from the Roman period onwards has produced examples of very distinctive assemblages associated with specific activities. For example, several Romano-British towns have produced significant accumulations of primary butchery waste from cattle. Typically, these consist of large numbers of skull, mandible, and metapodial fragments. The skulls were broken open to remove the brain, and the metapodials were broken to remove the marrow. Good meat bones, horncores, and sometimes phalanges are grossly underrepresented (Maltby, 1984). Although no detailed meat utility indices have been developed for domestic cattle, there can be no doubt that these assemblages would fit an inverse index, with the major meat-bearing bones taken elsewhere. In addition, phalanges may have been removed with the skins, and the horncores either removed in the same manner or taken away for horn-working.

Other large-scale processing activities of cattle carcases have been found on Roman sites. At Cirencester (Gloucestershire), excavations near the centre of this important Roman town uncovered a midden consisting mainly of the systematically processed bones of cattle. Here, good and poor meat bones were not spatially separated, although fragments of mandible and skull predominated. Most of the longbones had been split open longitudinally to extract marrow, and the meat stripped crudely from their shafts. Cattle bones formed over 90% of the identifiable fragments, whereas sheep and pig were grossly underrepresented compared with assemblages recovered elsewhere in the town. There seems little doubt that this assemblage was produced by an establishment specialising in cattle butchery and processing. Its products may have been destined for sale in the nearby Forum Maltby 1984:130–132.

In the southern Netherlands, assemblages from the *vicus* associated with the

Roman *castellum* at Zwammerdam and at Xanten were both dominated by cattle upper limb bones, carpals and tarsals, with the rest of the skeletal elements virtually unrepresented. At Zwammerdam, all bones, apart from a few carpals and tarsals, had been chopped through longitudinally. Most of the articulations of the limb bones had been halved or quartered in this way. These accumulations were interpreted as bones that had been boiled up for broth (van Mensch 1974). King (1978:225) suggests that these bones could also have been kept on the boil for the extraction of bone grease and marrow. Many of the elements represented correspond to the parts of high white grease utility in sheep and caribou (Binford 1978:32–38), although the Nunamiut usually pulverised these bones to facilitate grease extraction (Binford 1978:158–159). Schmid (1972:48–49) suggests that an assemblage consisting just of the fragments of longbone shafts from Augst (*Augusta Raurica*), in Switzerland, may have been the waste from large-scale glue-boiling activities.

The virtual absence of scapulae and pelves from these assemblages suggests that they became separated spatially from the major meat-bearing limb bones. The scapula and pelvis can be important meat bones, but they are not good marrow bones. The separation of these bones from bones of low meat value and high marrow content may therefore be expected in certain circumstances. Several Romano-British assemblages have produced disproportionately high numbers of such bones. For example, a late Roman assemblage at Gloucester was dominated by fragments of cattle scapula, pelvis, and the proximal articulation of the femur (Maltby 1979b, 1984). The mid-first century A.D. levels at Balkerne Lane, Colchester, also produced a large proportion of cattle scapulae (Luff 1982:142). Schmid (1972:42–43) suggests that the meat from the scapula could often have been smoked during the Roman period. Preserving processes such as smoking or salting are additional sources of potential faunal variability, although we lack a clear understanding of the types of assemblages to expect from large-scale processing of this sort. Large-scale bone-working may also have had a significant bearing on the distribution of faunal elements, depending on which parts were selected as raw material. In the early Roman period at Winchester (Hampshire), for example, one deposit was dominated by thousands of small splinters of large mammal bones (mostly cattle), the offcuts of bone-working. The identifiable cattle fragments in this case consisted mainly of scapulae and parts of the lower limb bones (J. P. Coy, personal communication).

It is clear, therefore, that the large-scale processing of cattle carcases in the Roman period can leave quite distinct and spatially separate accumulations of bones. Most of the examples included here do not appear to have been severely modified by taphonomic processes, probably due to their rapid burial. However, even in this period the majority of assemblages fail to display such marked contrasts. As our knowledge of the range of processes applied to cattle carcases increases, it should be possible to obtain a better understanding of such composite assemblages from Romano-British sites. Although we do not know how much the practices varied, it appears that on some occasions skulls and mandibles, metapodia, phalanges, horncores, scapulae (and pelves), and the shafts and articulations of the major limb bones were all treated quite differently from each other. On urban and military settlements in particular, it should sometimes be possible to explain smaller variations in assemblage content using knowledge of these processes.

Distinct patterning resulting from carcase processing can also be recognised in the remains of other domestic species. For example, some Medieval and Postmedieval assemblages in England have a marked bias towards the major meat bones. The Medieval sheep assemblages from Okehampton Castle (Devon) contained very few fragments of the mandible, skull, metapodia, and phalanges and were dominated by the principal meat bones (Maltby 1982a; see also Figure 2.6). Clearly, such an imbalance cannot be ascribed simply to differential recovery or preservation, although canid gnawing had modified the assemblage quite heavily (1982a:Figure 2.4, no. 38). The assemblage consisted almost entirely of prime joints of meat that had been brought to the castle for consumption. This assemblage contrasts clearly with a subsequent early postmedieval (late sixteenth century) sample from the same excavation, in which sheep mandibles were found in much greater abundance (Figure 2.6). Excavations in Buckingham produced a sample of sheep bones dated to the thirteenth century A.D. consisting entirely of

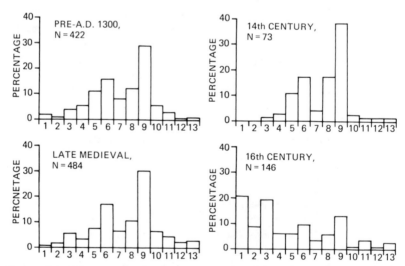

Figure 2.6 Relative percentages of sheep–goat skeletal elements from Okehampton Castle (Devon). 1, skull fragments including maxilla; 2, mandible; 3, loose teeth; 4, scapula; 5, humerus; 6, radius, ulna; 7, os coxae; 8, femur; 9, tibia; 10, carpals, tarsals; 11, metapodia (metacarpal, metatarsal); 12, phalanges; 13, others (mostly vertebrae fragments).

mandible, skull, and metapodia fragments (Rackham 1977), the types of bone so poorly represented in the medieval deposits at Okehampton. Although the two samples are otherwise unrelated, they provide evidence for the identical treatment of sheep carcases during primary butchery.

Analysis of activity patterns can therefore be quite productive, especially if serially or spatially diverse activities connected with carcase utilisation took place on a large scale. Assemblages that are distinctive of specific activities have been recognised, particularly in large urban settlements, although the full range of faunal variability on such sites is unlikely to be met because of the limited percentage of the settlements that can usually be excavated. Theoretically, it should be possible to obtain a better overall picture of settlement activity on smaller rural settlements, where researchers can uncover a substantial proportion of the settlement. However, the relatively small amounts of bone waste likely to be produced on such sites create fewer problems of disposal; bones are more likely to be scattered on middens or in an open space rather than be deliberately buried, resulting in the destruction of many bones through weathering and disturbance, or through scavenging. The limited ethnoarchaeological work on animal bone distributions from rural settlements supports this premise. Kramer (1982: 44) notes that the villagers of Aliabad in Turkey deliberately buried bones only when there was a large wedding or burial feast. Most of the other bones were disposed of casually, either in streams or in open areas where they were much disturbed by dogs. In Kenya, Hodder (1982a) observes that of the cattle or pig bones discarded outside the compound, only those that lodged in crevices escaped destruction by dogs. We may therefore expect that the majority of faunal assemblages from rural settlements will be small (compared to the original number of carcases exploited), scattered, badly disturbed, and poorly preserved.

Attempts to explain the intrasite variability of faunal remains in terms of differential activity face severe problems. Such difficulties hampered Halstead et al. (1978) in their examination of pottery, plant remains, and bones from the late iron age and Romano-British settlements at Wendons Ambo (Essex). Although such a multidisciplinary approach is much welcomed, the results from faunal analysis are unconvincing because of the small sample size, the lack of consideration of factors such as differential preservation, and the unsubstantiated assumptions that have been made about the use of different parts of the carcase. Meadow (1978) found significant differences in the types of bone deposited in interior and exterior locations at the neolithic settlement of Hajji Firuz (northwest Iran). However, the explanations offered for the observed variations were inconclusive as a result of the small number of bones involved. Similar studies at Winnall Down show that most of the Middle Iron Age (third to first centuries B.C.) pits contained a relatively high number of sheep–goat bones, compared with the number of cattle bones found (Maltby 1981b:166; n.d.a). Generally, however, the density of bones in the deposits was low, and there was evidence of a significant amount of canid gnawing, although there were some notable exceptions.

Some pits with high densities of bone contained a much larger proportion of cattle and horse bones. One pit included complete skeletons of a pig and a dog sealed with packed chalk; above these, there was a concentration of well-preserved bones dominated by those of cattle and horses, consisting mainly of complete or substantial portions of mandible and limb bones, which butchery marks revealed had been disarticulated and filleted. The assemblage was notable for its excellent preservation and lack of modification by scavengers; the bones must have been buried soon after butchery. At least twelve cattle (although not their whole carcases) were represented. It seems probable that these carcases were butchered over a short period of time, since the immediate disposal of bones is more likely when a relatively large amount of waste is created. The association of these bones with the burials of the pig and the dog may imply the slaughter of several animals in connection with some ritual or ceremonial event. Similar concentrations of butchery waste have been found in other Iron Age deposits at Winnall Down and at Old Down Farm, Andover (Maltby 1981a).

It is important to stress that such assemblages are exceptional on these Iron Age sites. Most of the pits at both settlements contained a relatively low density of bones, with sheep and pig bones generally better represented than in the examples described here. The butchery evidence implies that meat from large mammals was often stripped from them, whereas meat from sheep and pigs was more often cooked on the bone. As a result, when cooking and meat-stripping events took place in different locations, distinctive accumulations of bone were sometimes deposited. However, spatial variation was much less marked than in the large Romano-British examples discussed earlier. Because of the secondary deposition of many of the bones and the low level of bone survival, any significant patterns in the distribution of different bone elements were likely to be greatly disturbed. However, it is often possible to distinguish general patterning at least. At Winnall Down, for example, examination of the associations of different bones in the pits revealed that cattle humeri, radii, and ulnae were more commonly associated than, for example, cattle humeri and metapodia. Cattle and horse bones generally had more associations with each other than with sheep bones, although this picture was complicated by factors of differential preservation (Maltby, n.d.a). This type of analysis can be expanded to include a wider range of bones, provided that taphonomic factors are also taken into account.

It can be shown that faunal remains from sedentary settlements sometimes display distinct patterning, resulting from the purely functional utilisation of the carcase and the disposal of waste. However, we would be deluding ourselves to expect that all sites will provide clear, unequivocal evidence for such activities. Indeed, the most convincing examples of specific carcase utilisation events are, by their size, unusual and atypical of the everyday disposal of bone waste. With our present sketchy understanding of assemblage formation and destruction processes, added to further complications to be discussed in the following sections, any reconstruction of such activities from archaeozoological data can still be only partial and poorly detailed.

Symbolism and Faunal Variation

It has been pointed out by several authors that purely functional explanations for animal bone distributions can be misleading. Since animals are important in the belief systems of many societies, it is possible that the symbolic roles of animals may be reflected in the treatment of their carcases. This may be manifested in taboos of eating the flesh or drinking the milk of certain species, or in the assignation of symbolic meaning to particular species and/or parts of their bodies. There are many ethnographic examples of such symbolic behaviour. Hodder (1982b) and Moore (1982) provide ethnoarchaeological examples where such cognitive behaviour has resulted in the distinct patterning of bones of different species. Tilley (1981) argues that the division of animal carcases may provide both a framework for social classification and a powerful source of symbolism. He suggests that these may be reflected in the distinct spatial patterning of different classifications of bones—for example, left-sided as opposed to right-sided bones, forelimbs against hindlimbs, and so on.

There is, of course, still the problem of distinguishing this sort of variability from that created by differential functional usage of bones and differential preservation. One envisages the development of a debate among archaeozoologists favouring either strictly functional or cognitive explanations for observed faunal variability. A similar discussion has long engaged anthropologists concerning the economic rationality of food taboos such as Islamic food prohibition or the Indian sacred cow. Neither extreme view seems satisfactory, and the same is probably true for archaeological studies of rubbish disposal. As Moore (1982:76) states:

> It seems more probable that differential distribution of refuse types will always be the product of interaction between functional requirements and cognitive categories. . . . In only a few cases is it likely to be possible to interpret the spatial patterning of refuse purely in terms of either functional or cognitive factors.

Although the emphasis of different workers will inevitably vary, the interpretation of refuse disposal requires much more rigorous analysis than has been practised so far by proponents of either school of thought. Detailed analysis has to be carried out on the contents of each distinct archaeological layer or context, but only rarely have such data been recorded, let alone analysed.

Redistribution and Trade of Animal Products

There can be no doubt that the exchange, redistribution, or trade of animals and their products was an important factor in most late prehistoric and early historic societies. Yet the possible repercussions on faunal assemblages have rarely been considered. Whereas there has been much discussion relating to theories of exchange and trade and the analysis of artefact distributions, discussions concerning the redistribution of food, generally presumed to have been the commodity exchanged most commonly, have been limited. O'Shea (1981) argues that food exchanges can be viewed as a form of social storage, a mechanism to cope with periodic scarcity. Halstead (1981) discusses the evidence of sheep and wool management embodied in the Linear B tablets at Knossos in Minoan Crete from a similar standpoint. Sherratt (1982:23) suggests that seasonal cattle fairs took place at certain sites in Neolithic northwestern Europe. Rowlands (1980) argues that exchange in societies in the Late Bronze Age of northwestern Europe was important for the establishment and maintenance of control by dominant groups. For example, he proposes that there was a regional trade in livestock and their products from the upland settlements in southern England to the elites of the lowland river settlements, and that cattle circulated as a wealth item in ceremonial exchange (Rowlands 1980:35–36). Bradley (1980) also suggests that feasting and the control of food resources and distribution may have been important in some parts of Late Bronze Age Britain. At the same time, Gilman (1981) argues that local self-sufficiency would have precluded the large-scale regional exchange of food in Bronze Age Europe. Champion (1982) suggests that increased management of food storage and distribution may have become a feature of certain areas of western Europe from 1250 b.c. onwards. Unfortunately, similar discussions of the possible exchange of livestock or their products in the Iron Age are rare. It is not until the Late Iron Age, when classical sources such as Strabo and Tacitus mention the export of food, hides, and hunting dogs from Britain and western Europe, that archaeologists have ventured to pay due consideration to such matters.

In the Roman period, the situation is rather different. Trade was obviously important, and the debate here has recently centred more upon how exchange systems operated. However, the question of food distribution has figured only occasionally in the discussions, and little archaeological evidence has been used (Maltby, 1984). The same criticism can be levelled against studies of exchange in later historical periods.

Given the potential importance of food exchanges, it is worth assessing the extent to which archaeozoological studies can assist in recognising various modes of distribution.

SMALL-SCALE INTRASETTLEMENT EXCHANGE

Most food distribution takes place between residents of the same settlement. Most such transactions within or between households take place under the principle of "generalised exchange" (Sahlins 1974). Although such reciprocal exchanges exist in all societies, their importance may vary. Detailed analyses of such exchanges are limited in anthropological studies. Henry (1951) studied food distribution in a Pilagà village in Argentina where 95% of the transactions between villagers involved food. He made detailed records of 196 distributions by 36 residents during a 6-month period. The most important of these distributions were those of fish, palms, and parts of sheep butchered by the villagers. The analysis demonstrated that the more productive villagers made more distributions than they received. In a similar study of a Sallumiut Eskimo village, Pryor (1977:69–101) recorded 1250 distribution episodes between the inhabitants over a 6-week study period. He observed that a considerable amount of food was distributed by hosts during visits by members of other households. Pryor concluded that a significant percentage of most people's diets was obtained in households other than their own. He also notes that many of these exchanges were not strictly reciprocated and that there was a structured imbalance in the amounts of food distributed by and to different villagers. Both Pryor (1977:89) and MacCormack (1981:162) support Sahlin's (1974:215) conclusion that food has a special element of sociability and can be given away without reciprocal obligations in more cases than other commodities.

The most detailed ethnoarchaeological studies of intrasettlement meat-sharing have been made amongst hunting groups. Both Yellen (1977:305), in his study of the !Kung Bushmen, and Binford (1978:472), in his observations of the Nunamiut, claim that meat-sharing may leave distinct spatial patterning in faunal remains. They both point out that the amount of sharing may depend upon the size and number of animals culled in relation to consumer needs. There are, however, severe difficulties in applying such knowledge to archaeological material. As Binford (1978:471) states:

> The social criteria that are conditioning the decisions to give good parts to some people and marginal parts to others are not evident in the spatial (logistical) situation or the time utility (storage) sequence. Also, confusion arises from the fact that most such judgements of distribution are egocentric relative to the person procuring the meat. Thus the patterns of distribution shift with the individual conducting the distribution relative to the recipients. In any site where there are multiple consumer units, the likelihood increases that there will be multiple distributional acts by different people. This results in a very confusing distribution of anatomical parts at any one consumer location.

Most late prehistoric and early historic settlements contain such multiple consumer units. Since in most cases it is impossible to assign closely dated refuse to a particular household, any subtle variations in assemblage content between, for example, households of different productive capabilities will not be visible. Indeed, given all the additional modifications resulting from disposal strategies and taphonomic factors, only in exceptional cases will it be possible to monitor even the existence of small-scale intrasettlement exchanges of meat, let alone their extent and nature.

FEASTS AND FESTIVALS

In contrast to small-scale exchanges, large-scale intrasettlement distributions may be visible. Reference has already been made to Kramer's observation (1982:44) that only bones deposited from feasts tended to be deliberately buried in the Turkish village of Aliabad. In many societies, the slaughter of large mammals in particular and the subsequent division of the meat take place at a communal feast. Apart from the social and possible ceremonial or religious importance of such occasions, there is the practical consideration that sharing in this way is an efficient method of disposing of a large quantity of meat and an alternative to storage preparation through drying, smoking, freezing, or salting. Given that the amount of waste may be of some magnitude on these occasions, it is more likely that the deliberate burial of rubbish may take place. It is tempting to view the Iron Age examples of concentrations of cattle and horse bones in certain pits in this light (see "Carcase Utilisation and Disposal Strategies").

Of course, feasts may also be held on an intersettlement basis, and extreme examples of such large-scale reciprocal meat-sharing have been observed in many Melanesian groups. Gilbert and Singer (1982:26) focus the attention of archaeozoologists on the observations of Rappaport (1968) concerning the distribution of thousands of kilograms of pork by the Tsembaga in the Papua New Guinea highlands. In the same region, a study of exchange amongst the Wola (Sillitoe 1979) illustrates a similar phenomenon. Apart from many other exchanges of pigs, large kills are organised by members of a territorial group at approximately 5-year intervals. Data collected from observations of such pig kills in 1973–1974 revealed that more meat was distributed to persons resident elsewhere than to those belonging to the hosts' settlement. The size of the portions distributed tended to vary according to the closeness of the relationship between recipient and donor, as well as the amount of pork available. Of 133 pigs killed by 33 owners, legs of pork were given to 230 recipients, of whom 139 were resident elsewhere. The distribution of smaller portions of meat followed the same pattern.

Little is known of how such large-scale feasts and slaughter may be visible in the archaeological record. Much would depend on the butchery methods and subsequent disposal strategies. Nevertheless, one suspects that such large-scale slaughtering activities as those described in Melanesia or the potlatches in North America would leave significant traces. Apart from the disposal of large amounts of waste bones, such activities may be reflected in other aspects of the archaeozoological record. Strathern (1978) notes that at Wiru village festivals in Papua New Guinea, the build-up of pigs to be slaughtered resulted in the killing of 325 male and 181 female animals in festivals monitored between 1967 and 1974. This imbalance ensured that sufficient sows remained for breeding purposes. It is possible that the sex ratios in bone assemblages derived from such festivals may be quite different from the residues of small-scale pig slaughtering.

Although no clear evidence has emerged of comparable meat exchanges between communities on British prehistoric sites, their possible existence, perhaps on a smaller scale, certainly cannot be ruled out. Perhaps the concentrations of well-preserved animal bones on certain British Neolithic sites, such as Hambledon Hill (Legge 1981), could be viewed in the light of such possible food exchanges. Large dumps of bone at Thwing, a Late Bronze Age settlement in Yorkshire, have also been interpreted as residues of occasional feasting (Mounteney 1981).

OTHER INTERSETTLEMENT EXCHANGES

A common fallacy of archaeozoological reports is the assumption that in societies without markets, all the bones represented in an assemblage must belong to animals bred by the inhabitants of the settlement under study. In fact, the amount of meat imported either through reciprocal exchanges or through the exchange of other commodities is extremely variable. Once again, detailed figures are rarely encountered in the anthropological literature. However, several studies of complementary exchanges of proteins for carbohydrates between hunting or pastoralist groups and agriculturalists have been made. In the Philippines, Peterson (1977) has quantified the food exchanges between Agta (principally hunter–gatherer groups) and Palanan farmers near the northeast coast of Luzon. Although the amounts of the major food resources exploited (corn, yams, manioc, fish, deer, and pigs) for consumption and exchanges varied in the three selected areas studied, it was found that about two-thirds of the Palanan farmers were dependent on the Agta for 30–50% of their protein foods. In exchange, nearly all of the Agta obtained 70–100% of their carbohydrate foods from the Palanan. In addition to utilising wild resources, 37% of the Agta raised domestic animals simply for sale to the Palanan (the Agta themselves observed a taboo on eating the meat of domestic animals). The Palanan raised relatively few domestic animals, and these were usually slaughtered only for cash sales or on special occasions. Most of the transactions between the two groups took place between individual exchange partners. Smiley (1980) made a similar study of exchanges between the Birhor (predominantly hunter–gatherers) and Dravidian–Oraon agriculturalists in the Chota Nagpur region of Bihar, in northeast India. Among other exchanges, the Birhor traded live hares for rice from the village markets or from individual exchange partners. In the rainy season, when hunting conditions were poor, the Birhor also obtained some domestic animals from the farmers for consumption.

It is clear from these and many other examples of food exchanges between different groups that considerable amounts of food may be transferred between settlements. The degree to which such interaction is visible in the archaeological record is uncertain. Smiley (1980:166–174) is pessimistic about the correct interpretation of the Birhor–Dravidian exchanges from archaeological evidence. The Agta–Palanan interchanges would also be difficult to monitor. It is possible that environmental data, combined with locational analysis, may give some indication of potential food exchanges. Animal bones or plant remains of species found on settlements located in areas unsuitable for their husbandry are probably indicative of exchanges of some sort, but the wide ecological tolerance of many species severely limits this type of approach (compare Jones, Chapter 4, on the role of weed species in this respect). In some cases it is possible to demonstrate, for example, that sheep farming was practised by the inhabitants of many chalkland settlements in southern England during the Iron Age, simply because of the presence of many neonatal mortalities of little food value. Conversely, it has been argued that the absence of bones of young horses from contemporary sites suggests that they were not bred by the inhabitants (Harcourt 1979). The use of environmental evidence to recognise consumer and producer settlements of particular commodities may be a step forward. O'Shea (1981) suggests that the amount of food exchanged will vary according to the diversity of the environment. In broad and undifferentiated environments, such exchanges are less likely, except in times of localised shortages, than between groups exploiting different ecological niches. As Rubel and Rosman (1978:1) point out, this argument does not explain why similar food commodities are exchanged on a large scale in areas of similar environments. Nevertheless, it is clear that we are not going to be in a position to understand possible food exchange systems without a broad regional approach (O'Shea 1981:180). Even when food exchange systems between settlements are dominated by small-scale individual transactions of a reciprocal nature, the full complexity of such activity may never be fully appreciated.

LARGE-SCALE REDISTRIBUTION AND MARKETS

When exchanges of animal products are transacted consistently on a large scale and are organised either through redistributive or marketing mechanisms, the potential archaeological visibility of such exchanges increases. Polanyi

(1977) discusses the importance of the redistribution of commodities through an established centre in some societies. The control of such redistribution may be vested in a chief, an elite, or a bureaucratic institution. Its purpose is to collect and reallocate goods produced from various quarters. Such systems facilitate the specialised production of commodities. Complex and large-scale redistributive systems have been recognised in or postulated for many ancient societies. For example, Polanyi (1977) demonstrates that redistribution was a major factor in the economies of archaic Greek states. In addition, the impressive system for the organisation of sheep flocks and the redistribution of wool through the Minoan Palace has been revealed by the Linear B inscriptions (Renfrew 1972), and La Lone (1982) argues that much of the redistribution in the Inca Empire was centrally administered. Similarly, regular and substantial exchanges of commodities by means of market transactions should be visible in the archaeological record. The importance of the marketplace in urban development may have a significant bearing on the faunal assemblages at such centres.

In societies where either large-scale redistribution or marketing plays a significant role, the scale of organisation involved may be expected to leave evidence of the regulated flow of produce. This may be reflected in patterned variations in the ages and sex of animals represented at different settlements. In the case of market exchange, there are several well-documented examples of preferential sales of particular age groups of animals for slaughter. To take just one example, the Yörük nomadic pastoralists in southeast Turkey sell off male yearling sheep for slaughter, which enables the nomads to purchase flour and wheat. The Yörük themselves rarely consume their own stock unless the animals are close to death or slaughtered on special occasions (Bates 1973:144–154). The mortality profiles of sheep bones deposited at Yörük camps should therefore show a significant contrast from those in the towns.

Similar anthropological evidence for such variations in redistributive systems is rare, but it seems probable that the operation of such systems would result in the preferential acquisition of animals of particular ages and sex. This can be monitored by comparing the mortality profiles and sex ratios of animals represented by their bones in various settlements within the redistribution network, provided that other biasing factors contributing to variation in mortality profiles are taken into account (Maltby 1982b). We should, for example, expect a dichotomy in the ages and sex of animals represented on 'producer' and 'consumer' settlements. In addition, it is possible that the centre of redistribution may itself produce a faunal assemblage distinctive from those of its satellite settlements. Jones (Chapter 4, this volume) argues from botanical evidence that the Iron Age hillfort at Danebury (Hampshire) operated as such a centre for cereal production. It should thus be possible to monitor similar phenomena in the faunal record.

Unfortunately, in most cases suitable data have not been collected, or else insufficient attention has been paid to other possible causes of variability. It should also be pointed out that any patterning may be much more complicated than that resulting from simple exchanges between consumers, producers, and redistributive settlements. To measure these possible variations, we require well-dated and stratified contemporary assemblages from different types of settlements in the postulated redistribution or marketing network. These are rare in the prehistoric or early historic periods in Britain. The possibilities of the changing importance of Exeter (Devon), which was an important urban centre in Roman and Medieval times, have been discussed in relation to observed changes in the mortality profiles of the animals represented there (Maltby 1979a:88–93). It is suggested in that study that urban growth would in itself have necessitated special adaptations in the regional pastoral economy and the marketing of its products.

This phenomenon has been well documented in many African societies. Swift (1979) considers the options open to Somali nomadic pastoralists when faced with increasing commercialism and marketplace exchange. He lists six strategies: (1) they could sell more males surplus to breeding stock; (2) they could reduce the number of animals distributed in traditional reciprocal and redistributional networks and sell them instead; (3) they could sell more old female animals; (4) they could reduce their milk consumption to improve the nutrition and the chances of survival of their stock; (5) they could change the composition of their herds and flocks within the environmental constraints. In the Somali case, this allows choices between the safer subsistence animals (camels and goats) and those of higher market value (sheep and cattle); a pastoral economy can respond to market demand by shifting resources from the former to the latter. As a last resort, they could sell reproductive males and females (6). Swift (1979:454) suggests that these alternatives can be seen as a hierarchy of responses to the demands of the market.

If these sorts of responses could be applied generally, archaeozoological data might be used to monitor these adaptations. Unfortunately, the Exeter data still stand in isolation, since no assemblages from neighbouring settlements have become available for comparison. However, we may be encouraged by other examples. Luff (1982) has shown significant contrasts between contemporary sheep–goat mortality profiles from closely dated early Romano-British deposits at the legionary fortress and succeeding *colonia* at Colchester (Essex) and from Sheepen Hill, a site specialising in metal-working situated 1.6 km from Colchester. Pits from the latter site produced animal bones that included a large number of first-year sheep mortalities, whereas a much higher proportion of the sheep represented at Colchester were second-year mortalities (Luff 1982:60, 129). Although other possible biases from an admittedly limited range of deposits cannot be ruled out, the samples provide one of the few examples where 'real' variability in slaughter patterns can be demonstrated with a fair degree of confidence. As neither settlement can be regarded primarily as a pastoral producer settlement, the explanation of this particular variability requires further samples from these and neighbouring settlements.

It seems likely that the greater the role of large-scale marketing or redistribution, the more unlikely it is that the animal bones from a settlement will provide an accurate representation of the overall slaughtering pattern. In this respect, it is interesting that Cribb's simulations of herd structures, derived from archaeological mortality data (Chapter 3, this volume), show that only the Iron Age examples could conceivably represent a viable slaughtering strategy; mortality profiles from sheep mandibles from the late Romano-British and Anglo-Saxon periods at Portchester Castle could not easily be translated into realistic herd management strategies. The same would be true if the simulations were made on most other samples dated to these periods. The critical examination of age and sex profiles on a regional basis has great potential as a means of recognising trading patterns in livestock.

Similarly, the development of large-scale redistribution or marketing systems may result in greater variability in the type and size of the animals represented at different settlements. Swift (1979) suggests in the Somali example that improvements in the nutrition of stock may result, which in turn may improve stock size. Variations in bone morphology and size result from a complicated mix of genetic, gender, nutritional, and environmental factors, and it is extremely difficult to establish which is the principal cause of observed change. It would be valuable for archaeozoologists to unravel these causes of variation, since it seems that there were some significant variations in the size of stock represented on British sites, particularly from the Roman period. Animals larger than the Iron Age stock appear in fluctuating numbers in different regions and on different settlement types both in Britain and elsewhere (Boessneck and von den Driesch 1978:31–33; Bökönyi 1974:128–133; Maltby 1981b:185–192). Given the degree of variation in stock size and the diversity of Romano-British settlements, it is conceivable that some of the diversity could be the result of differential redistribution of different types of stock. In sixteenth-century London, the cattle brought to the wealthy inhabitants of Baynard's Castle were on average larger than those found nearby in deposits associated with less privileged inhabitants of the city (Armitage 1982:96–98).

In addition, the importance of different species involved in the marketing or redistribution networks may vary. King (1978:225–226) notes the small number of horse bones in Romano-British towns and military sites, compared with rural settlements. Of course, intersite comparisons of species frequency are greatly handicapped by the types of variability discussed in previous sections. However, subsequent studies of large samples from early 'Romanised' settlements such as Exeter (Maltby 1979a), Colchester, and Sheepen Hill (Luff 1982:61, 130) have also produced very small numbers of horse bones, whereas many contemporary rural settlements in southern England continue to produce them in relatively large numbers. This discrepancy may be linked to cultural preferences for the meat of other species, or to a change in the exploitation of the horse. Whatever the cause, horses do not appear to have been involved in meat redistribution. Cattle, on the other hand, were involved; the demand for beef may have gradually encouraged or coerced farmers to rear more of them to supply the urban centres with meat. As noted earlier, the importance of this process has been witnessed in the large-scale dumps of primary butchery waste consisting of cattle bones recovered from several Romano-British towns. The high market value of cattle in Medieval towns in Europe generally (Bourdillon 1980:183) is again an indication of the great demands that urban populations can have on the pastoral economy for the supply of meat, and ultimately on the relative numbers of different species reared.

It is clear, therefore, that faunal data can be used to monitor the large-scale marketing of animal produce. It must be emphasised that the transition or artic-ulation between such marketing systems and traditional reciprocal or re-distributive exchanges is likely to have involved complex processes. The ex-change of food in permanent marketplaces may have played only a minor role in the total exchange system, even where such foci existed. The common occur-rence of periodic markets in Africa, for example (in which marketplaces are present but transactions via them play only a minor role, resulting in a regular pattern of small markets held in different places on different days), may have some relevance to many historic systems (Bohannan and Bohannan 1968; Bohannan and Dalton 1962). Thus, Shaw (1979) offers a convincing argument for the existence of such rural periodic markets in northern Africa during the Roman period. In such circumstances, the majority of food transactions take place outside of the marketplace, and the overall influence of market centres on the organisation of food redistribution (and hence the potentially greater im-balance of the types of animals represented on different settlements) is lessened. Reece (1980) argues that in Roman Britain, the influence of major urban centres declined in the later Roman period, to be replaced by an agricultural economy based principally on the villa estates. It will be interesting to observe whether faunal samples in the latter period generally show less variation than in the earlier period, when the divergence between producer and consumer settlements may have been greater.

Conclusion

It should be clear that the questions that the animal bone specialist might ask of the data are much broader than such traditional ones as which species were exploited, how much meat each provided, and so on. There is considerable potential for faunal studies to provide valuable information about settlement organisation, cultural attitudes towards animals, and modes of production and redistribution. However, to bring archaeozoology into the realm of social studies requires a better understanding of the observed variability in faunal samples and a more sophisticated statistical treatment of the data. Those who argue that the development of a more rigorous methodology involving the detailed recording of bone fragments and their contexts is of secondary importance to the traditional role of the faunal specialist (palaeoeconomic reconstruction) are suffering from the delusion that current methodologies are providing accurate 'answers'. Unless all causes of faunal variability have been considered, no claims about the pastoral economy can be regarded as reliable. Undoubtedly, it will be impossible to attain a full appreciation of the factors causing faunal variability in many cases, and the limitations have been discossed at length here. Nevertheless, we urgently need to come to terms with such factors, unless we are to fall into the trap outlined by Binford (1981) at the beginning of this chapter. The middle-range research that he advocates must be extended in our attempt to explain the additional variations in the complex societies responsible for the majority of faunal assemblages studied in Europe.

References

Anschutz, K.
 1966 *Die Tierknochenfunde aus der mittelalterlichen Siedlung Ulm-Weinhof.* Unpublished Ph.D. dissertation, Stuttgart University.
Arbinger-Vogt, H.
 1978 *Vorgeschichtliche Tierknochenfunde aus Breisach am Rhein.* Unpublished Ph.D. dissertation, Munich University.
Armitage, P. L.
 1982 Studies on the remains of domestic livestock from Roman, medieval and early modern London: objectives and methods. In *Environmental archaeology in the urban context,* edited by A. R. Hall and H. K. Kenwood, pp. 94–106. Council for British Archaeology, Research Report 43, London.
Barker, G. W. W.
 1975 To sieve or not to sieve. *Antiquity* 49:61–63.
Bates, D. G.
 1973 *Nomads and farmers: a study of the Yörük of southeastern Turkey.* University of Michigan, Anthropological Paper 52, Ann Arbor.
Becker, C. and F. Johannson
 1981 *Die neolithischen Ufersiedlungen von Twann 11: Tierknochenfunde* (zweiter Bericht). Staatlicher Lehrmittelverlag, Bern, Switzerland.
Behrensmeyer, A. K.
 1978 Taphonomic and ecologic information from bone weathering. *Paleobiology* 4:150–162.
Behrensmeyer, A. K., D. Western, and D. E. D. Dechant-Boaz
 1979 New perspectives in vertebrate paleoecology from a recent bone assemblage. *Paleobiology* 5:12–21.
Binford, L. R.
 1978 *Nunamiut ethnoarchaeology.* Academic Press, New York.

Binford, L. R.
    1981 *Bones: ancient men and modern myths.* Academic Press, New York.
Binford, L. R., and J. B. Bertram
    1977 Bone frequencies and attritional processes. In *For theory building in archaeology,* edited
    by L. R. Binford, pp. 77–153. Academic Press, New York.
Boessneck, J., and A. von den Driesch
    1978 The significance of measuring animal bones from archaeological sites. In *Approaches to
    faunal analysis in the Middle East,* edited by R. H. Meadow and M. A. Zeder, pp. 25–39.
    Harvard University, Peabody Museum Bulletin 2.
Boessneck, J., A. von den Driesch, U. Meyer-Lemppenau, and E. Wechsler-von Ohlen
    1971 *Die Tierknochenfunde aus dem Oppidum von Manching.* Steiner, Wiesbaden, Germany.
Bohannan, P., and L. Bohannan
    1968 *Tiv economy.* Northwestern University Press, Evanston, Illinois.
Bohannan, P., and G. Dalton (editors)
    1962 *Markets in Africa.* Northwestern University Press, Evanston, Illinois.
Bökönyi, S.
    1974 *History of domestic mammals in central and eastern Europe.* Akadémiai Kiadó, Budapest.
Bourdillon, J.
    1980 Town life and animal husbandry in the Southampton area, as suggested by the excavated
    bones. *Proceedings of the Hampshire Field Club and Archaeological Society* 36:181–191.
Bourdillon, J., and J. P. Coy
    1980 The animal bones. In *Excavations at Melbourne Street, Southampton 1971–76,* edited by
    P. Holdsworth, pp. 79–121. Council for British Archaeology, Research Report 33, London.
Bradley, R.
    1980 Subsistence, exchange and technology: a social framework for the Bronze Age in southern
    England *c.* 1400–700 b.c. In *Settlement and society in the British Later Bronze Age,* edited
    by J. Barrett and R. Bradley, pp. 56–75. British Archaeological Reports, British Series 83,
    Oxford, England.
Brain, C. K.
    1967 *Hottentot food remains and their bearing on the interpretation of fossil bone assemblages.*
    Namib Desert Research Station, Scientific Paper 32.
Brain, C, K.
    1969 *The contribution of the Namib Desert Hottentots to the understanding of Australopithecine
    bone accumulations.* Namib Desert Research Station, Scientific Paper 39.
Brain, C. K.
    1976 Some principles in the interpretation of bone accumulations associated with man. In
    Human origins: Louis Leakey and the East African evidence, edited by G. L. Isaac and E.
    McCown, pp. 97–106. Benjamin, New York.
Brain, C. K.
    1981 *The hunters or the hunted? An introduction to African cave taphonomy.* University of
    Chicago Press.
Carter, H. H.
    1975 A guide to the rates of toothwear in English lowland sheep. *Journal of Archaeological
    Science* 2:231–233.
Champion, T. C.
    1982 Fortification, ranking and subsistence. In *Ranking, resource and exchange,* edited by C.
    Renfrew and S. Shennan, pp. 61–66. Cambridge University Press, Cambridge, England.
Clason, A. T., and W. Prummel
    1977 Collecting, sieving and archaeozoological research. *Journal of Archaeological Science*
    4:171–175.

Coy, J. P.
    1982 The animal bones. In *Excavation of an Iron Age enclosure at Groundwell Farm, Blunsdon St. Andrew, 1976–7*, edited by C. Gingell. Wiltshire Archaeological and Natural History Magazine 76:68–72.
Crader, D. C.
    1974 The effects of scavengers on bone material from large mammals: an experiment conducted among the Besa of the Luangwa Valley, Zambia. In *Ethnoarchaeology*, edited by C. B. Donnan and C. W. Chewlow, pp. 161–173. UCLA, Institute of Archaeology, Monograph 4.
Cunliffe, B., and D. W. Phillipson
    1968 *Excavations at Eldon's Seat, Encombe, Dorset*. Proceedings of the Prehistoric Society 34:191–237.
Fasham, P. J.
    1978 Winnall Down—R17. In *M3 archaeology 1976–1977*, edited by P. J. Fasham, pp. 14–17. M3 Motorway Rescue Committee, Winchester, England.
Gamble, C. S.
    1978 Optimising information from studies of faunal remains. In *Sampling in contemporary British archaeology*, edited by J. Cherry et al., pp. 321–353. British Archaeological Reports, British Series 50, Oxford, England.
Gifford, D. P.
    1978 Ethnoarchaeological observations on natural processes affecting cultural materials. In *Explorations in ethnoarchaeology*, edited by R. A. Gould, pp. 77–101. University of New Mexico Press, Albuquerque.
Gifford, D. P.
    1981 Taphonomy and paleoecology: a critical review of archaeology's sister disciplines. In *Advances in archaeological method and theory* (Vol. 4), edited by M. B. Schiffer, pp. 365–438. Academic Press, New York.
Gilbert, A. S. and B. H. Singer
    1982 Reassessing zooarchaeological quantification. *World Archaeology* 14:21–40.
Gilman, A.
    1981 The development of social stratification in bronze age Europe. *Current Anthropology* 22:1–23.
Grant, A.
    1975 The animal bones. In *Excavations at Portchester Castle* (Vol. I), edited by B. Cunliffe, pp. 378–408. Research Committee of the Society of Antiquaries, Report 32, London.
Grant, A.
    1976 The animal bones. In *Excavations at Portchester Castle* (Vol. II), edited by B. Cunliffe, pp. 262–287. Research Committee of the Society of Antiquaries, Report 33, London.
Grant, A.
    1977 The animal bones. In *Excavations at Portchester Castle* (Vol. III), edited by B. Cunliffe, pp. 213–233. Research Committee of the Society of Antiquaries, Report 34, London.
Grayson, D. K.
    1973 On the methodology of faunal analysis. *American Antiquity* 38:432–439.
Grayson, D. K.
    1978 Minimum numbers and sample size in vertebrate faunal analysis. *American Antiquity* 43:53–65.
Grayson, D. K.
    1979 Quantification of vertebrate archaeofaunas. In *Advances in archaeological method and theory* (Vol. 2), edited by M. B. Schiffer, pp. 199–237. Academic Press, New York.

Halstead, P.
1981 From determination to uncertainty: social storage and the rise of the Minoan Palace. In *Economic archaeology,* edited by A. Sheridan and G. Bailey, pp. 187–213. British Archaeological Reports, International Series 96, Oxford, England.

Halstead, P., I. Hodder, and G. Jones
1978 Behavioural archaeology and refuse patterns: a case study. *Norwegian Archaeological Review* 11:118–131.

Hanschke, G.
1970 *Die Tierknochenfunde aus der Wüstung Wülfingen, 11: die Wiederkäuer.* Unpublished Ph.D. dissertation, Munich University.

Harcourt, R. A.
1979 The animal bones. In *Gussage All Saints: an iron age settlement in Dorset,* edited by G. J. Wainwright, pp. 150–160. Department of the Environment, Archaeological Report 10, London.

Henry, J.
1951 The economics of Pilagà food distribution. *American Anthropology* 53:187–219.

Hill, A. P.
1976 On carnivore and weathering damage to bone. *Current Anthropology* 17:335–336.

Hill, A. P.
1979 Butchery and natural disarticulation: an investigatory technique. *American Antiquity* 44:739–744.

Hodder, I.
1982a *The present past.* Batsford, London.

Hodder, I.
1982b *Symbols in action.* Cambridge University Press, Cambridge, England.

Hornberger, M.
1970 *Gesamtbeurteilung der Tierknochenfunde aus der Stadt aus dem Magdelensberg in Karnten (1948–1966).* Vetlag des Landesmuseums fur Karnten, Klagenfurt, Germany.

Ijzereef, G. F.
1981 *Bronze age animal bones from Bovenkarspel: the excavation at Het Valkje.* Rijkdienst voor het Oudheidkundig Bodemonderzoek, Amersfoort, Holland.

Isaac, G. L.
1967 Towards the interpretation of occupational debris: some experiments and observations. *Kroeber Anthropological Society Paper* 37:31–57.

Kent, S.
1981 The dog: an archaeologist's best friend or worst enemy? *Journal of Field Archaeology* 8:367–372.

King, A.
1978 A comparative survey of bone assemblages from Roman sites in Britain. *Bulletin of the Institute of Archaeology of London* 15:207–232.

King, A.
1982 The animal bones. In *Excavations at Canterbury Castle,* edited by P. Bennett et al., pp. 193–205. Canterbury Archaeological Trust, Maidstone, England.

Klein, R. G.
1975 Palaeoanthropological implications of the non-archaeological bone assemblage from Swartklip 1, southwestern Cape Province, South Africa. *Quaternary Research* 5:275–288.

Klumpp, G.
1967 Die Tierknochenfunde aus der Mittelalterlichen Burgruine Niederrealta, Gemeinde Cazis/Graubunden (Schweiz), University of Munich, Germany.

Kramer, C.
1982 *Village ethnoarchaeology: rural Iran in archaeological perspective.* Academic Press, London.

La Lone, D. E.
    1982 The Inca as a non-market economy: supply on command versus supply and demand. In *Contexts for prehistoric exchange,* edited by J. E. Ericson and T. K. Earle, pp. 291–316. Academic Press, London.
Lauk, H. D.
    1976 *Tierknochenfunde aus bronzezeitlichen Siedlungen bei Monachil und Purullena (Provinz Granada).* Studien über frühe Tierknochenfunde von der Iberischen Halbinsel 6, Munich.
Legge, A. J.
    1981 Aspects of cattle husbandry. In *Farming practice in British prehistory,* edited by R. Mercer, pp. 169–181. Edinburgh University Press, Edinburgh, Scotland.
Levitan, B.
    1982 *Excavation at West Hill, Uley 1979: the sieving and sampling programme.* Western Archaeological Trust, Occasional Paper 10, Bristol, England.
Luff, R-M.
    1982 *A zooarchaeological study of the Roman northwestern provinces.* British Archaeological Reports, International Series 137, Oxford, England.
Lyon, P. J.
    1970 Differential bone destruction: an ethnographic example. *American Antiquity* 35:213–215.
MacCormack, C. P.
    1981 Exchange and hierarchy. In *Economic archaeology,* edited by A. Sheridan and G. Bailey, pp. 159–166. British Archaeological Reports, International Series 96, Oxford, England.
Maltby, J. M.
    1979a *Faunal studies on urban sites: the animal bones from Exeter 1971–1975.* Sheffield University, Department of Prehistory and Archaeology, Exeter Archaeological Reports 2.
Maltby, J. M.
    1979b The animal bones. In Excavations at 1 Westgate Street, Gloucester, 1975, edited by C. M. Heighway et al. *Medieval Archaeology* 23:182–185.
Maltby, J. M.
    1981a The animal bones. In Excavations at Old Down Farm, Andover, part II: prehistoric and Roman, edited by S. M. Davies. *Proceedings of the Hampshire Field Club and Archaeological Society* 37:81–163.
Maltby, J. M.
    1981b Iron age, Romano-British and Anglo-Saxon animal husbandry: a review of the faunal evidence. In *The environment of man: the Iron Age to the Anglo-Saxon period,* edited by M. Jones and G. Dimbleby, pp. 155–204. British Archaeological Reports, British Series 87, Oxford, England.
Maltby, J. M.
    1982a The animal bones. In Excavations at Okehampton Castle, Devon, part 2: the Bailey, edited by R. A. Higham et al. *Proceedings of the Devon Archaeological Society* 40:114–135.
Maltby, J. M.
    1982b The variability of faunal samples and their effects on ageing data. In *Ageing and sexing animal bones from archaeological sites,* edited by B. Wilson et al., pp. 81–90. British Archaeological Reports, British Series 109, Oxford, England.
Maltby, J. M.
    1983 The animal bones. In *The East and North Gates of Gloucester,* edited by C. Heighway, pp.228–245 (plus microfiche). Western Archaeological Trust, Bristol.
Maltby, J. M.
    1984 Animal bones and the Romano-British economy. In *Animals and archaeology* (Vol. 4),

edited by J. Clutton-Brock and C. Grigson, pp. 125–138. British Archaeological Reports, International Series 227, Oxford England.

Maltby, J. M.

   n.d.a. *The animal bones from Winnall Down, Hampshire.* Unpublished report 3453, Ancient Monuments Laboratory.

Maltby, J. M.

   n.d.b *The animal bones from the excavations at Balksbury, Hampshire.*

Maltby, J. M.

   n.d.c *The animal bones from the excavations at 1 Bleachfield Street, Alcester, Warwickshire.*

Meadow, R. H.

   1976 Methodological concerns in zooarchaeology. In *Thèmes, spécialisés, prétirage,* pp. 108–123. Union Internationale des Sciences Préhistoriques et Protohistoriques, IX Congrès, Nice.

Meadow, R. H.

   1978 Effects of context on the interpretation of faunal remains: a case study. In *Approaches to faunal analysis in the Middle East,* edited by R. H. Meadow and M. A. Zeder, pp. 15–21. Harvard University, Peabody Museum Bulletin 2.

Meadow, R. H.

   1980 Animal bones: problems for the archaeologist together with some possible solutions. *Paleorient* 6:65–77.

Mensch, P. J. A. van

   1974 A Roman soup-kitchen at Zwammerdam? Berichten van de Rijksdienst voor het Oudheidkundig Bodemonderzoek 24:159–166.

Moore, H. L.

   1982 The interpretation of spatial patterning in settlement residues. In *Symbolic and structural archaeology,* edited by I. Hodder, pp. 74–79. Cambridge University Press, Cambridge, England.

Mounteney, G.

   1981 Faunal attrition and subsistence reconstruction at Thwing. In *Prehistoric communities in northern England: essays in economic and social reconstruction,* edited by G. Barker, pp. 73–86. Sheffield University, Department of Prehistory and Archaeology.

O'Shea, J.

   1981 Coping with scarcity: exchange and social storage. In *Economic archaeology,* edited by A. Sheridan and G. Bailey, pp. 167–183. British Archaeological Reports, International Series 96, Oxford, England.

Payne, S.

   1972a On the interpretation of bone samples from archaeological sites. In *Papers in economic prehistory,* edited by E. S. Higgs, pp. 65–81. Cambridge University Press, Cambridge, England.

Payne, S.

   1972b Partial recovery and sample bias: the results of some sieving experiements. In *Papers in economic prehistory,* edited by E. S. Higgs, pp. 49–64. Cambridge University Press, Cambridge, England.

Payne, S.

   1975 Partial recovery and sample bias. In *Archaeozoological studies,* edited by A. T. Clason, pp. 7–17. North Holland, Amsterdam.

Payne, S.

   1980 The animal bones. In Excavations at Park Street, Towcester, edited by G. Lambrick. *Northamptonshire Archaeology* 15:105–113.

Peterson, J. T.

   1977 Ecotones and exchange in northern Luzon. In *Economic exchange and social interaction in*

Southeast Asia: perspectives from prehistory, history and ethnography, edited by K. L. Hutterer, pp. 55–71. Michigan Papers on South and Southeast Asia, Ann Arbor.

Piehler, W.
1976 *Die Knochenfunde aus dem Spätrömischen Kastell Vemania.* Ph.D. dissertation, Munich University.

Polanyi, K.
1977 *The livelihood of man.* Academic Press, New York.

Pryor, F. L.
1977 *The origins of the economy: a comparison of distribution in primitive and peasant economies.* Academic Press, New York.

Rackham, D. J.
1977 The animal bones. In An excavation at Hunter Street, Buckingham, 1974, edited by R. A. Hall. *Records of Buckinghamshire* 20:125–133.

Rappaport, R.
1968 *Pigs for the ancestors.* Yale University Press, New Haven, Connecticut.

Reece, R.
1980 Town and country: the end of Roman Britain. *World Archaeology* 12:77–92.

Renfrew, C.
1972 *The emergence of civilisation.* Methuen, London.

Rowlands, M. J.
1980 Kinship, alliance and exchange in the European Bronze Age. In *Settlement and society in the British Later Bronze Age,* edited by J. Barrett and R. Bradley, pp. 15–55. British Archaeological Reports, British Series 83, Oxford, England.

Rubel, P. G., and A. Rosman
1978 *Your own pigs you may not eat.* Chicago University Press.

Sahlins, M. D.
1974 *Stone age economics.* Tavistock, London.

Schiffer, M. B.
1976 *Behavioural archaeology.* Academic Press, New York.

Schmid, E.
1972 *Atlas of animal bones/Knochenatlas.* Elsevier, Amsterdam.

Shaw, B. D.
1979 Rural periodic markets in Roman North Africa as mechanisms of social integration and control. In *Research in economic anthropology* (Vol. 2), edited by G. Dalton, pp. 91–117. JAI Press, Greenwich, Connecticut.

Sherratt, A.
1982 Mobile resources: settlement and exchange in early agricultural Europe. In *Ranking, resource and exchange,* edited by C. Renfrew and S. Shennan, pp. 13–26. Cambridge University Press, Cambridge, England.

Sillitoe, P.
1979 *Give and take: exchange in Wola society.* Australian National University Press, Canberra.

Smiley, F. E.
1980 The Birhor: material correlates of hunter–gatherer/farmer exchange. In *The archaeological correlates of hunter–gatherer societies: studies from the ethnographic record,* edited by F. E. Smiley et al., pp. 149–176. Michigan Discussions in Anthropology 5, Ann Arbor.

Strathern, A.
1978 Finance and production revisited: in pursuit of a comparison. In *Research in economic anthropology* (Vol. 1), edited by G. Dalton, pp. 73–104. JAI Press, Greenwich, Connecticut.

Swift, J.
1979 The development of livestock trading in a nomad pastoral economy: the Somali case. In *Pastoral production and society,* edited by L'Equipe écologie et anthropologie des sociétés pastorales, pp. 447–465. Cambridge University Press, Cambridge, England.
Tappen, N. C., and G. R. Peske
1970 Weathering cracks and split-line patterns in archaeological bone. *American Antiquity* 35:383–386.
Thomas, D. H.
1969 Great Basin hunting patterns: a quantitative method for treating faunal remains. *American Antiquity* 34:392–401.
Tilley, C.
1981 Economy and society: what relationship? In *Economic archaeology,* edited by A. Sheridan and G. Bailey, pp. 131–148. British Archaeological Reports, International Series 96, Oxford, England.
Uerpmann, H. P.
1971 *Die Tierknochenfunde aus der Talayot-Siedlung von S'Iliot (San Lorenzo/Mallorca).* Studien über frühe Tierknochenfunde von der Iberischen Halbinsel 2, Munich.
Uerpmann, H. P.
1973 Animal bone finds and economic archaeology: a critical study of osteo-archaeological method. *World Archaeology* 4:307–322.
Watson, J. P. N.
1972 Fragmentation analysis of animal bone samples from archaeological sites. *Archaeometry* 14:221–227.
Yellen, J. E.
1977 Cultural patterning in faunal remains: evidence from the !Kung bushmen. In *Experimental archaeology,* edited by D. W. Ingersoll et al., pp. 271–331. Columbia University Press, New York.

3

The Analysis of Ancient Herding Systems:
An Application of Computer Simulation
in Faunal Studies

ROGER CRIBB

One technique employed by faunal analysts in their investigations of animal domestication in the past, namely the analysis of age–sex structures of faunal assemblages, may hold considerably greater potential within the new problematic of subsistence systems and cultural dynamics. Earlier studies sought to differentiate domesticated age structures from wild or "natural" ones (Ducos 1978; Perkins 1964), but there are grounds for questioning the existence of a 'natural' structure for any wild faunal assemblage. For example, Collier and White (1976) have shown that there is great variation in the kill-off patterns of wild herds under human predation, and that some of the age structures may closely resemble those of domesticated herds. (Certain of the age structures from early Middle Eastern sites considered wild by Ducos (1978) in fact fall within the pattern for some kinds of domestic herds kept primarily for meat production [Cribb n.d.].) We are now in a position to explore the full range of variability within the domestic category itself, which promises to unlock a much more fertile store of information than the simple domestic–wild categorisations of the past. I hope to demonstrate in this chapter that by treating the age structure of a faunal assemblage as the end state of a systemic process, it is possible not only to facilitate interpretation but also to provide a basis for evaluating hypotheses.

Prerequisites

Age structures or kill-off patterns are obtained by inference from the condition of specific items in the faunal assemblage. Therefore, an essential prerequisite is

75

the existence of sound techniques for establishing the age of species within archaeological assemblages. Consideration here will be restricted to the primary herd domesticates—sheep, goats, and cattle—with the emphasis on sheep and goats. Two ageing techniques are currently in common use. The first of these, epiphyseal fusion, is based on the assumption that closure of the epiphyses of different bones occurs at a certain age and in a prescribed sequence. By measuring the proportion of fused and unfused specimens for each bone type, a comparative scheme can be obtained of the relative age distribution of slaughtered animals, though this becomes increasingly imprecise for the higher age groups (Harcourt 1979; Morris 1972:83; Noddle 1974; Silver 1969). The second technique is based on tooth development and wear. It employs the sequence of eruption of different teeth, as inferred from that of known contemporary breeds, and the degree of attrition on tooth enamel (Carter 1975; Ewbank et al. 1964; Grant 1975; Klein et al. 1981; Payne 1973; Silver 1969; Wilson et al. 1982).

All of these techniques are beset by three major problems. First, ages of epiphyseal fusion (Healy and Ludwig 1965; Noddle 1974) and of the eruption and wear of teeth (Arrowsmith et al. 1974) vary considerably between individuals and populations. Second, it is difficult to arrive at an estimate for the actual number of individual animals (minimum number) being dealt with, due to the presence of both right and left elements. Third, most techniques rely on *relative* ages, and much accuracy may be lost in the attempt to convert these into units of time, such as years or months. Absolute ageing techniques based on the incremental growth of cementum, similar in principle to the accretion of tree rings, have been investigated (Coy et al 1982) but are not yet widely used and would in any case fail to detect units of age less than 1 year.

These considerations are fundamental to any attempt to treat age structures in a rigorous quantitative fashion. While many of the problems involved may seem insoluble, a recognition of the limitations of our database is an important first step from which significant, if limited, progress is then possible.

Statistical Considerations

The next step involves the statistical treatment of age structures. Any statements about herd structure need to be made with some knowledge of how reliable these statements are likely to be, which in turn requires an understanding of the kind of population being addressed and the representativeness of the sample under study.

POPULATIONS

A problem that is rarely discussed in faunal studies is the nature of the population from which a bone sample is thought to be derived (Gamble 1978).

There is little point in trying to assess the nature of a faunal sample unless some attempt is made to refer back to a population. Two different kinds of population may be involved. On one level we are dealing with the population of bones—or the individuals from which they arise—deposited on a site; this can be defined as the target population. On another level we are dealing with a total population of animals, the herd or herds of which this first population is a segment. The distinction between these two population types is reflected in the two alternative assumptions used in inferring from an aged sample to a population: (1) the sample represents all the bones deposited on the site, or (2) the sample represents the animal population exploited by the inhabitants of the site. Quite apart from problems of sampling, many difficulties of inference in age studies arise from the complexity of the relationship between these two kinds of populations. The former is a 'population' in the accepted statistical sense; the latter is a more abstract entity, difficult to arrive at from the knowledge of a sample alone because of complications introduced by both temporal and spatial factors.

Temporally, a faunal sample cannot be representative of a complete herd, since the latter accumulates over time, perhaps over a number of generations; nor is the sample population a single age cohort, as is often assumed in the construction of 'survival curves' (Grant 1975; Payne 1973). Rather, a faunal sample may be regarded as being drawn ultimately from the death population of a series of generational cycles accumulating over time. Assuming that the herd structure perpetuates itself over time, this death population may be treated as if it were that arising from a single, discrete herd.

In spatial terms, difficulties arise because the target population deposited in a site may have been drawn from part of a herd (for example, from certain age categories within the herd kept at a certain location) or from slaughtered animals originating from many different herds. Factors of scale may also be involved. For instance, the target population of faunal elements may comprise all the animals reared and slaughtered on a single farm, hamlet, or village, or those acquired from a surrounding hinterland for consumption in an urban settlement. Alternatively, a population may be spread over many locations. Spatial and temporal factors interact where a single population is kept in different places at different times, as in the case of transhumant or nomadic management systems.

The nature of the target population will therefore change depending on the scale of the spatial unit involved (whether farmstead, village, or region) and on certain animal management strategies such as herd-splitting, buying and selling of breeding stock, and the presence of exchange networks arising from kinship and ceremonial obligations. The population parameters of the herd are therefore likely to be unknown and, to a large extent, unknowable.

SAMPLES

The controlled selection of representative samples is impossible in archaeozoology. However, a faunal assemblage or a part thereof may be treated *as if* it were a sample of a wider population of bones of herd animals. It is essential that samples of ageable items be as large as possible, since numerically small samples are more likely to yield distorted results. Ideally, a sample should comprise upwards of 100 items, though we may often need to be content with considerably fewer, perhaps as low as 50. Apart from being of adequate size, the sample should be as representative as possible. With many archaeological materials this would be impossible to assess, but with biological data we are fortunate. The known composition of anatomical elements and the symmetry of animal remains—that is, the existence of both left and right sampling units (assuming, of course, that these are independently drawn)—can provide the basis for an estimate of the target population (Bourdillon and Coy 1980; Fieller and Turner 1982). In practice, however, we deal with a sample not of the *target* but of the *sampled* population—all the bones that are potentially recoverable after natural and cultural processes have whittled down the target population. The symmetry of biological data allows us to estimate the degree of loss between these two populations.

Problems and Opportunities

The problems of interpreting archaeological herd structure are formidable, as the previous chapter has described. Even assuming complete recovery of all ageable items from an ancient population, there is no direct correspondence between the age structure of a faunal assemblage and the composition of the death population of the herd from which it originated. Only under special conditions—for example, the 'catstrophic kill-off' (Klein et al. 1981) or a controlled cull drawn proportionately from all age groups—will the age profile resemble the mortality profile. Nor, as has been suggested by Grant (1975), is there a reciprocal relationship whereby the former represents a 'negative impression' of the latter. Quite apart from problems of differential deposition, preservation, and other formation processes, the tendency for herds to increase rapidly in size introduces a dynamic component that destroys the assumptions of any static model seeking direct links between the archaeological sample and the original herd (Cribb, n.d.).

One of the biggest problems is that we cannot assume either complete or representative preservation and recovery. Much has been written about the kinds of factors that may intervene (e.g., Behrensmeyer and Hill 1979; Grant 1975; Maltby, this volume; Payne 1973). These include the killing of animals away from the site, their introduction onto the site, as well as differential preservation between older and younger specimens and differential deposition within the site (e.g., Wapnish et al. 1977). But it is insufficient simply to enumerate factors which may or may not have distorted the record without attempting to arrange these factors in some kind of logical order, together with the procedures involved with sampling and analysis. This has been attempted in Figure 3.1. Transformations of the faunal material are arranged in a possible chronological order from the live herd to the mortality profile as finally constructed by the archaeologist on the basis of surviving faunal material. These transformations have been grouped into three categories, the first two corresponding to Schiffer's (1976) 'cultural formation processes' (C-transforms) and 'natural formation processes' (N-transforms), and the third occurring in the process of analysis itself (Meadow 1976). These three categories correspond roughly to Schiffer's 'systemic context' and 'archaeological context', with the third being designated 'analytical context'. Each transformation results in a further reduction of the faunal material, though it should not be forgotten that this may have the effect of generating rather than destroying information in the process (Gifford 1981).

This last point is illustrated by the fact that various cultural formation processes such as herd management, carcase disposal, and butchery result in the patterned deposition of certain bones from all or part of a mortality structure while they are still part of the systemic context. Such behaviour breaks down the animal skeleton but adds information. Natural formation processes then take over, acting on the faunal material in the archaeological context to produce the primary population of ageable elements potentially available for recovery. This constitutes a sampled population (Cherry et al 1978:Figure 1.2). Further reduction occurs through excavation itself, in the course of which an archaeological 'sample' is drawn from the sampled or primary population with all the attendant problems of recovery.

We now have within our archaeological sample a set of ageable elements, but the sequence of sample reduction does not end here. Further selection occurs through the choice of age categories and ageing technique. Finally, errors in classification and the faulty assignment of elements, together with various adjustments to arrive at comparative indices such as minimum numbers, can introduce further inaccuracies in the final archaeological age structure (or 'mortality profile,' as I shall refer to it here). It is with this final winnowed sample of elements that interpretation begins and from which any attempt to argue back to a previous state must start.

In making inferences from a mortality profile to an ancient herding system, we are in effect trying to jump backwards over at least five different steps in the sequence outlined above. This is best done in small hops rather than a single reckless leap. For example, information may be obtained from the excavation strategy employed at the site, which may help to reduce errors arising in the analytical context. Problems arising from the archaeological context may be controlled for to some extent through knowledge of the physical and chemical properties of the soil and the context of deposition—for example, whether in pits, ditches, or destruction levels (Mounteney 1981). Further clues to some of

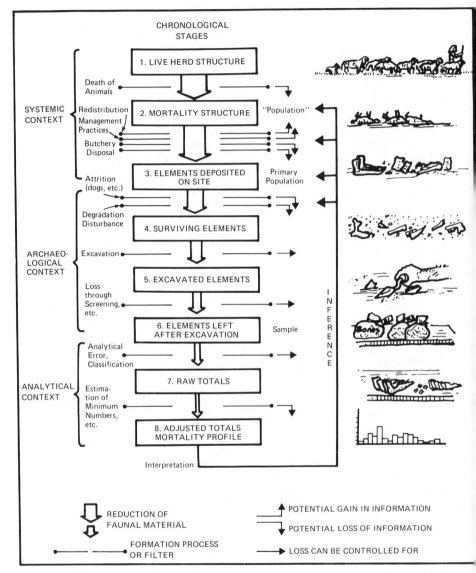

Figure 3.1 Formation processes involved in the reduction of ageable faunal material.

the systemic processes involved may be obtained from other cultural attributes revealed through excavation: "It is the lack of integration of faunal evidence with the result of the archaeological record that has been the major drawback of much previous work. Faunal analysis, for example, is only one source of information that may be drawn upon to study pastoral husbandry.'' (Maltby 1981:193).

The simulation model of the herd is primarily concerned with stages 1, 2, and 8 in Figure 3.1. It is expected that inconsistencies or anomalies detected in the course of simulation may point to the influence of cultural and natural formation processes occurring between stages 2 and 3, and 3 and 4. The effects of other processes may be more difficult to infer, but to some extent other processes, particularly those operating in the analytical context, can be controlled for or reduced through careful and systematic excavation and analysis.

Attempts have already been made to infer directly from stage 8 to stages 1 and 2 (e.g., Grant 1975; Payne 1973). However, these have mostly been on an ad hoc basis, using the overall shape of the age histogram as a guide. It is often unclear just what is being attempted—an account of the use of the animals on the site, or a reconstruction of an ancient herd and the herding strategy lying behind it. Attempts to reconstruct the ancient mortality structure—let alone the age structure of the live herd—may often be misplaced.

The reason for this criticism stems from the simulation of many different kinds of herds (Cribb n.d.). This work has demonstrated that any attempt to arrive at the original age composition of the live herd is an unrewarding exercise since, regardless of the kind of kill-off pattern involved, the proportions of adults, juveniles, and young tend to be quite similar for different kinds of herds. Even if some kind of pure herd structure lying behind the various distortions could be obtained, this would add little information of any value, since it would represent an ideal construct of limited practical applicability. Instead, I propose to explore a different approach, one that focuses on the so-called distortions themselves as a source of information about the cultural factors that went into the formation of the sample. The analysis of age structure tells us less about the highly elusive original herd than about the cultural filter through which its remains have passed, with the latter comprising information of greater accuracy and utility. Consequently, each distortion of the original material contains its own opportunities to explain what happened to the herd and why, which is after all what we as archaeologists (rather than faunal analysts) are trying to discover.

The problem of interpreting herding systems from kill-off patterns is therefore a particular case of the fundamental archaeological problem—that of inferring dynamic processes from their static consequences (Binford 1981, 1983). My approach to this problem is to use simulation to investigate the relationship between faunal data and past human behaviour. Simulation has been employed in archaeology mostly in spatial studies, where settlement patterns and the sampling of archaeological sites have been investigated (Hamond 1978; Hodder 1978). Simulation studies of a contemporary pastoralist system have been made by Dahl and Hjort (1976), although their model does not consider the mortality structures, and hence is of limited use to the archaeologist.

The Herd as a System

Certain properties of the pastoral herd lend themselves readily to modelling in terms of a dynamic equilibrium system (Clarke 1968). The existence of a growth potential, together with constraints on the values and proportions of the various components, means that the herd can be regarded as a dynamic system, with balances between reproduction and attrition maintained in statistical equilibrium by a birth rate and mortality rates for each age–sex category. Three interdependent sets of variables are therefore involved in its simulation: (1) age–sex categories, (2) reproduction, and (3) mortality or attrition. These variables are related not to balances between the herd and its physical environment, but to the management options and productive strategies of the humans under whose aegis the herd is constituted. The herd is primarily a human creation, and the aggregate patterning of faunal remains is a cultural artefact (Daly 1969:152; Yellen 1977:328), not simply a collection of ecofacts as is sometimes implied in current faunal research.

The three key variables mentioned above govern the systemic properties of the herd. These can be assigned quantitative values that constitute, in the case of age and mortality structures, certain demographic rules that determine how the system will run. A further feature of the herd relates to the constraints under which the system operates. The values that can be assigned to the different variables of the system can occur only within realistic tolerance limits, dictated either by biological facts or economic viability. At the most basic level, a herd that fails to reproduce itself (in which the ratio of births over deaths of potential breeders is less than one) cannot be considered viable. Consequently, a faunal assemblage with an age structure implying such a birth–death ratio cannot be considered as representing any past population, and hypotheses must be considered to account for biases in the sample. Indeed, the shape of the age profile may suggest which of these is likely to be correct. In short, only a full awareness of the constraints under which a system operates will make it possible to exclude some hypotheses as unsound, while ranking others on a scale of probability. A systematic, qualitative approach to the problem enables us not only to detect the imponderable factors distorting our data set, but also to take maximum advantage of the opportunities that this knowledge affords.

At this point, many faunal specialists will probably retort: ''Ah, but this is what we've been doing all along!'' This is to some degree correct, but the effect has been minimised by unsystematic procedures, with little correspondence between the interpretations of different experts and no precise explication of the steps leading to the conclusions drawn. A standardised framework for the analysis of archaeological age structures and the evaluation of alternative hypotheses would be of great value, if for no other purpose than the communication of ideas and observations.

The Simulation Procedure

A simulation is set to run by inputting values for the key variables involved. For a number of reasons, sex has been dropped as a variable for simulation, although, as we shall see, certain assumptions can be made that have the effect of controlling the proportions of males and females. The addition of the male–female distinction as an optional variable would greatly complicate the model without necessarily adding a great deal of information. In view of the inaccuracies inherent in the model, it seems preferable to keep it as simple as possible.

AGE CATEGORIES

For reasons of economy, the age categories employed have been reduced to the three major stages through which an animal passes: young (Y, less than one year), immature (I, between one and two years), and adult (A, two years and over). The sum of these input values gives the total number of animals ($T = Y + I + A$) at any given time. By limiting the simulation model to only three age categories, it is considered that a suitable trade-off is achieved between information content on the one hand and criteria of simplicity, precision, and parsimony on the other.

REPRODUCTION

A single birth rate (B) is input, comprising the number of young per female per year. This is then converted into the birth rate per adult (male or female) per year (Ba), derived from B and depending on the proportion of the adult population calculated to be female according to the following assumptions: (1) births are 50% male and 50% female, (2) deaths in the first year are divided equally between males and females, and (3) all deaths in the immature category are of males, up to 50% of the total of immatures, and thereafter all are female. The birth rate per adult is calculated according to the following formula:

$$Ba = B \times 0.5/sI$$

where Ba is the birthrate per adult, B is the birthrate per adult female, and sI is the survival rate of immatures. The birth rate operates within certain tolerance limits of between 0.5 and 1.0 for sheep.

Mortality

An attrition rate is set for each age category: young mortality (mY), immature (mI), and adult (mA). These rates also operate under certain constraints. For instance, as explained above, if adult mortality falls below a certain level, the system begins to run down—that is, the herd fails to reproduce itself and dies out.

Time

The simulation is set to run over a certain number (N) of annual cycles. New values for Y, I, and A are arrived at with the end of each cycle and serve as the base line for calculations in the next cycle.

The simulation routine itself is extremely simple and is currently being run on

```
a.  AM= 0.3
    IM= 0.29   B= 1.16
    YM= 0.3                     GROWTH PROFILE

        0      100      200      300      400      500      600
        J----+----I----+----I----+----I----+----I----+----I----+----I
     0  JAAAAAAAAAAAAAAAAAAAAA*
     1  JAAAAAAAAAAAAAAAYYYYYYY*
     2  JAAAAAAAAAIIIIIYYYYY*
     3  JAAAAAAAAAAIIIYYYYYY*
     4  JAAAAAAAAAAIIIYYYYYY*
     5  JAAAAAAAAAAIIIIYYYYY*
     6  JAAAAAAAAAAIIIIYYYYY*
     7  JAAAAAAAAAAIIIIYYYYY*
     8  JAAAAAAAAAIIIIYYYYY*
     9  JAAAAAAAAAIIIIYYYYY*
    10  JAAAAAA^AAIIIYYYYY*

    AGE        A= 9.70159   I= 3.98785   Y= 5.54767
    MORT.      A= 4.10683   I= 1.60882   Y= 2.37757
               ANNUAL GROWTH RATE = -0.873245 %P.A.
    -----------------------------------------------------------------


    AGE STRUCTURE OF FLOCK      (PERCENT) %

        0      20      40      60      80      100
        I----+----I----+----I----+----I----+----I----+----I
    0-1 JYYYYYYYYYYYYYY                       28.8384
    1-2 JIIIIIIIII                            20.73
    2+  JAAAAAAAAAAAAAAAAAAAAAAAAA            50.4316

    MORTALITY STRUCTURE OF FLOCK    (PERCENT) %

        0      20      40      60      80      100
        I----+----I----+----I----+----I----+----I----+----I
    0-1 JYYYYYYYYYYYYYY                       29.3773
    1-2 JIIIIIIIII                            19.8786
    2+  JAAAAAAAAAAAAAAAAAAAAAAAAA            50.7441


    -----------------------------------------------------------------

    EFFICIENCY INDICES:
              MEAT  =   0.358913
              MILK  =   0.267785
              WOOL  =   0.252158
```

Figure 3.2 Computer simulation of idealised kill-off patterns for meat, milk, and wool production. (Data derived from Payne, 1973: Figs. 1–3.) (a) meat production; (b) milk production; (c) wool production.

a VDU interactive terminal or line printer using the BASIC programming language. The equations controlling the buildup of the herd over time are as follows:

$$T_{(t1)} = Y_{(t1)} + I_{(t1)} + A_{(t1)}$$

where $T_{(t1)}$ is the total animals at time $t1$, $Y_{(t1)}$ is the number of young at time $t1$, $I_{(t1)}$ is the number of immatures at time $t1$, and $A_{(t1)}$ is the number of adults at time $t1$.

$$A_{(t1)} = (I_{(t)} \times sI) + (A_{(t)} \times sA)$$

$$I_{(t1)} = Y_{(t)} \times sI$$

$$Y_{(t1)} = A_{(t)} \times Ba \times sY$$

b. AM= 0.22
   IM= 0.125 B= 0.8
   YM= 0.6   GROWTH PROFILE

```
        0       100      200      300      400      500      600
        ]----+----I----+----I----+----I----+----I----+----I----+----I
   0    JAAAAAAAAAAAAAAAAAAAAA*
   1    JAAAAAAAAAAAAAAAAAYYYY*
   2    JAAAAAAAAAAAAIIIIYYYY*
   3    JAAAAAAAAAAAAIIIYYYY*
   4    JAAAAAAAAAAAAIIIYYYY*
   5    JAAAAAAAAAAAAIIIYYYY*
   6    JAAAAAAAAAAAAIIIYYYY*
   7    JAAAAAAAAAAAAIIIYYYY*
   8    JAAAAAAAAAAAAIIIYYYY*
   9    JAAAAAAAAAAAAIIIYYYY*
  10    JAAAAAAAAAAAAIIIYYYY*
```

AGE   A= 12.6472   I= 3.54588   Y= 4.04711
MORT.   A= 3.56248   I= 0.505889 Y= 6.07066
        ANNUAL GROWTH RATE = -0.105042 %P.A.

AGE STRUCTURE OF FLOCK   (PERCENT) %

```
        0       20       40       60       80       100
        I----+----I----+----I----+----I----+----I----+----I
   0-1  JYYYYYYYYY                         19.9954
   1-2  JIIIIIIII                          17.519
   2+   JAAAAAAAAAAAAAAAAAAAAAAAAAAAAAAAA  62.4856
```

MORTALITY STRUCTURE OF FLOCK   (PERCENT) %

```
        0       20       40       60       80       100
        I----+----I----+----I----+----I----+----I----+----I
   0-1  JYYYYYYYYYYYYYYYYYYYYYYYYYYYYYY    59.8742
   1-2  JII                                4.98952
   2+   JAAAAAAAAAAAAAAAAAA                35.1363
```

EFFICIENCY INDICES:
            MEAT =   0.35097
            MILK =   0.399908
            WOOL =   0.312428

Figure 3.2 (*Continued*)

```
C. AM= 0.2
   IM= 0.071  B= 0.7
   YM= 0.3                         GROWTH PROFILE

       0      100     200     300     400     500     600
       ]----+----I----+----I----+----I----+----I----+----I
    0  JAAAAAAAAAAAAAAAAAAAA*
    1  JAAAAAAAAAAAAAAAAYYY*
    2  JAAAAAAAAAAAAIIIYYY*
    3  JAAAAAAAAAAAAIIIYYY*
    4  JAAAAAAAAAAAAAIIIYYY*
    5  JAAAAAAAAAAAAAIIIYYY*
    6  JAAAAAAAAAAAAAIIIYYY*
    7  JAAAAAAAAAAAAAIIIYYY*
    8  JAAAAAAAAAAAAAIIIYYY*
    9  JAAAAAAAAAAAAAIIIYYY*
   10  JAAAAAAAAAAAAAIIIYYY*

AGE       A= 12.9665   I= 3.18746   Y= 3.41959
MORT.     A= 3.2308    I= 0.242791  Y= 1.46554
          ANNUAL GROWTH RATE = -0.275868 %P.A.
---------------------------------------------------------------------


AGE STRUCTURE OF FLOCK      (PERCENT) %

       0      20      40      60      80      100
       I----+----I----+----I----+----I----+----I
   0-1 JYYYYYYYY                          17.4704
   1-2 JIIIIIIII                          16.2845
   2+  JAAAAAAAAAAAAAAAAAAAAAAAAAAAAAAAAA 66.2451

MORTALITY STRUCTURE OF FLOCK    (PERCENT) %

       0      20      40      60      80      100
       I----+----I----+----I----+----I----+----I
   0-1 JYYYYYYYYYYYYYYYY                  29.672
   1-2 JII                                4.91567
   2+  JAAAAAAAAAAAAAAAAAAAAAAAAAAAAAAAAA 65.4123
---------------------------------------------------------------------


EFFICIENCY INDICES:
              MEAT  =   0.2149
              MILK  =   0.162226
              WOOL  =   0.331225
```

Figure 3.2(c) *(Continued)*

where sY is the survival rate of young $(1 - mY)$, sI is the survival rate of immatures $(1 - mI)$, sA is the survival rate of adults $(1 - mA)$, and Ba is the birth rate per adult. This continues until the last cycle (tn) has been reached. The total number of animals dying in each age category is then calculated for cycle $t(n + 1)$ according to the formula

$$A_{(tn + 1)} = A_{(tn)} \times mA$$

and so on.

The values of A, I, and Y are printed out graphically in Figure 3.2 for each successive yearly cycle, resulting in a steadily rising growth curve. A growth rate G is calculated and expressed as a percentage:

$$100(T_{tn + 1)} - T_{(tn)})/T_{(tn)}$$

AGE AND MORTALITY PROFILES

The final values for Y, I, and A are expressed as a percentage of T and printed out in histogram form. The values for the mortality occurring in each age category, expressed as a percentage of total mortality (mT), are printed out graphically, also in histogram form, immediately below this.

PRODUCTIVITY INDICES

Three productivity or efficiency indices are printed out for meat, milk, and wool production. The indices are derived from the demographic structure of the flock or herd; that is, that proportion of the total population of animals whose age–sex status predisposes it to produce certain commodities. For example, milk production depends on the proportion of lactating females, and meat production on the proportion of animals being killed and the age at which this occurs. It should be stressed that the indices are arbitrary figures and serve only as a rough guide. They do not take account of variations in either demand or productive capacity produced by artificial selection for good milkers and wool producers, nor do they allow for the plane of nutrition. The indices are measures of the proportion of animals able to produce each product, rather than of the quantities produced. This approach is preferable to one in which an estimate is made of the level of production for each commodity from the general shape of the mortality profile (Payne 1973). These indices provide concrete values that may be compared with each other and with values derived from other herd simulations. Moreover, they are measures of productive *efficiency* as well as relative measures of the overall levels of production.

Assuming that all animals slaughtered or dying are eaten or sold, the meat production index is calculated as follows:

$$E(\text{meat}) = (aM + iM + 0.5yM) / T$$

where aM = mortality among adults, iM = mortality among immatures, and yM = mortality among young. Milk production is measured by the formula

$$E(\text{milk}) = (0.5Y + yM) / T$$

which gives a rough measure of the proportion of females with young (i.e., those lactating), enhanced by the number of young killed off, thereby leaving more milk for human consumption. Wool production depends on the overall proportion of adults in the flock (Maltby 1981:174) and is therefore calculated as follows, divided by a factor of 2 in order to keep the ratio within the same range as that for meat and milk:

$$E(\text{wool}) = A\ /\ 2T$$

In each case, T (the total number of live animals) gives a rough approximation of the costs involved in maintaining the herd.

Options

A number of options are built into the programme that may be selected or suppressed at will. The growth curve and the age and mortality profiles may be suppressed in order to restrict output to that needed at the time. In order to simulate the effects of unpredictable ecological disasters or animal epidemics, a randomiser is employed that designates certain years as disaster years, during which mortality rates are enhanced by a constant factor. However, this option will not be used in the present study. Another option permits the user to exclude all neonatals from the mortality profile. This is achieved by automatically cutting out 25% of the young—an arbitrary figure for expected losses in the first few weeks of life—and dropping them from further consideration. Consequently, the input mortality rate for young animals applies to deaths in excess of this total. Under appropriate conditions, it is also possible to specify that all adults are female. This can be done by overriding the assumption that the mortality of the young included 50% male and 50% female animals.

An Heuristic Example

The interpretation of economic emphasis on the basis of summary statistics for meat, milk, and wool productivity permits a far greater degree of precision than is possible through the 'eye-balling' of kill-off pattern histograms or survival curves. Attempts to compare archaeologically derived kill-off patterns against the ideal ones derived by Payne (1973) for meat, milk, and wool production have proved both cumbersome and uninformative (e.g., Griffith 1979:338–339). In the latter case, it is possible to say only that the observed pattern is more similar to meat production than wool production, or somewhere in between.

In view of the almost infinite variety of shapes that it is theoretically possible for a kill-off pattern to assume, visual comparisons of this kind, even if supported by statistical tests for significance, are of limited utility. The present method, on the other hand, provides measures, albeit arbitrary, that permit comparison between a large number of cases, and is thus a more convenient tool for measuring changes in productive strategy at discrete points in time over long periods (see Figure 3.9). Whereas the inspection of kill-off patterns yields information only on subsistence practices—that is, the mix of age groups—the present measure is more nearly an economic index, in that it is concerned not only with the subsistence pattern, but also with its relative efficiency. The loss of information brought about by reducing the number of age classes to three needs to be balanced against these advantages in deciding whether or not to use the model in any particular instance.

These points are illustrated in Figure 3.2, where the ideal kill-off patterns for meat, milk, and wool production employed by Payne (1973:Figures 1–3) have been converted to the three-category scheme outlined earlier and replicated through the simulation routine, FLOCKS (Cribb n.d.). In order to avoid the problem of 'equifinality' (the same pattern being produced by different combinations of birth and mortality rates), it has been assumed that the flocks are in a state of no-growth. This means that there is only one possible solution, since any alteration in rates that preserves the static growth profile would inevitably distort the desired mortality profile that one is attempting to replicate. The results of the experiment serve as both a vindication of Payne's (1973) ideal herd structures and a validation of the algorithms used to arrive at the productivity indices in the FLOCKS programme.

Meat production is highest in Figure 3.2a, as expected; the milk and wool indices are also highest in the appropriate cases (Figures 3.2b and 3.2c, respectively). Note, however, that in Figure 3.2b (the flock programmed for high milk production), the other productivity indices are also relatively high. These simulations draw attention to a very real and important property of all sheep–goat herding systems, one that I have observed many times in the course of repeated simulations of different herding scenarios: Selective biases towards one productive strategy or another are not necessarily mutually exclusive. For example, a system geared to meat production will also maintain a certain component of milk production. In another study (Cribb 1984), I have been able to show that a herding system oriented primarily towards milk production is likely to be highly productive in other departments as well. Conversely, a primary focus on meat production would appear to give rise to a more specialised strategy—thus, increments in meat productivity need not have any major effect on milk and wool productivity indices.

The implication of this study, namely that subsistence-based herders interested in security and high overall productivity will tend to select over time for a strategy based on milk and secondary milk products, would appear to be confirmed by ethnographic accounts of sheep–goat pastoralists, and of nomads in particular (Bates 1973; Cribb 1982; Dahl and Hjort 1976; Irons 1975). It would also appear that an exclusive focus on meat production can be a highly inefficient and wasteful strategy on the basis of studies of modern pastoralists and in terms of the assumptions of the simulation model outlined in this chapter. On the other hand, wool production tends to be associated with moderate levels of all-round efficiency. In short, the problem of interpreting kill-off patterns and deducing herding strategies is one that involves not only productive strategies and economic biases, but also the overall adaptive posture of the culture of which the herding system is a part.

In order to apply the simulation to a specific data set, the model must be set to run under certain conditions and constraints. These may differ from region to region, from period to period, and from one type of stock to another. Birth and mortality rates, as well as overall growth rates, must be set within certain realistic tolerance limits specific to a time and place. These may be derived from environmental evidence or in some cases—as for the Saxon period in Britain (Finberg 1972)—from written records. Furthermore, knowledge of such constraints may override certain quantitative results from the simulation. For instance, a high index for wool production on an Early Iron Age site would be negated by the knowledge from metrical studies of faunal samples that have confirmed that iron age sheep were relatively unspecialised and were poor producers of wool (Applebaum 1972; Malty 1981).

Simulating British Iron Age, Roman, and Saxon Flocks

Archaeological evidence and historical sources have now charted the major changes in pastoralism from Neolithic to Medieval times in Britain (e.g., Applebaum 1972; Bourdillon 1980; Bourdillon and Coy 1980; Finberg 1972; Grant 1975; King 1978; Legge 1981; Maltby 1979, 1981; Noddle 1974). Several archaeozoologists are now exploring the potential of elaborating these broad trends using faunal data as the primary evidence. The purpose of this section is to show how the simulation of age structure can make a positive contribution towards this objective.

Not only have there been historical shifts in the relative emphasis on different species (sheep, cattle, and pig), but within species there appear to have been major changes in herd structure through time. While the data are patchy and the observed changes may reflect no more than random variations in the preservation of bone or sampling error, there is strong circumstantial evidence to suggest that these changes may in fact be linked to major transformations in the pattern of land use and settlement, economic integration, and political stability.

I shall concentrate here on the practical application of the simulation model FLOCKS to the substantive problem of documenting and explaining changes in the pattern of sheep–goat pastoral production in British prehistory and early history, on the basis of ageable faunal elements. I am concerned here only with the kill-off data, for while there is much additional contextual and environmental evidence from the sites considered, the faunal data and the interpretations based upon them may be regarded as independent test cases.

In each case, the simulation routine FLOCKS will be used to arrive at a plausible scenario from which the specified mortality profile may have arisen. This is achieved by adjusting the various mortality rates until convergence on the desired mortality profile is achieved. By invoking the option of excluding neo-natals, it is then possible to review the same mortality profile as a structure from which the deaths of very young animals—the kind that are unlikely to show up in archaeological assemblages—are excluded.

IRON AGE (BALKSBURY, WINNALL DOWN, AND MICHELDEVER WOOD)

Three Iron Age kill-off patterns have been selected for study: two Middle Iron Age patterns from the sites of Balksbury and Winnall Down (Maltby 1981), and the aggregated results from Micheldever Wood (Griffith 1979). These sites are all in a small area of Hampshire in southern England (Figure 3.3). The patterns from Balksbury and Winnall Down were very similar and could be replicated through almost identical herding scenarios (Figures 3.4a and 3.5a). Although different mortality rates were employed in each case, the age structures and productivity profiles were similar. With a birth rate of 0.8/adult female/year, the two herding scenarios operate well within the acceptable limits for northern European flocks. Assuming these samples to be representative of animals dying at the site from a discrete local population, the results suggest a conservative herding strategy in which surplus young were killed while most surviving animals were allowed to reach an advanced age. This conclusion is in substantial agreement with Maltby's (1981:172–175) visual assessment of the same kill-off patterns.

Such a strategy would tend to maximise the production of wool from adult animals, both male and female, though the indices of high productivity for wool at 0.349 (Balksbury) and 0.352 (Winnall Down) may be misleading due to a low level of individual efficiency among Iron Age sheep. Meat and milk indices remain low. We might therefore postulate a herding strategy aimed at conserving the adult population and oriented towards secondary products (with some degree of specialization on wool), together with a minor spin-off in the form of surplus lambs. The low proportion of immatures (Maltby 1981:174) may conceivably have resulted from the export of surplus males, but there is no particular reason to expect such behaviour among Iron Age herders. In any case, this would alter the suggested scenario only slightly, requiring a marginally higher birth rate.

Changing the assumptions of the simulation so that neonatal mortality is not

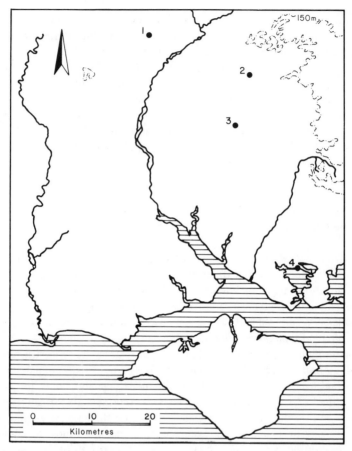

Figure 3.3 Location of the Hampshire archaeological sites used in the simulation. 1. Balks-
bury (hillfort, Iron Age); 2. Micheldever Wood (enclosed agricultural settlement, Iron Age); 3.
Winnall Down (enclosed agricultural settlement, Iron Age); 4. Portchester (military site, Roman and
Saxon).

considered as part of the mortality profile, it becomes increasingly difficult to
reproduce the same mortality profile, since the effect of this adjustment is to limit
the recruitment of adults. This modification can be accommodated if it is assumed that only male young are culled, in which case all those reaching adult-
hood are part of the breeding flock. The effect of this scenario is to produce a
flock that is more demographically viable, and to modify the productivity indices
in the direction of a more eclectic productive strategy, with less emphasis on
wool and more on milk (Figures 3.4b and 3.5b).

The Micheldever Wood sample exhibits a slightly different herding strategy in
which there is a higher kill-off of adult stock and immatures (Figure 3.6a).

Again, the scenario is an entirely plausible one in demographic terms. While the system differs in some respects from the previous Iron Age examples, the productivity indices are similar. However, changing the assumptions to exclude neonatals from consideration has the opposite effect on the productivity profile, enhancing the wool index at the expense of meat and milk (Figure 3.6b).

ROMAN (PORTCHESTER CASTLE)

The Roman pattern at Portchester seems to represent a straightforward herding strategy aimed at maximum meat production (Figure 3.7a). This is consistent

```
a.  AM= 0.12
    IM= 0.17  B= 0.8
    YM= 0.5                      GROWTH PROFILE

        0        100       200       300       400       500       600
        ]----+----I----+----I----+----I----+----I----+----I----+----I
     0  ]AAAAAAAAAAAAAAAAAAAA*
     1  ]AAAAAAAAAAAAAAAAAAAYYYY*
     2  ]AAAAAAAAAAAAAAAAIIIYYYY*
     3  ]AAAAAAAAAAAAAAAAAIIIYYYY*
     4  ]AAAAAAAAAAAAAAAAAIIIYYYY*
     5  ]AAAAAAAAAAAAAAAAAAAIIIYYYY*
     6  ]AAAAAAAAAAAAAAAAAAAAIIIYYYY*
     7  ]AAAAAAAAAAAAAAAAAAAAAIIIYYYY*
     8  ]AAAAAAAAAAAAAAAAAAAAAAIIIIYYYYY*
     9  ]AAAAAAAAAAAAAAAAAAAAAAAIIIIYYYYY*
    10  ]AAAAAAAAAAAAAAAAAAAAAAAAIIIIYYYYY*

    AGE        A= 23.1213    I= 4.41268    Y= 5.57139
    MORT.      A= 3.30407    I= 0.947136   Y= 5.57139
               ANNUAL GROWTH RATE =   3.98782 %P.A.
    ----------------------------------------------------------------------


    AGE STRUCTURE OF FLOCK       (PERCENT) %

        0        20        40        60        80       100
        I----+----I----+----I----+----I----+----I----+----I
    0-1 ]YYYYYYYYY                                  16.8293
    1-2 ]IIIIII                                     13.3292
     2+ ]AAAAAAAAAAAAAAAAAAAAAAAAAAAAAAAAAAA        69.8415

    MORTALITY STRUCTURE OF FLOCK    (PERCENT) %

        0        20        40        60        80       100
        I----+----I----+----I----+----I----+----I----+----I
    0-1 ]YYYYYYYYYYYYYYYYYYYYYYYYYYYYYYY            56.7201
    1-2 ]IIIII                                       9.64242
     2+ ]AAAAAAAAAAAAAAAA                           33.6375

    ----------------------------------------------------------


    EFFICIENCY INDICES:
               MEAT  =    0.212561
               MILK  =    0.252439
               WOOL  =    0.349208
```

Figure 3.4 Computer simulation of the Balksbury sample. (a) including neonatals; (b) excluding neonatals.

```
b. AM= 0.15
   IM= 0.17  B= 0.8
   YM= 0.5                      GROWTH PROFILE

      0       100      200      300      400      500      600
      ]----+----I----+----I----+----I----+----I----+----I----+----I
   0   JAAAAAAAAAAAAAAAAAAAAA*
   1   JAAAAAAAAAAAAAAAAAAYYYY*
   2   JAAAAAAAAAAAAAAIIIIYYYY*
   3   JAAAAAAAAAAAAAAAIIIYYYY*
   4   JAAAAAAAAAAAAAAAAIIIYYYY*
   5   JAAAAAAAAAAAAAAAAAIIIIYYYYYY*
   6   JAAAAAAAAAAAAAAAAAAIIIIYYYYYY*
   7   JAAAAAAAAAAAAAAAAAAAAIIIIYYYYYY*
   8   JAAAAAAAAAAAAAAAAAAAAAIIIIYYYYYY*
   9   JAAAAAAAAAAAAAAAAAAAAAAIIIIIYYYYYYY*
  10   JAAAAAAAAAAAAAAAAAAAAAAAIIIIIYYYYYYYY*

AGE          A= 22.3855   I= 5.30191   Y= 6.71565
MORT.        A= 4.15311   I= 1.14166   Y= 6.71565
             ANNUAL GROWTH RATE =  4.13009 %P.A.
-----------------------------------------------------------------

AGE STRUCTURE OF FLOCK    (PERCENT) %

      0       20       40       60       80      100
      I----+----I----+----I----+----I----+----I----+----I
  0-1 JYYYYYYYYY                                 19.5205
  1-2 JIIIIIII                                   15.4111
   2+ JAAAAAAAAAAAAAAAAAAAAAAAAAAAAAAAAAAAAA     65.0683

MORTALITY STRUCTURE OF FLOCK   (PERCENT) %

      0       20       40       60       80      100
      I----+----I----+----I----+----I----+----I----+----I
  0-1 JYYYYYYYYYYYYYYYYYYYYYYYYYYYYY             55.9152
  1-2 JIIII                                      9.50558
   2+ JAAAAAAAAAAAAAAAA                          34.5792

-----------------------------------------------------------------

EFFICIENCY INDICES:
             MEAT  =    0.251507
             MILK  =    0.292808
             WOOL  =    0.325342
```

Figure   3.4(b)   *(Continued)*

with what is known about sheep husbandry during Roman times on the basis of historical sources (Applebaum 1972:215). Assuming a representative sample, we could plausibly reconstruct a flock with a birth rate of 0.9/adult female/year and kill-off rates of 21% for adults, 47% for immatures, and 24% for young, resulting in an overall growth rate of 3.21% per year. The productivity index for meat is quite high at 0.346, accompanied by moderate figures for milk and wool. Such a herding strategy implies a high level of all-round efficiency alongside a marked bias towards meat production from juvenile and adult animals.

The possibility still remains that we are not dealing with a representative sample, in which case it might be suggested that juveniles were being brought onto the site from elsewhere. In fact, it is not beyond the bounds of possibility

```
a.  AM= 0.12
    IM= 0.12  B= 0.8
    YM= 0.5

                         GROWTH PROFILE
     0      100     200     300     400     500     600
     I---+---I---+---I---+---I---+---I---+---I---+---I---+---I
  0  JAAAAAAAAAAAAAAAAA*
  1  JAAAAAAAAAAAAAAAAYYYY*
  2  JAAAAAAAAAAAAAAAIIIYYY*
  3  JAAAAAAAAAAAAAAAAIIIYYY*
  4  JAAAAAAAAAAAAAAAAAIIIYYY*
  5  JAAAAAAAAAAAAAAAAAAIIIYYY*
  6  JAAAAAAAAAAAAAAAAAAAIIIYYY*
  7  JAAAAAAAAAAAAAAAAAAAAIIIYYY*
  8  JAAAAAAAAAAAAAAAAAAAAAIIIYYY*
  9  JAAAAAAAAAAAAAAAAAAAAAIIIYYYY*
 10  JAAAAAAAAAAAAAAAAAAAAAAAIIIYYYYY*

AGE     A= 23.1213   I= 4.41269   Y= 5.25483
MORT.   A= 3.30407   I= 0.63058   Y= 5.25483
        ANNUAL GROWTH RATE = 4.02632 %P.A.

AGE STRUCTURE OF FLOCK   (PERCENT) %
     0      20      40      60      80      100
     I---+---I---+---I---+---I---+---I---+---I
0-1  JYYYYYYY                        16.0263
1-2  JIIIIII                         13.4579
2+   JAAAAAAAAAAAAAAAAAAAAAAAAAAAAAA 70.5158

MORTALITY STRUCTURE OF FLOCK   (PERCENT) %
     0      20      40      60      80      100
     I---+---I---+---I---+---I---+---I---+---I
0-1  JYYYYYYYYYYYYYYYYYYYYYYYYY       57.1831
1-2  JIII                            6.86197
2+   JAAAAAAAAAA                     35.9549

EFFICIENCY INDICES:
     MEAT =  0.200132
     MILK =  0.240395
     WOOL =  0.352579
```

```
b.  AM= 0.15
    IM= 0.13  B= 0.8
    YM= 0.5

                         GROWTH PROFILE
     0      100     200     300     400     500     600
     I---+---I---+---I---+---I---+---I---+---I---+---I---+---I
  0  JAAAAAAAAAAAAAAAAAA*
  1  JAAAAAAAAAAAAAAAAAYYYY*
  2  JAAAAAAAAAAAAAAAIIIYYY*
  3  JAAAAAAAAAAAAAAAAIIIYYY*
  4  JAAAAAAAAAAAAAAAAAIIIYYY*
  5  JAAAAAAAAAAAAAAAAAAIIIYYY*
  6  JAAAAAAAAAAAAAAAAAAAIIIYYY*
  7  JAAAAAAAAAAAAAAAAAAAAIIIYYYY*
  8  JAAAAAAAAAAAAAAAAAAAAAAIIIYYYY*
  9  JAAAAAAAAAAAAAAAAAAAAAAAIIIYYYYY*
 10  JAAAAAAAAAAAAAAAAAAAAAAAAIIIIYYYYY*

AGE     A= 23.8609   I= 5.87846   Y= 7.15827
MORT.   A= 4.4609    I= 0.930575  Y= 7.15827
        ANNUAL GROWTH RATE = 4.78836 %P.A.

AGE STRUCTURE OF FLOCK   (PERCENT) %
     0      20      40      60      80      100
     I---+---I---+---I---+---I---+---I---+---I
0-1  JYYYYYYYY                       19.4003
1-2  JIIIIIII                        15.9318
2+   JAAAAAAAAAAAAAAAAAAAAAAAAAAA    64.6678

MORTALITY STRUCTURE OF FLOCK   (PERCENT) %
     0      20      40      60      80      100
     I---+---I---+---I---+---I---+---I---+---I
0-1  JYYYYYYYYYYYYYYYYYYYYYYYYY       57.0391
1-2  JIII                            7.41509
2+   JAAAAAAAAAA                     35.5458

EFFICIENCY INDICES:
     MEAT =  0.243122
     MILK =  0.291005
     WOOL =  0.323339
```

Figure 3.5 Computer simulation of the Winnall Down sample. (a) including neonatals; (b) excluding neonatals.

a.

```
AM= 0.19
IM= 0.27   B= 0.8
YM= 0.26                GROWTH PROFILE

     0         100       200       300       400       500       600
     J---+---I---+---I---+---I---+---I---+---I---+---I---+---I
  0  JAAAAAAAAAAAAAAAAAAAA*
  1  JAAAAAAAAAAAAAAAAAAAYYYYY*
  2  JAAAAAAAAAAAAAAAAAAIIIIYYYY*
  3  JAAAAAAAAAAAAAAAAAIIIIIYYYY*
  4  JAAAAAAAAAAAAAAAAAAIIIIIYYYY*
  5  JAAAAAAAAAAAAAAAAAIIIIIYYYYY*
  6  JAAAAAAAAAAAAAAAAAIIIIIIYYYYY*
  7  JAAAAAAAAAAAAAAAAAIIIIIIYYYYY*
  8  JAAAAAAAAAAAAAAAAAIIIIIIYYYYY*
  9  JAAAAAAAAAAAAAAAAAAIIIIIIYYYYY*
 10  JAAAAAAAAAAAAAAAAAAAIIIIIYYYYY*

AGE    A= 18.9489   I= 5.39087   Y= 7.68338
MORT.  A= 4.62455   I= 2.07451   Y= 2.69957
       ANNUAL GROWTH RATE = 3.07377 %F.A.
```

```
AGE STRUCTURE OF FLOCK    (PERCENT) %

     0    20    40    60    80    100
     I----+----I----+----I----+----I----+----I----+----I
 0-1 JYYYYYYYYY                                23.9932
 1-2 JIIIIIII                                  16.8343
 2+  JAAAAAAAAAAAAAAAAAAAAAAAAAAAAAA           59.1725
```

```
MORTALITY STRUCTURE OF FLOCK   (PERCENT) %

     0    20    40    60    80    100
     I----+----I----+----I----+----I----+----I----+----I
 0-1 JYYYYYYYYYY                               28.723
 1-2 JIIIIIIIII                                22.0725
 2+  JAAAAAAAAAAAAAAAAAAAAAAAAA                49.2045
```

```
EFFICIENCY INDICES:
   MEAT =  0.251345
   MILK =  0.204267
   WOOL =  0.295862
```

b.

```
AM= 0.14
IM= 0.25   B= 0.8
YM= 0.24                GROWTH PROFILE

     0         100       200       300       400       500       600
     J---+---I---+---I---+---I---+---I---+---I---+---I---+---I
  0  JAAAAAAAAAAAAAAAAAAAA*
  1  JAAAAAAAAAAAAAAAAAYYIIYYY*
  2  JAAAAAAAAAAAAAAAAIIIIYYYY*
  3  JAAAAAAAAAAAAAAAAAIIIIYYYY*
  4  JAAAAAAAAAAAAAAAAAAIIIIYYYYY*
  5  JAAAAAAAAAAAAAAAAAAIIIIYYYYY*
  6  JAAAAAAAAAAAAAAAAAAAIIIIYYYYY*
  7  JAAAAAAAAAAAAAAAAAAAIIIIYYYYY*
  8  JAAAAAAAAAAAAAAAAAAAAIIIIYYYYY*
  9  JAAAAAAAAAAAAAAAAAAAAAIIIIYYYYY*
 10  JAAAAAAAAAAAAAAAAAAAAAIIIIYYYYY*

AGE    A= 22.1051   I= 4.81263   Y= 6.71994
MORT.  A= 3.76848   I= 1.67999   Y= 2.12209
       ANNUAL GROWTH RATE = 3.77993 %F.A.
```

```
AGE STRUCTURE OF FLOCK    (PERCENT) %

     0    20    40    60    80    100
     I----+----I----+----I----+----I----+----I----+----I
 0-1 JYYYYYYYY                                 19.9774
 1-2 JIIIIIII                                  14.3073
 2+  JAAAAAAAAAAAAAAAAAAAAAAAAAAAAAAAA         65.7153
```

```
MORTALITY STRUCTURE OF FLOCK   (PERCENT) %

     0    20    40    60    80    100
     I----+----I----+----I----+----I----+----I----+----I
 0-1 JYYYYYYYYYYYY                             28.0308
 1-2 JIIIIIIIII                                22.1911
 2+  JAAAAAAAAAAAAAAAAAAAAAAAA                 49.7781
```

```
EFFICIENCY INDICES:
   MEAT =  0.193519
   MILK =  0.162974
   WOOL =  0.328576
```

Figure 3.6 Computer simulation of the Micheldever Wood sample. (a) including neonatals; (b) excluding neonatals.

96

a.
```
AM= 0.21
IM= 0.47  B= 0.9
YM= 0.24        GROWTH PROFILE

     0        100       200       300       400       500       600
     ]----+----I----+----I----+----I----+----I----+----I----+----I
  0  ]AAAAAAAAAAAAAAAAAA*
  1  ]AAAAAAAAAAAAAAAYYYYYYYYY*
  2  ]AAAAAAAAAAAAAIIIIYYYYYYYY*
  3  ]AAAAAAAAAAAAIIIIYYYYYYYY*
  4  ]AAAAAAAAAAAAIIIIYYYYYYYY*
  5  ]AAAAAAAAAAAAAIIIIIYYYYYYYY*
  6  ]AAAAAAAAAAAAAAIIIIIIYYYYYYYY*
  7  ]AAAAAAAAAAAAAIIIIIIYYYYYYYYY*
  8  ]AAAAAAAAAAAAAAAIIIIIIYYYYYYYYY*
  9  ]AAAAAAAAAAAAAAAAAIIIIIIYYYYYYYYY*
 10  ]AAAAAAAAAAAAAAAAAAIIIIIIIYYYYYYYYY*

AGE   A= 19.31   I= 6.30252  Y= 12.4604
MORT.  A= 5.37863  I= 5.8564  Y= 3.93487
      ANNUAL GROWTH RATE = 3.21854 %P.A.
```

```
AGE STRUCTURE OF FLOCK    (PERCENT) %

     0        20        40        60        80        100
     I----+----I----+----I----+----I----+----I----+----I
0-1  ]YYYYYYYYYYY                               32.7278
1-2  ]IIIIIIII                                  16.5538
2+   ]AAAAAAAAAAAAAAAAAAAAAAAA                  50.7185
```

```
MORTALITY STRUCTURE OF FLOCK    (PERCENT) %

     0        20        40        60        80        100
     I----+----I----+----I----+----I----+----I----+----I
0-1  ]YYYYYYYYYY                                25.9387
1-2  ]IIIIIIIIIIIIIIII                          38.6054
2+   ]AAAAAAAAAAAAAAAA                          35.4559
```

```
EFFICIENCY INDICES:
       MEAT =  0.346768
       MILK =  0.26699
       WOOL =  0.253592
```

b.
```
AM= 0.17
IM= 0.47  B= 0.9
YM= 0.24        GROWTH PROFILE

     0        100       200       300       400       500       600
     ]----+----I----+----I----+----I----+----I----+----I----+----I
  0  ]AAAAAAAAAAAAAAAA*
  1  ]AAAAAAAAAAAAAAAYYYYYYYY*
  2  ]AAAAAAAAAAAIIIIYYYYYYY*
  3  ]AAAAAAAAAAAIIIIYYYYYYY*
  4  ]AAAAAAAAAAAAIIIIYYYYYYY*
  5  ]AAAAAAAAAAAAAIIIIYYYYYY*
  6  ]AAAAAAAAAAAAAIIIIIYYYYYY*
  7  ]AAAAAAAAAAAAAAIIIIIYYYYYY*
  8  ]AAAAAAAAAAAAAAAIIIIIYYYYYY*
  9  ]AAAAAAAAAAAAAAAAIIIIIYYYYYYY*
 10  ]AAAAAAAAAAAAAAAAAIIIIIIYYYYYYY*

AGE   A= 18.9722  I= 4.69918  Y= 9.18184
MORT.  A= 4.02414  I= 4.31546  Y= 2.89953
      ANNUAL GROWTH RATE = 2.56363 %P.A.
```

```
AGE STRUCTURE OF FLOCK    (PERCENT) %

     0        20        40        60        80        100
     ]----+----I----+----I----+----I----+----I----+----I
0-1  ]YYYYYYYYY                                 27.948
1-2  ]IIIIIII                                   14.3035
2+   ]AAAAAAAAAAAAAAAAAAAAAAAAAAA               57.7484
```

```
MORTALITY STRUCTURE OF FLOCK    (PERCENT) %

     0        20        40        60        80        100
     ]----+----I----+----I----+----I----+----I----+----I
0-1  ]YYYYYYYYYY                                25.7985
1-2  ]IIIIIIIIIIIIIIIII                         38.3968
2+   ]AAAAAAAAAAAAAAAA                          35.8047
```

```
EFFICIENCY INDICES:
       MEAT =  0.297973
       MILK =  0.227997
       WOOL =  0.288742
```

Figure 3.7 Computer simulation of the Roman sample from Portchester. (a) including neonatals; (b) excluding neonatals.

that the entire sample may have been derived from imported carcases, since this was a Roman military site. In the latter case, it would be uncertain to what extent this structure would reflect the herding strategies of surrounding pastoral populations from which meat supplies were drawn. Grant (1975), however, sees little reason to doubt that the sample was produced by a local pastoral economy.

If it is assumed that neonatals do not enter the mortality profile, the productivity profile appears slightly less specialised, with the meat index even marginally lower than that for wool (Figure 3.7b).

SAXON (PORTCHESTER CASTLE)

The Saxon sample quickly shows itself to be an implausible mortality profile. In simulating a herding system conforming to such a pattern (Figure 3.8a), it soon becomes clear that the pattern cannot be maintained while keeping the mortality, birth, and growth rates within acceptable limits. In order to achieve a minimally viable growth rate of more than 3% per year, a birth rate of 1.2/female per year is required, which is considered to be far too high for early British flocks. Far too many adults were being killed off for the flock to reproduce itself. An alternative hypothesis is that only male adults were being deliberately culled out. Such a herd does not seem to be oriented towards any particular commodity—the productivity indices are all low, especially those for milk. In short, such a herding strategy would have been not only demographically unfeasible but also economically inefficient. It is highly unlikely that the sample is representative of the mortality profile of any animal population attached to the site, with young and immature animals being grossly underrepresented. It would therefore be unwise to attempt any inferences about the herding strategies that produced such a profile, other than the possibility that younger animals were exported; instead, we should consider the possibility that the sample represents provisioning for the inhabitants of the site who were not themselves engaged in pastoral activities.

Modifying this scenario to exclude neonatals has little effect on the demographic viability of the simulated flock; a negative growth rate still occurs (Figure 3.8b). However, it does produce a change in the productivity profile, with the wool index now exceeding that for meat.

DIACHRONIC COMPARISONS

If the simulation output from all five cases (Table 3.1) is plotted over time in graph form (Figure 3.9), certain tendencies can be observed in the data. Since each simulation run represents an independent experiment, the results are assumed to reflect actual differences in past herding systems as modelled by

```
a. AM= 0.3
   IM= 0.18  B= 0.9
   YM= 0.14            GROWTH PROFILE

        0        100       200       300       400       500       600
        ]---+----I----+----I----+----I----+----I----+----I----+----I
     0  ]AAAAAAAAAAAAAAAAAAAAA*
     1  ]AAAAAAAAAAAAAAAAYYYYY*
     2  ]AAAAAAAAAIIIIYYYY*
     3  ]AAAAAAAAAIIIIYYYY*
     4  ]AAAAAAAAAIIIIYYYY*
     5  ]AAAAAAAAAIIIIYYYY*
     6  ]AAAAAAAAAIIIIYYYY*
     7  ]AAAAAAAAAIIIIYYYY*
     8  ]AAAAAAAAAIIIIYYYY*
     9  ]AAAAAAAAAIIIIYYYY*
    10  ]AAAAAAAAAIIIIYYYY*

    AGE    A= 8.8631   I= 3.51004   Y= 4.18295
    MORT.  A= 3.71194  I= 0.752931  Y= 0.680945
           ANNUAL GROWTH RATE = -1.70284 %P.A.
    -------------------------------------------------------

    AGE STRUCTURE OF FLOCK   (PERCENT) %
        0        20   40   60   80       100
        I---+----I----+----I----+----I----+----I
    0-1 JYYYYYYYYYY                     25.2653
    1-2 JIIIIIIII                       21.2009
    2+  JAAAAAAAAAAAAAAAAAAAAAAAAAAAA   53.5538

    MORTALITY STRUCTURE OF FLOCK  (PERCENT) %
        0        20   40   60   80       100
        I---+----I----+----I----+----I----+----I
    0-1 JYYYYY                          13.233
    1-2 JIIIIII                         14.6319
    2+  JAAAAAAAAAAAAAAAAAAAAAAAAAA     72.1351
    -------------------------------------------------------

    EFFICIENCY INDICES:
        MEAT  =  0.290246
        MILK  =  0.167456
        WOOL  =  0.267669


b. AM= 0.24
   IM= 0.18  B= 0.9
   YM= 0.14            GROWTH PROFILE

        0        100       200       300       400       500       600
        ]---+----I----+----I----+----I----+----I----+----I----+----I
     0  ]AAAAAAAAAAAAAAAAAAAAA*
     1  ]AAAAAAAAAAAAAAAYYYYY*
     2  ]AAAAAAAAAIIIIYYYY*
     3  ]AAAAAAAAAIIIIYYYY*
     4  ]AAAAAAAAAIIIIYYYY*
     5  ]AAAAAAAAAIIIIYYYY*
     6  ]AAAAAAAAAIIIIYYYY*
     7  ]AAAAAAAAAIIIIYYYY*
     8  ]AAAAAAAAAIIIIYYY*
     9  ]AAAAAAAAAIIIYYY*
    10  ]AAAAAAAAAIIIYYY*

    AGE    A= 10.7216  I= 3.16209  Y= 3.79505
    MORT.  A= 3.33208  I= 0.68311  Y= 0.617799
           ANNUAL GROWTH RATE = -1.24523 %P.A.
    -------------------------------------------------------

    AGE STRUCTURE OF FLOCK   (PERCENT) %
        0        20   40   60   80       100
        I---+----I----+----I----+----I----+----I
    0-1 JYYYYYYYYY                      21.4668
    1-2 JIIIIIII                        17.8864
    2+  JAAAAAAAAAAAAAAAAAAAAAAAAAAAAAA 60.6468

    MORTALITY STRUCTURE OF FLOCK  (PERCENT) %
        0        20   40   60   80       100
        I---+----I----+----I----+----I----+----I
    0-1 JYYYYY                          13.3348
    1-2 JIIIIII                         14.7445
    2+  JAAAAAAAAAAAAAAAAAAAAAAAAAAAA   71.9208
    -------------------------------------------------------

    EFFICIENCY INDICES:
        MEAT  =  0.244593
        MILK  =  0.14228
        WOOL  =  0.303234
```

Figure 3.8 Computer simulation of the Saxon sample from Portchester. (a) including neonatals; (b) excluding neonatals.

Table 3.1

Summary of Data from Five Simulated Herding Systems[a]

| | Iron Age | | | | | | Roman | | Saxon | |
	Micheldever		Winnall Down		Balksbury		Portchester		Portchester	
Mortality (%)										
Young	28.7	28.0	57.2	57.0	55.1	55.9	25.9	25.8	13.2	13.3
Immature	22.1	22.2	6.9	7.4	9.4	9.5	38.6	38.4	14.6	14.7
Adult	49.2	49.8	35.9	35.5	35.5	34.6	35.5	35.8	72.1	71.9
Productivity										
Meat	.251	.194	.200	.243	.220	.251	.347	.298	.290	.244
Milk	.204	.163	.240	.291	.252	.293	.267	.228	.167	.142
Wool	.296	.328	.352	.323	.349	.325	.253	.289	.268	.303
Mean productivity	.250	.228	.264	.285	.273	.290	.289	.271	.240	.233
Growth rate (%)	3.074	3.780	4.026	4.788	3.135	4.130	3.218	2.564	-1.70	-1.24

[a]For each system, the number in the first column includes neonatals, and the number in the second column excludes neonatals.

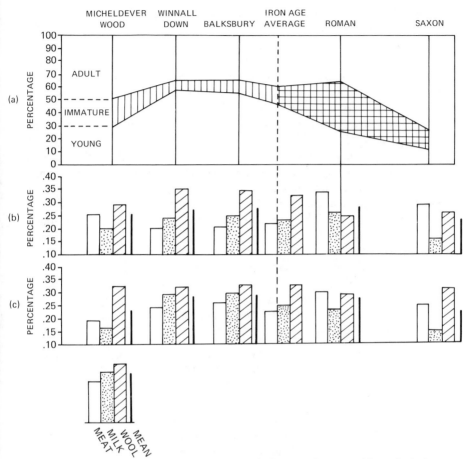

Figure 3.9 Diachronic trends in simulation output for Iron Age, Roman, and Saxon flocks from Hampshire. (a) mortality profiles; (b) productivity indices for meat, milk, and wool production including neonatals; (c) productivity indices for meat, milk, and wool production excluding neonatals. The column to the right of each bar graph in (b) and (c) represents the overall efficiency index, the mean of the three productivity indices.

FLOCKS. Of course, in view of the likely intervention of a variety of formation processes, the extent to which this is true remains uncertain.

Looking at changes in the mortality profiles (Figure 3.9a), differences appear between the three iron age cases in the proportions of adults, immatures, and young. These differences, however, are less extreme than the ones observed between all the iron age cases—and their average—and the Roman and Saxon examples. The width and positioning of the immature group serve as a summary of the changes in the mortality structure, or kill-off pattern, over a period of some nine centuries. The kill-off of immatures—probably young males—was moderate to low throughout the Iron Age, increasing markedly in Roman times and dropping back to a moderate level in Saxon times. A high kill-off of young occurred in all iron age cases, decreasing in Roman times (coinciding with an increased kill-off of immatures) and dropping even further in the Saxon case.

The productivity indices for meat, milk, and wool production display even greater consistency within the Iron Age, as well as sharp contrasts between the Iron Age and the later periods (Figure 3.9b). There is a consistent bias towards the kind of productivity profile that one would associate with wool production throughout the Iron Age. The pattern is reversed for Roman Portchester, where meat production dominated but wool productivity was still relatively high. Again, a major qualitative change occurred in the Saxon case, where milk productivity dropped sharply. In summary, a period of specialised meat production occurred during the Roman period against a background of subsistence herding. Tracing the same sequence with neonatals excluded from the mortality profile, we find that the general effect was to enhance the wool productivity index in all cases (Figure 3.9c). The only instance in which the meat productivity index exceeds that for wool is the Roman case.

Maltby (1981:178) summarises the changes in productive patterns from the Iron Age to the Saxon period as

> an underlying trend from a low level of subsistence husbandry in the Iron Age, through improvements and emphasis on better meat production during the Romano-British period, to the development of wool production as the most important component of sheep husbandry in the late Saxon period.

The results of the present study are broadly consistent with this picture, except in two respects. First, the productivity indices point to an emphasis on wool production during the Iron Age—an emphasis that may be partly offset by low percapita productivity in terms of wool weight. Second, in view of the evident incompleteness of the Saxon sample, it is difficult to confirm a bias towards wool production, or indeed to accept any productivity profile based on this sample.

Conclusion

The computer simulation of herd structures represents an attempt to explore the properties of an abstract system derived from the real-life conditions and constraints governing the practice of sheep husbandry. Although the model assumes perfect information and representative samples, its potential applications are not limited by these assumptions. In my view, the simulation using FLOCKS and the model of herd structure on which the programme is based are representative of the kinds of theoretical and methodological machine tools that are currently necessary for the advancement of archaeological science. By focusing on subsistence strategies and concepts such as productivity and degree of specialization, it is possible to derive information about the past which, though lacking in precision, is more attuned to current developments in archaeozoology than are visual inspection or the subjective assessment of kill-off patterns. Though reduced to simplified categories—and therefore meeting the requirement of 'robustness'—the model has revealed trends in the original data that would not otherwise have been observable or quantifiable. The potential applications of the model will increase as the number of usable kill-off patterns from archaeological sites increases.

Of course, indiscriminate use of the simulation model, free of the context of a particular research problem, can reduce it to a mere plaything. This was proved in the course of many fruitless hours spent juggling mortality and birth rates against each other in the initial phase of the operationalization of the system. But in the service of definite theoretical goals, simulations of simple and bounded natural and cultural systems, such as FLOCKS, have a great deal to offer in making possible perceptions and insights that would be impossible to achieve with the unaided mind.

References

Applebaum, S.
    1972 Roman Britain. In *The Agrarian history of England and Wales,* edited by H. P. R. Finberg, pp. 3–282. Cambridge University Press, Cambridge, England.
Arrowsmith, S. P., D. G. Steenkamp, and P. LeRoux
    1974 The influence of breed and plane of nutrition on the chronology of tooth eruption in sheep. *South African Journal of Animal Science* 4:127–130.
Bates, D. G.
    1973 *Nomads and farmers: a study of the Yörük of southeast Turkey.* University of Michigan, Museum of Anthropology, Anthropological Paper 52.
Behrensmeyer, A. K., and A. Hill
    1979 *Fossils in the making.* Chicago University Press.
Binford, L. R.
    1981 *Bones: ancient men and modern myths.* Academic Press, New York.
Binford, L. R.
    1983 *In pursuit of the past.* Thames and Hudson, London.
Bourdillon, J.
    1980 Town life and animal husbandry in the Southampton area, as suggested by the excavated bones. *Proceedings of the Hampshire Field Club and Archaeological Society* 36:181–191.
Bourdillon, J., and J. P. Coy
    1980 The animal bones. In *Excavations at Melbourne Street, Southampton 1971–76,* edited by P. Holdsworth, pp. 79–121. Council for British Archaeology, Research Report 33, London.

Carter, H. H.
  1975 A guide to the rates of toothwear in English lowland sheep. *Journal of Archaeological Science* 2:231–233.
Cherry, J. F., C. Gamble, and S. Shennan (editors)
  1978 *Sampling in contemporary British archaeology.* British Archaeological Reports, British Series 50, Oxford, England.
Clarke, D. L.
  1968 *Analytical archaeology.* Methuen, London.
Collier, S., and P. White
  1976 Get them young? Age and sex inferences on animal domestication in archaeology. *American Antiquity* 41:96–102.
Coy, J. P., R. T. Jones, and K. A. Turner
  1982 Absolute ageing of cattle from tooth sections and its relevance to archaeology. In *Ageing and sexing animal bones from archaeological sites,* edited by R. Wilson et al., pp. 127–140. British Archaeological Reports, British Series 109, Oxford, England.
Cribb, R. L. D.
  1982 *The archaeological dimensions of Near Eastern nomadic pastoralism.* Unpublished Ph.D. dissertation, Southampton University.
Cribb, R. L. D.
  1984 Computer simulation as an interpretive and heuristic device in the study of kill-off strategies. In *Animals and archaeology 3: herding in western Asia and the Mediterranean region,* edited by C. Grigson and J. Clutton-Brock, pp. 161–170. British Archaeological Reports, International Series 202, Oxford, England.
Cribb, R. L. D.
  n.d. The logic of the herd: on the meaning of archaeological age structure—a computer simulation model. Ms. on file, University of Southampton, Department of Archaeology.
Dahl, G., and A. Hjort
  1976 *Having herds: pastoral herd growth and household economy.* Stockholm University Studies in Social Anthropology 2.
Daly, P.
  1969 Approaches to faunal analysis in archaeology. *American Antiquity* 24:146–153.
Ducos, P.
  1978 Domestication defined and methodological approaches to its recognition in faunal assemblages. In *Approaches to faunal analysis in the Middle East,* edited by R. H. Meadow and M. A. Zeder, pp. 53–56. Harvard University, Peabody Museum Bulletin 2.
Ewbank, J. M., D. W. Phillipson, R. D. Whitehouse, and E. S. Higgs
  1964 Sheep in the Iron Age: a method of study. *Proceedings of the Prehistoric Society* 30:423–426.
Fieller, N. R. J., and A. Turner
  1982 Number estimation in vertebrate samples. *Journal of Archaeological Science* 9:49–62.
Finberg, H. P. R. (editor)
  1972 *The agrarian history of England and Wales.* Cambridge University Press, Cambridge, England.
Gamble, C.
  1978 Optimising information from studies of faunal remains. In *Sampling in contemporary British archaeology,* edited by J. F. Cherry et al., pp. 321–353. British Archaeological Reports, British Series 50, Oxford, England.
Gifford, D. P.
  1981 Taphonomy and palaeoecology: a critical review of archaeology's sister disciplines. In *Advances in archaeological theory and method* (Vol. 4), edited by M. B. Schiffer, pp. 365–438. Academic Press, New York.

Grant, A.
1975 The animal bones. In *Excavations at Portchester Castle* (Vol. I), edited by B. Cunliffe, pp. 378–408. Research Committee of the Society of Antiquaries, Report 32, London.

Griffith, N. J. L.
1979 Animal Bones from R-27, M3 motorway excavations. In *Faunal remains project, Southampton 1975–78*, pp. 272–375. Ancient Monuments Laboratory Report 2647, London.

Hamond, F. W.
1978 RQS "The contribution of simulation to the study of archaeological processes." In *Simulation studies in archaeology*, edited by I. Hodder, pp. 1–9. Cambridge University Press, Cambridge, England.

Harcourt, R. A.
1979 The animal bones. In *Gussage All Saints: an iron age settlement in Dorset*, edited by G. J. Wainwright, pp. 150–160. Department of the Environment, Archaeological Report 10, London.

Healy, W. B., and T. G. Ludwig
1965 Wear of sheep's teeth: the role of ingested soil. *New Zealand Journal of Agricultural Research* 8(4):737–752.

Hodder, I. (editor)
1978 *Simulation studies in archaeology*. Cambridge University Press, Cambridge, England.

Irons, W.
1975 *The Yomut Turkmen: a study of social organisation among a central Asian Turkic-speaking population*. University of Michigan, Anthropological Paper 58, Ann Arbor.

King, A.
1978 A comparative survey of bone assemblages from Roman sites in Britain. *Bulletin of the Institute of Archaeology of London* 15:207–232.

Klein, R. G., C. Wolf, L. G. Freeman, and K. Allwarden
1981 The use of dental crown heights for constructing age profiles of red deer and similar species in archaeological samples. *Journal of Archaeological Science* 8(1):1–32.

Legge, A. J.
1981 Aspects of cattle husbandry. In *Farming practice in British prehistory*, edited by R. Mercer, pp. 169–181. Edinburgh University Press, Edinburgh, Scotland.

Maltby, J. M.
1979 *Faunal studies on urban sites: the animal bones from Exeter 1971–1975*. Sheffield University, Department of Prehistory and Archaeology, Exeter Archaeological Reports 2.

Maltby, J. M.
1981 Iron age, Romano-British and Anglo-Saxon animal husbandry: a review of the faunal evidence. In *The environment of man: the Iron Age to the Anglo-Saxon period*, edited by M. Jones and G. Dimbleby, pp. 155–203. British Archaeological Reports, British Series 87, Oxford, England.

Meadow, R. H.
1976 Methodological concerns in zooarchaeology. In *Thèmes, spécialisés, prétirage*, pp. 108–123. Union Internationale des Sciences Préhistoriques et Protohistoriques, IX Congrès, Nice.

Morris, P.
1972 A review of mammalian age determination methods. *Mammal Review* 2(3):69–103.

Mounteney, G. A.
1981 Faunal attrition and subsistence reconstruction at Thwing. In *Prehistoric communities in northern England: essays in economic and social reconstruction*, edited by G. Barker, pp. 23–36. Sheffield University, Department of Prehistory and Archaeology.

Noddle, B.
1974 Ages of epiphyseal closure in feral and domesticated goats and ages of dental eruption. *Journal of Archaeological Science* 1:195–204.

Payne, S.
   1973 Kill-off patterns in sheep and goats: the mandibles from Asvan Kale. *Anatolian Studies*
      23:281–303.
Perkins, D.
   1964 Prehistoric fauna from Shanidar, Iraq. *Science* 144:1565–1566.
Schiffer, M. B.
   1976 *Behavioural archaeology.* Academic Press, New York.
Silver, I. A.
   1969 The ageing of domestic animals. In *Science in archaeology,* edited by D. Brothwell and E.
      S. Higgs, pp. 283–302. Thames and Hudson, London.
Wapnish, P., B. Hesse, and A. Ogilvy
   1977 The 1974 collection of faunal remains from Tell Dan. *Bulletin of the American School of
      Oriental Research* 227:35–62.
Wilson, R., C. Grigson, and S. Payne (editors)
   1982 *Ageing and sexing animal bones from archaeological sites.* British Archaeological Re-
      ports, British Series 109, Oxford, England.
Yellen, J. E.
   1977 Cultural patterning in faunal remains: evidence from the !Kung bushmen. In *Experimental
      archaeology,* edited by D. Ingersoll et al., pp. 271–351. Columbia University Press, New
      York.

4

Archaeobotany beyond Subsistence Reconstruction

MARTIN JONES

Introduction

In the majority of archaeobotanical studies, the human landscape has been perceived as being made up of discrete 'sites' distributed within an 'environment'. The environment is seen as the theatre of global processes, of forest advance and retreat, of climatic change, and from time to time the 'impact' of man. The site is seen as the locus of human activity, and of particular processes relating to production and consumption. Human behaviour within the environment is treated differently from human behaviour within the site. Within the environment it is discussed in general functionalist terms, using concepts such as optimisation, least effort, and cost–benefit ratios (Roper 1979), whereas within the site, the emphasis has steadily moved to the fine detail of human activity influencing the archaeological record (Hillman 1981).

This dichotomy within the perceived human landscape is reflected in the division between current approaches to the botanical record, on the one hand placing emphasis on the region, on the other hand the site. In the regional approach, the landscape is described in terms of general parameters drawn from palynological studies, such as arboreal to non-arboreal pollen ratios and arable to pastoral ratios (Godwin 1968; Roberts et al. 1973; Turner 1964). The sites, which in this approach are thought of as points in the landscape, may also yield general parameters such as crop ratios, dominance ratios, and presence values (Godwin 1975; Hubbard 1975; Renfrew 1972:276). The site-based approach has developed into a behavioural study (in the sense of Schiffer 1976) in which variations in the database are associated with particular crop-related activities rather than with the general parameters described above.

This dichotomy is frequently the result of practical limitations of the archaeological record, and in certain cases it may provide the most feasible framework for archaeobotanical research. Nonetheless, it should be recognised that the view of the human landscape behind this dichotomy becomes increasingly unrealistic as our appreciation develops of the complexity of the societies we study. The growth of aerial photography in recent years has clearly shown the inadequacy of viewing late prehistoric landscapes as well-defined sites scattered within an unstructured environment (Benson and Miles 1974; Bowen and Fowler 1978). Instead, whole landscapes show signs of social organisation, and it is these structured landscapes, rather than individual sites, that should form the arena within which the complexities of human behaviour can then be explored. In order to understand man–plant relationships within these structured landscapes, it is necessary to remove the division between the two approaches outlined above and to combine the more critical behavioural analysis of the site-based approach with the more realistic scale of the region-based approach.

In order to take the behavioural approach out of the site and into the landscape, the terms of reference of excavation need to be expanded beyond the traditional foci of habitation areas to include fields, trackways, and other intermediate zones. Indeed, the few examples that exist of excavations of fields, lynchets, and dry valleys (e.g., Bell 1977, 1981; Fowler and Evans 1967) clearly demonstrate the potential of such exercises. But while the majority of excavated data come from the more traditional sites, this chapter considers some of the possibilities of extending the behavioural approach into the landscape, using archaeobotanical data from settlement foci within that landscape. Following a consideration of the developments within archaeobotany that have led to a behavioural approach, that approach is applied to aspects of iron age landscapes in southern Britain.

The Development of a Behavioural Approach within Archaeobotany

By the time Clement Reid's *Origin of the British Flora* was published in 1899, a large body of archaeobotanical data from Europe was already in existence (Buschan 1895; Heer 1866; Kunth 1826). Most of the work conducted in the nineteenth century involved the use of archaeological evidence to explore botanical problems, such as those relating to vegetation history and plant evolution. Individual components within the environment, such as man, were not thought of as playing an active role in the process of environmental change; rather, they were seen as pawns in the intractable progress of global events. Thus, detailed knowledge of the interaction between man and other components of the environment was not considered to be of central importance, since archaeological information was considered essentially a means of dating the botanical evidence.

Nonetheless, an interest in the dynamics of interactions within an environment was beginning to develop amongst botanists at this time. Key landmarks in this field are the works of Warming (1895) and Schimper (1898), which mark the fusion of such interests into the 'new' study of ecology. This area of study gained momentum in the first half of the twentieth century, and by the time Tansley (1935) had coined the term 'ecosystem', the emphasis in archaeobotany had begun to shift from vegetation history to ecology. This development can be seen clearly in the work of Clark and Godwin at Cambridge (Clark et al. 1935), and in the growing awareness in Britain and Denmark of neolithic man's involvement in vegetation change (Godwin 1944; Iversen 1941, 1969).

While the classic study of the mesolithic site at Star Carr in Yorkshire was clearly ecological in concept, the archaeobotanical method used by Walker and Godwin (1954) is clearly rooted in the study of vegetation history. Although Clark gives considerable attention to the spatial variation among the artefacts from the site, the botanical study is more concerned with variations through time. The work belongs to a tradition in which interactions between man and the environment are explored in terms of deviation from an expected sequence of vegetation changes, and in terms of the appearance and disappearance of 'indicator species'. Much research on man–plant relationships continues to be carried out within this tradition, an emphasis clearly reflected in Godwin's *History of the British Flora* (1975) and in the compilation of crop records by Jessen and Helbaek (Helbaek 1952; Jessen and Helbaek 1944).

However, the emphasis on temporal variation obscured the potential of other forms of variation, in particular spatial variation, to elucidate man-plant relationships. These were not fully explored until Körber-Grohne's archaeobotanical investigations at Feddersen Wierde, a first-to-fourth-century A.D. settlement mound on the north German coast excavated by Haarnagel in the late 1950s (Körber-Grohne 1967, 1981). In this study, the spatial distribution of plant remains and their relation to structural features on the site are associated with the processes of collecting, threshing, storing, and using crop plants. In addition, Körber-Grohne calls attention to what would now be described as cultural and noncultural formation processes (Schiffer 1976). For example, the intact state of whole plants of flax, gold of pleasure, and horsebean is related to the method of harvesting and the short distance the harvest must have travelled. The effects of different forms of preservation on assemblage composition are also discussed. Körber-Grohne's study has become the model for subsequent work on the North Sea coasts of Germany and Holland (Behre 1976; van Zeist 1974).

At both Star Carr and Feddersen Wierde, the extensive waterlogging of sediments resulted in the anaerobic preservation of a wide variety of plant remains. Well-preserved material could therefore be studied in the context of the wooden structures with which it was associated. In this respect, the sites were atypical; it is far more usual for prehistoric settlements to be located on sediments conducive to the rapid decay of organic matter, in which plant remains survive chiefly in the form of carbonised debris from the various fires in the settlement, and where structural evidence is more limited in range. Körber-Grohne's approach was, however, adapted by Knörzer (1971a, b, 1972) at a series of sites of this type along the lower Rhine valley, ranging from the early neolithic to the medieval period. Knörzer collected large bodies of carbonised material and inferred crop-related activities from the internal structure of these assemblages—the relative proportions of the major components, the precise state of carbonisation, and the ecological character of the weeds present. Where information could be inferred from the archaeological context, it was used.

Similar approaches were taken by Hillman (1973) to Turkish material and by Dennell (1972, 1974) to Bulgarian material. Dennell was concerned not only to argue from particular instances, but also to construct a predictive scheme that would be generally applicable to archaeobotanical studies. His scheme takes the form of a flow-diagram in which a comprehensive sequence of activities from the harvesting of the crop to its consumption is related to the expected form and context of the associated plant debris. The activity of cleaning a grain crop, for example, would be expected to produce debris rich in weed seeds, in which any grains present would be small ones that had slipped through a cleaning sieve. This debris would be associated with the cleaning floors. In contrast, the consumption of grain would lead to debris free of weeds and chaff in such contexts as domestic ovens. Dennell's research was undertaken as part of the Cambridge University research project on the early history of agriculture directed by E. S. Higgs. This group was particularly concerned with the formulation of predictive models for palaeoeconomic studies, and Dennell's approach should be seen in the context of procedures advocated by the group for the assessment of environmental potential (Higgs 1975; Higgs and Vita-Finzi 1972) and for the complete extraction of archaeobotanical material (Jarman et al. 1972).

The kind of predictive model that Dennell attempted to produce was both necessary, if spurious temporal and ecological trends were to be avoided, and of clear value in any unified approach to the detection of human activity in the archaeobotanical record. To be effective, however, such a model would have to match the complexity of human activity. This was recognised in subsequent publications in the field, as was the further complexity inherent in the transition of archaeological material from the cultural system to the archaeological record. In her analysis of plant remains from Assiros Toumba in Greece, Jones (1979, 1981) proposes a model of cereal processing in which three stages are added to those indicated by Dennell. The order of stages is slightly rearranged, and there are a number of alternative routes through the model. A thorough analysis of the formation of botanical debris from agricultural activities of a technologically unsophisticated nature in modern Turkey led Hillman (1981) to propose separate models for different cereal species involving up to 28 stages of crop-processing.

The additional variation that is introduced once material leaves a cultural system to enter the archaeological record has been considered in some detail by Schiffer (1976) for archaeological material as a whole. His argument, that models of archaeological transformation at these stages should develop just as critically as models of cultural transformation, is as relevant for plant material as for any other category of evidence. As some indication of the further complexity this may add to models for botanical data, Gilbert and Singer (1982) list 37 transformations that may contribute to the nature of a bone assemblage, of which 16 affect the material after it leaves the cultural system. The progress towards a behavioural approach in archaeobotany has been considerable, but such an approach is constantly in danger of foundering under the weight of its own intricacy.

Methodological Adaptations: From Context to Site

The difficulty of passage through the depositional labyrinth is demonstrated in a study of carbonised plant material from a small Romano-British villa at Barton Court Farm in Oxfordshire (Miles, in press). This was the first of a series of iron age Romano-British sites excavated in the upper Thames valley in southern England to be examined for botanical evidence (Figure 4.1).

In many ways, a villa site would seem well suited for the implementation of a sampling strategy developed from Dennell's model. Many of the structural contexts could be assigned to a function with some confidence. Ovens and hearths, for example, could be related to a room whose purpose was established from other evidence. These inferred functions formed the basis for selection of a series of samples for flotation. Unfortunately, the resulting analysis shows no clear relationship between these inferred functions and the composition of their associated plant assemblages. To take a single example, a feature identified as a smithy oven yielded an assemblage of charred cereals, even though the oven would normally have operated at too high a temperature for burned plant material to survive in a recognisable state, and this material in any case would not be expected to include cereals.

This kind of disparity is explicable in terms of the details of refuse deposition. As with a number of sites, many of the contexts at Barton Court Farm contained secondary refuse (see Schiffer 1976) relating to the final use of the structure concerned, which was often quite different from its original use—sometimes no more than a depository for rubbish after its abandonment. The experience at Barton Court Farm lends support to a conclusion also reached by Hillman (1981), namely that the internal structure of the carbonised assemblage *alone* provides the most reliable evidence of factors leading to its deposition. This should be only subsequently related to the context in which the assemblage is found, and should never be used to infer the 'activity' of a context except for its

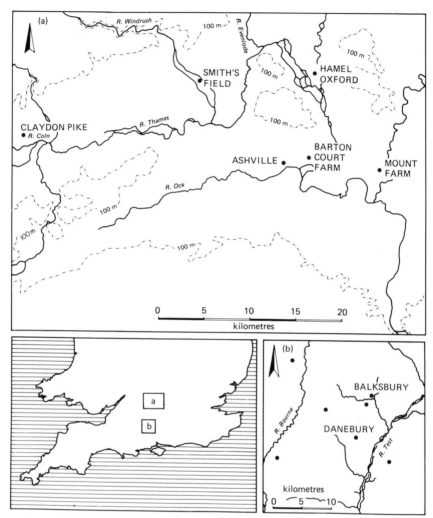

Figure   4.1   The location of the sites mentioned in the text. (a) upper Thames valley; (b) central
Hampshire downs between the rivers Test and Bourne.

use as a disposal location. Both Hillman and Jones (1979, 1981) emphasise the
diversity of parameters that may be derived from this internal structure.

Subsequent investigations of carbonised material from the upper Thames valley took a different course from that pursued at Barton Court Farm. While the
purposive sampling strategy outlined above was employed at Barton Court Farm,
on more recent excavations a probabilistic sampling strategy was employed
which aimed at relating assemblages to general zones of the site without refer-

ence to particular structural contexts (Jones 1978a, b; Redman 1974). The greater clarity of the results of this strategy can be illustrated by reference to the iron age farmstead investigated at the Ashville site (Jones 1978a). This settlement, located on a gravel terrace above a tributary of the Thames, took the form of a series of penannular gullies presumed to have surrounded thatched wattle-and-daub roundhouses, a number of associated irregular ditches and postholes (perhaps denoting farmyard areas), and a dense cluster of pits of the type commonly linked with grain storage.

An area of the site that included each of these elements was completely excavated and a random sample of the features analysed for carbonised plant material. A great deal of information was gleaned about the arable landscape, but only certain features relevant to the processing of crops will be mentioned here. First, the proportions of weeds and cereal chaff in the assemblages were clearly correlated (coefficient of regression significant at the 99.9% level), indicating that crop-cleaning activities were the main source of this variation. The second

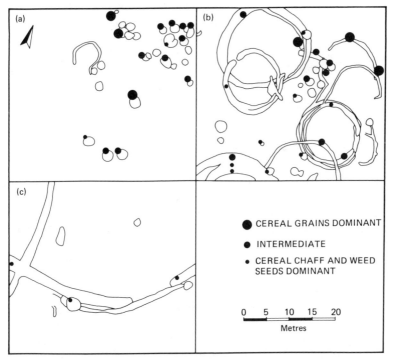

Figure 4.2 The Ashville site: plan showing the relationship between the composition of carbonised assemblages and their location, for each of the major phases of occupation: (a) Iron Age 1; (b) Iron Age 2; (c) Iron Age 3. All the features are cuts into the subsoil: the small ones are pits, the circular ditches denote houses, and the long ditches probably denote field boundaries.

feature relates to the spatial distribution of 'clean' and 'unclean' samples (respectively poor or rich in weeds and chaff) across the excavated area in each of three phases of the Iron Age. In Figure 4.2, circles indicating the positions from which carbonised assemblages were derived are superimposed on features in each of three phases of the Iron Age. The size of the circles indicates the predominance of cereal grains within each assemblage. The larger the circle, the greater the number of grains in comparison with the number of weed seeds and chaff fragments.

In the early phase (Figure 4.2a), virtually every sample is dominated by cereal grains, representing the fully processed material deposited at the core of the settlement. In the latest phase (Figure 4.2c), all three samples are rich in weeds and chaff. It is clear from the site plan that the core of the settlement had moved away from the area excavated, and the carbonised debris would appear to reflect crop-cleaning activities taking place on the periphery of the settlement. In the middle phase, both types of assemblage occur: grain-rich assemblages from the harvest product around the pit group northeast of the excavated area, and crop-cleaning debris around the enclosures to the west of the hut compound.

This approach to the carbonised material revealed a degree of order relating to agricultural activity that had survived the complexities of preservation and deposition and was still perceptible in the archaeological record. By shifting our attention from particular contexts to general zones of the site, the emphasis is drawn away from particular (but often ephemeral) activities to the more general and stable trends in site activity.

Methodological Adaptations: From Site to Landscape

The examples from the upper Thames valley demonstrate the possibilities that stem from broadening our terms of reference from the context to the site. This chapter began by emphasising the need to broaden them still further, from the site to the landscape. This second extension is greatly facilitated by the implementation of probabilistic sampling strategies. Intersite comparisons based on purposively or haphazardly sampled data can only be made in intuitive terms. If on one site samples are taken from all the 'blackish' layers, on another site from every context, and on two other sites from contexts selected on site-specific criteria, intersite variation may merely reflect differences in sampling strategy. By contrast, a probabilistic strategy can be designed to be repeated on any site, regardless of its individual character, and comparison is consequently easier.

An approach with considerable potential for intersite comparisons arose in the study of bones, rather than plants, and centres on the concept of 'complementarity'. The idea behind this concept, as outlined by Sebastian Payne (personal communication) may be summarised as follows:

Individual archaeological contexts may yield skeletal elements in proportions that differ from those in the living animal. However, if the refuse deposits derived from each stage in the overall sequence of processes affecting that animal resource (e.g., from maintenance through utilisation to deposition) were collected together, then the combined assemblage of skeletal elements would occur in the same proportions as in the living animal, and the age and sex ratios would relate to those of the original herd or flock. In other words, the original components are known and their remains must be accountable. The concept of complementarity allows complementary assemblages and sites to be linked within a sequence of animal-related activities. Equally important, this concept also allows missing links in the sequence to be detected. The idea of complementarity is essentially encompassed in Schiffer's (1976:54) equation:

$$Y = rdC + rdc_2 \ldots + rdC_n$$

where Y is the total number of exhausted elements of each type (in this case the original skeletal composition of the herd or flock), r is a coefficient of recycling, d is a coefficient of decay, and C is the respective output fraction of elements of an activity (in this case the composition of individual bone assemblages from contexts 1 to n).

Vertebrate bones are clearly well suited to studies of complementarity. It is possible to quantify skeletal debris and to determine the frequency with which the corresponding element occurs in the living animal. By contrast, not all parts of a crop plant are recognisable in the carbonised state, and some parts that are recognisable are difficult to quantify. In addition, the proportions in which the various organs occur in the living plant are rarely fixed in the same way as vertebrate skeletal elements.

Figure 4.3 indicates which fragments of plant material from a field of cereals tend to be recognisable in the carbonised state. Other fragments are no doubt preserved, but they bear insufficient morphological detail to allow recognition. For each taxon, the general ratios between recognisable fragments may be assessed. For spelt wheat (*Triticum spelta*) and emmer wheat (*T. dicoccum*), for example, each separate stalk or tiller will bear in the region of three culm nodes, and a grain-bearing head or ear will have some 20 rhachis internodes. Running along the ear are the grain-bearing spikelets in which the grains are enclosed by glumes. There will be two glumes and one to three grains to every spikelet, and one spikelet to every internode. In varieties that bear awns, there will be one awn to every grain. The ratios for spelt and emmer wheats among culm nodes : rhachis internodes : glumes : grains : awns are therefore of the order 3 : 20 : 40 : 40 : 40. Bread wheat (*T. aestivum*) may contain more grains per spikelet but will be similar in other respects. These ratios are depicted as a histogram in Figure 4.4a, alongside histograms derived from three bodies of archaeobotanical data: a single twelfth-century A.D. assemblage from the Hamel site in the city of Oxford (Palmer

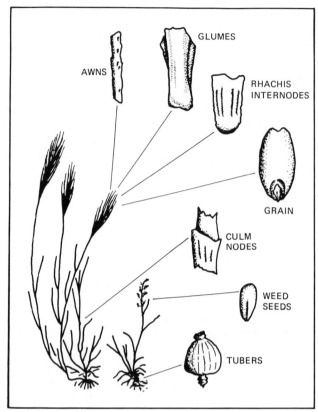

Figure 4.3 Components of a cereal harvest that may be recognised in carbonised debris recovered from excavations.

1980) (Figure 4.4b), and the combined figures from the series of probabilistic samples from the Ashville site (see previous section), and from a hillfort at Danebury, Hampshire (Cunliffe, 1984), both of Iron Age date (Figure 4.4c, d).

The Medieval assemblage from Oxford appears to be derived from a sheaf of wheat from which 90% of the grains have been threshed, leaving culm nodes and rhachis internodes in proportions similar to those in which they occur in the living plant, and with the floral parts greatly reduced. The Iron Age assemblages, by contrast, show glumes and grains in roughly their original proportions, but all other fragments are comparatively rare. The association of glumes and grains is not surprising, since the first sequence of mechanical disturbance of ripe spelt wheat is the removal of spikelets from the straw and the shattering of the awns, leaving the grains tightly locked within their glumes. What is surprising is the absence of the fraction corresponding to the threshed straw, especially as, with

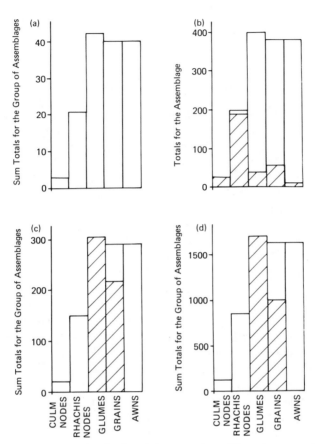

Figure 4.4 Bar diagrams showing the relative proportions of the various recognisable parts of the wheat plant in (a) the modern plant, (b) a twelfth century assemblage bread wheat from the Hamel site, Oxford, (c) Iron Age assemblages of spelt wheat from Danebury, and (d) Iron Age assemblages of spelt wheat from the Ashville site.

one exception, straw debris tends to occur in very low quantities in iron age assemblages from southern Britain. The single assemblage and the medieval assemblage illustrated in Figure 4.4a and b, respectively, rule out the possibility of differential survival as an explanation. It would seem instead that while one portion of the cereal harvest, the grain crop, was ubiquitous in iron age settlements, the other portion, the straw crop, failed to reach the settlement fires that preserved evidence of the grains.

A consideration of complementarity (comparing what is missing as much as what is present) has some immediate implications in terms of the general composition of carbonised assemblages. In combination with a repeatable probabilistic sampling strategy, it holds further potential in an examination of crop-related activities in the landscape.

Behavioural Analysis within the Landscape

In addition to the Barton Court Farm and Ashville sites, a number of other upper Thames valley excavations revealing iron age and Romano-British settlement have been analysed for carbonised plant material (Figure 4.1). While these sites share a number of structural elements, they are not all located in a similar topographic position in the valley, nor are they all surrounded by environments suited to crop production (Robinson 1981). The Iron Age phases of four of these sites are examined here in detail. The Ashville and Mount Farm sites are both located on the second gravel terrace above the Thames and its tributaries and have in their immediate vicinity an expanse of free-draining, level, and reasonably fertile land well suited to cereal agriculture. Neither site has produced water-logged environmental evidence of Iron Age date, but studies of waterlogged plant and insect remains of Roman date at Mount Farm would suggest an immediate landscape dominated by arable agriculture in this subsequent period (Robinson 1983). Two other sites, one at Claydon Pike near Lechlade and another at Smith's Field at Hardwick, lie closer to the river, on the first gravel terrace. On the basis of his extensive study of waterlogged material from the upper Thames valley, Robinson (1981, 1983) undoubtedly views open pasture as a key element in these parts of the valley.

Evidence relating to cereal agriculture comes from carbonised remains collected probabilistically in the manner already outlined for the Ashville site. Triangular scattergrams are used here to present data in a manner that facilitates intersite comparison (Figure 4.5). Each circle represents a single assemblage of carbonised material. Its position in the scattergram indicates the relative proportions of grains, weeds, and chaff fragments (see legend, Figure 4.5). The size of each circle indicates a further value—the density of carbonised material (the sum of cereal grains + weed seeds + chaff fragments) in the deposit.

It is immediately evident from a comparison of the scattergrams that the difference in topographic position of the two pairs of sites is mirrored by a difference in the general spread of assemblage composition. At the two sites located on the second gravel terrace, Ashville and Mount Farm, at least 30% of all fragments in the great majority of assemblages are cereal grains, and in a few assemblages 80–100% are grains (Figure 4.5a, b). No sample has more than 50% chaff fragments or 70% weed seeds. By contrast, assemblages from the two sites situated on the first gravel terrace may be composed of up to 80% chaff fragments or 100% weed seeds, and cereal grains make up no more than 50% of any individual sample (Figure 4.5c, d). Thus, the spread of assemblage compositions and the environmental setting of a site are clearly linked.

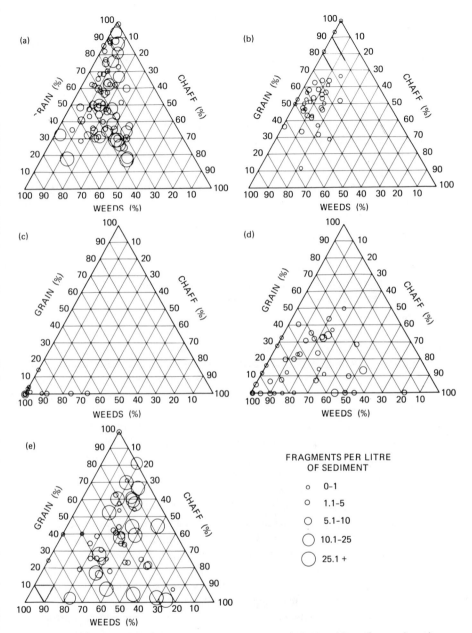

Figure 4.5 Composition of grains, chaff, and weed seeds in assemblages from various sites, displayed as triangular scattergrams. The category 'chaff' includes glumes, rhachis internodes and culm nodes, but excludes awns, which fragment to such an extent that they are unquantifiable. In each scattergram a circle corresponds to an individual assemblage, its position to assemblage composition, and its size to the density of fragments (comprising grains, weed seeds, and chaff as defined above) in each sediment. (a) Ashville; (b) Mount Farm; (c) Smith's Field; (d) Claydon Pike; (e) Danebury.

That the assemblages on some sites are dominated by weeds and chaff is less surprising than the fact that on others they are dominated by grain. The grain is the part of the harvest least likely to be treated as waste material, and for that reason its deposition as charred debris is least expected. The most likely place for this unlikely event to occur is at its place or production. For example, at harvest time in many parts of the Third World today, farming settlements become inundated with the harvest product because every family is out in the yard and in the thoroughfares threshing, winnowing, and sieving. The floor sweepings at such a time may pick up a substantial number of the billions of grains passing through the settlement. It is this kind of situation that produces assemblages rich in grain.

With further processing and transportation, the perceived unit value of the crop accrues, while its quantity at any single point lessens. The chance of the prime product itself being discarded into a fire consequently drops. A nonproducer site receiving the harvest product through exchange is likely to allow only the waste material from any final processing to be discarded into the settlement fires. Consumption on a nonproducer site would therefore be expected to produce the kind of assemblage distribution found at the two sites on the first gravel terrace.

The patterns that emerge from Figure 4.5 can thus be explained in terms of the activities of production and consumption of the cereal crop. This explanation is substantiated by Robinson's reconstruction from waterlogged material of the Iron Age landscape of the upper Thames valley, with arable production on the second terrace contrasting with a greater emphasis on pasture on the lower ground towards the river (Robinson 1981). Such a thesis is further supported by the physical components of the respective sites. The clusters of pits that seem suited to grain storage are a feature of the sites on the second gravel terrace but not of those on the first, which instead show a greater emphasis on ditched enclosures, suggesting more concern with the control of animals.

The construction of a complete picture of crop movement through the landscape requires that all categories of sites within that landscape be inspected. While it has been possible, within the constraints of rescue archaeology, to examine a diverse range of rural Iron Age sites in the upper Thames valley (Lambrick 1978; Selkirk 1978), the associated hillforts have not been excavated since Harding's excavation of Blewburton Hill, which did not incorporate a strategy for plant evidence (Harding 1976). However, some idea of the information that could be derived from extending the strategy to this element of the landscape may be gleaned from the extensive excavations of the hillfort at Danebury in Hampshire (Cunliffe 1984), which have incorporated a probabilistic strategy for the collection of plant evidence.

Lying three miles northwest of Stockbridge in central Hampshire, the hillfort dominates a wide expanse of chalk downland between the rivers Test and Bourne (see Figure 4.1). Cunliffe's excavations have revealed an interior packed with pits, postholes, and, where surface layers were protected by the slump of the ramparts, traces of numerous roundhouses. The sediments related to this extensive usage all contained carbonised cereal grain, chaff, and weed seeds in various proportions (Cunliffe 1984). Some 40 taxa of weed species give some indication of the source from which the associated cereals within the hillfort had arrived. Not surprisingly, species that thrive on free-draining alkaline soils, such as those that surround the hillfort today, were very common. However, to accomodate the ecological requirements of all the weed taxa present, the source area must have extended to the riverside loams and gravel soils along the Test and its tributaries—in other words, to the limits of the hillfort's presumed territory. This area contains many smaller contemporary sites, raising the question of how these smaller settlements and the hillfort interacted in relation to their agricultural resources.

The data collected from Danebury are presented as a scattergram in Figure 4.5e. The range of assemblage compositions is different again from the two types of range observed on the upper Thames valley rural sites. The range is far greater at Danebury than at any of these sites, both in terms of composition (with some samples having in excess of 70% of one of the three categories of grain, chaff, and weeds) and in terms of fragment density within each deposit, which varies between deposits by a factor of over a thousand. This would suggest a broad range of agricultural activities within the hillfort. The presence of threshing debris, sometimes in quantity, indicates that crops were not fully processed before entering the hillfort, and that the final stages of threshing and cleaning took place within the fort. A number of the 'threshing debris' assemblages also include species of weed that would be associated with the riverside habitats at the edge of the presumed territory. (The term 'threshing' is used here in a broad sense to include any process in which cereal grains are separated from the chaff, however that separation is achieved.)

The Danebury scattergram cannot be explained simply in terms of a combination of all the activities detected on individual rural sites. In particular, the hillfort contains a series of assemblages that are distinguished by their very high quantities of weeds or chaff compared with other components. The composition of weeds within these assemblages is that of a mixture of ecological types, suggesting that they are derived from more than one source. It would seem reasonable to view these assemblages as the debris from individual processing activities conducted on a large volume of crops entering the hillfort from various parts of the territory.

The analysis of the Danebury material further emphasises the importance of a rationalised sampling strategy for archaeobotanical material. In the absence of such a strategy, the inferences from this site could well have been based only on the deposits of grain that were discernible to the naked eye as grain. These are the rich black layers of almost pure grain that are occasionally found within subsoil features and that appear to derive from a cereal product that has been stored in a threshed and cleaned state. The probabilistic sampling strategy employed places equal emphasis on deposits with a less promising appearance—those that reflect threshing and cleaning activities as much as storage. Indeed, the probabilistic survey of carbonised debris provides at least as much evidence of crop-processing as of storage activities within the hillfort at Danebury.

The Articulation of an Iron Age Landscape

The evidence discussed in the previous section shows how the range of crop-related activities may vary from site to site within an iron age landscape. It remains for us to consider how the various activities articulate and how crop products moved within that landscape.

Mention has already been made of the supply of crops to the hillfort at Danebury. It has been suggested that the fort was receiving cereal harvests in a semi-processed state from various parts of its territory and that the processing of these harvests was being completed en masse. The weed flora suggests that at least some of the harvests were derived from river valleys that contained a series of smaller contemporary settlements. It may be concluded that at least some of the harvests arriving at the hillfort were derived from these settlements. In the upper Thames valley, the Ashville site is the type of smaller settlement that could have supplied neighbouring sites with grain. Mount Farm also appears to have been a producer of cereals, but the lower density of cereal debris implies a lower turnover and consequently a lower available surplus.

Following storage of the processed cereals within the hillfort at Danebury, there are three possible routes the cereals could have taken: consumption within the hillfort, passing out of the territory along a network of external exchange, or distribution within the territory. Whichever route was taken, the carbonised debris at the receiving end would be expected to be relatively free of weed seeds and chaff, compared with the state of the material reaching the consumer sites in the upper Thames valley. The evidence suggests that cereals at the pastoral sites on the first gravel terrace were in the semi-processed state in which they left the arable sites on the second gravel terrace, rather than in the fully processed state in which they would leave a hillfort operating in the manner of Danebury. If the patterns discerned in each region are more generally applicable, this would imply that extracted cereal surpluses were not being redistributed within the system, but rather that smaller consumer sites were receiving cereals directly from the producer sites and that the cereals reaching the hillfort were either being consumed there or exchanged for goods from outside the system. Figure 4.6 gives an outline of this scheme. The value of testing this scenario further by examining a full range of classes of contemporary sites within a single territory is self-evident.

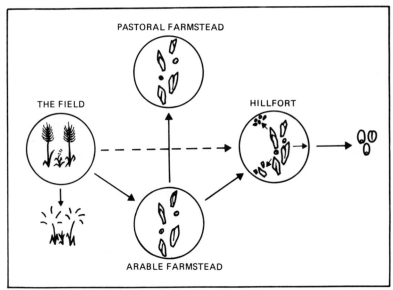

Figure   4.6   Schematic diagram showing the possible flow of cereals through an Iron Age economic system.

Further Potential of a Landscape Approach

The analyses and references presented here demonstrate how the removal of the barrier between 'site' and 'environment' allows man–plant relationships to be followed beyond a study of isolated activities in order to show how a broad range of activities articulate with one another. As the conceptual limits of investigation approach the actual limits within which a meaningful sequence of human activities is manifest, the questions that may be tackled pass from the anecdotal (Did seed-cleaning take place to the left or right of the pit group?) to those of more general interest (Did hillforts act as centres of redistribution?).

Of course, the barrier between site and environment is only one of many that may impede an understanding of human action within past environments. This chapter clearly illustrates a further barrier—that between studies of various categories of material, including plant remains, animal remains, and artefacts. A fuller understanding of behavioural systems would follow from an integrated approach to all these categories, not just the one that best fits the individual observer's research experience. With adequate cooperation between specialists and (of particular importance) the implementation of rationalised sampling strategies that allow material of different categories and from different sites to be included within a single analysis, we may be optimistic about detecting and following human behaviour, not on a scale that brings mere fragments into view, but rather on the scale at which that behaviour shaped and structured the pre-historic human landscape.

Acknowledgements

I would like to acknowledge Tim Allen, Barry Cunliffe, George Lambrick, David Miles, Simon and Nicholas Palmer, and Mike Parrington, whose excavations produced the material used in this chapter, and Colin Haselgrove, Mark Maltby, Martin Millett, and the editors of this volume for reading through and making invaluable comments on earlier drafts. Various members of the Oxford Archaeological Unit and Danebury excavation team—in particular Ann James, Cynthia Poole, and Chris Unwin—were involved in the processing of the plant material, and much of the research was conducted while the author was working under the supervision of Stanley Woodell and Dennis Britton, with the support of the S.E.R.C. Thanks are extended to all.

References

Allen, T.
  1981 Smith's Field, Hardwick with Yelford. *Council for British Archaeology Group IX News-letter* 11:112–146.
Barker, G. W. W., and D. Webley
  1978 Causewayed camps and early neolithic economies in central southern England. *Proceedings of the Prehistoric Society* 44:161–186.
Behre, K. E.
  1976 *Die frühgeschichtliche Marschensiedlung beim Elisenhof in Eidersfedt* (Band 2). Peter Lang, Frankfurt.
Bell, M.
  1977 Excavations at Bishopstone, *Sussex Archaeological Collections* 115:1–299.
Bell, M.
  1981 Valley sediments and environmental change. In *The environment of man: the Iron Age to the Anglo-Saxon period,* edited by M. K. Jones and G. W. Dimbleby, pp. 75–91. British Archaeological Reports, British Series 87, Oxford, England.
Benson, D., and D. Miles
  1974 *The upper Thames valley: an archaeological survey of the river gravels.* Oxford Archaeological Unit.
Bowen, H. C., and P. J. Fowler
  1978 *Early land allotment.* British Archaeological Reports, British Series 48, Oxford, England.
Buschan, G.
  1895 *Vorgeschichtliche Botanik der Cultur- und Nutzpflanzen der alten Welt auf Grund prähistorischer Funde.* J. U. Kern, Breslau.
Clark, J. G. D., H. Godwin, M. E. Godwin, and M. H. Clifford
  1935 Report on recent excavations at Peacock's Farm, Shippea Hill, Cambridgeshire, *Antiquaries Journal* 15:284–319.
Cunliffe, B. W.
  1984 *Danebury: an Iron Age hillfort in Hampshire.* Council for British Archaeology, London.

Dennell, R. W.
    1972 The interpretation of plant remains: Bulgaria. In *Papers in economic prehistory,* edited by
        E. S. Higgs, pp. 149–159. Cambridge University Press, Cambridge, England.
Dennell, R. W.
    1974 Botanical evidence for prehistoric crop-processing activities. *Journal of Archaeological
        Science* 1:275–284.
Fowler, P. J., and J. G. Evans
    1967 Ploughmarks, lynchets and early fields. *Antiquity* 41:289–301.
Gilbert, A. S., and B. H. Singer
    1982 Reassessing zooarchaeological quantification. *World Archaeology* 14:21–40.
Godwin, H.
    1944 Age and origin of the 'Breckland' heaths of East Anglia. *Nature* 154:6.
Godwin, H.
    1968 Organic deposits at Old Buckenham Mere, Norfolk. *New Phytologist* 67:95–107.
Godwin, H.
    1975 *History of the British flora* (second ed.). Cambridge University Press, Cambridge,
        England.
Harding, D. W.
    1976 Blewburton Hill, Berkshire: re-excavation and reappraisal. In *Hillforts: later prehistoric
        earthworks in Britain and Ireland,* edited by D. W. Harding, pp. 134–146. Academic Press,
        London.
Heer, O.
    1866 Treatise on the plants of the Lake Dwellings. In *The lake dwellings of Switzerland and
        other parts of Europe,* edited by F. Keller. Longmans Green, London.
Helbaek, H.
    1952 Early crops in southern England. *Proceedings of the Prehistoric Society* 18:194–233.
Higgs, E. S. (editor)
    1972 *Papers in economic prehistory.* Cambridge University Press, Cambridge, England.
Higgs, E. S. (editor)
    1975 *Palaeoeconomy.* Cambridge University Press, Cambridge, England.
Higgs, E. S., and C. Vita-Finzi
    1972 Prehistoric economies: a territorial approach. In *Papers in economic prehistory,* edited by
        E. S. Higgs, pp. 27–36. Cambridge University Press, Cambridge, England.
Hillman, G.
    1973 Crop husbandry and food products: a modern basis for the interpretation of plant remains.
        Anatolian Studies 23:241–244.
Hillman, G.
    1981 Reconstructing crop husbandry practices from charred remains of crops. In *Farming
        practice in British prehistory,* edited by R. Mercer, pp. 123–162. Edinburgh University
        Press, Edinburgh, Scotland.
Hubbard, R. N. L. B.
    1975 Assessing the botanical component of human palaeo-economies. *Bulletin of the Institute of
        Archaeology* 12:197–205.
Hubbard, R. N. L. B.
    1976 On the strength of evidence for prehistoric crop processing activities. *Journal of Archae-
        ological Science* 3:257–265.
Hubbard, R. N. L. B.
    1980 Development of agriculture in Europe and the Near East: evidence from quantitative
        studies. *Economic Botany* 34:51–67.

Iversen, J.
1941 Land occupation in Denmark's Stone Age. *Danmarks Geologiske Undersøgelse* II(66):1–68.
Iversen, J.
1949 The influence of prehistoric man on vegetation. *Danmarks Geologiske Undersøgelse* IV(3):1–25.
Jarman, H. N., A. J. Legge, and J. A. Charles
1972 Retrieval of plant remains from archaeological sites by froth flotation. In *Papers in economic prehistory,* edited by E. S. Higgs, pp. 39–48. Cambridge University Press, Cambridge, England.
Jessen, K., and H. Helbaek
1964 Cereals in Great Britain and Ireland in prehistoric and early historic times. *Wet Kongelige Danske Videnskaernes Selskab Biologiske Skrifter* 3(2):1–68.
Jones, G. E. M.
1979 *An analysis of the plant remains from Assiros Toumba.* Unpublished M. Phil. thesis, Cambridge University.
Jones, G. E. M.
1981 Crop processing at Assiros Toumba: a taphonomic study. *Zeitschrift für Archäologie* 15:105–112.
Jones, M. K.
1978a The plant remains. In *The excavation of an iron age settlement, bronze age ring ditches and Roman features at Ashville Trading Estate, Abingdon (Oxon) 1974–1976,* edited by M. Parrington, pp. 93–110. Council for British Archaeology, Research Report 28, London.
Jones, M. K.
1978b Sampling in a rescue context: a case study in Oxfordshire. In *Sampling in contemporary British archaeology,* edited by J. F. Cherry et al., pp. 191–205. British Archaeological Reports, British Series 50, Oxford, England.
Jones, M. K.
in press The carbonised plant remains. In *Archaeology at Barton Court Farm, Radley (Oxon),* edited by D. Miles. Council for British Archaeology, Research Report, London.
Jones, M. K., and D. Miles
1979 Celt and Roman in the Thames valley: approaches to culture change. In *Invasion and response: the case of Roman Britain,* edited by B. C. Burnham and H. B. Johnson, pp. 315–375. British Archaeological Reports, British Series 73, Oxford, England.
Knörzer, K. H.
1971a Urgeschichtliche Unkräuter im Rheinland: ein Beitrag zur Entstehungsgeschichte der Segetalgesellschaften. *Vegetatio* 23:89–111.
Knörzer, K. H.
1971b Eisenzeitliche Pflanzenfunde im Rheinland. *Bonner Jahrbücher* 71:40–58
Knörzer, K. H.
1972 Subfossile Pflanzenreste aus der bandkeramischen Siedlung Langweiler und 6, Kreis Julich, und ein urnenfelderzeitlicher Getreidefund innerhalb dieser Siedlung. *Bonner Jahrbücher* 72:395–403.
Körber-Grohne, U.
1967 *Feddersen Wierde: die Ergebnisse der Ausgrabung der vorgeschichtlichen Wurt bei Bremerhaven in den Jahren 1955–1963* (Band 1), Wiesbaden.
Körber-Grohne, U.
1981 Crop husbandry and environmental change in the Feddersen Wierde, near Bremerhaven,

northwest Germany. In *The environment of man: the Iron Age to the Anglo-Saxon period,* edited by M. K. Jones and G. W. Dimbleby, pp. 287–307. British Archaeological Reports, British Series 87, Oxford, England.

Kunth, C.
    1826 Examin botanique. In *Catalogue raisonné et historique des antiquities découvertes en Egypte.* J. Passalacqua, Paris.

Lambrick, G.
    1978 Iron age settlements in the upper Thames valley. In *Lowland iron age communities in Europe,* edited by B. Cunliffe and T. Rowley, pp. 103–119. British Archaeological Reports, International Series 48, Oxford, England.

Miles, D. (editor)
    in press *Archaeology at Barton Court Farm, Radley (Oxon).* Council for British Archaeology, Research Report, London.

Palmer, N.
    1980 A Beaker burial and medieval tenements in the Hamel, Oxford, *Oxoniensia* 45:124–225.

Redman, C. L.
    1974 *Archaeological sampling strategies.* Addison-Wesley, New York.

Reid, C.
    1899 *The origin of the British flora.* Dulau, London.

Renfrew, C.
    1972 *The emergence of civilisation.* Methuen, London.

Renfrew, J. M.
    1973 *Palaeoethnobotany: the prehistoric food plants of the Near East and Europe.* Methuen, London.

Roberts, B., J. Turner, and P. Ward
    1973 Recent forest history and land use in Weardale, northern England. In *Quaternary plant ecology,* edited by H. Birks and R. G. West, pp. 207–221. Blackwells, Oxford.

Robinson, M.
    1981 The iron age to early Saxon environment of the Upper Thames terraces. In *The environment of man: the Iron Age to the Anglo-Saxon period,* edited by M. K. Jones and G. W. Dimbleby, pp. 251–277. British Archaeological Reports, British Series 87, Oxford, England.

Robinson, M.
    1983 Arable-pastoral ratios from insects? In *Integrating the subsistence economy,* edited by M. K. Jones, pp. 19–55. British Archaeological Reports, International Series 181, Oxford, England.

Roper, D. C.
    1979 The method and theory of site catchment analysis: a review. In *Advances in archaeological method and theory* (Vol. 2), edited by M. B. Schiffer, pp. 120–142. Academic Press, London.

Schiffer, M. B.
    1976 *Behavioural archeology.* Academic Press, New York.

Schimper, A. F. W.
    1898 *Pflanzengeographie auf physiologischer Grundlage.* G. Fischer, Bonn.

Selkirk, A.
    1978 After Little Woodbury: village and farm in iron age Oxfordshire. *Current Archaeology* 63:106–113.

Tansley, A. G.
    1935 The use and abuse of vegetational concepts and terms. *Ecology* 16:284–307.

Turner, J.
1964 The anthropogenetic factor in vegetational history: Tregaron and Whixall mosses. *New Phytologist* 63:73.

Walker, D., and H. Godwin
1954 Lake stratigraphy, pollen analysis and vegetational history. In *Excavations at Star Carr*, edited by J. G. D. Clark, pp. 25–69. Cambridge University Press, Cambridge, England.

Warming, E.
1895 *Plantesamfund: Grundträk auf den Okologiske Plantegeografi*. Kjoenhavn.

van Zeist, W.
1974 Palaeobotanical studies of settlement sites in the coastal area of the Netherlands, *Palaeohistoria* 16:223–371.

5

Land Tenure, Productivity, and Field Systems

ANDREW FLEMING

Introduction

If we are to understand the major socioeconomic developments of later pre-history in northwestern Europe, we have to develop some kind of first-approximation model of land tenure. It makes a good deal of difference whether we envisage neolithic or iron age Europe as a mosaic of small, inalienable family farms or as a patchwork of larger territories without permanent internal property boundaries, where access to land was more flexible. For the first case it would be appropriate—with all the usual caveats about rents, prices, and market conditions—for prehistorians to assess the range of likely economic behaviour on the basis of our knowledge of recent European peasant economies. In the second case, it would be important to know something of the workings of various open-field or runrig systems, or of the economic organisation of commoners. The incentives and constraints for the 'peasant' model would be different from those of the 'collective' model, and so would the various developmental trajectories that might have occurred in each case. It is, of course, also possible to consider 'mixed' systems; for example, with permanent pastures grazed in common and arable land held by or allocated periodically to individual families, and where seasonal variations caused land used by individual families for cultivation to become a communal resource for winter grazing. There could also have been intercommoning systems where some resources were exploited outside the regular framework of territorial organisation.

In addition, we need to know something of the range and scope of labour organisation, whether we are dealing with the peasant household—its independence blighted by its recurring inadequacy as a unit of labour—or with a much larger social group, one with strong traditions of collectively organised labour

129

˙ and egalitarian attitudes inimical to smaller-scale economic enterprise. Only when we have the capacity to model these essential relations of production will we be able to identify the sets of circumstances in which, for example, productivity is likely to have increased, stimulating or responding to change in population density or social organisation.

Ideally, we should model these relations of production for initial agricultural populations and consider the various possible trajectories that might have ensued. Prehistoric land boundaries, which offer our best hope of modelling land tenure, have not often been studied seriously from this point of view (but see Müller-Wille 1965). Most work on land boundaries and field systems, when not concerned solely with recording, has concentrated on explaining their origins and functions, or on asking general questions like "What kind of farming was going on here?" (cf. Fowler 1981:30: "There is no mystery about our great extent of prehistoric landscape: the people who were using those areas were quite simply trying to be better farmers.") These approaches have a certain utility, but they are essentially *reactive;* their point of origin is the existence of field systems as artefacts. The reactive approach must be complemented by a *behavioural* approach whose starting point is structured curiosity about the evolution of past human group behaviour. Unfortunately, it is impossible at present to offer a magisterial survey of European prehistoric field systems and their behavioural correlates. It is feasible, however, to suggest what the important elements of such a behavioural approach might be.

Collective Land Ownership and Labour Organisation

Recent work in southern and eastern England has revealed, with increasing clarity, a second millennium b.c. settlement pattern consisting of houses scattered in ones and twos, or at best grouped in small hamlets, accompanied by field systems that look as if they were laid out by a larger community. The sites in question include Fengate in eastern England (Pryor 1978, 1980), Itford Hill (Burstow and Holleyman 1957; Ellison 1978) and Black Patch in Sussex (Drewett 1979, 1980, 1982), Shearplace Hill in Dorset (Rahtz and apSimon 1962), and Gwithian in Cornwall (Megaw et al. 1960–1961; Megaw 1967). The original size of the field system and the closeness of its relationship to the settlement are not always demonstrable, and major field systems like those described by Bradley (1978:268) as cohesive, as well as the Dartmoor parallel reave systems (Fleming 1978), must also be considered if we wish to understand the nature of land division at this period. The best-preserved parallel reave system on Dartmoor, the Dartmeet system, has walled fields and circular stone-walled houses that have survived as surface features. The houses are scattered in ones and twos, but they are also disposed in distinct clusters when viewed on the scale of the large field system in which they are set. The pattern is not unlike that recorded by Curwen at Black Patch in Sussex (Curwen 1937:Figure 55), although Drewett (1980:393) suggests that the house platforms might have been occupied successively.

The archaeological evidence forces us to consider the nature of the relationship between, on the one hand, the individual household so clearly revealed by some analyses (Drewett 1979, 1980, 1982; Ellison 1978, 1981) and, on the other, the community responsible for laying out the field systems. I use the word 'household' here to represent nuclear or small extended families conceived principally as child-rearing units occupying single houses, pairs of houses including 'major' and 'minor' structures (Bradley 1975:164; Ellison 1978), or house groups like the one discussed by Drewett at Black Patch (1979, 1980).

The kinship structures that link households of this type are well known ethnographically. Within Britain, they have been studied in some detail. Arensberg and Kimball (1948:95) described how

> through the workings in and out of the interlocking series of pyramids . . . an isolated area of small population can soon become inextricably intertangled . . . [and] through such intermingling, it very often happens that a comparatively large area will be peopled entirely by individuals standing within near degrees of kinship to one another.

A good impression of how a dispersed settlement pattern can represent a close-knit community is conveyed by Rees (1968:100):

> There exists in upland Wales a diffused form of society which is not only able to function without a unifying social centre but seems to be opposed to all forms of centralisation. The hearth of the lonely farm itself *is* the social centre. The farms are not outlying members of a nucleated community, but entities in themselves, and their integration into social groups depends on the direct relationship between them rather than upon their convergence on a single centre. The traditional social unit does not consist of the environs of a town or village: it is *cefn gwlad,* the neighbourhood in the countryside.

In prehistoric Europe, only large nucleated settlements could have been effectively endogamous, and there is little evidence for the widespread occurrence of settlements of this type before the first millennium B.C. If dispersed homesteads and hamlets were linked in a near-continous network of kinship and affinal ties, in what circumstances did groups define themselves as distinct entities for some behavioural purposes? Kinship itself is likely to have been the most important integrative mechanism:

> The demarcations between the kindred groups of one individual and the next are not rigidly drawn. The individual can expand and contract the group outward from the restricted family to whom he belongs. If he is important in the community, he can command the respect and the services of a great number of kindred; it becomes an advantage to the peripheral relatives to establish the reciprocals of behaviour which the system allows. (Arensberg and Kimball 1948:93–94)

If the household is defined as the primary level of organisation, secondary and tertiary organisational levels may also be recognised. The workings of the secondary level are frequently described by British rural sociologists; they comprise cooperative relationships between households physically located in the same neighbourhood, and sometimes between groups of households from more than one neighbourhood. The keynote here is economic cooperation. However, these groups, whose size makes them ideal for pooling labour and resources and sometimes for making joint economic decisions, are too small to make arrangements for territorial defence. Nevertheless, they have invested too much in specific areas of land to make flight a satisfactory defence mechanism, as it might be if they were a hunter–gatherer band. Territorial defence requires a tertiary level of organisation—the sociopolitical group occupying a defined territory that contains a broad enough array of resources to satisfy the economic aspirations of its component groups and that can organise the manpower to defend the territory. This level of organisation is not available for study by rural sociologists working in modern European contexts.

The essentials of second-level organisation may be explored further. Terray (1972:127, 151ff) points out that there are important distinctions between the work team and the production community, and between the production unit and the consumption unit, which may or may not be homologous. Cooperation at the secondary group level may relate to the collective ownership of land; the pooling of labour, tools, and other resources; the distribution of food and other materials produced; and economic decision-making at the local level. Obviously, the groups that cooperated could be polythetic—in other words, each household could be at the centre of several partially overlapping groups organised for different purposes but on the same general scale. Studies in British rural sociology make it quite clear that even in an age of farm machinery, the individual household is badly matched with the labour demands of a family farm. This is partly a matter of the fluctuating level of the age and sex composition of the family as it passes through its well-known demographic cycle. The need for pooling labour and resources has survived the partition of the countryside into individual holdings and the growth of a cash and market economy, and it is probably the most basic type of organisation at the secondary group level. Many rural sociologists have described the ramifications of traditions of collective labour; one of the best general descriptions is provided by Arensberg and Kimball (1948:269). Activities like hay-making, harvesting, turf-cutting, shearing, and threshing were often carried out by groups of individuals from different farms. Authorities stress the important social role of such gatherings and their psychological value to people working long hours at tedious tasks under pressure. Even in nineteenth-century England, where labourers were working for a money wage and piecework was often important, the tradition of feasting, drinking, and sexual licence was impossible to eradicate (Samuel 1975:3–133).

Rees (1968:94) describes the geographical and social implications of cooperation among dispersed settlements:

> Each farm is the centre of a circle of cooperation which differs slightly from those of its immediate neighbours while overlapping with them, and in this way the whole countryside is covered by a continuous network of reciprocities . . . Obligations have a different range for different tasks.

It is perhaps wise not to take the published maps of cooperating farms in Britain too literally (Hughes 1960:Figure 8; Williams 1956:Figure 9, 1963:Figure 15), but they do seem to imply that cooperation between farms 2 km apart was not uncommon, which suggests a series of overlapping circles perhaps 4 km across. Emmett (1964:67) records how 'shearing circles' in northern Wales often "cross the boundaries of the parish more, because the boundary often runs across the tops of mountains on which sheep farmers share grazing rights". Although "the neighbour group is much less definite in extent, and the emotional bonds which unite it are weaker than those of the kin group" (Williams 1956:143), the geographical proximity of kin is both inevitable and to some extent consciously contrived. Arensberg (1937:69) recalls how a Great Blasket Islander could not marry the girl of his choice, a mainlander, because her kin would be too far away when he needed aid. There is a context, therefore, in which the postulates of site catchment analysis should take account of labour pooling factors.

Both in Wales (Rees 1968:93) and Ireland (Arensberg and Kimball 1948:74), cooperation was apparently much more extensive in the period before the modern surveys took place and before the advent of modern machinery. In County Clare in Ireland, for example, when scythes were used for mowing, "cooperating groups would have been larger and a more pronounced rotation of the working groups from meadow to meadow could have been observed" (Arensberg and Kimball 1948:74). It is likely that this cooperation would have been still more pronounced in prehistoric times, and activities like forest clearance, fencing, and house-building may well have been included. Startin (1978) suggests that about 550 man-hours would have been needed to construct the neolithic house at Ballynagilly in County Tyrone, northern Ireland. This is perhaps 55 man-days, the equivalent of eight adults working for a week, or of 16 or 17 adults working for three days. Startin's estimates for the much larger houses of the early neolithic Linear Pottery culture in central Europe involve about five times as much work. For these houses, it seems likely that gangs comprising a couple of dozen adults and older juveniles were employed. In northwest Europe generally, the construction of ceremonial monuments such as megalithic tombs and earthen longbarrows much have been undertaken by communities thoroughly habituated to a tradition of collective labour. Indeed, gang construction is sometimes inferred from the heterogeneity or lack of standardisation of such monuments.

A small community of 'hamlet' size is also appropriate for decision-making on

day-to-day economic matters and those of strictly local concern. Ideally, the
number of decision-makers should be small and the families that each one represents relatively large, so that decisions may be made smoothly and uncontrover-
sially and be binding on as many people as possible. Much research is needed to
discover the extent to which the St. Kilda 'Parliament' (Steel 1975:44–46; see
also Figure 1.1, this volume) and the old men's *cuaird* of County Clare (Arensberg 1937:129–139) were examples of once more widespread and effective rural
institutions, as well as how such institutions functioned and what numbers were
concerned. The numbers involved in this kind of secondary organisation may be
partly determined by normative principles. Forge (1972: 374), describing a situation in New Guinea where status competition was involved, suggests that "when
the players in this game (of prestige) are all defined as potentially equal, the
game becomes static, i.e., unplayable, if the numbers are too low, and unplayable if the numbers are too high". In this case, 'too low' means fewer than 30
adult males; 'too high' means more than 75–80. Although further work needs to
be done on this topic, it is arguable that most groups organised at the secondary
level are within the range suggested for hunting bands, and that the numbers have
as much to do with organisational limits as with density-dependent factors. In
short, there must be a threshold above which a group of adult decision-makers
can no longer work together effectively; as numbers rise, the increasing frequency of disputes and personality clashes will inevitably result in fission.

To what extent should second-level organisation in prehistoric times be envisaged as extending to collective land ownership and use? This is a difficult
issue, because it cannot be considered separately from the land-owning functions
of larger groups at the tertiary level. It has already been suggested that the
successful defence of land may require the concerted action of a larger group
than one organised at the secondary level. Neolithic colonisation in northwest
Europe would have involved much more than the acquisition of small plots of
land for growing cereals. There is the question of game resources, especially
important in the early stages of colonisation (Case 1969:181) and in the event of
crop failure. The use of woodland browsing, also a probable early economic
strategy, would also have involed substantial areas of land (Fleming 1972),
especially if competition from wild and feral animals is taken into account. In
addition, wood was required for fuel and other purposes. In Somerset, southwest
England, it has been shown that from about 3000 b.c. there were carefully
managed coppices, in all probability fenced (Rackham 1977:71).

The situation is complicated by the need for, and choice of, more than one
type of land. The type of territory hypothesised for some past communities may
be labelled the *catena* territory, comprising a strip of land cutting across the grain
of a series of zones of different land-use potential, like the strip parishes of the
English chalklands (Ellison and Harriss 1972:947–951), or the model suggested
for the prehistoric inhabitants of the Somerset Levels, where the fens, the fen

edge, the nearby slopes, and the higher hills all had their respective uses (Coles 1978). Sometimes the blocks of land needed may not be contiguous; for example, a group could have used a zone of summer pasture that was so valuable that they were willing to accept its physical separation from their more regularly used territory (Ford 1976).

The control and colonisation of resources and land located over a broad and sometimes discontinous stretch of terrain carries implications of collective action by a group larger than the household, and often, I would suggest, larger than the secondary group. In this sense there must be a balance and a dialogue between the easy, day-to-day decision-making and collective action of the secondary group and the wider political control that could be exerted by the tertiary group. It is not surprising to find territorial units of 40–65 km^2 on South Dartmoor in the Bronze Age (Fleming 1978), or to find examples of hillfort spacing that suggest communities numbering in the hundreds (Stanford 1972).

The ancient land-holding systems of Wales (Seebohm 1904, 1911) apparently included tribal subgroups whose collective economic organisation was a good deal stronger than the systems of mutual aid referred to here. Seebohm describes the *trefgordd* as "a working unit of co-operative dairy farming . . . the natural group of homesteads of relatives or neighbours acting together as a single community as regards their cattle and their ploughing". The legal *trefgordd* was supposed to include "nine houses and one plough and one oven, and one churn and one cat and one cock and one bull and one herdsman" (Seebohm 1911:36,37). The former land-use systems of Scotland and Ireland ('runrig'), as well as those of medieval England, included the rotation of parcels or strips of land among tribesmen or tenants, as well as substantial rights of 'common', or grazing. It thus seems reasonable that we should seek to understand prehistoric systems within this kind of framework. Whether the study of ancient land boundaries will allow us to pick out secondary and tertiary levels of organisation on the ground is unclear at present. Our model of land tenure in prehistoric times, however, has implications for what we should expect in terms of land boundaries.

Neolithic fields had to be protected from deer and other crop predators by a fence or hedge of some kind. The advantages of collective land-taking are worth remembering. Twenty individual farmers, laying out spatially separate plots of land, each 1 ha in extent, would require a 350-m perimeter fence for each (circular) plot, involving a total of 7000 m of fencing. If the 20 farmers took in the land as one block, they would need only about 1600 m of fence, and each farmer would have to build only 80 m, as opposed to 350 m. If the plot size were increased to 2 has, the fence for an individual plot would have a 500-m perimeter, while the collective field would be surrounded by a fence 2250 m in length, with each man responsible for building a little over 110 m. Thus a group of farmers, by amalgamating their plots and refraining from building internal fences, could fence their land more rapidly and with much less individual effort. The energy saved could be used to make a more durable or effective barrier.

This approach can be carried further. Let us suppose that these same individuals decide to keep their land together, but that each one has to have a fence round his own farm. Figure 5.1 shows three possible arrangements. In Figure 5.1a, 20 square plots with side n are placed in a rectangle of sides $4n \times 5n$. In Figure 5.1b, the plots are packed in two rows of 10, in a rectangle of sides $10n \times 2n$—a long, narrow settlement zone as opposed to a compact one. If fence-building is to be shared equally, each individual has to build $2.45n$ or $2.6n$. Making internal boundaries involves the community in over twice as much work (see Table 5.1). Without internal boundaries, each individual only has to make his share of the outer fence, either $0.9n$ or $1.2n$. Figure 5.1c shows what happens if the farms are packed into the long, narrow territory in such a way that each farm is aligned along the long axis, as might be the arrangement in a catena territory. If individuals abandon the idea of building fences around their own farms, they save nearly 90% on boundary-building. Long territories are inconvenient from both fencing and defensive points of view; Figure 5.1 shows that the total boundary length increases as a plot of given area n^2 becomes longer and narrower.

Thus the pressures are towards individuals merging their land into one territory without internal fences, and they are all the stronger when the community has

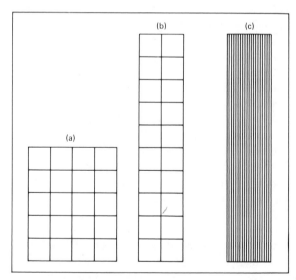

Figure 5.1 Three systems of collective land ownership for 20 prehistoric farms operating together. (See Table 5.1 for the amounts of work involved in fencing the boundaries of the different systems.) Each square represents one n.

Table 5.1

Boundary Divisions Created by the Three Systems of Collective Farming Illustrated in Figure 5.2

	$4n \times 5n$ (a)	$10n \times 2n$ (b)	$20n \times 1n$ (c)
Total boundary length (x)	$49n$	$52n$	$210n$
Total perimeter length (y)	$18n$	$24n$	$24n$
Perimeter of each plot	$4n$	$4n$	$20.2n$
Individual's work share with internal boundaries $(x/20)$	$2.45n$	$2.6n$	$10.5n$
Individual's work share if no internal boundaries $(y/20)$	$0.9n$	$1.2n$	$1.2n$

[a]a—rectangle of 5×4 holdings; b—rectangle of 10×2 holdings; c—rectangle of 20×1 holdings

chosen a long, narrow territory, as must have happened quite often. It can be argued, of course, that internal boundaries can be maintained without fences, and that individuals could have erected posts, cairns, and other types of markers to indicate their farm boundaries. But if the frequency of boundary disputes and related quarrels is proportional to the total length of boundaries within a community, the establishment of only *community* boundaries is highly desirable, both for second- and third-level communities. Such action would further the cohesion of the group, whose members were agreed on the boundaries of the unit to be defended against outsiders. The maintenance of an external boundary only could have allowed the group to claim an even larger territory, since the energies of individuals were not called into play to insist on the territorial integrity of their own farms.

The annexation of a relatively large territory would have delayed the time when internal conflict resulting from land shortages created new management problems for the community. In fact, however, the idea that the frequency of disputes is always proportional to total boundary length is simplistic. It is possible for a community to have too few boundaries in relation to the diversity of competing human groups within it or the economic activities being undertaken, in which case there are more disputes than necessary. Another community might have too many divisions, in the sense that excessive fragmentation of land creates disputes and absorbs labour on maintenance work. The latter situation is likely to result from previous conditions, and whether it can be corrected depends largely on the current political situation and, in some environments, on the nature of the boundaries themselves. That brutal 'corrections' were made in prehistory is suggested by the evidence from Wessex, where linear earthworks cut across field systems and barrow cemeteries have been put into former fields (Bowen 1975; Fowler 1971:171).

Collective Enterprise and Productivity

It is thus possible to build a model involving a high level of cooperation and collective land-taking in the northwest European Neolithic without recourse to Marxist theory or non-European ethnography. Whether such collectives were bound together by the mutual self-interest of their component households in the manner described by Dahlman (1980), or whether "they never regarded themselves as individuals", as Steel (1975:46) suggests was the case with the St. Kildans, is immaterial for our present purpose. The obvious question is: How productive and efficient might prehistoric 'collective economies' have been? The unexpectedly high yields of primitive cereals from the experimental 'iron age farm' at Butser Hill, Hampshire, stimulated Mercer to make calculations that resulted in the suggestion that about one million people could have been supported in an area the size of the modern county of Wiltshire (Mercer 1981:236). These figures help to illustrate the potential of prehistoric agriculture, even though it is highly improbable that carrying capacity was reached, or even seriously approached, in later prehistoric Britain. (The fact that grain was actually exported from southeast England in Late Iron Age times is probably good evidence for this proposition.) According to figures in Darby and Finn (1967), the population of Wiltshire in 1086 A.D. was probably about 50,000.

The Butser cereal yields, even viewed conservatively, suggest the potential elasticity of prehistoric economic performance. This provides a framework within which estimates of actual performance may be made. In assessing the performance of prehistoric 'collective economies', prehistorians would do well to avoid the pitfalls of present-day political debate (Jewell, 1981:224). The performance of collective economies in historic times is unlikely to be a reliable guide to their achievements in prehistoric times, since many could have been highly productive in some circumstances.

A number of these economies could fairly be described as 'decadent' owing to the proximity of urban societies, cash and market economies, the destruction of their original structure, and often the location of real political power outside their boundaries. A critical factor has often been the degree of social organisation and, in a hierarchical structure, the number of levels in that organisation. If tribute or taxation are involved, the situation resembles the familiar 'ecologists' pyramid', with its several levels of predation, and the members of the lowest level may even conceptualise the situation in this way. In medieval economies, for example, low productivity could be related to the number of levels in the sociopolitical hierarchy, and even to the existence of more than one predatory structure under the umbrella of a state organisation. In both medieval and prehistoric periods, burdens were placed on populations by ceremonialism, including the construction of ceremonial monuments, and by the building of fortifications and expenditures on weapons for furthering the ambitions of the ruling classes. It would be interesting to compare the weight of these burdens in the two periods concerned, since it is very possible that proportionally less of the productive surplus was spent in this way in prehistoric times.

Dahlman (1980:6,26), in an interesting consideration of Medieval English open field systems, correctly mentions the "overuse and underinvestment problems that are usually associated with communal property", but his theory also shows how "collective property rights and decision-making can be quite consistent with private wealth maximization", and he suggests that "under certain conditions with respect to transaction and decision costs, such arrangements will be superior to private ownership and control". For example, collective rights in the waste, he suggests, are cheaper because of lower transaction costs incurred in policing and maintaining the boundaries, "as long as the community is well-defined and outsiders can be kept at bay" (Dahlman, 1980:117). I have suggested, on the basis of a similar argument, that there was intercommoning on the high moors of Dartmoor from neolithic times (Fleming 1979:122). In the case of the waste, Dahlman mentions the economies of scale that are possible (the communal shepherd is a well-known figure in European ethnography) and suggests that the costs of established organisations to facilitate production and exchange are lower because no one is in a position to 'withdraw' land. It should be noted that Dahlman's analysis is unsentimental in the sense that it is concerned with correctly applied economic theory and makes no assumptions about the commitment of individuals to a collectivist ideal: "There is simply no incentive left for the individual tenant to make separate decisions when his strips are scattered. He participates naturally in the collective" (Dahlman 1980:129).

In Britain, comparisons have been made between the productivity of large and small holdings (Arensberg and Kimball 1948; Levy 1911; Thomas 1927). Levy quotes Vebbel, who wrote: "No argument is wanting at this time to show that a man can thrive on a small grass farm, who would starve on a small corn farm" (Levy 1911:111). Levy's general conclusion is that large holdings were successful for cereal production and sheep farming, while small holdings depended mainly on pigs, poultry, and dairying. This was the English experience of the eighteenth and nineteenth centuries, and although market forces and a money economy have to be taken into account, those factors that relate to labour supply and the size of holdings are relevant to all periods. Arensberg and Kimball (1948), using census figures from the early twentieth century, were able to compare the small holdings of western Ireland with the larger holdings further east. Despite the obvious ecological differences between the two areas, the small holdings were more productive in some respects. The authors comment that "the number of persons supporting themselves upon the small holdings is much greater than those upon large farms", and "the smaller farms produce more per person at work" (Arensberg and Kimball (1948:13,21).

A comparison between holdings of 30–50 acres and those of 100–200 acres (one acre equals approximately 0.4 ha) shows that, per 1000 acres, the former had 80% more pigs, 54% more milch cows, 53% more cattle less than one year old, 32% more ploughed land, 29% more hay, and 13% more poultry than the latter, which were more productive in terms of sheep (24% more than the small holdings) and dry cattle. Again, market forces are at work here, but labour force and holding size are also relevant. In this context, it is interesting that animal bone samples containing high proportions of pig bones, as at the Durrington Walls henge (Harcourt 1971) have been interpreted in terms of ritual practices, extensive local woodland cover, or paying tribute to a priestly caste (MacKie 1977:179–180), but not, as far as I know, in terms of the size of local holdings.

The limits within which farmers operate produce some results which at first sight seem odd to the economic prehistorian. Thomas's comparison of upland and lowland holdings in southwest Wales led him to comment: "The higher percentage of arable shown to obtain for the highlands is due probably to the poorer quality of the soil, making it necessary to grow crops for the sustenance of livestock" (Thomas 1927:36). In terms of head of cattle per 100 acres, the larger holdings had less stock, and so did the upland holdings, so that small- and medium-sized lowland farms were much more densely stocked than medium-sized and large upland farms (see Table 5.2).

Table 5.2 shows that the most intensive use of labour occurred on small lowland farms and the least intensive on large upland farms. Thomas also notes that more sheep were kept on the larger holdings. With sheep farming in general, however, access to common pasture on the mountains made a significant difference: "The two most common conditions for successful sheep farming—a large flock and a large run—made it unsuitable for the small holding" (Thomas 1927:43). Levy (1911:169) makes much the same point.

Table 5.2

Stock and Labour Rates of Farms in Southwest Wales[a]

Farm category (acres)	Cattle equivalents per 100 acres	Employed man equivalents per 100 acres
Highland		
< 30	38.1	6.3
30–60	32.8	5.6
60+	20.8	3.2
All holdings	29	4.9
Lowland		
< 25	47.2	10.8
25–50	48.9	6.3
50+	41.1	5.4
All holdings	46	6.4

[a]After Thomas 1927:Tables XII and XXIII.

In relatively recent times, those working large holdings have been able to make a good living for their immediate families by exploiting particular economic and technological conditions, without having to run an economy well balanced in subsistence terms, because of the development of regional and even international markets and appropriate transport facilities. They have reached high levels of productivity per unit of labour; however, modern productivity per unit of land cannot be readily or usefully compared with that under prehistoric conditions, given the innovations of the past few centuries. Machinery has obviously played a key role. In terms of subsistence, prehistoric economies would have had to achieve much more local self-sufficiency.

It is possible to envisage prehistoric economies in which (1) land was held collectively for the most part, (2) cooperative labour organisation was common and more fully developed than in recent British rural history, and (3) frequent exchange, bridewealth payments, and the like ensured the wide circulation of agricultural produce in the community. These economies would then combine the advantages of a plentiful labour supply with the economies of scale and the management advantages associated with large holdings. With concepts of 'tribute' or 'rent' underdeveloped or lacking, but with universal entitlement to agricultural land and an absence of influence from nearby urban systems, prehistoric economies could have been highly productive given certain incentives.

Naturally, different ratios between population and land area could imply high levels of productivity per unit area in some places. The circumstances in which prehistoric economies with strong collectivist tendencies reached these levels are largely a matter for future research. In the Early Neolithic, we may envisage high levels of agricultural production being translated into population increases and a relatively high standard of living. The apparent speed with which the Linear Pottery style spread across Europe—nearly 1 km per year, according to Ammerman and Cavalli-Sforza (1971:681)—might reflect these trends. At this stage, with a low population density and collective land management subject to few internal pressures, land boundaries would have been relatively rare and related more to land management than to the reinforcement of sociopolitical divisions.

Later, general prosperity accompanied by population increases would provide a plausible trigger for the changes suggested by Friedman and Rowlands (1977), where prestige competition between different groups develops and finds expression in various ways, including feast-giving. (Incidentally, the link between collective work and feast-giving is very strong and survived for a long time in Britain at times of harvesting, threshing, sheep-shearing, etc.) There is no reason to suppose that the growth of intergroup competition presaged the end of collectivist traditions. We have already noted how the Irish kinship system could be mobilised in support of more influential individuals. This can be compared with Sahlins's 'fish-tail' distribution of labour intensity (1972:Figure 3.3). He describes how, in 'big-man' systems of classic Melanesian type, there are ''on the one side, the big-men or would-be big-men and their followers, whose production they are able to galvanise, and on the other side those content to praise and live off the ambition of others''.

At this stage, collectively owned resources could become subject to disputes and overexploitation, and increasing regulation of access would become necessary. In societies with strong egalitarian traditions, this development might encourage the emergence of a headman or chief whose role as an impartial arbitrator was stressed—a person like the 'king' of Tory Island (Buchanan 1973:594). In more competitive societies, "the collective decision-making rule can best be understood as voting in relation to the size of the economic interest belonging to each farmer in the village" (Dahlman 1980:26). Most members of the community have an interest in maintaining and even strengthening the collective system. Economically and socially dominant families naturally wish to maintain a system in which they can continue to manipulate the distribution of labour and wealth, while the poorer groups will struggle to maintain their minimum stake in the community land, even if debts and obligations make it impossible for them to prosper. Groups in the middle range of prosperity are also securely locked into the system.

At this point, land boundaries must have become much more significant. An important early distinction may have been between *management* boundaries, often running *along* the line between land-use zones, and *sociopolitical* boundaries running *across* such lines. Another distinction can be made between boundaries separating tertiary groups and those separating secondary groups within a tertiary group's territory. Some field systems may represent strong collective traditions at the tertiary organisational level, with the wider community dominating the smaller-scale units involved in agricultural production. Others may be composed of well-defined blocks of land, suggesting a more 'federal' structure for the tertiary group. A good example of the dialogue between tertiary and secondary levels of organisation occurs in the Dartmeet parallel reave system, a 3000-ha field system on Dartmoor (Fleming and Ralph 1983) in southwest England that was laid out around 1300 b.c. The houses here are distributed in ones and twos in open clusters that may be termed 'neighbourhoods', though it is not possible to isolate 'individual farms' in the sense of groups of land parcels in close association with individual houses or pairs of houses. Details of the layout of the parallel system suggest that the inhabitants of a 'neighbourhood' laid out the land boundaries in their own area; between neighbourhoods, a 'community gang' completed the work. One is reminded of Arensberg and Kimball's distinction between work gangs operating at different sociopolitical levels (*comhair* and *meitheal*) in County Clare, Ireland (Arensberg and Kimball 1948:263–264).

Thus is is possible to see field system formation as an attempt to maintain collective economies by communities organised on segmentary principles and subject to increasing internal competition. More work needs to be done on the small-scale divisions within field systems to see whether they are likely to relate to management systems or to the growth of inalienable rights with regard to land. Fowler (1971:174), Brongers (1976:57, Plate 15c), and Bradley (1978:Figure 3) show how a field system may be divided into a number of primary blocks followed by 'infilling', and more detailed studies along these lines could be attempted with profit. The Dartmoor reave systems, which vary considerably with regard to their degree of infilling, might well be susceptible to this kind of analysis. The work of Müller-Wille (1965:40–56), who analysed fields to see whether they had been split into equal divisions, perhaps suggesting inheritance patterns, could be applied in other regions. Finally, the behaviour of droveways and trackways is often revealing (Fleming and Ralph 1983; Pryor 1978, 1980).

The spread of field systems could also have led to agricultural improvements unenvisaged by their makers. Smaller bounded units could have become units of observation and experiment by more 'progressive' farmers, thus encouraging more systematic approaches to manuring, crop rotation, and the provision of shelter and perhaps raising the productivity per unit area. Unfortunately, there is no space here to pursue the ramifications of this subject. More systematic, problem-orientated fieldwork is needed, as is a fuller investigation of the properties of collectively organised land-use systems, with emphases on decision-making, productivity, and the dialogue between competition and cooperation that is present in most human endeavours. Only then will we have established a framework within which other components of the study of economic prehistory can find their place.

References

Ammerman, A. J., and L. L. Cavalli-Sforza
    1971 Measuring the rate of spread of early farming in Europe. *Man* 6:674–687.
Arensberg, C. M.
    1937 *The Irish countryman.* Macmillan, London.
Arensberg, C. M., and S. T. Kimball
    1948 *Family and community in Ireland.* Harvard University Press, Cambridge, Massachusetts.
Bowen, H. C.
    1975 Pattern and interpretation: a view of the Wessex landscape from neolithic to Roman times. In *Recent work in rural archaeology,* edited by P. J. Fowler, pp. 44–55. Moonraker Press, Bradford-on-Avon.
Bradley, R.
    1975 The bronze age occupation in its wider context. In *Rams Hill,* edited by R. Bradley and A. Ellison, pp. 150–170. British Archaeological Reports, British Series 19, Oxford, England.
Bradley, R.
    1978 Prehistoric field systems in Britain and northwest Europe: a review of some recent work. *World Archaeology* 9:265–277.
Brongers, J. A.
    1976 *Air photography and Celtic field research in the Netherlands.* Nederlandse Oudheiden 6, Amersfoort, Holland.

Buchanan, R. H.
    1973 Field systems of Ireland. In *Studies of field systems in the British Isles,* edited by A. Baker
        and R. Butlin, pp. 580–618. Cambridge University Press, Cambridge, England.
Burstow, G. P., and G. A. Holleyman
    1957 Late bronze age settlement on Itford Hill. *Proceedings of the Prehistoric Society* 23:167–
        212.
Case, H.
    1969 Neolithic explanations. *Antiquity* 43:176–186.
Coles, J. M.
    1978 The Somerset Levels: a concave landscape. In *Early land allotment,* edited by H. C.
        Bowen and P. J. Fowler, pp. 147–148. British Archaeological Reports, British Series 48,
        Oxford, England.
Curwen, E. C.
    1937 *The archaeology of Sussex.* Methuen, London.
Dahlman, C. J.
    1980 *The open field system and beyond.* Cambridge University Press, Cambridge, England.
Darby, H. C., and R. W. Finn
    1967 *The Domesday geography of southwest England.* Cambridge University Press,
        Cambridge, England.
Drewett, P.
    1979 New evidence for the structure and function of middle bronze age round houses in Sussex.
        Archaeological Journal 136:3–11.
Drewett, P.
    1980 Black Patch and the Later Bronze Age in Sussex. in *The British Later Bronze Age,* edited
        by J. Barrett and R. Bradley, pp. 377–395. British Archaeological Reports, British Series
        83, Oxford, England.
Drewett, P.
    1982 Late bronze age downland economy and excavations at Black Patch, East Sussex. *Pro-
        ceedings of the Prehistoric Society* 48:321–400.
Ellison, A.
    1978 The Bronze Age of Sussex. In *Archaeology in Sussex to A.D. 1500,* edited by P. Drewett,
        pp. 30–36. Council for British Archaeology, Research Report 29, London.
Ellison, A.
    1981 Towards a socioeconomic model for the Middle Bronze Age in southern England. In
        Pattern of the past, edited by I. Hodder et al., pp. 413–435. Cambridge University Press,
        Cambridge, England.
Ellison, A., and J. Harriss
    1972 Settlement and land use in the prehistory and early history of southern England. In *Models
        in archaeology,* edited by D. L. Clarke, pp. 911–962. Methuen, London.
Emmett, I.
    1964 *A North Wales village: a social anthropological study.* Routledge and Kegan Paul,
        London.
Fleming, A.
    1972 The genesis of pastoralism in European prehistory. *World Archaeology* 4:179–188.
Fleming, A.
    1978 The prehistoric landscape of Dartmoor, part 1: South Dartmoor. *Proceedings of the
        Prehistoric Society* 44:97–123.
Fleming, A.
    1979 The Dartmoor reaves: boundary patterns and behaviour patterns in the second millennium
        b.c. *Proceedings of the Devon Archaeological Society* 37:115–130.

Fleming, A., and N. Ralph
    1983 Medieval settlement and land use on Hoine Moor, Dartmoor: the landscape evidence. *Medieval Archaeology* 26:101–137.
Ford, W. J.
    1976 Some settlement patterns in the central region of the Warwickshire Avon. In *Medieval settlement,* edited by P. H. Sawyer, pp. 274–294. Edward Arnold, London.
Forge, A.
    1972 Normative factors in the settlement size of neolithic cultivators (New Guinea). In *Man, settlement and urbanism,* edited by P. J. Ucko et al., pp. 363–376. Duckworth, London.
Fowler, P. J.
    1971 Early prehistoric agriculture in western Europe: some archaeological evidence. In *Economy and settlement in neolithic and early bronze age Britain and Europe,* edited by D. D. A. Simpson, pp. 153–179. Leicester University Press, Leicester, England.
Fowler, P. J.
    1981 Wildscape to landscape: 'enclosure' in prehistoric Britain. In *Farming practice in British prehistory,* edited by R. Mercer, pp. 9–48. Edinburgh University Press, Edinburgh, Scotland.
Friedman, J., and M. J. Rowlands
    1977 Notes toward an epigenetic model of the evolution of 'civilization'. In *The Evolution of social systems,* edited by J. Friedman and M. J. Rowlands, pp. 201–272. Duckworth, London.
Harcourt, R. A.
    1971 Animal bones from Durrington Walls. In *Durrington Walls: excavations 1966–68,* edited by G. J. Wainwright and I. Longworth, pp. 338–350. Society of Antiquaries, Reports of the Research Committee 29, London.
Hughes, T. J.
    1960 Aberdaron: the social geography of a small region in the Llyn peninsula. In *Welsh rural communities,* edited by E. Davies and A. D. Rees, pp. 120–181. University of Wales Press, Cardiff.
Jewell, P.
    1981 A summing-up. In *Farming practice in British prehistory,* edited by R. Mercer, pp. 223–230. Edinburgh University Press, Edinburgh, Scotland.
Levy, H.
    1911 *Large and small holdings.* Cambridge University Press, Cambridge, England.
MacKie, E.
    1977 *The megalith builders.* Phaidon, Oxford, England.
Megaw, J. V. S.
    1967 Gwithian, Cornwall: some notes on the evidence for neolithic and bronze age settlement. In *Settlement and economy in the third and second millenia b.c.,* edited by C. Burgess and R. Miket, pp. 51–66. British Archaeological Reports, British Series 33, Oxford, England.
Megaw, J. V. S., A. C. Thomas, and B. Wailes
    1960–61 The bronze age settlement at Gwithian, Cornwall. *Proceedings of the West Cornwall Field Club* 2:200–215.
Mercer, R.
    1981 Appendix. In *Farming practice in British prehistory,* edited by R. Mercer, pp. 231–237. Edinburgh University Press, Edinburgh, Scotland.
Müller-Wille, M.
    1965 *Eisenzeitliche Fluren in den festländischen Nordseegebiet.* Geographischen Kommission, Münster.

Pryor, F.
  1978 *Excavation at Fengate, Peterborough, England: the second report.* Royal Ontario Museum, Canada.
Pryor, F.
  1980 *Excavation at Fengate, Peterborough, England: the third report.* Northamptonshire Archaeological Society and Royal Ontario Museum, Northampton, England, and Ontario, Canada.
Rackham, O.
  1977 Neolithic woodland management in the Somerset Levels: Garvin's, Walton Heath and Rowland's tracks. *Somerset Levels Papers* 3:65–71.
Rahtz, P., and A. apSimon
  1962 Excavations at Shearplace Hill, Sydling St. Nicholas, Dorset, England. *Proceedings of the Prehistoric Society* 28:289–328.
Rees, A. D.
  1968 *Life in a Welsh countryside.* University of Wales Press, Cardiff.
Sahlins, M.
  1972 *Stone age economics.* Aldine, Atherton, Chicago.
Samuel, R. (editor)
  1975 *Village life and labour.* Routledge and Kegan Paul, London.
Seebohm, F.
  1904 *The tribal system in Wales* (second ed.). Longmans Green, London.
Seebohm, F.
  1911 *Tribal custom in Anglo-Saxon law.* Longmans Green, London.
Stanford, S. C.
  1972 The function and population of hill-forts in the Central Marches. In *Prehistoric man in Wales and the west,* edited by F. Lynch and C. Burgess, pp. 307–318. Adams and Dart, Bath, England.
Startin, W.
  1978 Linear pottery culture houses: reconstruction and manpower. *Proceedings of the Prehistoric Society* 44:143–157.
Steel, T.
  1975 *The life and death of St. Kilda.* Fontana, London.
Terray, E.
  1972 *Marxism and 'primitive' societies.* Monthly Review Press, New York.
Thomas, E.
  1927 *The economics of small holdings.* Cambridge University Press, Cambridge, England.
Williams, W. M.
  1956 *The sociology of an English village: Gosforth.* Routledge and Kegan Paul, London.
Williams, W. M.
  1963 *A west country village: Ashworthy.* Routledge and Kegan Paul, London.

6

Iron Age Transformations in Northern Russia and the Northeast Baltic

MAREK ZVELEBIL

Introduction

Models constructed to understand the workings of 'simple' societies, such as those of mesolithic or neolithic Europe, invariably emphasise the biological sectors of the cultural system. As a rule, hunting–gathering and early farming societies are perceived as 'egalitarian', 'unstratified', 'acephalous', and generally close to nature, while their cultural dynamism is more often explained in terms of interaction between the natural environment, subsistence, and population. From the infinite number of subsystems that comprise the cultural system, the clear favourites of the hunter–gatherer and early man specialists are subsistence or resource use, site location–land use, demography, and technology (Clark 1953, 1957, 1975; Dolukhanov 1979; Higgs and Vita-Finzi 1972; Jochim 1976), while the subsystems of the social environment suffer not only from the lack of evidence, but also from conceptual neglect. Models used to explain the development of social and economic complexity, on the other hand, accentuate the role of trade and/or social differentiation as the prime movers of culture change. The simple biological needs of mankind are downplayed in favour of the role of social hierarchies, trade in prestige objects and other valuables, warfare, and other aspects of the social system (Hodder 1982; Peebles and Kus 1977; Renfrew and Shennan 1982; Wells 1980), as if complex societies were exempt from basic subsistence and reproductive requirements.

To achieve a more balanced approach, we have to escape the conceptual dichotomy that produced such 'law and order' models of culture change. For simple societies, this means considering socially determined phenomena as po-

147

tential causes of cultural developments, a need that is gradually being recognised, especially for past forager societies (Bender 1978; Moore 1981). Conversely, in considering the development of cultural complexity, more attention has to be paid to basic economic and demographic processes. While for some forms of evidence, powerful operational models have been devised that help to identify patterns of social and economic organisation (Renfrew 1975, 1977; Smith 1976), such models are in short supply for subsistence data, as other chapters in this volume describe. Ecological models alone, though useful as indicators of adaptive fitness for different subsistence strategies (Jochim 1976; Odner 1972; Zvelebil 1981), operate within limits that are too broad to allow identification of the mechanisms responsible for cultural change.

The aim of this chapter is to evaluate the role of subsistence in the transition from what were essentially neolithic to iron age societies in northeast Europe, a transition involving a rapid transformation in social and economic complexity. Traditionally, these developments have been explained in terms of external events such as intervention from the more advanced societies in the south or west (Bulkin et al. 1978; Kivikoski 1967), or as a result of "the growth of productive forces" (Graudonis 1967). The emphasis in this chapter is on the internal developments of these societies, with a twofold objective: (1) to consider how subsistence data can release information about the development of complex social and economic organisation, and (2) to consider the interaction between changing conditions of subsistence and other aspects of society during the transition to the iron age system cf production. The eastern Baltic area of northeast Europe is examined during the first millennium A.D. (Figure 6.1). Characteristic features of the area include the marginality of the environment for cultivation, a long persistence of the hunting way of life, the virtual absence of a Bronze Age, and the peripheral location of northeast Europe in relation to the ancient and classical civilisations—in several senses, a pioneer location.

Iron Age Transformations: The European Context

The development of iron age society has been examined recently in several areas of temperate Europe (Collis 1984; Frankenstein and Rowlands 1978; Renfrew and Shennan 1982; Wells 1980). Models applied to these data form the background to the present analysis of cultural change in northeast Europe, and some discussion of the European context is therefore essential. In summary, society in Iron Age Europe underwent related and more or less simultaneous transformations in basic aspects of its organisation that set it apart from preceding Neolithic and Bronze Age communities, and from the succeeding states of the historical period. Most significantly, Iron Age society appears to have been on the threshold of state formation, yet most observers agree that the state level of economic and sociopolitical organisation was not achieved until the Roman or post-Roman period.

Despite the doubts expressed recently about the true impact of iron metallurgy (Cunliffe 1978), its introduction remains the most significant development in the technoeconomic system of the Iron Age. After the initial stages, iron tool production, improved and extended to objects of daily use, made possible basic improvements in the technology of agriculture, which then remained almost unchanged in more traditional agricultural areas until recently. Hence, the range of iron tools utilised by a Celtic farmer in the first century B.C. and by a Russian peasant earlier in this century was essentially the same (Clarke 1972; Pleiner 1978). Billhooks, scythes, knives, sickles, axes, and especially ploughshares all helped to improve agricultural production (Pleiner 1978). Through metallurgy, the mode of production ceased to be generalised, subsistence-oriented, and village-based and became instead more specialised, industrialised, and regionally oriented.

Because of the relatively high investment needed in terms of skill, labour, and capital—a combination not available to everyone—metallurgy encouraged the emergence of specialised craftsmen who could supply the basic means of production beyond the household and eventually beyond the village. The tools they supplied, if not essential to food procurement, could nevertheless greatly improve productivity. Moreover, Pleiner (1978) argues that the nature of production also changed, from the specialised production of a few artefacts for high-status individuals (as in the Late Bronze Age) to the mass production of standardised types in response to a general demand. The emergence of specialists in metallurgy helped to precipitate the development of craft specialisation in other areas of manufacturing as well, including pottery, glass production, and mining. As Clarke points out, intensification in one group of economic activities stimulates expansion in other groups "through an increased demand from the former group for the goods and services of the latter" (1972:863).

Sahlins (1972) argues that the domestic mode of production contains an anti-surplus principle. With craft specialisation, this principle is necessarily removed, because surplus production of foodstuffs has to exist to feed the craft specialist. At the same time, the existing exchange system is expanded or given new significance to include transfers of everyday goods that affect populations at a regional scale. Sahlins emphasises the regional nature of this type of exchange in the ethnographic context: to trade for food would be acceptable only at the regional scale, where the "insulation of the food circuit may be worn through by frictions of social distance" (1972:219). Hence, we have two other important features occurring intermittently in the European Iron Age: surplus production and the development of a regional exchange system.

Exchange networks, especially over long distances, are often thought to be the key factor in the development of iron age social organisation (Wells 1980).

Long-distance trade, dealing mainly in luxuries that could be used as 'social transfers' (Hodges 1982a), principally affected a restricted section of society: leaders, elders, warriors, chiefs, and other socially dominant groups (Frankenstein and Rowlands 1978). Such exchange systems served to stimulate the surplus production of goods that were traded in return for luxuries, to enhance the status and position of the social elite, and to encourage specialisation as a way of increasing the quantity of locally produced materials. Hodges (1982a), in the case of Dark Age Europe, and Wells (1980), in the case of the Late Hallstatt Iron Age, both illustrate how long-distance trade was used to stimulate production, support the established social order, and promote craft specialisation.

When dealing with common goods, it is more difficult to recognise exchange at the regional level in the archaeological record. As a result, this type of exchange is less clearly understood. Regional exchange probably involved transfers of foodstuffs, specialists' utilitarian items, and trinkets that were common enough to keep their social value relatively low. Whilst almost everyone is agreed about the likely significance of regional exchange, its extent and organisation remain elusive. As Collis (1984) argues, several systems might have operated, including centralised market exchange, individual redistribution systems, and communal exchange at the village level, each with their own set of socioeconomic implications. Despite recent attempts at operationalising these models in archaeological contexts (Hodges 1982a; Renfrew 1975, 1977; Smith 1976), no comprehensive picture has emerged for the Iron Age. The extent to which iron age communities depended on regional trade is equally unclear (Renfrew and Shennan 1982). The general impression is one of agrarian self-sufficiency, but there is clear evidence for the specialist production of utilitarian objects, which would have required some form of local or regional exchange.

These technological and economic changes took place in the context of the accelerated development of social hierarchies and the extension of social organisation to administer the increasingly complex production and redistribution sectors of society. Even so, the lack of efficient administration may have hampered the development of states and precipitated periodic breakdowns in the functioning of iron age society (Hodges 1982a). Indeed, it was not until the post-Roman period, and only with the benefit of Roman imperial experience, that the organisational element was able to administer the new levels of social and economic complexity attained during the Iron Age.

The priority of social evolution, as opposed to technological and economic change, is a much-debated subject. It is clear that the technological and economic changes introduced by the development of iron metallurgy provided the means for expressing as well as accentuating social differences that might have already been engendered within the society but that had been unable to find sufficiently tangible means of expression. Craft specialisation provided, at least potentially, a differential access to the means of destruction as well as the means of production: "The bow and arrow is a democratic weapon because anyone can make himself one; but weapons which can be monopolised may be used to maintain the position of authority" (Wilkinson 1973:110). It is equally clear that more complex forms of economy required more extensive administration—the kind that could be organised only through the hierarchical arrangement of distinct social groups commanding different sectors of production and redistribution. At the same time, it is obvious that a social elite, however incipient, would be the first and principal beneficiary of expanded trade and surplus production, and that both of these processes would operate to extend the control of the elite. What is not obvious, and yet is crucial to our understanding of the period, is the extent to which the 'take-off' point in cultural evolution during the Iron Age was achieved through external contact, as opposed to the internal articulation of various aspects of the cultural system. In the latter process, four factors seem to have combined to play a crucial role: iron metallurgy, craft specialisation, surplus production, and regional trade. The hypothesis that these should be reflected in subsistence patterns and associated material remains is investigated later in this chapter.

Early Farming in the Boreal Zone

The transition to Iron Age society in northeast Europe cannot be understood without being aware of the special nature of farming in the region. One characteristic feature of the area is that bronze was generally unavailable and therefore confined to the making of prestige goods; iron was the first widely available metal in the area. Moreover, the full transition from foraging to farming was made very late in northeast Europe and did not take place before the Iron Age. Thus, the full impact of the neolithic revolution coincided with the distribution of iron artefacts, a situation not found elsewhere in Europe. The context of this development must be sought in the conditions that control the role of farming in the overall subsistence pattern.

Farming in northeast Europe, as in northern Europe in general, is severely constrained by environmental factors. The most persistent limiting factors include a short growing season (150 ± 30 days), low temperatures, excessive precipitation, a paucity of suitable soils with the appropriate mixture of organic and mineral components, and unpredictable (noncyclic) fluctuations in climatic parameters (Stålfelt 1972; Zvelebil 1981). A certain amount of risk was inevitable upon introducing cultigens and domesticates originally adapted to temperate and semi-arid (Mediterranean) regions into such different climatic conditions.

A decade of studies on the development of farming in northern Europe have demonstrated that the dispersal of farming was checked and reversed several times after its initial introduction around 3000 B.C. The reversals coincided with periods of climatic deterioration (Moberg 1966; Bergelund 1969; Welinder 1975; Zvelebil 1980, 1981). The adoption of farming exposed the population to hazards of crop failures, which have been very disruptive in historic times (Jutikkala 1955; Melander and Melander, 1924) and must have been all the more so in the prehistoric period (Moberg 1968; Zvelebil 1981). The only advantage of farming in northern Europe, in comparison with the indigenous foraging economies, was its superior productive potential (Zvelebil 1981). In short, it proved difficult to adjust the agrarian system to the conditions of the northern regions. Adjustments included a greater emphasis on the animal rather than the cereal component of farming, the selection of cultigens best adapted to vigorous boreal conditions (rye in particular), the practice of slash and burn agriculture, and the development of a mixed economy in which foraging (hunting, fishing, and gathering) continued to play a significant role, not least as insurance against failures in the agrarian system.

Although the earliest traces of cultigens and domesticates in northeast Europe occur sporadically from approximately 2500 B.C., bones of domesticated animals constitute less than 5% of the total sample until the first millennium B.C. (Paaver 1965; Zvelebil 1981). The subsequent transition to farming as the principal means of subsistence occurred during the thousand years between 500 B.C. and 500 A.D. (Figure 6.1). This is evident not only in the osteological and palynological record (Huttunen 1980; Paaver 1965; Salo and Lahtiperä 1970; Tolonen et al. 1976), but also in the relocation of settlements in areas with light sandy clays and loams and other locations optimal for farming (Graudonis 1967; Jaanits 1959; Zvelebil 1978, 1981). On the northern and eastern fringes of the area, foraging remained an important diet source well into the Middle Ages (Jutikkala 1949; Vilkuna 1968). In general, prior to the late first millennium B.C. most 'farming' communities in northeast Europe in fact relied substantially on hunting, fishing, and gathering.

One reason for the greater stability of the farmer–forager adaptation in northeast Europe may have been the greater role played by slash and burn agriculture. Due to the ecology of northeast Europe, swidden farming presents a low-risk alternative to permanent arable. Although it will produce a higher yield in the short term (the first 1–3 harvests), the long period of fallow (up to 30–40 years) renders swiddening less productive than arable in the long term (Soininen 1974). The decline in harvest, however, could be avoided by shifting the field to a new location every two or three years. With frequent relocation, swiddening is more productive than permanent farming in terms of yield per labour input (Zvelebil 1981). Moreover, the social and ideological contexts of swidden farming and foraging are more comparable than is the case for either of them in comparison with permanent arable. Both modes of production require the seasonal pooling of labour (either by group cooperation or by an extended family system) and either frequent settlement relocation or a spatial alteration of resources. Both form a

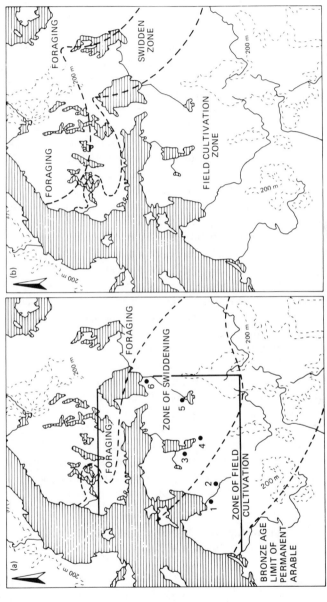

Figure 6.1 Land use history in northern Russia and the northeast Baltic. Solid line marks the principal research area, with the principal sites mentioned in the text. 1, Kentekalns; 2, Mukukalns; 3, Ryuge; 4, Pskov; 5, Novgorod; 6, Staraya Ladoga. (a) 500 B.C.–A.D. 400; (b) fifth through thirteenth centuries A.D. Approximate scale, 1:16,000,000

barrier against the ownership of resources (Sheldon 1952; Zvelebil and Rowley-Conwy 1984). Hence, the adoption of swidden by foragers in the study area did not require the cognitive and social changes that usually accompany permanent agriculture.

The extent and inception of swiddening are currently under review. Some authors contend that slash and burn was a late and insignificant development, at least in the western Baltic (Rowley-Conwy 1981; for opposite view, see Green 1979). In the eastern Baltic region, we rely partly on extrapolation back from the medieval period, when the slash and burn system was used extensively in northern Russia (Dorosenko 1959; Smith 1977; Tretyakov 1932), Finland (Vilkuna 1968), and Karelia (Soininen 1974; Teräsvuori 1928). In southern Finland, however, pollen profiles extending back to approximately 1400 B.C. indicate clearance and regrowth cycles accompanied by burning—evidence incompatible with the maintenance of open landscape (Zvelebil 1981). The successive rises and falls in cereal, grass, and arboreal pollen curves also argue for the existence of shifting rather than permanent cultivation (Huttunen 1980; Tolonen et al. 1976; Vuorela 1975). From the reconstruction of past landscapes in southern Finland, it seems likely that permanent arable did not become widely established until the mid-first millennium A.D. (Tolonen et al. 1976; Zvelebil 1981).

In summary, the present evidence suggests that early farming in northeast Europe combined small-scale arable farming, foraging, and swidden cultivation. Such a system appears to have been well adapted to the natural environment and to the conditions of an agricultural frontier zone. The expected effect would be to delay the development of permanent farming until the extensive swidden system had run out of land. General studies of the agricultural colonisation of temperate forest habitats (Green 1979) and historical sources relating to the northeast European fringes (Dorosenko 1959; Soininen 1974; Tegengren 1965; Teräsvuori 1928) both show how the availability of previously uncultivated land retarded agricultural intensification. Because of its organisation and low productivity, a system based primarily on swiddening and foraging would also have imposed severe constraints on the development of iron age social organisation. It is against this background that we should consider how subsistence conditions interacted with other forces in the formation of iron age society.

The Shift to the Iron Age Economy: Faunal and Botanical Data

As described earlier, the general features of the shift to an iron age economy in temperate Europe included the development of surplus production, craft specialisation, and regional trade. In considering a similar case of economic intensification, Maltby (1979) suggests that such changes ought to be reflected in subsistence by more intensive exploitation of food resources, generation of food surpluses, and redistribution of produce from producers to consumers. In this section, faunal and botanical data from the northeast Baltic region are assessed in light of these propositions.

FAUNAL REMAINS

Of several sources of evidence relating to food production in the area under study, faunal remains present the most complete record (Table 6.1). A comprehensive analysis by Paaver (1965) is supplemented by faunal reports from northern Russia (Ermolova 1976; Krasnov 1971; Ravdonikas 1949; Tsalkin 1962) and Finland (Salo 1968; Salo and Lahtiperä 1970). An obvious form of intensification in our area of study would be a shift from low-productivity foraging and slash and burn cultivation to greater reliance on permanent farming and animal husbandry. Such a shift should be reflected in the faunal record in two ways: first, as a decrease in the proportion of bones of wild animals in the total bone sample; and second (because permanent cultivation, unlike swidden, requires animals for traction and manure) as an increase in the number of domestic oxen and horses, as well as possible changes in the size and age of such animals. In addition, an increase in resources with industrial–commercial potential could indicate a growing market economy. Fur game fits this description (e.g., squirrel, fox, wolf, hare, beaver, otter, lynx, marten, wild cat, polecat, mink, wolverine, and badger). All such game except beaver represents a poor source of food (because of small size, low population density, and/or poor palatability) but a valuable source of fur. The furs of all these animals were a major object of trade in medieval Russia (Bulkin et al. 1978; Smith 1977); the *yasak,* a tax imposed on the indigenous inhabitants of Siberia, was also payable in furs. An increase in fur game could therefore indicate the development of a trading system using furs as the principal medium of exchange. Changes in resource-use strategies can also be detected in the composition of skeletal remains, which sometimes indicates selective butchering for industrial or commercial use such as the collection of furs and hides for tanning, or the removal of meat for market.

In Table 6.1, the sites with faunal material have been divided into four chronological groups corresponding to the major phases in the development of the Iron Age in this region (Graudonis 1967; Kivikoski 1967; Moora 1953, 1956). The first group covers the Metal Age or pre-Roman Iron Age (500 B.C.–0); the second group the Early Iron Age or Roman Iron Age (0–A.D. 400); the third group the Middle Iron Age or migration period (A.D. 400–800); and the fourth group the Late Iron Age or Viking–Crusader period (A.D. 800–1200). The data published by Paaver (1965) can also be divided into three groups that cross-cut these chronological divisions: those from sites with good preservation (A), where

Table 6.1

Faunal Data from Iron Age Sites in the Northeast Baltic Region

Site number	Site name	Site type[a]	Wild (%)	Domestic (%)	Wild fur (%)	Wild meat (%)	Cattle	Sheep–goat	Pig	Horse	Preservation[b]
Group 1 (500 B.C.–0)											
1	Asote	H	41.3	58.7	16.3	25.0	14.1	12.0	17.4	13.0	A
2	Mukukalns	H	52.3	47.7	26.7	25.5	13.2	10.8	12.3	10.4	A
3	Ridala	H	37.2	62.8	10.2	27.1	11.9	15.2	18.6	16.9	B
4	Asva	H	17.7	82.3	1.7	16.0	27.8	29.0	10.7	8.1	B
5	Tervete	H	10.0	90.0	2.0	8.0	36.1	21.7	14.0	18.0	A
6	Petrašjunaj	H	38.8	61.2	19.4	19.4	19.4	11.1	16.7	11.1	X
Group 2 (0–A.D. 400)											
7	Kivti	O	3.6	96.4	0.5	3.1	50.2	15.6	7.5	22.4	C
8	Batčkininkeliaj	O	62.5	37.5	6.3	56.2	18.8	0.0	12.5	6.2	C
9	Migonis	O	44.0	56.0	12.0	32.0	16.0	24.0	12.0	4.0	B/C
10	Aukštadvaris, I	O	30.0	70.0	9.0	16.6	22.7	18.2	15.2	12.1	A
11	Aukštadvaris, 1	H	42.9	57.1	7.1	35.7	14.2	14.2	14.2	14.2	A
12	Aukštadvaris, 2	H	43.5	56.5	10.4	33.0	15.3	16.1	16.1	8.8	A
13	Nemenčine, 1	H	41.9	58.1	12.4	28.5	21.9	12.4	20.0	3.8	B
14	Migonis	H	40.0	60.0	12.0	28.0	20.0	20.0	16.0	4.0	B/C
15	Batčkininkeliaj	H	75.0	25.0	12.5	62.5	0.0	0.0	12.5	12.5	C
16	Aukštadvaris	O	18.5	81.5	2.3	16.2	28.3	14.4	24.3	13.0	A
17	Asote, II	H	41.7	58.3	8.3	33.3	25.0	8.3	16.6	8.3	A

		Type[a]									Rating[b]
Group 3											
(A.D. 400–800)											
18	Ryuge (Rüüge)	H/O	46.0	54.0	21.2	25.0	15.0	7.4	11.9	19.6	B
19	Kenteskalns	H/O	14.0	86.0	5.0	9.0	41.0	13.5	7.0	23.5	B/C
20	Judonis	O	32.8	67.2	13.9	18.8	12.3	10.7	37.7	3.3	A
21	Ryuge (Rüüge)	H	62.2	37.8	33.2	29.0	12.3	10.4	10.1	12.3	B
22	Kentes Kalns	H	25.7	74.3	15.6	10.1	26.7	19.0	15.9	10.0	B
23	Peēdu	H	60.0	40.0	30.0	30.0	20.0	0.0	0.0	20.0	B
24	Tartu	H	16.9	83.1	10.7	6.2	27.8	23.0	24.0	5.9	B
25	Tervete	H	8.0	92.0	3.6	4.4	33.0	18.3	29.7	6.0	A
26	Dignaja	H	43.9	56.1	22.7	18.2	9.1	15.1	27.3	4.5	A
27	Veliuona	H	29.5	70.5	4.9	24.6	29.5	13.1	21.3	4.9	X
28	Aukštad, 3	H	18.2	81.8	3.9	14.3	24.7	70.2	25.0	9.8	A
29	Dovajnionis	H	15.4	84.6	0.0	15.4	30.7	7.7	23.0	7.7	C
Group 4											
(A.D. 800–1200)											
30	Olinkalns	H	19.6	80.4	10.9	8.7	22.7	22.7	23.1	10.0	A
31	Aizkraule	O	14.6	83.4	14.6	0.0	22.9	18.8	27.0	16.7	B
32	Tervete	O	38.8	61.2	25.2	13.6	14.9	8.7	21.4	10.6	A
33	Dobele	O	44.4	55.6	29.6	14.8	14.8	12.6	16.3	8.1	A
34	Tervete	H	38.8	61.2	25.2	13.6	14.9	8.7	21.4	10.6	A
35	Jersika	H	25.6	74.4	16.0	9.6	5.3	9.6	53.2	3.2	B
36	Mežotne	H	21.5	78.5	9.8	11.7	14.0	11.7	46.5	4.3	A
37	Talsi	H	41.6	58.4	21.8	19.8	13.6	14.4	16.3	10.5	A
38	Nemenčine	H	32.2	67.8	9.9	27.7	23.7	14.6	22.8	5.9	B

[a]H = hillfort; O = open settlement.

[b]A, good; B, average; C, poor; X, unspecified.

157

fragile bones and bones of small animals were preserved; and those with average (B) or poor (C) preservation, where fragile or small bones are rare or absent.

Average values were calculated for each chronological group as a first indication of the ratio of wild to domestic animals (Figure 6.2) and of fur-bearing animals to the rest of the wild fauna (Figure 6.3). However, it was important to counteract the biases in our sample caused by differential preservation conditions and wide variations in values within each chronological group. Therefore, the data were ranked and Man-Whitney and Kruskal-Wallis tests were applied to detect any significant differences between individual chronological groups in terms of (1) wild animal bones as a proportion of all bones, (2) bones of fur game as a proportion of all wild animal bones, and (3) horse bones as a proportion of all domesticates (Table 6.2). (Data on oxen were not available.) To guard against the possibility of any patterns resulting from the different preservation conditions of the sites, a Man-Whitney test was carried out to detect differences in the above-mentioned parameters between the A and B/C preservation groups. However, there were no significant differences in terms of fur game versus game, game versus all bones, or fur game versus all bones between the two groups, showing that preservation conditions do not significantly affect our variables.

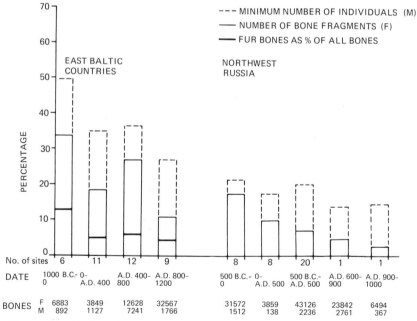

Figure 6.2 Northeast Baltic Iron Age fauna: wild animals expressed as a proportion of all bones. Columns 5–7 are Dyakovo culture; last two columns are (left) Krivitchi and (right) Staraya Ladoga.

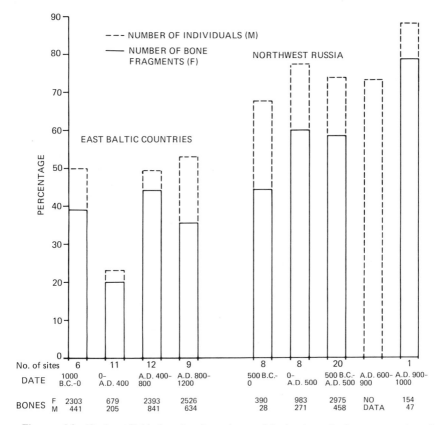

No. of sites	6	11	12	9	8	8	20		1
DATE	1000 B.C.-0	0-A.D. 400	A.D. 400-800	A.D. 800-1200	500 B.C.-0	0-A.D. 500	500 B.C.-A.D. 500	A.D. 600-900	A.D. 900-1000
BONES F	2303	679	2393	2526	390	983	2975	NO	154
M	441	205	841	634	28	271	458	DATA	47

Figure 6.3 Northeast Baltic Iron Age fauna: bones of fur-bearing animals as a proportion of bones of wild animals. Columns 5–7 are Dyakovo culture; last two columns are (left) Krivitchi and (right) Staraya Ladoga.

The results of the tests applied to the chronological groups indicate that, while there is no significant decline in wild resources up to A.D. 800, there is a significant increase in fur game within the category of wild resources. In other words, the continuing high contribution of wild resources to the total sample is maintained by the increasing share of fur game in the wild resources. At the same time, however, the average contribution of fur game to the total bone sample remains unchanged at about 5% (except for Group 1, where a high value of 13% is the result of a single site's anomalous contribution). This apparently paradoxical situation occurs because the mean values mask important variations in individual site values within chronological groups (Figure 6.4). The relative increase in fur game is not produced merely by the decline in game killed for meat. Rather, the increase identifies a type of site that is abundant in remains of fur game but poor in those of other game.

Table 6.2

Values Used in Man–Whitney and Kruskal-Wallis Tests of Faunal Data from Iron Age Sites in the Northeast Baltic Region

Site number[a]	Total number of bones	Bones, domestic species	Bones, wild species	Bones, fur species	Horse bones	Bones, wild species per total bones	Rank	Bones, fur species per total bones	Rank	Bones, fur species per bones, wild species	Rank	Horse bones per bones, domestic species	Rank	Preservation[b]
Group 1 (500 B.C.–0)														
1	537	385	152	45	70	0.283	11	0.084	11	0.296	19	0.182	8	A
2	3969	2272	1697	787	499	0.427	5	0.198	4	0.463	8	0.219	6	A
3	576	409	107	6	44	0.208	18	01.2	34	0.056	36	0.080	22.5	B
4	909	696	213	15	74	0.234	15	01.7	35	0.070	35	0.106	17	B
5	675	612	63	14	121	0.093	28	02.0	33	0.222	25	0.179	9	A
6	277	207	70	22	32	0.252	13	08.0	13	0.314	17	0.154	12	X
Group 2 (0–A.D. 400)														
7	641	618	23	3	144	0.030	38	0.5	37	0.130	32	0.233	4	C
8	35	21	14	1	2	0.480	6	2.9	29	0.071	34	0.095	19	C
9	187	145	42	13	4	0.289	10	7.0	16.5	0.310	18	0.027	36	B/C
10	235	198	37	7	16	0.157	24	3.0	28	0.189	27	0.080	22.5	A
11	110	71	39	9	11	0.354	7	8.2	12	0.230	23	0.155	11	A
12	965	684	281	63	71	0.291	9	6.5	18.5	0.224	24	0.103	18	A
13	454	321	133	21	12	2.293	8	4.6	22	0.158	29	0.037	32	B
14	166	133	33	5	2	0.199	19	3.8	24	0.151	30.5	0.015	37	B/C
15	11	6	5	1	0	0.454	4	9.1	9	0.200	26	0.000	38	C
16	941	872	69	7	95	0.073	33	0.7	16.5	0.101	33	0.109	16	A
17	64	52	12	6	3	0.188	21	9.3	7.5	0.500	7	0.058	30	A

Group	Site[a]													Rank[b]
Group 3 (A.D. 400–800)	18	575	299	276	145	118	0.480	3	25.2	3	0.525	6	0.394	1	B
	19	809	736	73	28	221	0.090	29	03.5	26	0.383	13	0.273	3	B/C
	20	1068	895	173	45	77	0.162	23	04.2	23	0.260	20	0.086	21	A
	21	1425	613	812	432	168	0.570	2	30.3	1	0.532	5	0.274	2	B
	22	2424	2082	342	177	231	0.141	26	07.3	15	0.517	1	0.110	15	B
	23	29	9	20	8	6	0.689	1	27.6	2	0.400	10	0.207	7	B
	24	746	603	143	82	44	0.191	20	11.0	6	0.573	2	0.073	24	B
	25	300	276	24	11	18	0.080	32	03.7	25	0.458	9	0.065	27	A
	26	1049	754	295	98	89	0.281	12	9.3	7.5	0.332	16	0.118	14	A
	27	304	259	45	8	18	0.148	25	2.7	30	0.178	28	1.069	25	X
	28	2842	2644	198	30	168	0.070	34	1.0	36	0.151	30.5	0.064	28	A
	29	57	55	2	0	5	0.035	37	0.0	38	0.000	37	0.091	20	C
Group 4 (A.D. 800–1200)	30	748	686	62	35	71	0.083	31	4.7	21	0.565	3	0.059	29	A
	31	158	150	8	8	21	0.050	36	5.0	20	1.000	0	0.140	13	B
	32	989	760	229	88	133	0.231	16	8.9	10	0.384	12	0.175	10	A
	33	1061	801	260	149	54	0.245	14	14.0	5	0.452	4	0.067	26	A
	34	10005	9350	655	223	284	0.065	35	2.3	31	0.340	14	0.030	34	A
	35	1305	1086	219	85	32	0.168	22	6.5	18.5	0.388	11	0.029	35	B
	36	5152	4700	452	111	193	0.087	30	2.1	32	0.246	22	0.041	31	A
	37	2769	2151	618	206	475	0.223	17	7.4	14	0.333	15	0.221	5	A
	38	380	320	50	13	10	0.131	27	3.4	27	0.260	21	0.031	33	B

[a] Site numbers as in Table 6.1.
[b] A, good; B, average; C, poor; X, unspecified.

The results of the tests and the distribution of ranks within each chronological group suggest that the most significant increases in fur-bearing game took place within Groups 3 and 4 (A.D. 400–1200), while the changes in fur game between Groups 1 and 2 (500 B.C.–A.D. 400) are statistically insignificant (see notes, Table 6.2). Prior to A.D. 400, fur game values reflected the overall contribution of wild remains; they were either high or low, reflecting the ecological conditions and the degree of transition to food production. From about the middle of the first millennium A.D., however, a new pattern emerges: in addition to sites high or low in wild resources, sites are found (almost all of them fortified settlements) where a high contribution of fur game contrasts with an otherwise

---

Notes to Table 6.2. Man-Whitney (MW) and Kruskal-Wallis (KW) test results

1. MW test for difference in representation of bones of fur animals between samples with A and B/C preservation: $U: 158$ (no significant difference can be demonstrated according to level of preservation).

2. MW test for difference in representation of bones of wild animals between samples with A and B/C preservation: $U: 203$ (no significant difference can be demonstrated according to level of preservation).

3. MW and KW tests for difference in proportion of horse bones among sites of different chronological groups: Groups 1/2 versus Groups 3/4: $Z: 0.190$ (no significant difference can be demonstrated in horse bones from Groups 1/2 and 3/4). All four groups: $H: 3.19$ (no significant difference can be demonstrated in horse bones among all four groups).

4. MW and KW tests for difference in proportions of wild animal bone among sites of different chronological groups: all four groups: $H: 3.00$ (no significant differences can be demonstrated in wild animal bone from the four chronological groups). Groups 1/2 versus Groups 3/4: $Z: 1.805 = H_0$ can be rejected at 0.05 level; there is a significant difference in wild animal bone between the bone assemblages dated 500 B.C.–A.D. 400 and those dated A.D. 400–1200. Group 1 versus Groups 2/3/4: $Z: 1.08$ (no significant difference can be demonstrated in wild animal bone between 500 B.C.– 0 and 0–A.D. 1200). Groups 1/2/3 versus Group 4: $Z: 1.805 = H_0$ can be rejected at 0.05 level; there is a significant difference in wild animal bone between the bone assemblages dated 500 B.C.–A.D. 800 and those dated A.D. 800–1200. Group 2 versus Group 3: $U: 55$ (no significant difference can be demonstrated in wild animal bone between assemblages dated 0–A.D. 400 and those dated A.D. 400– 800). Group 3 versus Group 4: $U: 43$ (no significant difference can be demonstrated in wild animal bone between assemblages dated A.D. 400–800 and those dated A.D. 800–1200).

5. MW and KW tests for difference in the representation of bones of fur animals, expressed as a proportion of bones of all wild animals, among sites of different chronological groups. All four groups: $H: 9.39 = H_0$ can be rejected at 0.05 level; there is a significant difference between all four groups. Group 1 versus Groups 2/3/4: $Z: 0.390$ (no significant difference can be demonstrated in fur animals between bone assemblages dated 500 B.C.–0 and those dated 0–A.D. 1200). Groups 1/2 versus Groups 3/4: $Z: 3.20 = H_0$ can be rejected at 0.001 level; there is a significant difference in numbers of fur animals between bone assemblages dated 500 B.C.–A.D. 400 and those dated A.D. 400–1200. Groups 1/2/3 versus Group 4: $Z: 2.21 = H_0$ can be rejected at 0.05 level; there is a significant difference in numbers of fur animals between bone assemblages dated 500 B.C.–A.D. 800 and those dated A.D. 800- 1200. Group 3 versus Group 4: $U: 48$ (no significant difference can be demonstrated in fur animals between bone assemblages dated A.D. 400–800 and those dated A.D. 800–1200).

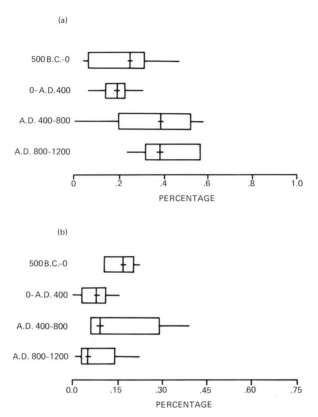

Figure 6.4 Box plots showing the range of variation of wild animal bone in different time periods. (a) fur bones as a proportion of wild animal bones; (b) wild animal bone as a proportion of all bone.

low occurrence of wild food remains (Tables 6.1, 6.2). It is unlikely that this pattern reflects only the ecological potential of the area; rather, it probably represents a concentration on fur for processing and redistribution in what were otherwise farming settlements.

One might ask why, if this was the case, the overall proportion of fur game did not increase. It is possible that fur animals were exploited to their full capacity, in which case any overall increase in exploitation would have resulted in overkill and a rapid decline in the game population. Such a decline did in fact take place in the late medieval period (Paaver 1965). Another feature to consider is the development of the agricultural landscape around more permanent settlements, among which the major fortified sites certainly belonged. Remains of wild fauna decline over time on sites with long periods of habitation, such as Mukukalns

(800 B.C.–A.D. 100) or Aukštadvaris (first to thirteenth centuries A.D.). This phenomenon must have been at least partly a function of the repeated use of the environment surrounding the settlements, leading to the establishment of permanent arable and open landscape—unfavourable conditions for most wild fauna of the region. Yet Paaver (1965) notes that wild faunal remains from fortified settlements are richer than those from open settlements. Thus it seems that fur game, which occurs mostly in the more permanent hillforts and fortified settlements, was brought to these sites from beyond the immediate vicinity of the settlement, indicating either an extended territory or some form of regional exchange.

These developments in the northeast Baltic region are paralleled in neighbouring northern Russia where, in the context of the Dyakovo culture, the proportion of fur game rose from 43% of all wild fauna in the early settlements to 60% in late Dyakovo horizons (Tsalkin 1962). At Staraya Ladoga, an eighth- to tenth-century settlement with definite traces of manufacturing and trading activity, fur game composed 87% of all wild resources (Ravdonikas 1949). The overall contribution of fur bones to the total bone sample remains within the 2–4% level (Figures 6.2, 6.3). (All of the above figures are based on numbers of identifiable fragments, a calculation that tends to produce a bias in favour of larger animals at the expense of smaller ones; hence, domesticated animals are probably overrepresented at the expense of game, and meat game at the expense of fur game, so the actual proportion of fur game is likely to have been even greater.)

More information about the industrial use of food resources can be extracted from the composition of skeletal remains. After taking into account the differential preservation of bones and some variation in the butchering patterns of individual resources, there still seems to emerge an additional pattern of exploitation for several species. Fortified sites and open settlements attached to hillforts contain from three to seven times the number of red deer and elk phalanges than other contemporary sites or the earlier sites of the hunting and gathering period. Metapodials and skull fragments are also more frequent, whereas meat bones occur in the same numbers on all settlements. The most frequent bones are all part of hide- and bone-working processes, implying that fortified and hillfort settlements served as centres of industrial activity where hides (with metapodials, phalanges, and skulls attached) were brought for tanning and bone-working. For example, tanning implements were found at Mukukalns (Graudonis 1967), one of the sites where phalanges occurred in disproportionately large numbers. At Osino, a hillfort in northwest Russia dating to the first millennium B.C., the only fractures found on beaver bones were on the metapodials. All distal ends were broken off, a pattern indicating that beaver was mainly used for its pelt, and that pelts were removed from the carcase in the same way as today (Ermolova 1976).

Taken together, the evidence indicates a gradual replacement of game killed for meat by that killed for fur. The contribution of hunting shifted from providing food to providing materials for manufacture and trade. The subsistence gap left by this change in foraging strategy was filled by a greater reliance on animal husbandry and cereal cultivation. The significant decline of wild fauna among bone samples dating to the period A.D. 800–1200 indicates the final demise of the diet-oriented foraging economy, rather than a decline in the hunting of fur game.

Changes in the composition of domestic fauna do not appear to form a pattern that would transcend local variation, with the possible exception of the horse. In the settlements of the Dyakovo culture (500 B.C.–A.D. 500), horse remains formed 20–35% of the total bone sample, with most horses belonging to young individuals, a pattern typical of stock raised for meat. The average number of horse bones then declined in the second half of the first millennium A.D., and the mortality structure shifted in the later first millennium from a predominance of young to old individuals. At the same time, the skeletal data suggest the development of heavier, larger forms (Graudonis 1967; Tsalkin 1962). In the eastern Baltic, the number of horse remains generally declined through time, although individual variations in the composition of the samples are so large that this decline is not significant statistically if the spread on either side of the mean is taken into consideration. Nevertheless, there does seem to have been a major change in horse husbandry in northeast Europe in the second half of the first millennium, just as there was across much of eastern Europe. Tsalkin (1962) suggests that there was a shift from keeping horses for meat to keeping them for traction, a thesis supported by finds of horse bits and other parts of horse gear in the eastern Baltic and adjacent areas of northern Russia.

PLANT REMAINS

Remains of cereals and other cultivated plants occur on far fewer sites than bones of domesticated animals. Prior to the fifth century A.D., evidence for cultivation in the eastern Baltic consists only of finds of barley from three sites, wheat from two, and beans from a single site. In southern Finland, intermittent evidence for farming can be found in pollen profiles (Zvelebil 1981). From the mid-first millennium A.D., two kinds of wheat (*Triticum aestivum* and *T. spelta*) and two kinds of barley (*Hordeum distichon* and *H. vulgare*) make up most of the samples, with two-row barley occurring most frequently. To this range of cereals can be added isolated finds of oats, millet, legumes, hemp, and flax (Kirianova 1979; Kruglikova 1967; Rasiņš 1959).

Perhaps the most important change in cultivation during the Iron Age was the appearance and rapid increase in the importance of winter rye. In eastern Europe, rye was found in small quantities as a weed of cultivation of spring-sown crops prior to the ninth century A.D. (Kirianova 1979). In the course of the ninth and tenth centuries, rye became the most commonly cultivated cereal. From its association with *Bromus secalinus,* we can conclude that we are dealing with winter-sown rye. Despite claims that rye reached Europe from the Near East (Helbaek 1971), the Russian evidence comes considerably later than evidence from central Europe (Lange 1975), where a winter-sown variety of rye appeared in the sixth century A.D. In Finland, too, analytical evidence of pollen suggests the field cultivation of rye from the fifth century A.D. onwards (Tolonen et al. 1976). It is clear that the arrival of rye, a crop well adapted to the rigours of the northern climate, provided a boost for both arable and swidden systems of cultivation. Rye was adopted as the principal crop of swidden cultivation, and its use in Finland coincided with the expansion of swiddening in the Late Iron Age and medieval periods to more peripheral areas in the north and east (Figure 6.1). At the same time, the winter cultivation of rye forms one element in the three-field system. As such, it represents an intensification of previous systems of cultivation (either swidden or alternate crop and fallow) in which crops were sown at greater intervals.

DISCUSSION

Assessing the contribution of swidden and permanent arable to the iron age economy remains one of the principal problems of the period. As noted previously, early farming in northeast Europe combined both methods. Both were part of the economy at the beginning of the medieval period, with swidden predominating in pioneer locations at the margins of the agricultural zone, such as central Finland, Karelia, and northeast Russia. In more central areas, such as southern Finland, the eastern Baltic, and northwest Russia, there is convincing though indirect evidence of a major shift to permanent farming in the mid-fifth century A.D., including changes in settlement location, the appearance of tools associated with arable, and the adoption of horses for traction (Graudonis 1967; Krasnov 1971; Moora 1953, 1956; Schmiedehelm 1956; Vassar 1956). Yet Laasimer (1964) estimates that in thirteenth-century Estonia, only 4–5% of the land was under permanent cultivation, compared with 20–25% under swidden.

Pollen analysis remains the principal means of distinguishing between the two systems of cultivation. To distinguish swidden reliably, large pollen counts at frequent intervals are needed, indicating a characteristic arboreal regrowth curve, an unmistakable *cerealia* curve, and the presence of NAP (non-arboreal pollen) species that thrive in early but not continuous cultivation (Huttunen 1980; Vuorela 1975, 1976). These requirements make the data from southern Finland, where such conditions exist, more reliable than the Russian evidence. The pollen evidence from southern Finland supports some evidence indicating a major shift to permanent field cultivation in the mid-first millennium A.D., but if Laasimer's figures are correct, permanent farming would have provided no more than half of the total crop yield once the differential period of fallow and the yield are taken into account (Zvelebil 1981). Additional evidence for more intensive land use comes from the extension of settlement to fertile morainic soil on higher ground during the first half of the first millennium A.D. This trend may indicate the extension of permanent field cultivation, since these lighter, more sparsely forested soils are more suitable for tillage than for slash and burn (Vassar 1956). Towards the middle of the first millennium A.D., a change in burial form took place from large communal burials to individual or family graves, perhaps reflecting the development of separate nuclear families from extended patriarchal bands (Moora 1953; Schmiedehelm 1956; Vassar 1956). Such a change would tend to confirm the thesis of a shift away from swidden farming, which traditionally relied on extended families for labour, to permanent cultivation based on nuclear family households.

To summarise, we can trace the development of the iron age economy in northeast Europe through four main stages: (1) (500 B.C.–0) mixed farming and foraging, with bones of domesticated animals forming 50–90% of the total faunal assemblage. Pollen analysis, where available, indicates small-scale and slash and burn farming rather than permanent field cultivation. (2) (0–A.D. 400) the extension of settlement to soils capable of permanent cultivation, coinciding with the appearance of iron agricultural equipment. (3) (A.D. 400–800) a decrease in the use of wild resources for meat; a decline in the number of horses, but an increase in their size and age; the appearance of iron shares for ards; a change in burial customs; an extension of settlement; and a major shift to permanent farming according to the pollen evidence. (4) (A.D. 800–1200) cultivation further intensified by the adoption of rye as the winter-sown crop, and by the introduction of the *sokha*, or forked plough (specially adapted to field cultivation in boreal conditions). A final shift was made to a reliance on domesticates for diet.

Although an increase in food production took place gradually, as foraging declined as the principal means of subsistence, the crucial period of economic intensification seems to have been between approximately A.D. 400 and 800. Exactly the same pattern of development took place in central Europe in the fifth century A.D.: an increase in arable farming, a shift to autumn-sown crops and more intensive soil cultivation, the adoption of iron-bound ploughs, and the use of horses as draught animals for tillage (Lange 1975).

The subsistence remains also indicate the use of animal products and fur animals in ways that suggest specialised bone- and leather-working and trade in furs. The scale of the evidence and its association with fortified settlements suggest that trade and craft production may have been organised beyond the household level. The decisive period in the emergence of these patterns was again between approximately A.D. 400 and 800.

The Development of Settlement Hierarchy, Specialisation, and Trade

The changes observed in subsistence during the first millennium A.D. are matched by an increase in the complexity of settlement patterns, exchange, and social organisation. In considering the causal links between subsistence and socioeconomic development, chronology is of crucial importance, and yet it is still very poorly defined. In the absence of a comprehensive series of radiocarbon dates, the data are summarised within the four typologically defined periods used earlier.

500 B.C.–0

Although there are differences in the size and sedentary nature of settlements, no differences of rank involving settlement organisation can be distinguished prior to the first millennium B.C., when the fortified settlements marking the development towards asymmetry and settlement hierarchy first appeared (Graudonis 1967; Moora 1956; Tretyakov 1963). Fortified villages rather than refuges, these settlements were positioned adjacent to shorelines and other major routes, such as the Daugava river. The presence of exotic materials such as amber or bronze alloy, as well as Scandinavian, East Prussian, Oriental, and Mediterranean imports, indicates a trade in prestige objects and materials, while traces of manufacturing activity in bronze-working, leather manufacture, and bone-working suggest the existence of local industry. There are no traces of local iron metallurgy until the first to second century A.D. in the eastern Baltic and adjacent parts of northwest Russia (Graudonis 1967).

Despite these developments, industrial production remained undifferentiated from food production and was carried out within individual households. Although pieces of bronze alloy, clay moulds, and semi-manufactured products were found at Mukukalns and other Latvian hillforts, no remains of workshops have been uncovered in layers dating to the first millennium B.C. The bronze work consisted of nonfunctional artefacts that would have had prestige rather than economic value, including bronze axes left with projected jets and displaying no traces of use (Graudonis 1967), while the number of imported iron tools was negligible. No structural remains or artefact scatters indicate the existence of special workshops for any industrial activities (Graudonis 1967; Vassar 1956). It would seem that metal objects were made 'to order' to satisfy social needs rather than for use in food production.

Long-distance trade with areas outside the eastern Baltic is thought to have been incidental and limited (Graudonis 1967), indicating a low level of social and economic organisation. At the same time, it is significant that the traces of manufacture and long-distance trade, meagre as they are, occur almost exclusively in fortified settlements. It appears that one function of fortified settlements was to provide a focus for nonsubsistence activity for the surrounding population. Thus it would seem that, while remaining within the household mode of production, early iron age societies also made the first tentative steps towards craft specialisation and the formation of regional centres of exchange during this period.

0–A.D. 400

During the first four centuries A.D., a shift in the function of fortified settlements took place, marked by the more extensive fortification of naturally defencible sites and by the abandonment of others with poor defences. Some authors contend that the fortified sites of this period served primarily as refuges for local dispersed populations (Graudonis 1967; Moora 1953), but this hypothesis is open to doubt because traces of permanent housing, manufacturing activity, and trade have been found on at least some of the settlements (Graudonis 1967; Šnore 1959). The development of local iron metallurgy was an important addition to the existing pattern of manufacture and trade during this period in both the eastern Baltic and southern Finland. Knives and shafthole axes became more common and new types appeared, including agricultural implements such as long, curved reaping knives, sickles, and adzes (Kivikoski 1967; Krasnov 1971; Moora 1953; Salo 1968; Vassar 1956). Local production is attested, albeit in only a few cases, by the presence of iron slag and manufacturing waste (Graudonis 1967; Kivikoski 1967).

A.D. 400–800

Important changes occurred in settlement and manufacturing activity during this period. The overall number of hillforts declined, and those remaining were centrally situated to surrounding dispersed settlements. The overall size of forts declined, and defences were strengthened by larger ditches, banks, and palisades. Structural differentiation developed within the forts, with some houses becoming larger and more elaborate. Industrial activity, previously concentrated within the fortified settlement, shifted to the adjacent open settlement, the 'forburg' (Moora 1953; Schmiedehelm 1959; Štubavs 1959). The concentration of prestige goods within forts and of tools within settlements indicates a clear dichotomy between the social elite and the commoners involved in production

(Stubavs 1959). Manufacturing activity was concentrated in specific areas or associated with separate features such as kiln remains, indicating specialist production. Some sites have even been interpreted as principally manufacturing (rather than food-producing) centres (Mugurevičs 1977; Schmiedehelm 1959; Štubavs 1959). At the settlement surrounding the Kentekalns hillfort, for example, most of the material remains were connected with iron and bronze manufacturing. Štubavs (1959) considers the site to be an incipient trading and manufacturing centre. A similar case can be found at Ryuge in the seventh and eighth centuries A.D. where, apart from blacksmithing, bone-working was especially well developed to a standardised and industrial (rather than household) level of production (Schmiedehelm 1959).

The manufacture of iron tools increased as a part of this general industrial development. Scythes and iron shares for ards were introduced in farming, and iron axes became frequent finds (Krasnov 1971, 1982). From his analysis of early iron tools, Kolchin (1967) places the beginnings of specialised iron metallurgy in the seventh and eighth centuries A.D.

A.D. 800–1200

Although the evidence for long-distance trade, such as the presence of exotic imports, glass beads, and coins, was increasing steadily in the previous period, it was not until the eighth and ninth centuries that the settlement hierarchy was enlarged by the growth of a new type of settlement—the open trading and manufacturing centre (Bulkin et al. 1978). One such site, Staraya Ladoga, has been extensively excavated down to the earliest levels of the settlement (Daushin 1960; Korzukhina 1961; Ravdonikas 1949, 1950). The first village dates from the mid-eighth century A.D. Two of the earliest three layers yielded remains of extensive metal, bone, and amber industries (Davidan 1975, 1976). At the beginning of the tenth century, a planned settlement was laid out on a grid, with the industrial quarter concentrated in one section of the town.

Staraya Ladoga proves beyond doubt the existence of specialised production and of organised trade from about A.D. 750. Based on the spatial patterning of finds and the structural remains, it seems that there were two types of industrial workers, blacksmiths and general craftsmen (Davidan 1976, 1979; Lvova 1967, 1970). The latter were engaged in the production of bronzework, beads, bone artefacts, and amber pendants; their workshops also contained scales and coins, emphasising the connection between craftsmanship and trade. Moreover, at least from the end of the eighth century, a regular trade was going on between the more accessible areas of northeast Europe and Scandinavia, central Europe, the bulgarian Empire on the Volga, and the eastern Mediterranean (Bulkin et al. 1978; Lvova 1967, 1970, 1976). Imports included a wide range of weapons, luxury objects, and bronze ingots for local industry, but no iron ore or tools (except weapons). A range of services and perishable goods may have been offered in return; as the subsistence analysis indicated, furs certainly played an important part in this exchange. Standardised unperforated glass beads, found in the tenth century layers in Staraya Ladoga as well as in other trading settlements in the region, may have served as a standard medium of exchange, reckoned by weight, prior to the introduction of local coinage (Lvova 1970). If so, this would underline the rapid development of organised trade at the end of the first millennium A.D.

The two phases of development at Staraya Ladoga superficially resemble the first two stages in the evolution of gateway communities as described by Hodges (1982b). However, the pattern of exchange at Staraya Ladoga was more complex than in Hodges's model of trading mass-produced prestige goods for local materials and foodstuffs, since four types of industrial and trading activities took place: (1) the manufacture of utilitarian objects intended for local and regional consumption; (2) the import of prestige goods and of raw materials (bronze and amber) for their production, intended for local and regional consumption by the elite; (3) the export of furs and other goods in return for prestige goods; and (4) the transfer of prestige goods among traders using Staraya Ladoga as a trading station along routes extending from the Near East to Scandinavia. It must be stressed that Staraya Ladoga was not an isolated case; a number of open trading centres and fortified settlements developed organisational features similar to those observed at Staraya Ladoga (Bulkin et al. 1978; Mugurevičs 1977; Tarankanova and Terenteva 1959).

From this account it can be seen that the period of major change in subsistence (A.D. 400–800) coincided with the development of craft specialisation and with an increase in settlement hierarchy. Evidence for sustained long-distance trade appeared only at the end of this period and belongs mainly to the ninth and tenth centuries. As far as we can judge, social differentiation was also a comparatively late development. Although status differences are evident in mortuary remains as early as the first millennium B.C., and although these differences increased from the mid-first millennium A.D. (Kivikoski 1967; Moora 1953; Mugurevičs 1977; Vassar 1956), there is no evidence of a social elite administering trade, food production, or industrial activity. In general, craft specialisation and trade preceded the structural expression of social control. At Staraya Ladoga, a trading and manufacturing centre existed for 150 years before the fort was erected and the town laid out. A similar order of events can be observed at Pskov, Velikie Luki, Toropets, Gorodok, Novgorod, Tervete, Jersika, and other settlements in Latvia, Estonia, and possibly Finland (Brivkalne 1959; Bulkin et al. 1978; Kivikoski 1967; Moora 1953).

It is difficult to estimate from this evidence the degree of control exercised by the social elite over the production of foods and crafts. On one hand, both long-distance trade and a large proportion of industrial production dealt in weapons and prestige goods, thus serving to enhance social differences and the power of a social elite. On the other hand, the first effective administrative structures in the area were not erected until the formation of the early Russian state in the ninth and tenth centuries. Thus it seems that although a social elite must have been an accelerating factor in the process of economic change throughout the period in question, it did not organise or control its development.

Conclusions

In considering alternative explanations for the rise of iron age societies in Europe, we are primarily concerned with core–periphery contact, as opposed to internal cultural dynamism, as a catalyst of cultural change. In the core–periphery model (Hodges 1982; Wells 1980), the culture change in the periphery is stimulated by trade or immigration from the more advanced core—in our case Viking Scandinavia to the west or Kievian Russia to the south. Although most of the later events described could be seen as the result of three major penetrations of the area (by Slavs, Vikings, and Crusaders), the cultural development prior to the sixth and seventh centuries A.D. would have remained unaffected. The subsequent establishment of a political administration at the end of the first millennium A.D., on the other hand, has been seen more as a result of social control introduced from outside than of indigenous social evolution (Bulkin et al. 1978). Nevertheless, these developments would affect our area only at the end of the period in question. The same applies to the mobilisation of the periphery by the core area through trade. As we have seen, effective long-distance trade did not develop until the end of the eighth century, while the more sporadic trade of the previous centuries failed to cause a rapid development of social hierarchies and the establishment of political control. The order of events in our area suggests, therefore, that while core–periphery relations helped to establish the political control that marked the end of the Iron Age and the beginning of the medieval period, they did not play a decisive role in the development of iron age society itself.

In the conditions that prevailed during the Early Iron Age in northeast Europe, two processes seem likely as possible forces for generating internal pressure for change: social competition arising from incipient social differentiation, and the need for economic intensification resulting from a decline in existing resources and/or population pressure (Figure 6.5). In northeast Europe a classic case of population stress, arising from a shortage of land for swiddening and necessitating a shift to more intensive farming, could at first appear to provide the original cause for intensification. However, calculations of the swiddening potential in at least one area (southern Finland) suggest that shortages of land for swidden could not have caused the transition to more widespread arable farming (Zvelebil

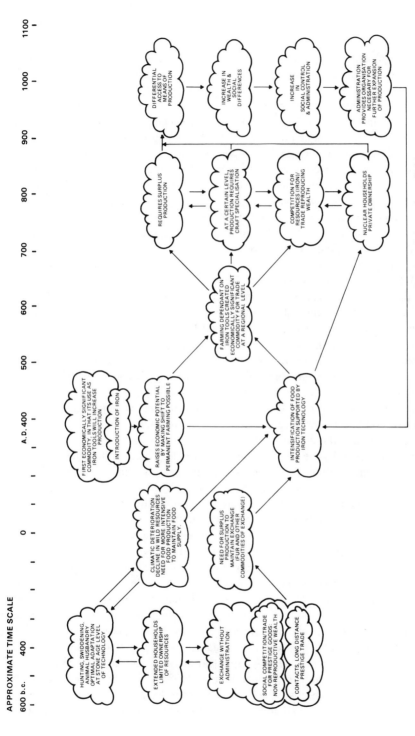

Figure 6.5 A model of Iron Age transformations in northern Russia and the northeast Baltic.

APPROXIMATE TIME SCALE

600 b.c.   400   0   A.D. 400   500   600   700   800   900   1000   1100

FIRST ECONOMICALLY SIGNIFICANT COMMODITY, IN THAT ITS USE AS IRON TOOLS WILL INCREASE PRODUCTION

INTRODUCTION OF IRON

RAISES ECONOMIC POTENTIAL BY MAKING SHIFT TO PERMANENT FARMING POSSIBLE

FARMING DEPENDANT ON IRON TOOLS CREATED ECONOMICALLY SIGNIFICANT COMMODITY FOR TRADE AT A REGIONAL LEVEL

REQUIRES SURPLUS PRODUCTION

AT A CERTAIN LEVEL, PRODUCTION REQUIRES CRAFT SPECIALISATION

COMPETITION FOR RESOURCES (IRON)/ TRADE REPRODUCING WEALTH

NUCLEAR HOUSEHOLDS PRIVATE OWNERSHIP

DIFFERENTIAL ACCESS TO MEANS OF PRODUCTION

INCREASE IN WEALTH & SOCIAL DIFFERENCES

INCREASE IN SOCIAL CONTROL & ADMINISTRATION

ADMINISTRATION PROVIDES ORGANISATION NECESSARY FOR FURTHER EXPANSION OF PRODUCTION

HUNTING, SWIDDENING, ANIMAL HUSBANDRY, OPTIMAL ADAPTATION AT STONE AGE LEVEL OF TECHNOLOGY

EXTENDED HOUSEHOLDS LIMITED OWNERSHIP OF RESOURCES

EXCHANGE WITHOUT ADMINISTRATION

SOCIAL COMPETITION/TRADE FOR PRESTIGE GOODS NON-REPRODUCTIVE WEALTH

CONTACTS, LONG DISTANCE PRESTIGE TRADE

CLIMATIC DETERIORATION DECLINE IN WILD RESOURCES NEED FOR MORE INTENSIVE FOOD PRODUCTION TO MAINTAIN FOOD SUPPLY

NEED FOR SURPLUS PRODUCTION TO MAINTAIN EXCHANGE (FUR AND OTHER COMMODITIES OF EXCHANGE)

INTENSIFICATION OF FOOD PRODUCTION SUPPORTED BY IRON TECHNOLOGY

1981). In other areas as well, the shift to more intensive farming seems to have taken place before the potential for swidden was exhausted (Smith 1977). The case can also be made for social competition creating a demand for surplus production and therefore generating economic intensification. However, the need for increased production could not have been met under the social and technological conditions prevailing at the beginning of the Iron Age.

Similarly, the increase in food production that was essential for the development of iron age society could not have taken place under the land-extensive system of farming augmented by foraging. This system was based on a risk-minimising, low-productivity strategy operating under ecological, economic, and social constraints that precluded economic intensification. This situation was changed by the introduction of iron metallurgy (Figure 6.5). The introduction of iron tools in agriculture made possible deeper ploughing and more effective harvesting technology (Aberg and Bowen 1960; Hansen 1969; Pleiner 1978; Smith 1959; for opposite view, see Reynolds 1979). This, in turn, increased the productivity of permanent agriculture in comparison with other modes of subsistence. Deeper ploughing also made possible the more widespread cultivation of oats and rye instead of millet, wheat, and barley (Balassa 1975), thus directly encouraging the cultivation of more reliable crops and the development of the three-field system. Moreover, the ploughing of a wider range of more fertile but heavier soils became possible with iron tools. Consequently, the previous ecological balance was altered and the productive potential of the environment increased, rendering permanent farming more productive, more competitive in relation to other subsistence activities, and more widely applicable.

Our evidence, though incomplete, suggests that these developments in subsistence, facilitated by the adoption of iron technology, set off the other social and economic changes that characterised iron age society: craft specialisation, surplus production, and the creation of regional markets. Workshops and specialised production (as opposed to mere traces of manufacture in general purpose structures) appear in the second half of the first millennium A.D.; from the ninth century onwards, the existence of both general and specialised blacksmiths can be postulated (Kolchin 1967). As we can see at Staraya Ladoga, craft specialists developed in other industries during this period. The specialised production of agricultural implements and other tools for daily use required the creation of a food surplus and the development of a regional system of trading. Although surplus production cannot be documented unequivocally in the archaeological record, there are clear traces of economic intensification and of the development of exchange patterns other than long-distance trade. From the middle of the first millennium A.D., the existence of regional markets can be postulated from the specialised manufacture of utilitarian objects, and later from the widespread distribution of glass beads, which are assumed to have served as local currency. Regional markets were probably also used to collect furs and to pass on goods in return. Within this framework, the relative contribution of long-distance trade and regional markets to the evolution of iron age social and economic organisation remains one of the most pressing problems of iron age studies.

Iron was the first metal technology with practical applications and a locally occurring supply of raw material to benefit the population at large. Through feedback, its use meant a constantly increasing need for surplus production (Figure 6.5). With its introduction, competition for prestige goods (which were incapable of reproducing wealth) was transformed into economic competition for technological resources. It was probably this transformation in technology and subsistence, rather than the core–periphery relations catering for elite competition, that in the long run generated the establishment of social hierarchy and political control in this part of Europe.

Acknowledgements

I would like to thank Nicholas Fieller (Department of Probability and Statistics, Sheffield University) for processing the statistical analysis of the faunal data, and for his general advice; and also Graeme Barker and John Collis (Department of Archaeology and Prehistory, Sheffield University) for commenting on earlier drafts of this chapter.

References

Aberg, F. A., and H. C. Bowen
    1960 Ploughing experiments with a reconstructed Donneruplund ard. *Antiquity* 34:144–147.
Balassa, I.
    1975 The earliest ploughshare in central Europe. *Tools and Tillage* II(4):242–254.
Bender, B.
    1978 Gatherer–hunter to farmer: a social perspective. *World Archaeology* 10:204–222.
Bergelund, B.
    1969 Vegetation and human influence in south Scandinavia. *Oikos,* Suppl. 12.
Boserup, E.
    1965 *Conditions of agricultural growth.* Allen and Unwin, London.
Brivkalne, E. P.
    1959 Gorodishche Tervete i ego istoricheskoe znachenie. In *Voprosy Etnicheskoi Istorii Narodov Pribaltiki,* edited by S. A. Tarakanova and L. N. Terentseva, pp. 254–274. Akademia Nauk, Moscow.
Bulkin, V. A., I. V. Dobov, and G. C. Lebedev
    1978 *Arkheologicheskiye Pamyatniki Drevnei Rusi 9–11 Vekhov.* Leningrad University.
Champion, T.
    1982 Fortification, ranking and subsistence. In *Ranking, resource and exchange,* edited by C. Renfrew and S. Shennan, pp. 61–66. Cambridge University Press, Cambridge, England.
Clark, J. G. D.
    1953 Archaeological theories and interpretations: Old World. In *Anthropology today,* edited by A. Kroeber, pp. 343–350. Chicago University Press.

176   Marek Zvelebil

Clark, J. G. D.
    1957 *Archaeology and society* (rev. ed.). Cambridge University Press, Cambridge, England.
Clark, J. G. D.
    1966 The invasion hypothesis in British archaeology. *Antiquity* 40:172-189.
Clark, J. G. D.
    1975 *The earlier stone age settlement of Scandinavia.* Cambridge University Press, Cambridge, England.
Clarke, D. L.
    1972 A provisional model of an iron age society and its settlement system. In *Models in archaeology,* edited by D. L. Clarke, pp. 801-871. Methuen, London.
Collis, J. R.
    1977 An approach to the Iron Age. In *The Iron Age in Britain: a review,* edited by J. R. Collis, pp. 1-8. Sheffield University, Department of Prehistory and Archaeology.
Collis, J. R.
    1978 The European Iron Age. *Current Archaeology* 61:51-54.
Collis, J. R.
    1984 *The Iron Age in Europe: a new perspective.* Batsford, London.
Cunliffe, B.
    1978 *Iron age communities in Britain.* Routledge and Kegan Paul, London.
Dauskin, K. D.
    1960 Razkopki v Staroi Ladoge. *Kratkie Soobshcheniya Instituta Arkheologii* 81:72-76.
Davidan, O.
    1975 Stratigrafiya nizhnego sloya staroladozhskogo gorodischcha: voprosy datirovkhi. *Arkheologicheskii Sbornik* 17:101-118.
Davidan, O.
    1976 K voprosu ob organizatsii kostoreznecovo remesla v drevnei Ladoge, *Arkheologicheskii Sbornik* 18:101-105.
Davidan, O.
    1979 Bronzoliteinoe delo v Staroi Ladoge. *Arkheologicheskii Sbornik* 21:59-61.
Dolukhanov, P.
    1979 *Ecology and economy in neolithic eastern Europe.* Duckworth, London.
Dorosenko, V. V.
    1959 Selskoe khozaistvo feodalnoi Liflandii v 13-17 vekakh. *Materialy i Issledovaniya Instituta Selskogo Khozaistva USSR* 3:41.
Ermolova, N. M.
    1976 Ostatki mlekopitayushchikh s drevnego gorodischa Osino. *Sovetskaya Arkheologiya* 3:217-227.
Frankenstein, S., and M. J. Rowlands
    1978 The internal structure and regional context of early iron age society in southwest Germany. *Bulletin of the Institute of Archaeology of London* 15:73-112.
Graudonis, I.
    1967 *Latvia v epokhu pozdnei bronzy i rannego zheleza.* Zinatne, Riga.
Green, S.
    1979 The agricultural colonization of temperate forest habitats: an ecological model. In *The frontier: comparative studies* (Vol. 2), edited by W. Savage and S. Thompson, pp. 69-104. University of Oklahoma Press, Tulsa.
Hansen, H. O.
    1969 Experimental ploughing with a Dostrup and replica. *Tools and Tillage* I(2):67-92.
Helbaek, H.
    1971 The origin and migration of rye: a palaeoethnobotanical study. In *Plant life of southwest Asia,* edited by P. H. David, pp. 265-278.

Higgs, E. S., and C. Vita-Finzi
1972 Prehistoric economies: a territorial approach. In *Papers in economic prehistory*, edited by E. S. Higgs, pp. 27–36. Cambridge University Press, Cambridge, England.
Hodder, I.
1982 *Symbols in action*. Cambridge University Press, Cambridge, England.
Hodges, R.
1982a *Dark age economics*. Duckworth, London.
Hodges, R.
1982b The evolution of gateway communities: their socioeconomic implications. In *Ranking, resource and exchange*, edited by C. Renfrew and S. Shennan, pp. 117–123. Cambridge University Press, Cambridge, England.
Huttunen, P.
1980 Early land use, especially the slash and burn cultivation in the commune of Lammi, southern Finland, interpreted mainly using pollen and charcoal analysis. *Acta Botanica Fennica* 113:1–45.
Jaanits, L.
1959 *Poselenie epokhi neolita i rannego metala v priuste reky Emaigi*. Akademia Nauk, Tallinn.
Jochim, M.
1976 *Hunter-gatherer subsistence and settlement: a predictive model*. Academic Press, New York.
Jutikkala, E.
1949 *Suomen Historian Kartasto*. Helsinki.
Jutikkala, E.
1955 The great Finnish famine in 1696–97. *Scandinavian Economic History Review 3:48–55*.
Kirianova, H. A.
1979 O sostave zemledelcheskikh kultur Drevnei Rusi X-XV vekhov. *Sovetskaya Arkheologiya* 46(4):72–84.
Kivikoski, E.
1967 *Finland*. Thames and Hudson, London.
Kolchin, B. A.
1967 Metallurgy and metalworking in ancient Russia. *Materialy I Issledovaniya Po Arkheologii SSSR* 32.
Koropotkin, V. V.
1967 *Ekonomiticheskiye svyazy vostochnoi Evropy v.1 tysichialetiya nashey epokhi*. Akademia Nauk, Moscow.
Korzukhina, G. F.
1961 O vremeni poyavleniya ukreplennogo poseleniya v Ladoge. *Sovetskaya Arkheologiya* 28(3):76–84.
Krasnov, Y. A.
1971 Rannee Zemledelie i zhivotovodstvo v lesnoi polose vostochnoi Evropy. *MIA* 174:3–165.
Krasnov, Y. A.
1982 Drevnie i srednevekhkovye rala vostochnoi Evropy. *Sovetskaya Arkheologiya* 49(3):63–79.
Kruglikova, I. T.
1967 *Voznikovenie i Razvitie Zemledeliya*. Akademia Nauk, Moscow.
Kruglikova, I. T.
1973 Zheleznyi vek vostochnoi Evropy. *Kratkie soobscheniye o dokladakh i polevykh issledovaniakh* 128:23–43.
Laasimer, L.
1964 *Eesti NSV taimkate*. Unpublished Ph.D. dissertation, Tallin.

Lange, E.
1975 The development of agriculture during the first millennium A.D. *Geologiska Foreningens i Stockholm Forhandlingar* 97:115–124.
Lvova, Z. A.
1967 Steklyannye busy Staroi Ladogi (Part 1). *Arkheologicheskii Sbornik* 9:64–95.
Lvova, Z. A.
1970 Steklyannye busy Staroi Ladogi (Part 2). *Arkheologicheskii Sbornik* 12:89–111.
Lvova, Z. A.
1976 K Voprosu o prichinakh proniknoveniya bus X - nachala XI veka. *Arkheologischeskii Sbornik* 15:106–109.
Maltby, J. M.
1979 *Faunal studies on urban sites: the animal bones from Exeter 1971–1975.* Sheffield University, Department of Prehistory and Archaeology, Exeter Archaeological Reports 2.
Melander, K. R., and G. Melander
1924 Katovuosista Suomessa. *Oma Maa* 5:350–359.
Moberg, C. A.
1966 Spread of agriculture in the north European periphery. *Science* 152:315–319.
Moora, H.
1953 Voznikovenniye klassovogo obshchestva v Pribaltike. *Sovetskaya Archaeologiya* 17:105–133.
Moora, H.
1956 Voprosy slozheniya estonskogo naroda i nekotorykh sosednikh narodov v svete dannykh arkheologii. In *Voprosy Etnicheskoi Istorii Estonskogo Naroda,* edited by H. Moora, pp. 49–140. Akademia Nauk, Tallin.
Moora, H.
1960 Voprosy o istoriko-kuturnykh podoblastyakh v raionakh Pribaltiki. *Sovetskaya Ethnografiya* 3:21–51.
Moore, J.
1981 The effects of information networks in hunter–gatherer societies. In *Hunter–gatherer foraging strategies,* edited by B. Winterhalder and E. A. Smith, pp. 194–217. Chicago University Press.
Mugurevičs, E.
1977 *Olinkalna un Lokstenes Pilsnovadi.* Zinatne, Riga.
Odner, K.
1972 Ethnohistoric and ecological settings for economic and social models of an iron age society. In *Models in archaeology,* edited by D. L. Clarke, pp. 623–652. Methuen, London.
Paaver, K.
1965 *Formirovanie Teriofaunyi i Izmenchivost Mlekopytayushchikh Pribaltiki v Golotsene.* Tartu.
Peebles, C., and S. Kus
1977 Some archaeological correlates of ranked societies. *American Antiquity* 42:421–448.
Pleiner, R.
1978 *Pravěké Dějiny Čech.* Academia, Prague.
Rasinš, A. P.
1959 Kulturnye i sorniye rasteniya v materialakh arkheologicheskikh raskopok na teritorii Latvii. In *Voprosy Etnicheskoi Istorii Narodov Pribaltiki,* edited by S. A. Tarakanova and N. L. Terenteva, pp. 316–340. Akademia Nauk, Moscow.
Ravdonikas, V. I.
1949 Staraya Ladoga (Part 1). *Sovetskaya Arkheologiya* 11:5–54.
Ravdonikas, V. I.
1950 Staraya Ladoga (Part II). *Sovetskaya Arkheologiya* 12:8–40.

Renfrew, C.
1975 Trade as action at a distance. In *Ancient civilizations and trade,* edited by J. Sabloff and C. C. Lamberg-Karlovsky, pp. 3–59. University of New Mexico Press, Albuquerque.
Renfrew, C.
1977 Alternative models for exchange and spatial distribution. In *Exchange systems in prehistory,* edited by T. Earle and J. E. Ericson, pp. 71–90. Academic Press, New York.
Renfrew, C., and S. Shennan (editors)
1982 *Ranking, resource and exchange.* Cambridge University Press, Cambridge, England.
Reynolds, P. J.
1979 *Iron age farm: the Butser experiment.* British Museum, London.
Rowley-Conwy, P.
1981 Slash and burn in the temperate European Neolithic. In *Farming practice in British prehistory,* edited by P. Mercer, pp. 85–96. Edinburgh University Press.
Sahlins, M.
1972 *Stone age economics.* Aldine, Chicago.
Salo, U.
1968 Die frührömische Zeit in Finnland. *Finska Fornminnesforeningens Tidskrift* 67:1–250.
Salo, U., and P. Lahtiperä
1970 *Metallikautinen Asutus Kokemäenjoen Suussa.* Satakunnan Museon Kannatusyhdistys, Pori.
Schmiedehelm, M. K.
1956 O plemenakh severo-vostochnoi Estonii vo vtoroi polovine 1. tysyacheletiya do nashei epokhi i pervoi polovine 1. tysyacheletiya n.e. In *Voprosy Etnicheskoi Istorii Estonskogo Naroda,* edited by H. Moora, pp. 172–186. Akademia Nauk, Tallin.
Schmiedehelm, M. K.
1959 Gorodishche Ryuge v yugo-vostochnoi Estonii, In *Voprosy Etnicheskoi Istorii Narodov Pribaltiki,* edited by S. A. Tarakanova and L. N. Terenteva, pp. 154–185. Akademia Nauk, Moscow.
Sheldon, R. C.
1952 *Socio-Economic development in a Karelian village.* Unpublished Ph.D. dissertation, Harvard University, Department of Anthropology.
Smith, C.
1976 *Regional analysis.* Academic Press, New York.
Smith, R. E. F.
1959 *The origins of farming in Russia.* Mouton, Paris.
Smith, R. E. F.
1977 *Peasant farming in Muscovy.* Cambridge University Press, Cambridge, England.
Šnore, E.
1959 Gorodishcha Drevnykh Latgalov. In *Voprosy Etnicheskoi Istorii Narodov Pribaltiki,* edited by S. A. Tarakanova and L. N. Terenteva, pp. 222–230. Akademia Nauk, Moscow.
Soininen, A. M.
1974 Vanha Maatalouteme. *Historiallisia Tutkimuksia* 96:1–459.
Stålfelt, M. G.
1972 *Plant ecology* (second ed.). Longmans Green, London.
Štubavs, A. J.
1959 Raskopki Gorodischa Kentekalns v 1954–1956. In *Voprosy Etnicheskoi Istorii Narodov Pribaltiki,* edited by S. A. Tarakanova and L. N. Terenteva, pp. 186–213. Akademia Nauk, Moscow.
Tarankanova, S. A., and L. N. Terenteva (editors)
1959 *Voprosy Etnicheskoi Istorii Narodov Pribaltiki.* Akademia Nauk, Moscow.

Tegengren, H.
    1965 Hunters and Amazons: seasonal migrations in older hunting and fishing communities. In *Hunting and fishing,* edited by H. Hvarfner, pp. 427–492. Norrbottens Museum, Luleå.
Teräsvuori, K.
    1928 The early settlement and agriculture in Savo. *Acta Agraria Fennica* 18(1):20–30.
Tolonen, K., A. Siiriäinen, and A. Hirviluoto
    1976 Iron age cultivation in southwest Finland. *Finskt Museum* 83:5–66.
Tretyakov, P. N.
    1932 Podsechnoye zemledelyie v vostochnoi Evrope. *Izvestiya Gosudarstvennyi Akademii Istorii Materyalnoi Kultury* 14(1):1–31.
Tretyakov, P. N.
    1963 Drevnie Gorodishcha Smolenshchiny. In *Drevnie Gorodishcha Smolenshchiny,* edited by E. A. Smiot and P. N. Tretyakov. Leningrad.
Tsalkin, V. I.
    1962 Zhivotnovodstvo i okhota v lesnoi polose vostochnoi Evropy v rannem zheleznom veke. *Materialy i issledovaniya po arkheologii SSSR* 107:1–79.
Vassar, A. K.
    1956 K izucheniu plemen 1-4 vekhov v zapadnoi i yugozapadnoi Estonii. In *Voprosy Etnicheskoi Istorii Estonskogo Naroda,* edited by H. Moora, pp. 187–217. Akademia Nauk, Tallin.
Vilkuna, K.
    1968 Narodnaya kultura Finlandii, *Sovetskaya Ethnografiya* 3:27–36.
Vuorela, I.
    1975 Pollen analyses as a means of tracing settlement history in southwest Finland. *Acta Botanica Fennica* 104:1–4.
Vuorela, I.
    1976 An instance of slash and burn cultivation in southern Finland investigated by pollen analysis of a mineral soil. *Memoranda Societatis pro Fauna et Flora Fennica* 52:29–45.
Welinder, S.
    1975 Prehistoric agriculture in eastern middle Sweden. *Acta Archaeologica Lundensia* 4.
Wells, P. S.
    1980 *Culture contact and culture change.* Cambridge University Press, Cambridge, England.
Wilkinson, R. G.
    1973 *Poverty and progress.* Methuen, London.
Zvelebil, M.
    1978 Subsistence and settlement in the northeastern Baltic. In *The early postglacial settlement of northern Europe,* edited by P. Mellars, pp. 204–241. Duckworth, London.
Zvelebil, M.
    1980 Northern Eurasia in the Holocene. In *Cambridge Encyclopaedia of Archaeology,* edited by A. Sherratt, pp. 320–324. Cambridge University Press, Cambridge, England.
Zvelebil, M.
    1981 *From forager to farmer in the boreal zone: reconstructing economic patterns through catchment analysis in prehistoric Finland.* British Archaeological Reports, International Series 115, Oxford, England.
Zvelebil, M., and P. Rowley-Conwy
    1984 The transition to farming in northern Europe: a hunter–gatherer perspective. *Norwegian Archaeological Review* 17(2):104–127.

7

Regional Survey and Settlement Trends: Studies from Prehistoric France

NIGEL MILLS

Introduction

It is often assumed that the differences between simple and complex agricultural societies are so radical as to prevent either useful comparisons between them or the identification of similar processes operating over the long term. One result is the view that subsistence analysis has little to offer studies of complex societies, leading to a failure to provide adequate analysis of such societies by overemphasising the uniqueness of their economic and social institutions without regard to processes of population–subsistence–environment interaction at the community level.

While rejecting a narrow determinist approach, it is argued here that human activities and development tend to be regionally circumscribed. The environment, through climate and variations in the range, quality, quantity, and availability of subsistence and raw material resources, imposes a series of constraints on settlement and societal development at a regional scale. These constraints are of great interest when studying long-term trends, beyond the level of simply stating what range of foods and other resources is likely to have been exploited.

The nature of these constraints and their contrasts across different areas may be assessed by considering the regional structure of subsistence and other resources, as well as their likely influence on the long-term dynamics of agricultural settlement. Particular emphasis is placed on the imbalances in resource distribution across different parts of a region, and on the ways in which these imbalances may affect societal development. By breaking a region down into component zones that offer contrasts in subsistence and raw material potential, we can assess how these zones may have been linked and used at different periods.

A simple example might start with the distinction between preferred and marginal arable land, defined according to local circumstances, and consider changes in settlement distribution and exploitation patterns between these zones over time. Recurring patterns might be found that would be of great interest in analysing long-term trends in societal development. Other categories can also be envisaged, including the cyclical drainage of marshland or the periodic cultivation of hillsides for vine and olive production (Mills 1981; Ward-Perkins 1981).

A key assumption in such an approach is that it is possible to isolate preferred areas within a given region in which agricultural settlement might normally be expected to concentrate. The fact that other areas are exploited or settled at different periods, or that the preferred area is abandoned, shows that particular economic, sociopolitical, demographic, or environmental changes are taking place. The nature of these changes is indicated by the type of exploitation in each area and the uses to which the area can be put. The more restricted the resource potential of a given zone, the better it will serve as an indicator of socioeconomic development.

Several points should be emphasised in order to clarify various aspects of this approach. First, it is not seen as an end in itself but as a means of designing research and providing a satisfactory basis for considering other aspects of societal development. In the studies that follow, existing archaeological data are considered against the environmental and historical background of specific regions. Anomalies can thus be distinguished between the existing distribution of prehistoric agricultural settlements and that of the historical period. These anomalies might be due to differences in subsistence systems and technology, environmental change, or sample bias; therefore, these factors are assessed through archaeological and environmental studies.

Second, our approach is essentially concerned with decision-making processes at the community level. Studies of agricultural communities in the Mediterranean and temperate Europe during the historical period (Bloch 1952; Braudel 1976; Chisholm 1968; Delano-Smith 1979; Duby and Whallon 1975; Mendras 1976; Slicher van Bath 1963) have noted a close interaction between population and food resources. Communities are often characterised by the relationship they have managed to establish with the particular structures and conditions of the local agricultural environment (Mendras 1976:17). Similarly, the distribution of settlement is largely determined by the available subsistence resources, population density, and the agricultural system, while the specific locations of settlements are constrained by basic subsistence needs: water, arable land, pasture, fuel, and building materials (Chisholm 1968:102). The agricultural system itself is usually organised according to four basic variables: technical needs (to maintain soil fertility, hence a fallowing or rotational system and methods of working the land); social needs (primarily to feed and clothe the domestic group); technological constraints (the available tools); and the natural potential of the area (Mendras 1976:33–34).

Of course, the community exists in a broader context of social and economic relations operating at two levels. The community functions primarily as an independent social and subsistence unit, and on one level it interacts as such with other similar communities. The nature of this interaction is geared towards the autonomous functioning of the individual community and is concerned with a variety of social (particularly marital) and economic relationships.

The second level of relations involves the degree to which external society impinges on the life of the group, acting as an additional variable affecting the community but not usually controlling it directly. Conditions imposed on the community by higher level social and economic institutions, and by environmental and other variables, must make sense at the community level in terms of the long-term survival of the community as a subsistence system.

Studies of prehistoric subsistence indicate considerable complexity amongst early agricultural communities that may be compared with aspects of agricultural systems in later periods: for example, the positioning of sites subject to available water, pasture, and the varying quality of arable land; crop rotation and sophisticated crop-processing activities; and complex systems of livestock husbandry. It is often supposed that the available technology would have been a critical limiting factor for early agriculturalists in Europe, and that a simple tool kit would have prevented the exploitation of soil types that were widely used later on in historical times. The latter assumption is questionable, however, since most peasant agriculturalists during the historical period were also dependent on an extremely limited range of simple implements, mainly of wood.

Particular importance is frequently attached to the introduction of the ard and plough and the effects these implements may have had on crop yields by increasing the variety of soils that could be cultivated. The ard is primarily a labour-saving device that merely scratches the surface of the soil rather than penetrating and turning it (as the plough does). Nevertheless, Sherratt (1980, 1981) argues that early agriculture may have been based on wet farming techniques using high-yielding but labour-intensive alluvial soils, and that in temperate Europe the introduction of the ard led to a major shift in settlement that allowed the extensive but lower-yielding and relatively more labour-demanding soils of the drier interfluves to be cultivated. (This model is not applicable to the Mediterranean case study presented in this chapter, since the difference between the marginal and preferred arable areas lies in the availability of suitable soils rather than in contrasts in type and natural productivity.) Sherratt's hypothesis may be applicable to parts of temperate Europe, but the argument that the appearance of the ard would have had little effect in extending or changing the settled and cultivated area is equally possible. Both hypotheses should be considered according to local conditions and data.

Unless there is firm evidence to the contrary, it seems reasonable to postulate that many prehistoric agricultural communities in Europe were subjected to similar constraints and responded with broadly similar subsistence strategies to those of the historical period. This does not imply, of course, that the social and economic structures were everywhere the same, regardless of time or place. It is nonetheless true that the environment imposes a set of contraints that delimit areas that can be satisfactorily cultivated under cereals, exploited by different animals, or that require particular techniques and organisational or labour inputs. At one level of analysis, these contraints result in broadly similar patterns of settlement through time that may underlie other processes of societal development. At another level, these constraints can be overcome, particularly with increased societal complexity making more options available and imposing new constraints on production.

Two case studies are presented below that illustrate our regional approach and its interest for considering long-term developments in social and economic organisation. The first study concerns settlement and economy in the Neolithic of southeast France, where the Mediterranean environment produces sharp and easily discernible contrasts in agricultural potential between adjacent ecological zones. The second study concerns iron age settlement in the Auvergne, central France, where the study of regional changes in settlement patterns through time, and the use of different ecological zones, assists our understanding of the development of complex societies.

Settlement and Population in the Southern French Neolithic

General Background

The study area is in lower eastern Languedoc around Montpellier and Nimes (Figure 7.1). This area consists of two main ecological zones—the coastal plain and the Garrigues—that offer sharply contrasted potentials for agricultural settlement and land use. The coastal plain is formed of soft marl and clay-rich rocks, covered in places by calcareous gravels and fringed by coastal lagoons. The plain slopes gently from sea level up to 50 m and is backed by limestone plateaus (the Garrigues) at an average height of 200–250 m. The area has a Mediterranean climate, with warm, dry summers and tepid winters; rainfall distribution is markedly seasonal, with peaks in spring and autumn.

The coastal plain has been the main settled and cultivated zone since Roman times, and cereals, particularly wheat, have been the principal subsistence crop

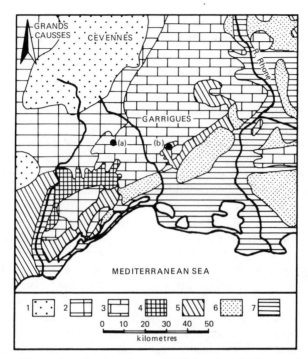

Figure 7.1   The southern French study area. (a) Viols-le-Fort; (b) Vaunage basin. Simplified geology: 1, crystalline massifs; 2, hard (Jurassic) limestones; 3, marly (Cretaceous) limestones; 4, mixtures of marly limestones, sands, and clays (Eocene); 5, sand and clay-rich rocks (Cretaceous, Miocene, Pliocene) and colluvium (Quaternary); 6, gravel terraces (Pliocene, Quaternary); 7, fine alluvium (Holocene).

(Leroy-Ladurie 1966). The Garrigues is a marginal arable area compared with the coastal plain. Soils suitable for cultivation are scarce and restricted to small depressions, while most of the plateau surface is covered by thin soils and scrub. During phases of population growth in historical times, the settled area expanded to include the marginal soils of the Garrigues, while the reverse occurred during intervening phases when population declined on a regional scale and the settled area retracted towards the coastal plain (Leroy-Ladurie 1966).

This simple picture of historical settlement at the subsistence level may be used as a model with which to make predictions concerning the development of prehistoric agricultural settlement and land use in the area. First, settlements based on cereal agriculture are likely to have concentrated initially over the coastal plain. If the population in this area grew to such a level as to put pressure on the available arable area, we might expect to see an expansion of settlement onto adjacent marginal land on the Garrigues. Alternatively, other resources such as sheep and goat may have been exploited to make up for the shortfall in cereal production, either directly or through the exchange of their produce. Since sheep and goats would then have competed with cereals for the allocation of land, such a development ought to be reflected in evidence for the increased use of rough grazing on the Garrigues without major permanent settlement.

ARCHAEOLOGICAL BACKGROUND AND RESEARCH DESIGN

These predictions are at variance with current data and interpretations of the development of neolithic settlement and economy. Agriculture appears to have been firmly established as the subsistence base by the fourth millennium b.c., with the advent of the middle neolithic Chasseen culture in approximately 3800 b.c. (Courtin 1977; Courtin and Erroux 1974; Erroux 1976; Guilaine 1977; Mills 1980, 1983; Phillips 1982; Poulain 1976). Most of the open air sites of this period are located over the extensive arable soils of the coastal plain, but these sites are rare and none has been adequately excavated. Final neolithic (Ferrieres culture, approximately 2600–2200 b.c.) open air sites are even scarcer over the coastal plain, but several settlements with dry-stone walled longhouses occur on the southern margins of the Garrigues at this period, and some dolmen (megalithic tomb) and numerous cave sites in the interior of the Garrigues have produced Ferrieres assemblages. The anomaly is complete for the Chalcolithic (Fontbouisse culture, approximately 2200–1800 b.c.), when numerous stone 'villages' appear over the whole area of the Garrigues but settlement evidence from the coastal plain is still rare. These stone settlements consist of groups of longhouses (Bailloud, 1973; Canet and Roudil, 1978; Gasco, 1976; Gutherz, 1975) and are usually located adjacent to small areas of cultivable soil, similar to the distribution of historical villages and farms.

These data have traditionally been interpreted in terms of environmental change, shifts in subsistence strategy, and cultural choice. It has been argued that the present thin soils and scrub that cover much of the Garrigues resulted from the long-term degradation of the agricultural environment by man (Braun-Blanquet 1936; Duchaufour 1970; Dugrand 1964; Emberger 1930; Flahault 1937; Kuhnholtz-Lordat 1945). Prior to man's intervention and resultant forest clearance and soil erosion, it is said, the Garrigues provided a much more favourable agricultural environment (Figure 7.2); indeed, the plateau soils were particularly attractive for settlement, since they were more easily tilled with the simple agricultural implements available than were the deeper, more humid soils of the plain (Delano-Smith 1972). It has also been suggested that there was a shift towards a pastoral, mobile economy in the Final Neolithic, as indicated by the numerous caves and dolmen on the Garrigues with scarce evidence for permanent settlement. Subsequently, the Fontbouisse economy was based on mixed agriculture, with cereals as a critical component of the subsistence strategy (Guilaine 1976).

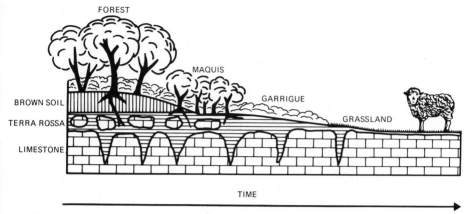

Figure 7.2 The traditional model of soil erosion and environmental degradation on the Garrigues.

There are several problems with these theories, the most obvious being that archaeological data have rarely been collected and assessed at a regional scale using research strategies aimed at obtaining samples representative of their variability in space and time. The present sample contains biases that may have led to false interpretations. Thus the small groups of middle neolithic sites clearly reflect the work of local researchers, while the numerous sites known from the Garrigues may simply reflect the high priority given to this zone by previous workers. Similarly, sites on the coastal plain are likely to be poorly preserved, since known remains consist of easily eroded structures such as pits and postholes, in contrast to the well-preserved stone structures known from the Garrigues. Furthermore, there is no firm evidence for anthropogenic degradation of the Garrigues environment to the degree usually supposed; the present scrub vegetation and thin soils have probably existed at least since the Late Quaternary (Couteaux 1974).

Research was therefore designed to assess these anomalies at a regional scale through case studies of environment and settlement distribution in representative sections of the coastal plain and the Garrigues. These studies were based on geomorphological research and systematic surface surveys.

FIELDWORK RESULTS

Two main conclusions were drawn from the geomorphological studies and are summarised here (for fuller discussion of the research, see D'Anna and Mills 1981; Mills 1980, 1983, in press a and b). The first conclusion was that the nature of soils and vegetation over the Garrigues has altered little during the

Later Holocene and that the area would have offered broadly similar potential for early agriculturalists as it does today.

The traditional model for the long-term degradation of the Garrigues environment is based largely on the hypothesis that *terra rossa* paleosols were once extensive over the limestones and provided critical support for soil and forest development in the postglacial period (Figure 7.2). However, available evidence, particularly the presence of abundant gelifracted rock debris over the limestone surfaces, suggests that these paleosols were eroded long before the Late Quaternary, and that since these soils take many thousands of years to develop, they could not have reformed in the relatively short period between the end of the Quaternary and the advent of the Neolithic. Nor is there evidence of extensive colluvial deposits that could be correlated with the supposed phases of clearance and consequent erosion.

The second major conclusion was that erosion and deposition have led to significant local changes in soil distribution over the soft rocks that underlie the coastal plain. These processes have resulted in the widespread destruction of archaeological sites and/or their burial beneath varying amounts of alluvium or colluvium. This effect has been differential, in that sites have been preferentially buried in some areas and eroded in others, dependent on local topography and land-use history. From a regional point of view, however, the erosion of soils over the soft rocks has not affected the essential imbalance between the Garrigues and the coastal plain, and the latter would always have been better suited for cereal cultivation and pasture than the former.

Systematic surface surveys were carried out in two sample areas—one on the coastal plain and one on the Garrigues—to check the validity of present data samples concerning settlement distribution, organisation, and density through time. The Vaunage basin forms part of the coastal plain and consists of an area of brown calcareous soils over marls, surrounded on three sides by limestone plateaus with thin, rendzina-like soils (Figure 7.3). Four middle neolithic and twelve final neolithic–chalcolithic open air sites were known from the basin and surrounding plateaus prior to the surveys, with an apparent preference for the plateau area during the Final Neolithic–Chalcolithic. My survey concentrated instead on the marls. Ten new final neolithic–chalcolithic sites were found, and three sites reported in earlier studies were visited and diagnostic assemblages collected. The surveys produced no new middle neolithic sites but almost doubled the number of final neolithic–chalcolithic sites over the marls. Where the most intensive work was done, involving detailed survey of a 4.3 km^2 segment of the plain, the number of sites was increased from one to seven. These data confirmed that the apparent low density of Final Neolithic–Chalcolithic settlement over the coastal plain was due to sample bias resulting from lack of research and/or site destruction (including masking by colluviation). About 10% of the 45 km^2 area of the basin was covered by intensive survey, producing five new sites.

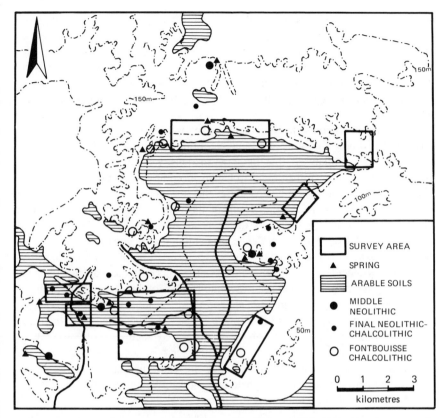

Figure   7.3   The Vaunage basin: distribution of Neolithic and Chalcolithic sites. Contours are in metres.

This suggests that a density of about one final neolithic site per square kilometre might be expected within the basin and on similar areas over the rest of the coastal plain.

Since there is no apparent reason why final neolithic–chalcolithic sites should be better preserved or more easily found than middle neolithic sites, the existing sample of the latter should be an accurate reflection of Chasseen settlement distribution and density in the Vaunage. The four sites are widely spaced and have easy access to arable land, but their specific locations seem determined by their proximity to major water sources. Other springs exist in intermediate positions, so the wide dispersion may reflect social and other factors. There are no data on settlement structures since none of the sites has been excavated, but the surface scatters are no larger than those of the Final Neolithic–Chalcolithic sites.

Three of the locations occupied in the Middle Neolithic continued in use during the Final Neolithic–Chalcolithic, and other spring-side locations were taken up, as well as intervening positions where water was less easily accessible. Spring-side locations therefore seem to have been the preferred locations, with intervening positions being occupied in the Final Neolithic–Chalcolithic as if the former were already occupied and as if the settlements were contemporary at some stage during their occupation, competing for available arable and water resources.

A considerable increase in settlement density thus appears to have taken place between the Middle Neolithic and Final Neolithic–Chalcolithic. The sizes of the settlements are similar, so this increase in density should reflect an overall increase in population rather than a change in community organisation. More significantly, the site assemblages show that the densest phase of settlement occurred during the Chalcolithic. Eight of the fifteen certain or probable final Neolithic–Chalcolithic settlements in the basin have produced clearly defined assemblages. All eight have evidence of Fontbouisse occupation, and four of these have Fontbouisse assemblages only. The proportion of Fontbouisse settlements to settlements of earlier periods is even more marked on the plateaus surrounding the basin, where six of the nine final Neolithic–Chalcolithic can be given a firm cultural and chronological context: all six show Fontbouisse occupation, and four have exclusively Fontbouisse material. These data are consistent with the hypothesis that the plateaus were extensively occupied only after taking up all the available arable land in the basin. This in turn ties in with the evidence of numerous Fontbouisse settlements over the Garrigues and suggests that a phase of population increase and spread onto surrounding marginal land occurred during the Chalcolithic, analogous to the historical cycles.

On the Garrigues, in the area north of Montpellier where extensive research has been done over the last 50 years, there are over 100 open air settlements, 90 dolmen, and 20 cave sites (Arnal 1963; Gasco 1976; Gutherz 1975). The few middle neolithic open sites are located on the southern margins of the Garrigues, while assemblages in the interior come from caves. The rest of the sites are dated to the Final Neolithic–Chalcolithic; most of the open settlements consist of groups of dry-stone walled huts that are easily identifiable on the surface of the stoney soils. The dolmen and caves are distributed widely over the plateaux, with the dolmen occurring both adjacent to settlements and elsewhere, often in groups on small eminences. The distribution of Final Neolithic–Chalcolithic sites with diagnostic assemblages confirms the impression of a spread of settlement across the interior of the Garrigues during the Chalcolithic. Thus, almost all the sites that have produced Ferrieres assemblages are located along the southern margins of the Garrigues, while the Fontbouisse settlements are more abundant and occur equally in the interior.

An area of 6.25 km^2 was surveyed around one of the major depressions in the central part of the Montpellier Garrigues as a check on the current sample of

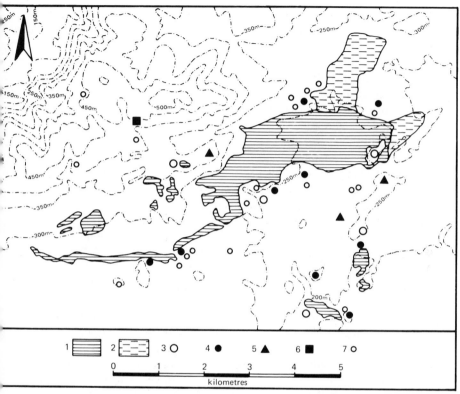

Figure 7.4 Chalcolithic settlement in the Viols-le-Fort area of the Garrigues. 1, good arable soils 2, marginal arable soils; 3, probable Chalcolithic settlement; 4, Chalcolithic settlement; 5, flint scatter; 6, cave with Chalcolithic occupation; 7, dolmen.

settlement density and chronology (Mills, in press a; see also Figure 7.4). Since no further examples of the easily recoverable sites were found, and since the whole of the Viols-le-Fort depression had previously been systematically covered by French archaeologists, the present sample seems a fairly accurate reflection of settlement distribution and density. Fifteen Final Neolithic–Chalcolithic settlements are known from the area, and all that have been partially excavated or sounded have produced Fontbouisse assemblages. It is therefore probable that most if not all of the settlements are chalcolithic.

DISCUSSION

In contrast with traditional models, it now appears that agricultural settlements were concentrated over the coastal plain from the Middle Neolithic onwards, with a few sites over the southern margins of the Garrigues in the Middle Neolithic and Final Neolithic. There is evidence for the exploitation of the interior of the Garrigues at these periods, as shown by the use of caves and the construction of dolmen, but this was probably on a seasonal basis for hunting, grazing, and other activities, since there are no permanent settlements. There is a marked increase in settlement density on the plain during the Chalcolithic, with a parallel spread of settlement over the interior of the Garrigues, a pattern that seems directly comparable to the phases of population growth and expansion during the historical period.

This analysis of regional settlement also provides a more satisfactory frame-work for studying other aspects of social and economic organisation than that provided by traditional cultural–historical models. The unity of Middle Neolithic assemblages has often been contrasted with the assemblage diversity of the Final Neolithic–Chalcolithic, with changes being interpreted in terms of cultural choice. In fact, the changes may be better seen in terms of economic adaptation and changing population levels affecting social interaction. Thus the unified middle neolithic blade-based flint industry with its extensive exchange system (Costantini 1976; Courtin 1974; Phillips et al. 1977) may reflect the establishment of a common subsistence system throughout southern France based on agriculture and employing a common technology and tool kit on a large scale for well-defined tasks (soil cultivation, harvesting, crop-processing, etc). This and the need for an extensive exchange system (since flint does not occur naturally in the coastal plain) in turn brought about a high degree of interdependence and interaction in conditions of relatively abundant arable and grazing, which is reflected in the unity of the ceramic assemblage.

Radical cultural changes occurred in the Final Neolithic–Chalcolithic, including increased diversity in the ceramic assemblage and the predominant use of local lithic sources and a flake-based industry (Arnal 1976; Courtin 1974; Guilaine 1976; Phillips 1975; Vaquer 1975). In Languedoc, the greatest ceramic variability occurs amongst Fontbouisse assemblages, at the time of maximum population growth. Following Hodder (1979), this variability could reflect the expression of community identity in response to demographically induced stress, while the lithic changes are probably the result of other factors. Most of the Final Neolithic–Chalcolithic flint assemblages are known from limestone areas where there are numerous outcrops of poor quality flint. These areas were not heavily settled in the Middle Neolithic, and most outcrops were not exploited. However, the Middle Neolithic settlements on the plain had to import the good quality flint used for their agricultural tools. Consequently, they employed a blade technique, since this reduced both the waste of raw materials and hence the costs of manufacturing and exchange. Several of the Final Neolithic–Chalcolithic sites that are known from the plain have produced blade-based industries (Gasco 1980), but a blade technique was not used by Final Neolithic–Chalcolithic communities on the Garrigues, since only poor quality flint was available there. The use of blade and flake techniques may therefore be a function of resource availability and production costs rather than of cultural variables (Mills 1983).

Iron Age Settlement in the Auvergne, Central France

GENERAL BACKGROUND

The Clermont-Ferrand area of the central Auvergne consists of a long depression containing the Grande and Petites Limagnes basins and the Allier valley, bounded by higher relief to the east and west (Figure 7.5). The volcanic chain of the Monts Dômes lies to the west, rising to a maximum height of 1500 m, over 1000 m above the Limagnes. Arable land is scarce and poor over the Volcanic mountains, but there are extensive areas of pasture suitable for cattle- and sheep-rearing. A series of lava-capped plateaus and volcanic outliers with poor arable soils lines the eastern edge of the mountains, dominating the Limagnes.

The vast plain of the Grande Limagne extends over the northern part of the central depression, reaching an average height of 300 m. The plain is covered by poorly drained, black, silty soils called *terres noires,* underlain by marly limestones. These terres noires are several metres deep in places, and initial work on their origin and chronology shows that they were laid down during the Late Holocene, from the Neolithic onwards, but particularly since the Late Iron Age (Collis et al., in press; Daugas and Raynal 1977; Daugas and Tixier 1977; Daugas et al. 1983; Gachon 1963). The terres noires today provide some of the most productive cereal lands in France, but they require extensive drainage before they can be cultivated, and fairly large areas were marshy until recent times.

The Petites Limagnes lie to the south of the Grande Limagne and comprise a series of more or less extensive basins divided by hilly areas and lava-capped plateaus. Apart from some volcanic intrusions and lava flows, the rocks are mainly marly limestones that give rise to thin, stoney rendzina soils on the hills. These hill soils provide poor arable, while soils in the lower parts of the basins are highly productive under cereals; nearly all are cultivated today.

The Allier valley is the third major geomorphic unit in the central depression. The valley forms a deep trench some 3 km wide with a series of gravel terraces in the bottom. The lowest terrace, up to 800 m wide in places, is of recent date, as shown by finds of modern pottery in its upper levels, 1 m below the present ground surface. Finds of Palaeolithic artefacts show that the upper terraces date to various phases of the Quaternary. The terrace soils are well drained and extensively cultivated with cereals.

The Limagnes and the Allier valley are dominated to the east by more broken

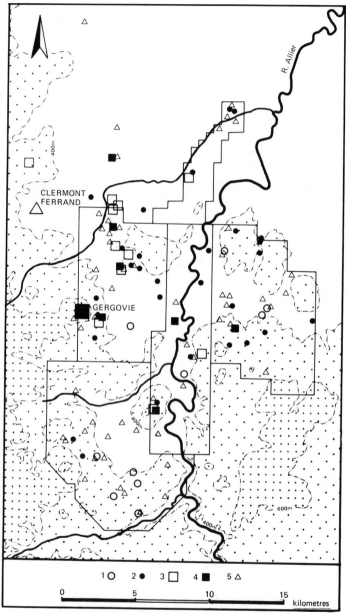

Figure 7.5 The central Auvergne, showing survey areas and the distribution of prehistoric and Roman sites. 1, Neolithic–Bronze Age; 2, Late Bronze Age–Early Iron Age; 3, Late Iron Age; 4, Early Roman; 5, Late Roman.

country, composed of sands and clays, that is presently devoted to pasture or forest.

ARCHAEOLOGICAL BACKGROUND AND RESEARCH DESIGN

The Auvergne was the centre of the Late Iron Age tribe of the Arverni, the largest Gallic tribe at the time of the Roman conquest. The area is therefore well suited to provide information concerning the emergence of state or quasi-state societies in western Europe during the last centuries B.C., characterised especially by the development of massive defended settlements—the *oppida* or 'towns' described by Caesar. In the study area, limited excavations have suggested that the large *oppidum* at Gergovie, some 10 km south of Clermont-Ferrand, is Gergovia, capital of the Arverni and supposed site of Caesar's defeat by Vercingetorix. Although there is little doubt that Gergovie was the major centre in the area from about 40–10 B.C. and was subsequently replaced by the Roman town of Augustonemetum (modern Clermont-Ferrand), there is no evidence of important occupation at the site in the earlier first century B.C. It had been suggested that the nearby low-lying settlement of Aulnat-Gandaillat may have been the earlier centre for the area, eventually being replaced by Gergovie after the Roman conquest. Systematic excavation at this site has produced evidence of an important settlement during the second and earlier first centuries B.C. with specialist artisanal workshops (bone-working, glass, iron, and coin manufacture), numerous imports of Mediterranean wine amphorae, coinage, and a rich ceramic assemblage (Collis 1975, 1980, 1983). The site was abandoned in the mid-first century B.C., at the time when the oppidum of Gergovia developed.

In this region as elsewhere in western Europe, Iron Age research has traditionally concentrated on the study of rich settlements and cemeteries in isolation from their rural settlement contexts. It is apparent that the processes of change in the Auvergne in the Late Iron Age cannot be understood without a firm grasp of the broader framework of settlement development. For instance, what was the relationship between the major settlements and other contemporary sites? Was there a change in the overall organisation of settlement between the Early and Late Iron Ages, or were the oppida superimposed on an otherwise unchanged settlement system Did these centres function as 'agricultural towns,' with the majority of the rural population concentrated within them, or did they function rather as political and commercial centres outside the rural system? A survey programme was started in 1979 that sought to obtain a representative sample of prehistoric settlement in the area at a regional scale. The contrasting opportunities for human settlement and land use in the various ecological zones formed the basis of the survey design. These contrasts have affected agricultural settlement in the area throughout the historical period, and, as in the Languedoc area, it seemed useful to use the historical pattern to establish an initial research framework.

The best cereal lands lie in the area formed by the Grandes and Petites Limagnes and the Allier valley, and it is here that agricultural settlements have been concentrated since the Roman period, apart from an apparent gap in the early Middle Ages. Within the general study area, the Grande Limagne and the upland areas are special cases that have only been occupied under particular conditions, and that may therefore serve as indicators of settlement organisation and development in the prehistoric period. Although agriculturally rich, the Grande Limagne is only likely to have been exploited extensively for agriculture either when changes in groundwater conditions made the area more attractive for settlement, or when socioeconomic conditions favoured drainage and cultivation of the *terres noires*. Such conditions would probably include a sufficient degree of centralised control or cooperative interest as to allow major communal drainage programmes and access to a redistribution system to meet demands for the specialised produce of the area.

The plateaus and uplands form a second special case, since these areas are covered by thin soils suitable for use as poor quality arable or for rough grazing. Large parts are covered by abandoned medieval and later field systems that were created in phases of demographic increase, when settled and cultivated areas expanded to include marginal arable soils. These soils may have been exploited in a similar way during the prehistoric period, and their occupation may therefore be an index of population pressure on the more favourable arable land below. Of course, it is also possible that the occupation of the plateaus and uplands reflects a need for defence, while sites such as Gergovia are central places whose positioning is affected as much by sociopolitical and economic variables as by subsistence concerns. However, such sites are separate cases and should be differentiated from a general spread of farming settlements over the uplands.

The surrounding mountainous and hilly country is also agriculturally marginal with respect to the general area of the Limagnes and the Allier valley, but it may also have provided opportunities for human settlement and economy. For instance, the primary economic basis in the volcanic country has traditionally been stock-raising, dependent on access to markets for the livestock and their produce. Occupation in these areas, whether to cultivate marginal land or to exploit particular raw materials or produce, must be seen in the context of what was happening elsewhere in the region.

FIELDWORK RESULTS

The first survey objective was to establish the pattern of settlement over the historically preferred zone of the central depression, and work was therefore concentrated over the Petites Limagnes and the Allier valley. Little work was done in the Grande Limagne since the area is difficult to survey using normal surface survey techniques, but previous work by Daugas and others gives a basic outline of settlement history there. Probability sampling techniques were used in the surveys, with individual basins of the Petites Limagnes and a segment of the Allier valley serving as the test units. These sites were stratified on the basis of agricultural criteria. Two distinctions were made: (1) good arable—gentle slopes, basin floors, and lower slopes; (2) poor arable—pasture, steep slopes, and upper slopes of basins and hilltops. The results of the surveys are shown in Figure 7.5. Detailed discussion of the survey methodology and results is given in Mills (in press c).

The majority of sites were located over the good arable soils of the first stratum in the Petites Limagnes and the Allier valley. The data confirmed that the previous sample of settlement distribution was heavily biased towards the Grande Limagne and the upland areas within the central depression. By the late Bronze Age, however, settlements of all periods appear to concentrate in the first stratum. Sites of the Late Bronze and Early Iron Age are numerous in this stratum, but several of the hills and plateaus of the Petites Limagnes and the Allier valley have also produced occupation evidence of this period. The relatively few settlements known from the Grande Limagne are located in footslope positions along the southern edge of the area. The data suggest a high density of settlement over the better quality soils, with the exception of the Grande Limagne. Settlements were also located in the marginal arable areas of the second stratum.

This pattern contrasts markedly with that of the Late Iron Age, by which time three radical changes had taken place. First, only a fifth of the sites remained in the areas previously occupied in the Petites Limagnes and the Allier valley. Second, abundant late iron age remains in and on the edges of the Grande Limagne show that this area was more heavily exploited at this time than previously. These remains consist both of isolated finds and burials revealed in ditch cutting, and of a string of rich settlements along the southern edge of the Grande Limagne. Third, there is no evidence of generalised occupation of the upland areas, although two important perched sites are known here, at Côtes de Clermont and Corent. Unfortunately, there are few published data from these two sites, and it is therefore difficult to assess their importance. However, a late iron age assemblage containing dies for gold coins, painted wares, and numerous amphorae has been reported at Corent, as has a similar asemblage at Côtes de Clermont.

Settlements of the later first century B.C. are scarce, occurring in similar numbers to those of the Late Iron Age, and there is a continuity of occupation between these periods. The large oppidum of Gergovie also appeared, with occupation that covered much of the plateau and included artisanal, habitation, and religious quarters, as well as an impressive stone rampart pierced by at least one monumental gateway. The pattern again changed markedly in the first and second centuries A.D., when numerous sites were spread widely over the main agricultural areas of the Petites Limagnes and the Allier valley. Sites were also plentiful across the Grande Limagne, spreading further into this area than during the Late Iron Age. Gergovia was abandoned after a brief occupation of about 30 years and was replaced by Augustonemetum.

DISCUSSION

The numerous late bronze and early iron age settlements suggest an increase in population at some stage during this period involving a spread of settlement onto the poorer agricultural land of the plateaus, while there appears to have been a radical change in the settlement system in the Late Iron Age. One explanation of these changes is that a decline in population occurred between the Early and Late Iron Ages, particularly in the Petites Limagnes and the Allier valley. While a decline in population probably did occur, as indicated by the retraction of settlement from the marginal areas away from the major perched sites, this explanation does not account for the evidence of increased exploitation of the Grande Limagne in the Late Iron Age.

An alternative explanation is that these changes reflect a total restructuring of the settlement system in the context of the social and economic transformations of late iron age Europe. These changes included increased artisanal specialisation, large-scale pottery production and exchange, the manufacture and use of coinage, and the development of extensive regional and extraregional trade networks. Several of the Late Iron Age sites found in the surveys have produced Mediterranean imports, and at least one of these covers a larger area than the site at Aulnat-Gandaillat. Late Iron Age pottery kilns have also been excavated at Clermont-Ferrand, where pottery was being produced on a large scale, including the wheel-turned forms from Aulnat-Gandaillat.

It is therefore possible that Aulnat-Gandaillat was in fact one of several large settlements that developed in the Late Iron Age. The change in settlement patterns from the Early to Late Iron Age might have involved the appearance of fewer, larger, more structured 'village'-type sites, each having artisanal industries and being integrated in important regional and extraregional exchange networks. We know from historical sources that this period was associated with a considerable increase in the power and influence of the Arverni, and probably with a greater hierarchisation of society as a whole and increased control by the ruling elite over both social and economic relations. The large-scale exploitation of the Grande Limagne at this time would have required both an organised system of drainage and markets for the specialised produce. The fulfillment of both these conditions is suggested by the historical and archaeological evidence.

It may be that produce from the Grande Limagne was exchanged directly for imported Mediterranean goods and formed the principal wealth of the Arverni. We might expect these changes in social and economic organisation to be associated with the appearance of political, social, and/or economic centres. In fact, Corent and Côtes de Clermont fit well here, with one controlling the traditionally settled areas of the Petites Limagnes and the Allier valley, and the other controlling the newly exploited land of the Grande Limagne. The development of Gergovia might thus be seen as a rationalisation of preceding centres at the time of the Roman conquest.

General Conclusions

The two case studies discussed here illustrate how regionally oriented research designs, based on an appreciation of contrasts in settlement and land use potential in different zones, allow clearer analysis of the development and dynamics of agricultural settlement amongst both simple and complex societies. Both studies bring to light patterns that appear to be cyclical, occurring both in prehistoric and historical contexts. It is not suggested that such patterns will be found everywhere, nor that the mechanisms are the same within each region over time; each region must obviously be considered according to local circumstances. However, in southern France in particular, I would argue that there is clear evidence of a prehistoric phase of population growth and settlement expansion that exhibits a very similar pattern to the population cycles of the historical period. The mechanisms behind the historical cycles are unclear and may include climatic change as well as both local and 'global' socioeconomic factors (Leroy-Ladurie 1966). The data are still inadequate for us to arrive at firm explanations of the prehistoric case, but the recognition of a pattern assists greatly in designing research and in understanding and ordering other aspects of current data.

These studies demonstrate the importance of regional and multiperiod surveys for settlement investigation. In both cases, the existing data samples were heavily biased and could not be used to answer many fundamental questions concerning processes of social and economic development. Previous research has tended to concentrate on atypical zones not normally or continuously used for agricultural settlement, resulting in false contrasts with the situation in later periods and, more generally, in the recognition of false patterns in the data. Once systematic surveys had established that the preferred settlement zones in both areas had remained substantially constant, it was then possible to use the occupation of particular zones with more limited or specific resource potential as a guide to more general processes of settlement and societal development. The occupation of marginal land seems to be an index of population growth and settlement expansion, while the use of the Grandes Limagne in the Late Iron Age gives us an important guide to processes of socioeconomic change associated with the growth of complex societies during this period. In both cases, study of these particular zones without an awareness of their regional and long-term contexts would have been of limited value.

Acknowledgements

The Sidney Perry Trust and the Sheffield University Research Fund contributed towards the costs of research in southern France. The Auvergne fieldwork was financed by grants from the British Academy, the Maison des Sciences de l'Homme, the Prehistoric Society, the Royal Anthropological Institute, the Explorer's Club, Sigma XI, the Service National des Fouilles, the Ernest Cassell Trust, and the Wenner Gren Foundation for Anthropological Research Inc. I should also like to thank all those who participated in the surveys for their unrelenting hard work, particularly Ian Cumming, Dave Fine, Colin Green, Peter Hayes, David Hosking, Clay Mathers, and Susan Stallibrass.

References

Arnal, G. B.
  1976 *La céramique néolithique dans le Haut-Languedoc.* Lodève.
Arnal, J.
  1963 Les dolmens du Département de l'Hérault. *Préhistoire* 15.
Bailloud, G.
  1973 Les habitations chalcolithiques de Conquette (St. Martin-de-Londres, Hérault). In *L'homme hier et aujourd'hui,* pp. 493–504. Cujas, Paris.
Bloch, M.
  1952 *Les caractères originaux de l'histoire rurale française.* Colin, Paris.
Braudel, F.
  1976 *The Mediterranean and the Mediterranean world in the age of Phillip II* (second ed.). Fontana, London.
Braun-Blanquet, J.
  1936 *La forêt d'yeuse languedocienne.* Mari-Lavit, Montpellier.
Canet, H., and J. L. Roudil
  1978 Le village chalcolithique de Cambous à Viols-en-Laval (Hérault). *Gallia Préhistoire* 21(1):143–188.
Chisholm, M.
  1968 *Rural settlement and land use.* Methuen, London.
Collis, J. R.
  1975 Excavations at Aulnat, Clermont-Ferrand: a preliminary report with some notes on the earliest towns in France. *Archaeological Journal* 132:1–15.
Collis, J. R.
  1980 Aulnat and urbanisation in France: a second interim report. *Archaeological Journal* 137:40–49.
Collis, J. R.
  1983 La stratigraphie du chantier sud d'Aulnat. In *Le deuxième Age du Fer en Auvergne et en Forez,* edited by J. Collis et al., pp. 48–56. Sheffield University, Department of Prehistory and Archaeology.

Collis, J. R., B. Hartley, M. Maltby, and G. Wells
    in press Fouilles de sauvetage dans la Grande Limagne. *Revue Archéologique du Centre.*
Costantini, G.
    1976 *Le Néolithique et le Chalcolithique des Grands Causses.* Millau.
Courtin, J.
    1974 *Le Néolithique de la Provence.* Klincksieck, Paris.
Courtin, J.
    1977 Les animaux domestique du néolithique provençal. In *L'elévage en Méditerranée Occidentale, pp. 67–76. Centre National de la Recherche Scientifique, Marseille.*
Courtin, J., and J. Erroux
    1974 Aperçu sur l'agriculture préhistorique en Provence. *Bulletin de la Société Préhistorique Française* 71(1):321–334.
Courteaux, M.
    1974 Présence de sols striés en région subméditerranéenne: Pédogenèse, végétation, et climat. *Bulletin de la Société Languedocienne de Géographie* 8(3–4):233–240.
D'Anna, A., and N. T. W. Mills
    1981 L'occupation néolithique du bassin de Trets (Bouches-du-Rhône). *Bulletin Archéologique de Provence* 8(4):3–46.
Daugas, J. P., and J. P. Raynal
    1977 Remarques sur le milieu physique et le peuplement humain en Auvergne à la fin des temps glaciaires. In *La fin des temps glaciaires en Europe,* edited by D. de Sonneville-Bordes, pp. 545–562. Centre National de la Recherche Scientifique, Paris.
Daugas, J. P., and L. Tixier
    1977 Variations paléoclimatiques de la Limagne d'Auvergne. In *Approche ecologique de l'homme fossile,* edited by H. Laville and J. Renault-Miskovsky, pp. 203–235. Association Française pour l'Etude du Quaternaire, Paris.
Daugas, J. P., J. P. Raynal, and L. Tixier
    1983 Variations du milieu physique et occupation du sol au Second Age du Fer en Grande Limagne d'Auvergne. In *Le deuxieme Age du Fer en Auvergne et en Forez,* edited by J. Collis et al., pp. 10–21. Sheffield University, Department of Prehistory and Archaeology.
Delano-Smith, C.
    1972 Late neolithic settlement and land use, and garrigue in the Montpellier region, France. *Man* 7(3):397–407.
Delano-Smith, C.
    1979 *Western Mediterranean Europe.* Academic Press, London.
Duby, G., and A. Whallon (editors)
    1975 *Histoire de la France rurale.* Seuil, Paris.
Duchaufour, P.
    1970 *Précis de pédologie.* Masson, Paris.
Dugrand, R.
    1964 *La Garrigue Montpellieraine.* Presses Universitaires de France, Paris.
Emberger, L.
    1930 La végétation de la région méditterranéenne: essai d'une classification des groupements végétaux. *Revue Générale de Botanique* 43: 641–662, 705–721.
Erroux, J.
    1976 Les débuts de l'agriculture en France: les céréales. In *La préhistoire française* (vol. 2), edited by J. Guilaine, pp. 186–191. Centre National de la Recherche Scientifique.
Flahault, C.
    1937 *La distribution géographique des végétaux dans la région méditerranéenne française.* Lechavalier, Paris.

Gachon, L.
1963 Contribution à l'étude du Quaternaire récent de la Grande Limagne marno-calcaire-morphogenèse et pédogenèse. *Annales Agronomiques* 14(1):1–191.

Gasco, J.
1976 *La Communauté Paysanne de Fontbouisse*. Laboratoire de Préhistoire et de Palethnologie, Carcassonne.

Gasco, J.
1980 Un habitat de plein air au néolithique recent: la Mort des Anes (Villeneuve-les-Maguelonne, Hérault). In *Le groupe de Veraza et la fin des temps néolithiques dans le sud de la France et la Catalogne*, edited by J. Guilaine, pp. 177–191. Centre National de la Recherche Scientifique, Toulouse.

Guilaine, J.
1976 *Premiers bergers et paysans de l'Occident Méditerranéen*. Moulton, Paris.

Guilaine, J.
1977 Sur les débuts de l'élévage en Méditerranée Occidentale, In *L'élévage en Mediterranée Occidentale*, pp. 39–48. Centre National de la Recherche Scientifique, Marseille.

Gutherz, X.
1975 *La culture de Fontbouisse*. Association pour la Recherche Archeologique en Languedoc Oriental, Caveirac.

Hodder, I.
1979 Economic stress and material culture patterning. *American Antiquity* 44(3):446–454.

Kuhnholtz-Lordat, G.
1945 La silva, le saltus, et l'ager des garrigues. *Annales de l'Ecole National d'agriculture de Montpellier* 26(4):1–84.

Leroy-Ladurie, E.
1966 *Les paysans de Languedoc*. S.E.V.P.E .N., Paris.

Mendras, H.
1976 *Sociétés paysannes*. Armand Colin, Paris.

Mills, N. T. W.
1980 *Prehistoric agriculture in southern France: case studies from Provence and Languedoc*. Unpublished Ph.D. dissertation, Sheffield University.

Mills, N. T. W.
1981 Luni: settlement and landscape in the Ager Lunensis. In *Archaeology and Italian society*, edited by G. Barker and R. Hodges, pp. 261–277. British Archaeological Reports, International Series 102, Oxford, England.

Mills, N. T. W.
1983 The Neolithic of southern France. In *Ancient France: neolithic societies and their landscapes 6000–2000 B.C.*, edited by C. Scarre, pp. 91–145. Edinburgh University Press, Scotland.

Mills, N. T. W.
in press a L'habitat ceinturé de Boussargues (Argelliers, Hérault) dans son contexte local et régional. *Bulletin de l'Ecole Antique de Nîmes* (June).

Mills, N. T. W.
in press b Geomorphology and regional archaeological research design. In *Palaeoenvironmental investigations*, edited by D. Gilbertson and N. Fieller. British Archaeological Reports, British Series, Oxford, England.

Mills, N. T. W.
in press c Iron age settlement and society in Europe: contributions from field surveys in central France. In *Archaeological field survey in Britain and abroad*, edited by S. Macready and F.

H. Thompson, pp. 74–99. Society of Antiquaries of London, Occaisional Papers Number 6, London, England.

Phillips, P.

1975 *Early farmers of west Mediterranean Europe.* Hutchinson, London.

Phillips, P.

1982 *The Middle Neolithic in southern France.* British Archaeological Reports, International Series 142, Oxford, England.ho

Phillips, P., A. Aspinall, and S. Feather

1977 Stages of 'neolithisation' in southern France: supply and exchange of raw materials. *Proceedings of the Prehistoric Society* 43:303–316.

Poulain, T.

1976 La faune. In *La préhistoire française* (Vol. 2), edited by J. Guilaine, pp. 104–116. Centre National de la Recherche Scientifique, Paris.

Sherratt, A.

1980 Water, soil, and seasonality in early cereal cultivation. *World Archaeology* 11(3):313–330.

Sherratt, A.

1981 Plough and pastoralism: aspects of the secondary products revolution. In *Pattern in the past: studies in memory of David Clarke,* edited by N. Hammond et al., pp. 261–305. Cambridge University Press, Cambridge, England.

Slicher van Bath, B. H.

1963 *The agrarian history of western Europe A.D. 500–1850.* Edward Arnold, London.

Vaquer, J.

1975 *La céramique chasséene du Languedoc.* Laboratoire de Préhistoire et de Palethnologie. Carcassone.

Ward-Perkins, B.

1981 Luni: the prosperity of the town and its territory. In *Archaeology and Italian society,* edited by G. Barker and R. Hodges, pp. 261–268. British Archaeological Reports, International Series 102, Oxford, England.

8

Social Factors and Economic Change in Balearic Prehistory, 3000–1000 b.c.

JAMES LEWTHWAITE

Introduction

V. G. Childe was the first scholar to state an explicit, logical correlation between the development of metallurgy and the process of social differentiation in Europe during the second millennium b.c. (Childe 1930). The bronze smith and miner, he argues, would have been the first specialist craftsmen. As such, they would have enjoyed a precarious independence; while liberated from primary production tasks, they would have been dependent on others for their subsistence. Although guaranteed a status superior to that of the peasant—through their monopoly of technical knowledge and craft skill and their (allegedly) itinerant life style—the only customers and patrons for their production would have been the emergent elites, since earlier Bronze Age artefacts were restricted to non-utilitarian functions such as the conspicuous demonstration of status. The division of labour would thus have developed alongside the growth of inequality. Childe further postulates that these Bronze Age social developments were set in motion from without, through the impact of the complex societies of the Near East on the barbarous inhabitants of the peripheral metalliferous regions of Europe such as the Balkans or Iberia. In the latter area, actual colonies of metal prospectors would have been established during the Copper Age (Childe 1957:270).

Although the details of the genesis and social organisation of Childe's model of the Bronze Age have been rejected (Renfrew 1967, 1969; Rowlands 1976), the contribution of the western Mediterranean Copper Age to the general debate remains critical. Few other areas demonstrate a transitional period (the later third

BEYOND DOMESTICATION
IN PREHISTORIC EUROPE

millennium B.C.) that offers such a tantalising opportunity to examine the interaction of local 'processual' and interregional 'diffusionist' factors. Generally, this period was one of demographic increase, artefactual and architectual elaboration, and a widening of horizons throughout the Mediterranean basin (Phillips 1975: 270; Renfrew 1972). Locally, as in central Portugal, Almeria, or Malta, this era represents a temporary climax of cultural achievement.

Four models have been offered that attempt to explain the configuration of the Bronze Age in terms of more or less rapid and radical transformations in the preceding Copper Age. Louis (1948, 1950), Puglisi (1959), and Lilliu (1963) propose that communities of transhumant pastoralists arose on the plateaus of the Midi, Baleares, Apennines, and Sardinia, exploiting areas marginal for agriculture. According to Lilliu, the constraints of the pastoral way of life would have determined a fragmentation and hierarchisation of the peaceful, egalitarian Neolithic village communities into competitive, patriarchal 'clans', and eventually into the complex society of the Later Bronze Age Nuraghic culture. Second, Renfrew (1972) proposes a detailed model for the corresponding period in the Aegean (the Early Bronze Age), outlining the positive functions of an emergent entrepreneurial elite in managing redistributive systems. The complex, differentiated society of the resultant Minoan-Mycenaean civilisation would have been functionally superior as an adaptive system to that of the Neolithic period. Third, Gilman (1981) suggests that by impeding demographic mobility, the cumulative stabilisation of subsistence through capital intensification (such as ard technology, irrigation, and polyculture) prevented the formerly free cultivator from resisting encroaching 'elites'—the proverbial sale of the birthright for a mess of pottage. Finally, Shennan (1982) argues that the proliferation of prestigious 'Beaker' assemblages throughout western Europe signified no more than the ideological rationalisation of the subsistence and social differentiation that had already been accomplished earlier in the third millennium B.C.

The factors least understood in the key areas of theoretical interest and research endeavour (central Europe, Wessex, Portugal, and southeast Spain) are demography and subsistence, primarily as a result of the lack of definition brought about by the long history of continuous occupation in these favourable environments. In this chapter, as in the previous one by Mills, a particularly marginal environment is investigated where cereal cultivation and pastoralism are precarious subsistence strategies, in the belief that subsistence change and settlement fluctuation will be less ambiguously attested. Our ultimate objective is an understanding of the adaptation involved in the transmission to an island milieu and in the reproduction of social systems rather than mere population aggregates.

An environment may be considered 'marginal' only when the other factors in the equation are defined: the size and structure of the population (including internal differentiation by sector or ranking), and the technical means available for settlement and subsistence for a specified period. Given these variables, one or more environmental zones may be considered 'marginal'—that is, deficient in terms of crop production or other limiting conditions for the low-risk maintenance of population. Changing configurations of settlement patterns and, insofar as it can be inferred, of zonal land use may then be interpreted as reflecting changed values of the invisible variables. Technical innovations and demographic fluctuations are the most frequently invoked, but social, political, and/or ideological factors should not be excluded. Such changes can be classified variously as directional and cumulative, cyclical, or even distinguished by inversion, which must affect application of the term 'marginal'.

An example of the former pattern is the long-term expansion of Neolithic settlement in the Cracow region of Poland, from the river valleys to the plateau interfluves (Kruk 1980). Mills (Chapter 7, this volume) offers an example of a cyclical or saw-toothed pattern of colonisation of another upland interfluve. Such plateaus might therefore be regarded as 'marginal' over such a long period, marked by so many technical advances and social configurations that they might well be classified as absolutely marginal compared to the adjacent plains. The islands of Corsica and Sardinia, however, experienced an actual inversion of settlement during the historic period (Blanchard 1914; Le Lannou 1941), in that the plains, exposed to malaria and piracy, were abandoned in favour of the previously marginal uplands. As a result, the logic of land-use evaluation has to be understood in relation to the actual, and not the hypothetically optimal, situation. Given the location of permanent settlement, distant plains of undoubted fertility became effectively marginal, although their exploitation was not less rational (Pieretti 1947). In general, however, for the purposes of long-term patterns, the western Mediterranean can be divided into sharply contrasted classes of fertile *huertas* (irrigable land suitable for the intensive cultivation of high-value crops such as rice, vegetables, and fruits) and marginal wastes (Delano Smith 1979:13).

The Balearic islands (Table 8.1) may be considered such a marginal area for three reasons: first, their physical isolation and limited extent within the western Mediterranean basin (Figure 8.1); second, the aridity of the climate, which increases progressively from Menorca in the north to the Pithyusae (Eivissa and Formentera) in the south, and from the northwestern range to the coastal lowlands within Mallorca (Figure 8.2); and third, the almost entirely calcareous geological composition, which further reduces surface water availability (there are no permanent rivers). Landscape types include jagged folded ranges of hard limestone, glacis of quaternary alluvium, low plateaus of softer limestone dissected by gorges and marly basins, coastal lagoons, and dunes. Present-day vegetation consists of evergreen oak, pine, macchia, and garrigue.

Table 8.1

The Major Geographic Variables of the Balearic Islands[a]

	Land area (km²)	Interdistance (km)	Distance from nearest mainland (km)	Maximum altitude (m)	Mean annual precipitation (mm)		Mean July temperature (°C)	Mean January temperature (°C)	Ecological zone	Principal vegetation climax
Menorca	701	37	200	357		607	24	11	semi arid	Quercion Ilicis
Mallorca	3640	81	191	1443	Lluc Pollença Inca Palma	1115 901 628 468	24–25	9–10	humid (mountains) subhumid (piedmont) semi-arid (coastal)	
Eivissa	541	10 (direct) 4 (via islets)	92	475		408	25	11	semi-arid/arid	Oleo-Ceratonion (wild olive lentisk)
Formentera	82			202		434	26	13	semi-arid/arid	
Total	5014[b]									

[a]After Bisson 1977.

[b]0.6% area of Western Mediterranean basin; 8.0% area of island surface within basin.

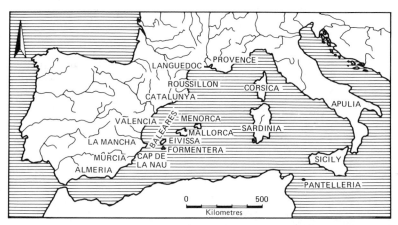

Figure 8.1 Location of the Baleares or Balearic islands within the west Mediterranean basin, with principal regions mentioned in the text.

The historical geography of the Baleares does not reveal independent cycles of population growth and expansion such as those of Languedoc (see Chapter 7, this volume). The turning points in medieval and modern settlement history have been the Catalan conquest of 1229–1235 and the cycle of abandonment and reoccupation caused by the depredations of the Barbary corsairs, which affected Formentera and the coastal areas of the larger islands. Historical Mallorca offers no examples of true subsistence economies. The fertile centre and the montane basins in particular have long specialised in the commercial production of cereals or a succession of tree crops (Bisson 1977:45). The arid calcareous plateaus of the southern and eastern wasteland (Sa Marina) were historically depopulated through the fear of piracy, and were exploited in the form of great estates through extensive pastoralism and sharecropping. On the island of Formentera there was a viable subsistence economy integrating permanent agriculture, animal husbandry, and fishing, despite exceptional aridity (Vilà Valentí 1950). Menorca, in contrast, reveals an enduring tradition of settlement on the southern, calcareous tableland, with an avoidance of the wind-swept, hummocky north (Bisson 1977). In general, the Baleares have been densely populated and entirely devoted to the classic Mediterranean farming system of cereals, legumes, small stock, and orchard crops, without the differentiation of a specialised pastoral way of life typical of Sardinia or Corsica (Lewthwaite 1981; Ravis-Giordani 1983), or the survival of large areas of climax forest yielding subsistence resources (Lewthwaite 1982b).

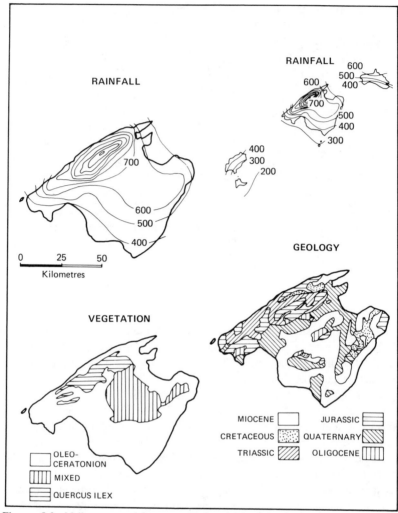

Figure   8.2   Mallorca: natural features, with (top right) rainfall for the Baleares as a whole.

Early Balearic Prehistory (5000–2700 b.c.)

The prehistory of the Greater Baleares (Mallorca and Menorca) has long been dominated by the study of the Talaiotic culture, named after dry-stone towers that are believed to have been used as defended habitations and watchtowers (*talaiots*). These were constructed in approximately 1400 b.c. and used until and even after the Roman conquest of 123 B.C. (Pericot Garcia 1972; Rosselló

Bordoy 1973). Talaiotic culture reached the Pithyusae only in the form of a few ceramic imports (Fernández Gomez and Plantalamor Massanet 1975). In 1972, Pericot Garcia wrote: "The first dividing line is obvious. Everything prior to the adoption of cyclopean, or megalithic, building techniques must be considered together" (1972:21). At that time, the only megalithic constructions known to predate the 'cyclopean' Talaiots comprised a few dolmens dating to 1800–1500 b.c. Since then, the discovery of an indubitably megalithic enclosed settlement has aligned the introduction of megalithic architecture with major changes in artefactual assemblages, settlement distribution, and subsistence in approximately 2000 b.c. (Fernández-Miranda and Waldren 1979; Pericot Garcia 1972; Rosselló Bordoy 1973; Veny 1968). This major threshold distinguishes the pre-Talaiotic culture proper from the first three millennia of settlement. It is used here to structure an outline of Balearic prehistory. The still earlier horizon of approximately 2700 b.c. marks the date of the introduction of ceramic technology and domestic animals (Waldren 1982, 1983:227–253), and very probably the beginning of the construction of rock-cut tombs traditionally assigned a much later date because of the assemblage found within them (Rosselló Bordoy 1984).

There is no evidence of human settlement on either of the Pithyusae prior to 2000 b.c., and only very questionable material from Menorca, specifically the disturbed deposits of the Cova Murada (Ciutadella) (Pericot Garcia 1972). Two sites in the northwestern range of Mallorca have yielded proof of earlier occupation: one from approximately 4000 b.c. in the cave of Muleta, in Sóller (Waldren and Rossello Bordoy 1975); and one from approximately 4700 b.c. in the rock shelter of So'n Matge, in Valldemossa (Figure 8.3). The latter site dominates a pass of major importance linking the central lowlands with the Valldemossa basin and the coast beyond, at a point where the range is only six kilometres wide. It is the key stratification on which Mallorcan chronology and cultural history rest (Fernández-Miranda and Waldren 1974, 1979; Rosselló Bordoy and Waldren 1973; Waldren 1981a, 1982, 1983; Waldren and Plantalamor Massanet 1976).

The artefactual material from So'n Matge is poor and culturally undiagnostic, consisting of flint flakes and bone needles (Waldren 1982). There is a surprising absence of the impressed ceramics associated with the neolithic settlement of other islands in the western basin such as Corsica, Sardinia, Malta, or the Aeolian archipelago (Cherry 1981; Lewthwaite 1982a). The paucity of this inventory is matched by the absence of evidence for the importation of domestic animals, particularly sheep, which were introduced by sea into the coastlands and other islands of the western basin during the early sixth millennium b.c. (Geddes 1983a, b; Uerpmann 1979; Vigne 1984). There is no direct evidence for cereal cultivation, although cereal-type pollen has been found in deposits of the Muleta cave (Gottesfeld and Martin 1968; Waldren 1982, 1983:539–545).

The only positive insight into the subsistence basis during the first two millen-

Figure   8.3   Principal archaeological sites in the Baleares.

nia of settlement on Mallorca consists of evidence for the exploitation of the largest endemic species to have survived the Quaternary: *Myotragus balearicus*, an animal resembling the mountain goat or chamois (Antoni Alcover et al. 1981:79–134). The deposits at So'n Matge contain not only butchered bones in association with hearths and a few artefacts but also extensive deposits of dung, suggesting that the animals were corralled for some time before slaughter. There are also horn cores that appear to have been trimmed, possibly to prevent damage from butting within the corral (Waldren 1979, 1982).

Even if the species was subjected to some rudimentary form of husbandry, it is unlikely that a human population of viable breeding size could be supported from the exploitation of *Myotragus* alone. Fishing and the gathering of acorns, fruits, and bulbs would have been an essential complement. *Myotragus* may also have been exploited as much for its skin (for winter clothes) as its meat, as are the feral goats that still roam the ranges today (Parrack 1973:158).

Around 2700 b.c. there is evidence for the first time of renewed mainland contact, in the form of a few sherds at So'n Matge resembling those of the contemporary Véraza group of western Languedoc, Roussillon, and Catalunya (Fernández-Miranda and Waldren 1979; Guilaine 1980). At the same period, the first domestic animals were imported: goats, pigs and small cattle, but not, apparently, sheep (Waldren 1982, 1983:253).

Subsistence, Settlement, and Social Change
(2700–1400 b.c.)

The chronological and cultural ordering of the pre-Talaiotic period has been profoundly revised as a result of the excavation of the key stratified site of So'n Matge (Valldemossa) by Waldren and his colleagues (Fernández-Miranda and Waldren 1979; Rosselló Bordoy and Waldren 1973; Waldren 1982, 1983:137–189; Waldren and Plantalamor Massanet 1976; Waldren and Rosselló Bordoy 1975), and of his accumulation of a corpus of radiocarbon dates (Waldren 1981a). A tripartite subdivision is suggested, the first phase of which (approximately 2700–2200 b.c.) would include sparse habitation evidence from So'n Matge and some burials; however, no major settlements are attested. Subsequently (approximately 2200–1700 b.c.), a Chalcolithic florescence occurred, marked by the extension of settlement to smaller islands, the first visual evidence of permanent settlement on Mallorca and Menorca, and a climax of funerary architecture. One aspect of the latter was the apogee of rock-cut tomb development, another the introduction of the megalithic style; both are linked by a common range of prestige artefacts. During the third phase (approximately 1700–1400 b.c.), there is little evidence of new developments or widespread contact, although existing facilities continued to be used.

There is no direct evidence for the occupation of the Pithyusae in the early second millennium b.c.; ceramics from certain caves and enclosures are either undiagnostic or typologically late. Nevertheless, typologically early material (incised ware, v-perforated buttons, and simple copper daggers) from three megalithic chamber tombs indicates the antiquity of pre-Talaiotic settlement (Fernández 1977; Gordillo Courcières 1981; Topp et al. 1976, 1979; Trias and

Roca 1975). Similar material is known on Menorca, from four megalithic chamber tombs and the Nau d'Es Tudons *naveta*. (*Navetes* are above-ground megalithic structures, apsidal in plan. Although they were once assumed to have been tombs, excavations at So'n Mercer de Baix, Ciutadella, suggest that many may have been domestic in function; see Anglada Gomila 1976.) The beginning of construction on the Menorcan examples has now been extended to approximately 2000 b.c. (Plantalamor Massanet and Rita 1984). All the navetes of Menorca conform to the historical preference for the dissected calcareous tableland of the *Migjorn* (south) rather than the windswept *Tramuntana* (north) (Mascaró Pasarius 1967b).

Three categories of pre-Talaiotic settlement are known on Mallorca. The most numerous category comprises 40–50 apsidal habitations termed 'navetiformes' (from their similarities to navetes) (Mascaró Pasarius 1967b; Pericot Garcia 1972; Rosselló Bordoy 1966). They are often curiously paired or tripled, as at Ca'n Roig Nou (Felanitx), and sometimes form loose aggregates, as at Es Closos de Ca'n Gaià (Frey and Rosselló Bordoy n.d.). Such sites show a marked avoidance of the piedmont glacis and central lowlands of the island and a corresponding concentration on the dissected calcareous tablelands of the southern and eastern coastal area (Migjorn) and the cemented quaternary sand dunes (marès) of Calvià in the southwest and Santa Margalida in the north. The second category consists of the numerous habitation caves and shelters such as So'n Matge, in which activities such as metallurgy were carried out (Waldren 1979). Only in the last few years has a third category of settlement been recognised: the enclosed settlement. One example is the older settlement of So'n Ferrandell-So'n Oleza (Figure 8.4), which covered some 3600 m² and was occupied continuously from approximately 2000 b.c. until the transition to the Talaiotic period (Waldren 1981b). Another may be the bastioned enclosure of Ets Antigors (Ses Salines) in the most arid corner of Mallorca (Figure 8.5). It is normally interpreted as a Talaiotic village (Rosselló Bordoy 1973), but incised sherds found during excavations by J. Malbertí Marroig indicate pre-Talaiotic origins. Finally, incised sherds have been found in a single structure that may be a pre-Talaiotic bastioned enclosure (Fernández-Miranda 1981) underlying the first millennium b.c. ritual enclosure at Torralba d'En Salord (Alaior) on Menorca (W. H. Waldren, personal communication, 1976).

Direct evidence for the subsistence system associated with these settlements is minimal. Charred grain was found during an old excavation of the navetiforme of Sa Punta (Felanitx) (Pericot Garcia 1972:60); caprids and bovids were identified at the navetiforme Ca N'Alemany (Magalluf, Calvià) (Enseñat Estrany 1971); and caprids, bovids, and pig were identified at Ca Na Cotxera (Muro) (Cantarellas Camps 1972). The extinction of *Myotragus balearicus* occurred between 2150 and 2000 B.C. at So'n Matge (Burleigh and Clutton-Brock 1980). The principal indication of pre-Talaiotic subsistence consists of the distribution of

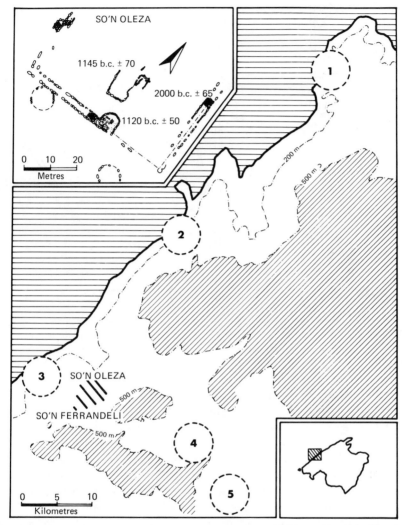

Figure 8.4 The enclosure of So'n Ferrandell-So'n Oleza (Valldemossa) and its hinterland. Circles mark other contemporary sites. 1, Muleta; 2, So'n Gallard; 3, So'n Sabater; 4, So'n Matge; 5, So'n Puig.

settlements. On Mallorca, the distribution of the navetiformes is the reverse of the historical pattern; that is, navetiformes are concentrated on the periphery (Enseñat Estrany 1971:41), whereas historical peasant settlement was densest in the centre (Bisson 1977:153). Although this distribution might be attributed to the destruction of the prehistoric monuments of the central zone by subsequent agricultural activity, there are two reasons for accepting the navetiforme pattern

216   James Lewthwaite

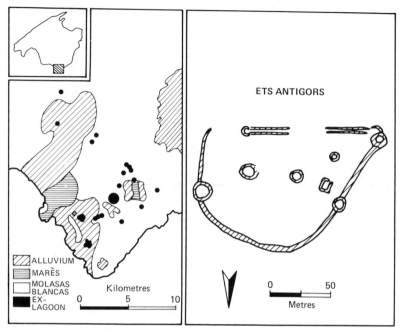

Figure 8.5 The enclosure of Ets Antigors (Ses Salines): soil selection and site hierarchy. The large circle marks the enclosure, the smaller circles mark other *navetes*. Right: detail of the enclosure.

as reasonably reliable. First, the distribution of rock-cut tombs (less likely to be destroyed by agriculture) agrees with that of the navetiformes (Veny 1968:17). Second, the navetiforme pattern on Menorca agrees with that of historical settlement, despite the effects of later agriculture (Bisson 1977:55).

The pre-Talaiotic settlements are densest on the *marines* (littoral wastelands) of Llucmajor, Campos, and Ses Salines, which form the arid calcareous plateau of southern and eastern Mallorca. Here, marginal populations (the *roters*) lived in simple dry-stone dwellings very like some of the prehistoric structures. They also cultivated cereals in temporary clearings using slash-and-burn techniques (*rotes*). However, there is no reason to project this way of life back into prehistory. Social, rather than ecological, factors explain the precarious existence of the roters, just as commercial considerations and defence factors underlay their historical reliance on swine and small stock (Lewthwaite 1984).

The navetiformes are invariably located beside small marly basins and alluvial valleys offering limited areas of deep, humid soil, and a system of permanent cultivation, particularly one integrated with animal husbandry, is far more likely than rotes. Each species could have performed a complementary and essential function: Small stock would have maintained arable productivity through manuring, cattle could have supplied traction, and pigs could convert sundry vegetable produce into high quality protein. For such a system to function, an extensive zone of pasture and open forest would have been required to complement the arable sector. Since the islands are only slightly differentiated ecologically, there is no reason to suppose that transhumance was ever systematically practised in order to exploit complementary resources. The limited evidence for sheep or goat pastoralists in caves of the northern range above the Sóller basin (Enseñat Estrany 1963, 1967) can be interpreted in at least two ways. Stock may have been moved away from the arable land in the basin for a brief period whilst the grain ripened and was harvested later, returning to graze the stubble, or larger populations may have moved up to the high, humid plateaus to sow crops there in times of drought.

Such a pattern of mixed farming is applicable not only to individual navetiformes but also to larger settlements, such as the enclosed settlement of So'n Ferrandell-So'n Oleza, which lies adjacent to the most fertile soils (Pliocene marls) in the Valldemossa basin (Waldren 1981b). The shelter of So'n Matge, on the edge of the basin close to a pass leading to the central lowlands, would have been ideally situated for subordinate pastoral, gathering, and processing activities (Figure 8.5). The Ets Antigors enclosure is not adjacent to high quality soils, but there are three clusters of navetiformes within a radius of a few kilometres of the site, all located near such soils. Thus it is reasonable to suppose that the inhabitants of Ets Antigors obtained their subsistence staples indirectly (Rosselló Bordoy 1963).

The discovery that bastioned enclosures coexisted with simpler navetiforme dwellings and—on the evidence of Ets Antigors—possibly dominated a two-tier system of land use raises the possibility that a ranked society was already established in the Balearic islands by the Chalcolithic. Despite the unresolved chronological problems and the absence of a systematic study of the expression of social differences through mortuary ritual, it is reasonable to suppose that the variation in the size and complexity of tomb types and in the quantity and quality of grave goods is at least partly due to social factors (Veny 1968). The question of the emergence and maintenance of such a ranked society is particularly acute, given that previously the Balearic archipelago was largely uninhabited, so that population pressure could hardly have been a relevant factor.

Of the four models considered earlier, two may be rejected without hesitation. Lilliu's (1963) scenario of the emergence of ranking from the tensions of pastoral societies is unlikely, since there is no reason to believe that the pastoral sector was more important than the arable in terms of the production of subsistence staples, although this sector was probably preeminent from a sociopolitical perspective. Shennan's (1982) model—a Beaker ideological transformation legitimising previously established social differentiation due to economic intensification—presupposes precisely the dense settlement and developed economy that is far from evident in the period prior to the Chalcolithic in the Baleares. Both Renfrew (1972) and Gilman (1981) envisage a diverse economy integrated by an elite in a central place, although they disagree over the extent of redistribution as opposed to exploitation. Either of these models is compatible with the two-tier agricultural system hypothesised for Ets Antigors, and at a more general level with the settlement division of bastioned enclosures and navetiforme hamlets. However, three of the four variables listed by Gilman (1981) are missing from the Baleares: There is no evidence for tree crop cultivation before the Punic period (Pericot Garcia 1972:98), nor for irrigation or deep sea fishing, even in the early historical period. The use of ards, Gilman's fourth variable, is the only plausible form of intensification likely to have preceded the Chalcolithic period. Sherratt's postulated horizon of diffusion, predicted to occur at 2700–2500 b.c. in the Mediterranean (Sherratt 1981:271), has been vindicated by the discovery of ard marks dated to approximately 2650–2600 b.c. at the ritual site of St. Martin-de-Corléans in the Val d'Aosta in northern Italy (Mezzena 1982:33,50). Therefore, since the Mediterranean wooden ard is easily constructed in itself, it is worth considering whether the practice of cereal cultivation with the ard depended on some other variable that could be denied to the potential user by one segment of the population. It is also worth attempting to establish that the employment of the ard was a critical factor for subsistence.

Historical studies of west Mediterranean farming suggest that labour, rather than land, has been the principal constraint for the small agricultural enterprise. Only 10 or 11 ha are needed for a nuclear family (Delille 1977:132; Rosselló Verger 1964:302), but small population nuclei find it impossible to provide the necessary labour supply over the growing season, even when children are pressed into service as full-time stock minders (Delille 1977:103–133). Furthermore, a wide range of other activities is necessary for self-sufficiency, such as firewood gathering (Vilà Valentí 1950:426), the care of several species of livestock, domestic processing, and general maintenance work. Given these labour demands, permanent cultivation based on the hoe is not likely to have been possible for the dispersed pattern of navetiforme settlement (whether individual homesteads or hamlet-sized clusters). However, this settlement pattern could have been supported by a cultivation system using the ard and animal traction, which together increase productivity by a factor of at least two or three (Delille 1977:128).

The substitution of ox traction for manual labour would have solved the problem of the labour shortage inherent in dispersed population nuclei but would have brought additional problems. For example, more pasture would have been necessary, since oxen need some 10–12 ha per head in southern Mediterranean environments (Delille 1977:135). Worn-out stock also needs to be replaced. By analogy with Sardinia today, the working lifetime of oxen may not have exceeded 10 years out of a total lifespan of 18–20 years (Angioni 1976:104). Above all, the maintenance of a bull would have been an impossible investment for every household (Delille 1977:135–136). Moreover, although sheep would have been an essential component of the farming system, looking after the small numbers appropriate to a single family or small community would have made disproportionally heavy demands on the limited labour available. Hence, for a dispersed population such as that envisaged for the Baleares in the Chalcolithic, it would have been far more efficient in terms of cost and labour inputs for the cattle-raising and (to a lesser extent) shepherding to be practised by a specialised segment of the population.

A small group controlling the critical means of production (the herds) would clearly have been in a powerful position to exploit the remainder. Historically, one of the most characteristic features of Mediterranean latifundist regimes has been the dependence of the small proprietor on the feudal landlord for the provision of traction animals (Delille 1976:136). Delille also notes that the infrequent renewal of the feudal class in Sicily has always taken place from the ranks of the *gabelotti*, the possessors of cattle (1977:136); in fact, *gabelotto* is practically synonymous with *mafioso* (Rochefort 1961:47, 110–111). In the Baleares, therefore, the subordinate elements of the chalcolithic population may thus have been dependent not on permanent facilities such as terraces or irrigation systems, as envisaged in Gilman's (1981) model, but on access to sources of energy and fertiliser that they could not maintain or reproduce themselves. Since meat is almost universally esteemed, and since the slaughter of surplus young or worn out cattle would provide large quantities of a perishable food ideal for a 'big man' sharing–feasting system, control of the reproduction of live herds would also have enabled the elite segment of the population to grant or withhold further benefits. It therefore seems plausible to suggest that at least those enclosures that occupy nodal positions in a two-level site hierarchy may have been inhabited in the Chalcolithic by a dominant element of the population able, through their manipulation of the herds, to practise an asymmetric system of exchange or simply to extort grain from a dispersed subordinate population engaged in permanent agriculture. Barker's (1978) model of the *zimbabwe* economy of iron age southern Africa provides a striking analogy.

Settlement Changes of the Talaiotic Period

The demarcation of a pre-Talaiotic–Talaiotic boundary during the fourteenth century b.c. (Fernández-Miranda and Waldren 1979:364) does not signify a rapid and radical transformation of settlement, subsistence, or social organisation at that time. The horizon is not based on the date of construction of a large sample of talaiots but on the single analysis from the talaiot of Pula, So'n Servera (Fernández-Miranda and Waldren 1979:366), and on the appearance of ceramic assemblages different in form and fabric from those of the pre-Talaiotic in a variety of contexts (navetes, navetiformes, rock-cut tombs, shelters, and sites of ritual importance) between 1300 and 1000 b.c., which clearly indicates the continued use of such structures (Fernández-Miranda and Waldren 1979:364; Rosselló Bordoy 1973:160–166, 187–188). A more significant date is that of 1000 b.c., which marks the final abandonment of many sites and the date of construction of a large sample of talaiots and of talaiotic villages, including the talaiots that succeeded the older enclosure of So'n Ferrandell-So'n Oleza (Fernandez-Miranda and Waldren 1979:364, 368).

The two phenomena of most significance for this study are, first, the evidence for a concentration of population into a few large sites (Talaiotic walled villages) ranging in size from 0.8 to 1.7 ha, with populations estimated at 200–400 (Rosselló Bordoy 1973:137); and second, the probability of much more organised settlement systems consisting of central villages and peripheral, subordinate talaiots (Lewthwaite 1983). In pursuing the theme of progressive architectural elaboration, the orthodox models (Pericot Garcia 1972:41; Rosselló Bordoy 1973:106) assume that the simpler talaiots fall into an earlier period (before 1000 b.c.) than that of the villages. However, this hypothesis remains unverified, and the spatial patterning of talaiots and Talaiotic villages within natural territorial cells such as the Puigpunyent basin suggests an integrated settlement system (Rosselló Bordoy 1953). Thus it seems more likely that both classes of structure began to be constructed around 1000 b.c. in response to profound social transformations (Fernández-Miranda and Waldren 1979:368).

Such a transformation can best be interpreted as a further step in the control of primary food production by local dominant groups. Whereas the pre-Talaiotic two-tier settlement system suggests indirect exploitation over a distance through unequal exchange or the exaction of tribute, the concentration of the bulk of the population into talaiotic villages after 1000 b.c. would have enabled a more direct and continuous system of control and coercion.

Balearic Developments in the Western Mediterranean Regional Context

It might be argued that the settlement transformations of the Chalcolithic period in the Baleares can best be explained in terms of sustained population pressure elsewhere in the western Mediterranean and the resulting colonisation. In this scenario, the agricultural potential of the archipelago was largely ignored or at least underexploited during the third millennium b.c. because of its geographical isolation. When the pressure of population on resources in an adjacent mainland zone surpassed the threshold set by this barrier, colonisation occurred. In effect, since the ecological and archaeological variables are very similar to those of the Garrigues of Languedoc, the Balearic case could be regarded as an extension of the process of population increase and settlement expansion discussed by Mills (Chapter 7, this volume). The model would remain relatively intact even if the evidence for later third millennium settlement in Mallorca were to increase with future research, since Menorca and the Pithyusae are as handicapped by size and location in comparison with Mallorca as the latter is with the mainland. The process, perhaps underway on Mallorca by 2700 b.c., nevertheless accelerated dramatically between approximately 2200 and 1800 b.c. However, this model would fail to predict the extent of social differentiation apparent at such an early date in both settlement and mortuary contexts. I would argue instead that pre-Talaiotic settlement cannot be understood in isolation from comparable and concurrent phenomena common to the west Mediterranean. These can be described in terms of three interacting processes.

First, there was admittedly a major increase in the number of permanent agricultural settlements during the second millennium b.c., particularly in the upland interiors. This process is especially evident in southern Spain, where Argaric, Valencian, and Manchegan bronze age villages were established in areas devoid of copper age settlement (Coles and Harding 1979:216–226; Molina and Nájera 1978:70–74), and in Sicily, where a fivefold increase in site numbers occurred between the Copper and Early Bronze Ages, and where large areas of the centre were first settled in the latter (Castelluccio) period (Fairbank 1978:16). However, this purely demographic increase cannot be divorced from a second phenomenon, namely the emergence of coherent networks of sites that can be defined at the regional scale, suggesting the development of polities concurrent with a trend towards the selection of defensible positions and the fortification of sites. In Spain, for example, Argaric Bronze Age systems linking lowland villages with adjacent upland sites have been identified in the province of Murcia. These have been interpreted as federations or chiefdoms (Ayala Juan 1979, 1981), and analogous models have been proposed for regional groupings of Sardinian *nuraghi* and Corsican *torri,* which are structures similar to the Balearic talaiots (Lewthwaite 1983).

Third, and perhaps most critical, a 'maritime interaction sphere' can be observed across the Mediterranean during the later third and early second millennia b.c. There are striking similarities in the plans and architectural details of a large series of enclosures, often occupying coastal locations, from Spain through southern France and on to Sicily and the Aegean. In the western basin (Figure 8.6), the enclosures are sometimes associated with Beaker pottery ('primary–maritime' or regional derivative styles), and from Sicily eastwards with a class of bossed bone plaques (Lewthwaite 1983). The few radiocarbon dates and associated assemblages suggest an approximate synchronism, but the archaeology is not so identical as to indicate a single migration or diffusion 'package'. For example, the bastioned enclosures of Cabezo de la Cueva del Plomo (a coastal

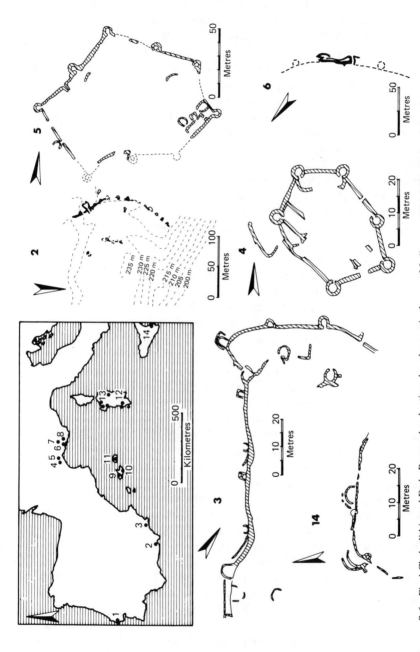

Figure 8.6 Final Chalcolithic and Early Bronze Age bastioned enclosures in the west Mediterranean basin. 1, Tagus (Vila Nova da São Pedro, etc.); 2, Los Millares; 3, Cabeza del Plomo; 4, Boussargues; 5, Lébous; 6, Camp de Laure; 7, Les Lauzières; 8, La Citadelle; 9, So'n Ferrandell–So'n Oleza; 10, Ets Antigors; 11, Torralba d'En Salord; 12, S'Urecci; 13, Monte Claro sites; 14, Petraro di Melilli.

site in Murcia, Spain) and of Lébous and Boussargues (inland sites in Hérault, France) are associated only with local material (Arnal 1973; Colomer et al. 1980; Muñoz Amilibia 1982). The Monte Ossoni enclosure on the northern coast of Sardinia probably has no bastions (the site is much disturbed) and has revealed Monte Claro pottery together with a few Beaker sherds (Moravetti 1979:332–333). Some of the Spanish and French enclosures were abandoned by 2200 b.c., or even 2500 b.c., yet the Camp de Laure (Bouches-du-Rhône, southern France), which is enclosed by a rampart of distinctively 'Aegean' appearance, continued in use until approximately 1500 B.C. (Courtin 1978:26; Coutel et al. 1981:8; Sangmeister and Schubart 1977). The extent to which the variables coincide in the Baleares, particularly in the case of the So'n Ferrandell-So'n Oleza enclosure, is therefore extremely significant.

In addition to this class of site, there is a great deal of other evidence for maritime connections across the Mediterranean during this period, and the re-futation of diffusionist models for the origins of the Iberian and Italian Copper Ages (Renfrew 1967; Whitehouse and Renfrew 1974) does not eliminate the clear evidence for indirect contacts along a chain extending from the Iberian peninsula to the eastern Mediterranean established especially between approximately 2200 and 1800 b.c. There was particularly strong contact between the Aude region of southern France and Sardinia (Bray 1964). The next closest parallels for Mallorcan chamber tombs are Sardinian or Corsican (Plantalamor Massanet 1977; Rosselló Bordoy et al. 1980). As early as 3000 b.c. there is suggestive evidence of Cypriot and Aegean influences on the Ozieri culture of Sardinia by way of Malta (Bernabò Brea 1980; Tanda 1980). Besides the distribution of the enclosures and associated artefacts, there is now tentative evidence from southeastern Spain for direct ceramic analogies with Cyprus and the Levant in Copper and Early Bronze Age contexts (Walker 1981:188–190). Groups with affinities to the Sicilian Castelluccio and Capo Graziano cultures settled the arid and inhospitable island of Pantelleria (Tozzi 1968, 1978) and introduced the Tarxien cemetery culture into Malta in place of the civilisation of the temples (Bernabò Brea 1980). Corsica provides a striking negative instance of a large island that appears to have been completely by-passed at this time, with traffic from northwest Sardinia taking the deep sea route to Provence (Camps 1975: 118–121). The use of the Baleares for navigation was surely a crucial link in the maritime interaction sphere that embraced so much of the Mediterranean basin from Spain to Cyprus.

The strategic position of the Baleares must surely be regarded as at least as powerful an attraction as their subsistence opportunities, particularly for entrepreneurial elements within the population. Access to or even control over traffic in exotic products, including almost certainly by this time the regional circulation of metal axes, ingots, or artifacts, could well have decided between locations of equal potential for subsistence. Only by giving equal weight to both subsistence and nonsubsistence factors can the simultaneous development of elite differentiation and population increase be adequately explained.

Conclusions

It is argued here that the transformations that propelled the Baleares into the centre stage of western Mediterranean cultural activity in approximately 2000 b.c. cannot be explained in purely palaeoeconomic terms (for example, the hypothesis of sustained population growth optimising the use of resources). Isolation and a dearth of indigenous sources of subsistence may have retarded initial settlement by foragers, and the same isolation and environmental constraints may have handicapped the local adoption of mixed farming. However, neither technical innovation nor subsistence stress alone appears to have overcome these limitations. (In fact, by far the greatest expansion in population appears to have taken place within the archipelago itself, most probably on Mallorca, despite the problems of aridity and the maintenance of soil fertility.) The explanation proposed here is that the strategic location of the Baleares provided opportunities for entrepreneurial activity, particularly within the triangle of Sardinia-southern France-southeastern Spain, the apices of which are roughly equidistant from Mallorca. Similar entrepreneurial activity, in the form of control over critical elements in the agricultural system (particularly traction cattle and less certainly flocks of sheep and goats), appears to provide the best explanation for the settlement pattern.

Such a model enables the most positive elements of the Renfrew (1972) and Gilman (1981) scenarios to be combined. Gilman recognises three variables: the subordinate group practising the domestic mode of production, the aggrandising elite, and the fixed facilities resulting from labour investment necessary for sustained intensive production. The subordinate group cannot evade the exactions of the elite without sacrificing the investments, while the elite finances its conspicuous wealth, consumption, and waste through a protection racket. Gilman's logic can be simplified if perishable facilities (traction cattle, in this case) are involved, which need to be periodically renewed and constantly maintained. However, in a situation of rapid population growth in an island environment such as the Baleares, it is possible to question his twin assumptions of the scarcity of land and capital rather than labour, as well as his antagonistic model of elite emergence. Since every elite group must ultimately be descended from a domestic group, and since people rather than space or ploughs may have been the actual limit on systemic growth, dominance might have been achieved through a favourable initial position, differential reproductive success, and the 'management' of fissile tendencies within one domestic group. The transition from a purely subsistence to a partly politicised economy with a prestige element may thus have occurred within a single growing lineage without the tensions assumed by Gilman.

In effect, Gilman's model of class tension appears anachronistic in a chalcolithic context in which it seems more appropriate to envisage competitive lineages or clans occupying shifting positions of relative dominance and subordination. In this sense (and only in this sense), Renfrew's model of a managerial node organising diverse sectorial activities, and hence catalysing a 'multiplier effect' appears valid, though at the very much reduced scale of communities of a few hundred kinsmen occupying a restricted territory. For instance, in the case of the Valldemossa basin, some form of organisation and differentiation can clearly be detected between the main settlement at So'n Ferrandell-So'n Oleza, where a wide range of food production and processing activities were carried out besides copper- and flint-working and perhaps ceramic manufacture, compared with the So'n Matge 'out station'. There is no evidence, however, of such 'modules' approaching the density of population or degree of social differentiation evident in the contemporary Aegean.

This model may appear to function only in the very peculiar and restricted circumstances of the Balearic example, combining extreme marginality with a potential for considerable growth due to the favourable strategic location at a specific conjuncture—that is, in the context of the growth of maritime interaction. However, many comparable patterns of development doubtless recurred in marginal areas of continental Europe in the form of small settlement enclaves, perhaps in mineral-endowed mountainous regions. These would have prospered from the extension of value from subsistence to nonsubsistence resources at the inception of the local Bronze Age.

Acknowledgements

I would like to thank the many scholars who supplied offprints, books, and welcome advice: A. d'Anna, J. Arnal, M. M. Ayala Juan, A. Arribas, G. Barker, M. Brunswig, G. Camps, J. Courtin, C. Delano Smith, J. Estévez, M. Fernández-Miranda, C. Gamble, J. Gascó, A. Gilman, X. Gutherz, C. Lassure, C. Mathers, F. Mezzena, N. Mills, R. Montjardin, A. M. Muñoz, T. Nájera, H. Osmaston, V. M. Rosselló Verger, H. Schubart, S. J. Shennan, C. Topp, C. Tozzi, P. Villari, and M. Walker. Particular thanks are due to Andrew Sherratt, Richard Harrison, Bill Waldren, Fred Hamond, Alison Sheridan, José and Teresa Morais Arnaud, Catherine Delano Smith, and Pat Phillips for discussions, although the remaining errors and omissions are entirely mine. John Howell prepared the originals for the illustrations.

References

Angioni, G.
    1976 *Sa Laurera: il lavoro contadino in Sardegna*. Editrice Democratica Sarda, Cagliari.

Anglada Gomila, J.
1976 Estudio de una naveta de habitación de Son Mercer de Baix, Menorca. *Mayurqa* 15:271–289.
Antoni Alcover, J., S. Moyà-Solà, and J. Pons-Moyà
1981 *Les quimeres del Passat: els vertebrats fòssils del Plio-Quaternari de les Balears i Pitiüses.* Institució Catalana d'Història Natural and Editorial Moll, Ciutat de Mallorca.
Arnal, J.
1973 Lébous. *Gallia Préhistoire* 16:131–200.
Ayala Juan, M. M.
1979 Un yacimiento argárico de llanura: 'la Alcanara'. *Anales Universidad Murcia-Filosofía y Letras* 36(1–2):5–10.
Ayala Juan, M. M.
1981 La cultura del Argar en la provincia de Murcia. *Anales Universidad Murica-Filosofía y Letras* 38(4):147–179.
Barker, G. W. W.
1978 Economic models for the Manekweni *zimbabwe,* Mozambique. *Azania* 13:71–97.
Bernabò Brea, L.
1980 Beziehungen zu Malta, Sizilien und zu den Äolischen Inseln. In *Kunst und Kultur Sardiniens,* edited by J. Thimme, pp. 192–200. C. F. Müller, Karlsruhe.
Bisson, J.
1977 *La Terre et l'homme aux Iles Baléares.* Edisud, Aix-en-Provence.
Blanchard, R.
1914 Les genres de vie en Corse et leur évolution. *Recueil Travaux Institut Alpin Grenoble* 2:187–238.
Bray, W.
1964 Sardinian Beakers. *Proceedings of the Prehistoric Society* 28:75–98.
Burleigh, R., and J. Clutton-Brock
1980 The survival of *Myotragus balearicus* Bate, 1909, into the Neolithic on Mallorca. *Journal of Archaeological Science* 7:385–388.
Camps, G.
1975 La place de la Corse dans la Préhistoire Méditerranéenne. *Etudes Corses* 5:109–134.
Cantarellas Camps, C.
1972 Excavaciones en 'Ca Na Cotxera' (Muró, Mallorca). *Noticiario Arqueológico Hispánico-Prehistoria* I:179–226.
Cherry, J. F.
1981 Pattern and process in the earliest colonisation of the Mediterranean islands. *Proceedings of the Prehistoric Society* 47:41–68.
Childe, V. G.
1930 *The Bronze Age.* Cambridge University Press, Cambridge, England.
Childe, V. G.
1957 *The dawn of European civilisation.* Routledge and Kegan Paul, London.
Coles, J., and A. Harding
1979 *The Bronze Age in Europe.* Methuen, London.
Colomer, A., J. Coularou, X. Gutherz, and J. Vallois
1980 L'enceinte en pierres sèches de Boussargues, Argelliers, Hérault. In *Le Groupe de Véraza et la fin des temps néolithiques dans le sud de la France et la Catalogne,* edited by J. Guilaine, pp. 257–262. Centre National de la Recherche Scientifique, Toulouse.
Courtin, J.
1978 Quelques étapes de peuplement de la région de l'étang de Berre au post-glaciaire. *Bulletin Archéologique de Provence* 1:1–36.

Coutel, R., J. Courtin, and A. d'Anna
  1981 *Les Lauzières (Lourmarin, Vaucluse) Fouilles 1981*. Ministère Affaires Culturelles, Rapport
Delano Smith, C.
  1979 *Western Mediterranean Europe*. Academic Press, London.
Delille, G.
  1977 *Agricoltura e demografia nel Regno di Napoli nei secoli XVIII e XIX*. Guida editore, Napoli.
Enseñat Estrany, B.
  1963 Noticias sobre el hallazgo en Mallorca de unas cerámicas incisas del estilo del vaso campaniforme. *Congreso Nacional de Arqueología, Actas* 8:184–187.
Enseñat Estrany, B.
  1967 Aportación al conocimiento de los primitivos pobladores de Mallorca. *Congreso Nacional de Arqueología, Actas* 10:67–74.
Enseñat Estrany, C.
  1971 Excavaciones en el naviforme 'Alemany' Magalluf (Calvià, Mallorca). *Noticiario Arqueológico Hispánico* 15:39–73.
Fairbank, J.
  1978 *The Castelluccio culture*. Ph.D. dissertation, Institute of Archaeology, London, BLLD D 25487/79.
Fernández, J.
  1977 Ultimos descubrimientos prehistóricos en la isla de Formentera (Baleares). *Congreso Nacional de Arqueología, Actas* 14:471–478.
Fernández Gomez, J,, and L. Plantalamor Massanet
  1975 Cerámicas de tipología talayótica en el Museo de Ibiza. *Congreso Nacional de Arqueología, Actas* 13:377–382.
Fernández-Miranda, M., and W. H. Waldren
  1974 El abrigo de Son Matge (Valldemosa) y la periodización de la Prehistoria Mallorquina mediante los análisis de carbono-14. *Trabajos de Prehistoria* 31:297–304.
Fernández-Miranda, M., and W. H. Waldren
  1979 Periodificación cultural y cronología absoluta en la prehistoria de Mallorca. *Trabajos de Prehistoria* 36:349–377.
Frey, O. H., and G. Rosselló Bordoy
  n.d. Es Closos de Ca'n Gaià. *Trabajos del Museo de Mallorca* 2.
Geddes, D.
  1983 Neolithic transhumance in the Mediterranean Pyrenees. *World Archaeology* 15(1):51–66.
Geddes, D.
  1983b *De la Chasse au Troupeau en Méditerranée Occidentale: les débuts de l'élevage dans la Vallée de l'Aude*. Centre d'Anthropologie des Sociétés Rurales, Toulouse.
Gilman, A.
  1981 The development of social stratification in bronze age Europe. *Current Anthropology* 22(1):1–8.
Gordillo Coucières, J. G.
  1981 *Formentera: historia de una isla*. Albatros ediciones, Valencia.
Gottesfeld, A., and P. Martin
  1968 Palynological analysis of the soil of Muleta. In *Myotragus balearicus: palaeopathology and the palynological study of the soil of the deposit*. DAMARC, Deyà.
Guilaine, J. (editor)
  1980 *Le groupe de Véraza et la fin des temps néolithiques dans la sud de la France et la Catalogne*. Centre National de la Recherche Scientifique, Toulouse.

Kruk, J.
1980 *The earlier Neolithic of southern Poland.* British Archaeological Reports, International Series 93, Oxford, England.
Le Lannou, M.
1941 *Pâtres et Paysans de la Sardaigne.* Arrault, Tours.
Lewthwaite, J. G.
1981 Plains tails from the hills: transhumance in Mediterranean archaeology. In *Economic archaeology,* edited by A. Sheridan and G. Bailey, pp. 57–66. British Archaeological Reports, International Series 96, Oxford, England.
Lewthwaite, J. G.
1982a Ambiguous first impressions: a survey of recent work on the early Neolithic of the West Mediterranean. *Journal of Mediterranean Anthropology and Archaeology* 1(2):242–307.
Lewthwaite, J. G.
1982b Acorns for the ancestors: the prehistoric exploitation of woodland in the west Mediterranean. In *Archaeological aspects of woodland ecology,* edited by S. Limbrey and M. Bell, pp. 217–230. British Archaeological Reports, International Series 146, Oxford, England.
Lewthwaite, J. G.
1983 La culture des castelli de la Corse: dernier témoin d'un genre de vie ouest-Méditerranéen d'autrefois? *Archaeologia Corsa* 6–7:19–33.
Lewthwaite, J. G.
1984 Works and days: archaeological implications of recent settlement and subsistence activities in marginal regions of the western Mediterranean. In *Progress in Mediterranean studies,* edited by J. L. Bintliff. Bradford Archaeological Publications, Bradford, England.
Lilliu, G.
1963 *La civiltà dei Sardi.* Edizioni RAI, Turin.
Louis, M.
1948 *Préhistoire du Languedoc Méditerranéen et du Roussillon.* Brugier, Nîmes.
Louis, M.
1950 Notes de voyage aux Îles Baleares. *Zephyrus* 1:39–48.
Mascaró Pasarius, J.
1967a *Monumentos prehistóricos y protohistóricos de la Isla de Menorca.* Ministerio de Educación y Ciencia, Palma de Mallorca.
Mascaró Pasarius, J.
1967b *Monumentos prehistóricos y protohistóricos de la Isla de Mallorca.* Ministerio de Educación y Ciencia, Palma de Mallorca.
Mezzena, F.
1982 *Archeologia in Valle d'Aosta dal Neolitico alla Caduta dell'Impero Romano 3500 a.c.-V Secolo d.c.* Assessorato del Turismo, Aosta.
Molina, F., and T. Nájera
1978 De Motillas von Azuer und los Palacios. *Madrider Mitteilungen* 19:52–74.
Moravetti, A.
1979 Notiziario-Sardegna: Neolitico e Metalli. *Rivista Scienze Preistoriche* 34(1–2):332–334.
Muñoz Amilibia, A. M.
1982 Poblado eneolitico del tipo 'Los Millares' en Murcia, España. *Congreso Nacional de Arqueologia, Programa 16*:71–75.
Parrack, J.
1973 *The naturalist in Majorca.* David and Charles, Newton Abbot.
Pericot Garcia, L.
1972 *The Balearic Islands.* Thames and Hudson, London.
Phillips, P.
1975 *Early farmers of West Mediterranean Europe.* Hutchinson, London.

Pieretti, A.
1947 Les formes d'exploitation et de peuplement d'une plaine Méditerranéenne. *Bulletin de la Société Géographique et d'Economie Coloniale de Marseille* 63:7–20.

Plantalamor Massanet, L.
1977 Algunas consideraciones sobre los sepulcros megalíticos de Menorca. *Trabajos del Museo de Menorca* 1.

Plantalamor Massanet, L., and M. C. Rita
1984 Formas de población durante el II y I milenio antes de J. C. en Menorca. In *Early settlement in the western Mediterranean islands and their peripheral areas.* British Archaeological Reports, International Series 229, Oxford, England.

Puglisi, S.
1959 *La Civiltà Appenninica: origini delle comunità pastorali in Italia.* Sansoni, Florence.

Ravis-Giordani, G.
1983 *Bergers Corses: les communautés villageoises du Niolu.* Edisud, Aix-en-Provence.

Renfrew, C.
1967 Colonialism and Megalithismus. *Antiquity* 41:276–288.

Renfrew, C.
1969 The autonomy of the southeast European Copper Age. *Proceedings of the Prehistoric Society* 35:12–47.

Renfrew, C.
1972 *The emergence of civilisation in the Cyclades and the Aegean: the third millennium b.c.* Methuen, London.

Rochefort, R.
1961 *Le Travail en Sicile.* Presses Universitaires de France.

Rosselló Bordoy, G.
1953 Los núcleos talayóticos del término de Puigpuñent. *Boletín de la Sociedad Arqueológica Luliana* 31:385–390.

Rosselló Bordoy, G.
1963 Ses Salines: avance al estudio de sus yacimientos arqueológicos. *Boletín de la Sociedad Arqueológica Luliana* 32:1–17.

Rosselló Bordoy, G.
1966 Las navetas en Mallorca. *Studi Sardi* 19:261–314.

Rosselló Bordoy, G.
1973 *La Cultura Talayótica en Mallorca.* Ediciones Cort, Palma de Mallorca.

Rosselló Bordoy, G.
1984 Cuevas Mallorquinas excavadas en la roca y su problemática. In *Early settlement in the western Mediterranean islands and their peripheral areas,* edited by W. H. Waldren et al. British Archaeological Reports, International Series, 229. Oxford, England.

Rosselló Bordoy, G., and W. Waldren
1973 Excavaciones en el Abrigo del Bosque de Son Matge (Valldemosa, Mallorca). *Noticiario Arqueológico Hispánico* 2:3–76.

Rosselló Bordoy, G., L. Plantalamor Masanet, and A. Lopez Pons
1980 Excavaciones arqueológicas en Torre d'En Gaumés (Alayor, Menorca). *Noticiario Arqueológico Hispánico* 8:71–138.

Rosselló Verger, V. M.
1964 *Mallorca: el sur y sureste.* COCIN, Palma de Mallorca.

Rowlands, M. J.
1976 *The organisation of middle bronze age metalworking.* British Archaeological Reports, British Series 31, Oxford, England.

Sangmeister, E., and H. Schubart
1977 Zambujal: eine befestigte Siedlung der Kupferzeit in Portugal. *Antike Welt* 3:23–34.

Shennan, S.
  1982 Ideology, change and the European Bronze Age. In *Symbolic and structural archaeology,* edited by I. Hodder, pp. 155–161. Cambridge University Press, Cambridge, England.
Sherratt, A. G.
  1981 Plough and pastoralism: aspects of the secondary products revolution. In *Pattern of the past,* edited by I. Hodder et al., pp. 261–305. Cambridge University Press, Cambridge, England.
Tanda, G.
  1980 Beziehungen zum östlichen Mittelmeer. In *Kunst und Kultur Sardiniens,* edited by J. Thimme, pp. 171–179. C. F. Müller, Karlsruhe.
Topp, C., J. Fernández, and L. Plantalamor Massanet
  1976 Ca Na Costa: a megalithic chamber tomb on Formentera, Balearic Islands. *Bulletin of the Institute of Archaeology of London* 13:139–173.
Topp, C., J. Fernández, and L. Plantalamor Massanet
  1979 Recent archaeological activities on Ibiza and Formentera. *Bulletin of the Institute of Archaeology of London* 16:215–231.
Tozzi, C.
  1968 Relazione preliminare sulla I e II campagna di scavi effettuati a Pantelleria. *Rivista Scienze Preistoriche* 23:315–388.
Tozzi, C.
  1978 Nuovi dati sul villaggio dell'età del Bronzo di Mursia a Pantelleria. *Quaderni de la Ricerca Scientifica* 100:149–157.
Trias, M., and L. Roca
  1975 Noves aportacions al coneixement de les coves de Sa Mola (Formentera) i de la seva importancia arqueológica. *Endins* 2:15–33.
Uerpmann, H. P.
  1979 *Probleme der neolithisierung des Mittelmeeraums.* Reichert, Wiesbaden.
Veny, C.
  1968 *Las cuevas sepulcrales del Bronce Antiguo de Mallorca.* CSIC, Madrid.
Vigne, J. D.
  1984 Premières données sur le début de l'élevage du mouton, de la chèvre et du porc dans le sud de la Corse (France). In *Animals and archaeology* (Vol. 3), edited by C. Grigson and J. Clutton-Brock, pp. 47–65. British Archaeological Reports, International Series 202, Oxford, England.
Vilà Valentí, J.
  1950 Formentera: estudio de geografía humana. *Estudios Geográficos* 11:389–442.
Waldren, W. H.
  1979 A Beaker workshop area in the rockshelter of Son Matge, Mallorca. *World Archaeology* 11:43–67.
Waldren, W. H.
  1981a *Radiocarbon determination in the Balearic Islands: an inventory 1962–81.* DAMARC, Deyà.
Waldren, W. H.
  1981b *The settlement complex of Ferrandell-Oleza.* DAMARC, Deyà.
Waldren, W. H.
  1982 *Early prehistoric settlement in the Balearic Islands.* DAMARC, Deyà.
Waldren, W, H.
  1983 *Balearic prehistory, ecology and culture: the excavation and study of certain caves, rock shelters and settlements.* British Archaeological Reports, International Series 149, Oxford, England.

Waldren, W. H., and L. Plantalamor Massanet
   1976 Campaña de excavaciones en el abrigo de Son Matge, Valldemosa (Mallorca) 1973. *Noticiario Arqueológico Hispánico* 5:240–246.
Waldren, W. H., and G. Rosselló Bordoy
   1975 Excavaciones en la cueva de Muleta (Sóller, Mallorca): los niveles arqueológicos. *Noticiario Arqueológico Hispánico* 3:73–108.
Walker, M. J.
   1981 Climate, economy and cultural change: the southeast Spanish Copper Age. In *Miscelenea del X Congreso UICPP*, edited by J. García-Bárcena and F. Sánchez Martínez, pp. 171–197. Mexico, D.F.
Whitehouse, R., and C. Renfrew
   1974 The Copper Age of peninsular Italy and the Aegean. *Annual of the British School of Archaeology at Athens* 69:343–390.

9

Subsistence and Settlement in Northern Temperate Europe in the First Millennium A.D.

KLAVS RANDSBORG

Introduction

The first millennium A.D. is a crucial and most complex phase in the social history of Europe. At the beginning of the period, the Roman Empire was establishing itself in the temperate zones of Europe and bringing profound political, economic, and wider cultural changes to societies that were previously all but excluded from the development of the Mediterranean basin. Even more remote areas such as southern Scandinavia were also exposed to Roman influence for many centuries. By the time of the collapse of Roman power in the northwest in approximately A.D. 400, the Germanic societies beyond the frontier (the *limes*) had already been transformed into very organised entities. Some, like the Franks on the Rhine, inherited much of what was left of the imperial political and economic system. By this time, the empire had already developed into a confederacy of provinces, with Italy playing a less prominent role than in the early years of Roman rule (Reece 1980, 1981), a trend that coincided with a reduction in the importance of towns and growth in the rural economy. The late imperial system was less exploitative in terms of natural resources than the earlier system of government had been. By the late Roman period, political and economic structures were rather similar on either side of the frontier, and the old dichotomy between the Roman and Germanic worlds became increasingly less meaningful.

Cultural and social differentiation in time and space have been the main foci of archaeological and historical research in the regions on either side of the imperial limes during the first millennium A.D.; economies, especially subsistence econo-

BEYOND DOMESTICATION
IN PREHISTORIC EUROPE

233

mies, are still relatively poorly understood. In this chapter subsistence trends are reconstructed using the evidence of animal bones and plant remains from excavations. We also examine the organisation of the agricultural economy on the basis of settlements and settlement patterns. The principal study area is a broad zone stretching from the Rhine estuary to Denmark, with extensions north to Sweden and south and east across the northern German plains (Figure 9.1). In some instances the temporal framework has been extended on either side of the first

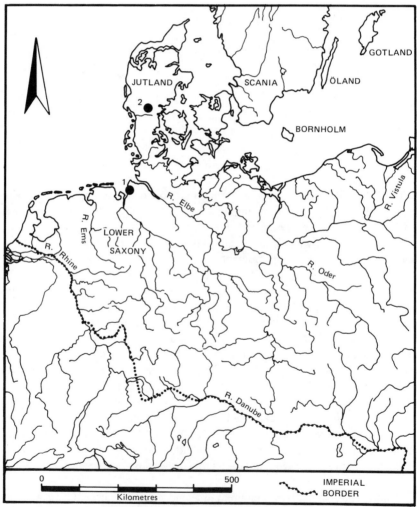

Figure 9.1 Parts of central and northern Europe, showing the frontier (*limes*) between the Roman empire and 'Germania libera'. 1, Feddersen Wierde; 2, Vorbasse.

millennium A.D. to provide a wider perspective. The areas under consideration are characterised by considerable environmental variation, from open marshlands to heavily forested parts of central Denmark and the northern perimeter of central Europe. Soils vary from rich marine and alluvial deposits to heavy morainic clays and sandy plains, offering very different potentials for crop and animal husbandry.

Pollen diagrams from southern and central Scandinavia show that levels of human influence on the landscape (according to cereal and plantain pollen) were high at the beginning and higher still at the end of the first millennium A.D. (Berglund 1969; Lange 1971, 1976; see also Behre [1976] for areas further south). The expansion at the beginning of the millennium was in fact already underway in the pre-Roman Iron Age towards the end of the first millennium B.C. In the second quarter of the first millennium A.D. there is a marked increase in arboreal pollen. Similar trends are recorded further south, including regions inside the Roman Empire. The high cereal and plantain levels at the beginning of the first millennium A.D. suggest intensive use (and perhaps overuse) of the natural resources (Randsborg 1982; Widgren 1977). This phenomenon should not be attributed simply to the impact of the Roman Empire (see Groenman-van Waateringe 1980), for it is unknown to what extent the northwestern part of the empire received foodstuffs and other agricultural products from regions beyond the limes. Apparently only the area up to the river Elbe (and probably only the coastal margin) was in a position to provide such goods, and it is highly unlikely that Norway, Sweden, or Finland was in any way involved (Berglund 1969; Tolonen 1976). Thus the reduction in cereal and plantain pollen across the whole region in the second quarter of the first millennium A.D. must reflect other (local) factors.

Different types of climatic information are also difficult to compare (Randsborg 1980:45). The best comparisons are often based on cultural phenomena such as changing depths of wells. Long sequences, such as the tree lines and glacier movements of the Alps or the annual layers of the Greenland ice cap, are also very useful (Hammer et al. 1980). Another recent branch of study concerns humification trends in Danish bogs (Aaby 1976). The correlation of such climatic data with the pollen diagrams confirms the picture of warm periods at the beginning and end of the first millennium A.D., separated by a cold and wet phase (Aaby 1976; La Marche 1974; Lamb 1981; Willerding, 1977). In several pollen diagrams, the recession phase is marked by relatively high values for cattle indicators, implying less labour-intensive subsistence than in the first expansion phase. On the island of Bornholm, for example, the collection of wild grasses increased as cereal farming decreased, and cattle ranching increased at the expense of sheep-rearing (Helbaek 1957; Møhl 1957). It seems likely that the recession was characterised by a real stagnation and probably even a decline in population levels. There are also several references to plagues from the third century A.D. onwards, including the well-known 'Justinian plague' of the early sixth century, which may have spread to areas outside the former empire (Biraben and Le Goff 1975).

The second expansion phase, at the end of the first millennium A.D., did not bring a return to earlier agricultural practices; pollen diagrams show very high values for cereals (including rye, relatively new to northwestern Europe), compared with indicators for animal husbandry (Iversen 1973; Lange 1971, 1976). This period was marked by strong population growth, a labour-intensive form of subsistence, and the development of early medieval society (Randsborg 1982). The technology and organisational structures also differed significantly from those of the Roman Empire and the Germanic Iron Age.

Domestic Animals

The available faunal data from the study area are scarce and unevenly distributed in time and space; the more sophisticated techniques of faunal analysis have been applied only to relatively few samples; hence, percentage enumerations of the main species are often the best available guide to regional variations in husbandry (Randsborg 1980:54). Samples of fewer than 100 fragments were excluded from this analysis. For the first centuries of the first millennium A.D., samples are known principally from the Netherlands and the North Sea coast of Germany, and to a lesser extent from the northern parts of central Germany, from Denmark, and from the Baltic islands of Öland and Gotland. The main samples for the second half of the millennium (particularly from approximately A.D. 800–1000, the Viking Age) are from Denmark and the adjacent regions of Germany and Sweden; others are from the Netherlands, Slavonia, and elsewhere in northern and eastern Germany.

The material has been divided into three regional groups in Figures 9.2 to 9.4. A long chronological sequence is available from the Netherlands (Figure 9.2) covering the Bronze Age; the pre-Roman Iron Age; the Roman period, divided into three groups—rural settlement north of the limes, rural settlement within the empire, and nonrural settlement within the empire (fortresses, towns, etc); and post-Roman or Carolingian, with material from the town of Dorestad separated from the other (rural) assemblages. The second group (Figure 9.3) consists of assemblages from the northern European plain to the east of the Netherlands, in three main regional clusters: the coastal zone of Lower Saxony between the Ems and Elbe rivers; the area north of the Elbe at the foot of the Jutland peninsula, and the east German and Polish lowlands between the Elbe and the Vistula. Most of the assemblages of this group date to the first phase of settlement expansion in the early first millennium A.D., although some late prehistoric sites are also included. From Denmark and southern Sweden (Figure 9.4) there is a faunal sequence comparable to that of the Netherlands: Bronze Age, Early Iron Age, Viking age (with data from towns and rural settlements separated), and material from the islands of Öland and Gotland dating to the second quarter of the first millennium A.D. and to the critical but otherwise poorly documented period around A.D. 500. Game in general played a minimal role in the meat diet of the first millennium (Reichstein et al. 1980:15), which consisted almost exclusively of beef supplemented by pork, mutton, and horse flesh.

In the Netherlands (Figure 9.2), the average cattle (C) percentage in the Bronze Age is very high (78%), pig (P) is relatively low (7%), sheep–goat (S/G) is moderate (13%), and horse (H) is extremely low (1%). For the pre-Roman Iron Age, the figures for these four species (counting sheep–goat henceforth as a single species) are, respectively, C = 65%, P = 10%, S–G = 21%, and H = 5%. Similar values exist for the post-Roman period apart from the atypical sample from the West Frisian island of Texel, which is dominated (like the island landscape today) by sheep. For the intervening Roman period, however, the

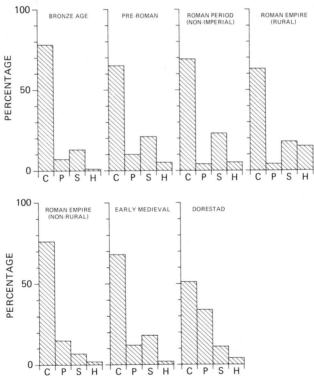

Figure 9.2 Averages of bone samples from the Netherlands. (The sources for the data are listed in the Appendix.) C, cattle; P, pig; S, sheep–goat; H, horse.

situation is somewhat more complex: Within the empire, the rural settlements have average figures of C = 63%, P = 4%, S–G = 18%, and H = 15%. It is evident that the new Roman economic system favoured the breeding of horses first and foremost as working animals. The Roman centres have very high figures for cattle (76%), rather high figures for pigs (15%), and low frequencies of sheep–goat and horse. Cattle and pigs were supplied by the countryside, with fewer numbers of these species being consumed in the production areas. The rural settlements outside the empire have extremely low levels of pigs P (4%) and were probably supplying pigs to the military sites on the frontier; cattle were also produced for this market, though on a more modest scale (Clason 1978). According to Tacitus, writing in the first century A.D., the Frisians living in this region paid tribute to the Romans in cow hides.

Tacitus also tells us that the area between the Ems and the Elbe (now Lower Saxony) was inhabited by the Chauci, a stable and peaceful nation rich in both men and horses. The faunal data from this part of the study area are C = 63%, P = 10%, S–G = 16%, and H = 12% (Figure 9.3); most horses are young, probably kept for their flesh. There is no sign of any major export of meat, but there may have been trade in secondary animal products such as hides (rather as with the Frisians), as well as in small numbers of animals such as horses. The same mixture of subsistence farming and small-scale surplus production was probably practised north of the Elbe (C = 65%, P = 9%, S–G=21%, and H = 5%). The high cattle frequencies in general suggest a well-fed human population with a successful reliance on animal husbandry. In fact, the settlements were on land that was well suited to such a regime but very marginal for plant cultivation (Behre 1970). The distinction between the faunal assemblages from town and countryside in the Roman period was mirrored in the post-Roman period. The Carolingian trading town of Dorestad in the Netherlands (Figure 9.2) has a very

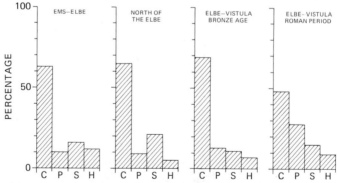

Figure 9.3 Averages of bone samples from the North Sea coast and from the German–Polish lowlands. (The sources for the data are listed in the Appendix.) C, cattle; P, pig; S, sheep–goat; H, horse.

high level of pig (34%) but relatively low levels of cattle (51%), and very low levels of sheep–goat (11%) and horse (4%), whereas the average figures for contemporary rural sites are cattle 68%, pig 12%, sheep/goat 18%, and horse 2%. Smaller towns, however, have assemblages very much like those of the rural sites.

The sites of the early part of the first millennium A.D. on the east German and Polish lowlands (Figure 9.3) have low levels of cattle (48%) and high levels of pig (28%), a ratio to be expected in this region, which was heavily forested. Sheep–goat levels are approximately 15%, less than on the coast, and horses 9%—a relatively high figure that may reflect their importance for land transport, warfare, and status rivalry. The contemporary sites in Denmark (Figure 9.4) have similarly low levels of cattle (51%), but pig was less important than on the lowlands (12%), sheep–goat more important (28%), and horses much the same (9%). On the Viking age rural sites in Denmark there were still lower levels of cattle (39%) and rather similar levels of sheep–goat (25%) and horse (10%),

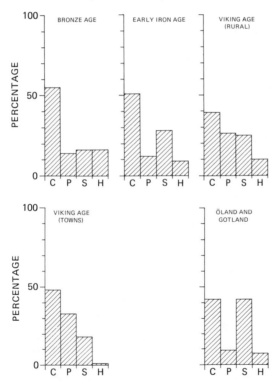

Figure   9.4   Averages of bone samples from Denmark and from the Baltic islands of Öland and Gotland. (The sources for the data are listed in the Appendix.) C, cattle; P, pig; S, sheep–goat; H, horse.

compared with a far greater reliance on pig than before (26%). The rural sites were supplying meat to the towns, where pork was increasingly important (C = 48%, P = 33%, S–G = 18%, H = 1%) (Randsborg 1980). There was a similar relationship in eastern Germany between the Slavonic town-fortresses and the rural sites in their vicinity (Gehl 1981.) The increasing reliance on pigs developed as populations grew and forested areas were used more intensively. The greater importance of sheep in Denmark and southern Sweden than on the east German and Polish lowlands was in response to the presence of zones of marginal sandy soils, although the trading opportunities of wool production were certainly exploited. Significantly, the levels for sheep–goat are highest (42%) in the Baltic islands, where sandy soils are very common.

Despite the obvious sampling and analytical problems in these data, two clear

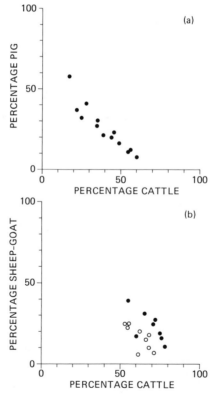

Figure 9.5 Percentages of (a) cattle and pig on rural sites from the Viking Age in Denmark, and (b) cattle and sheep on settlements of the Roman period in the North Sea coastal zone: In (b), solid circles represent sites north of the frontier in the Netherlands, and open circles represent sites in Germany between the Ems and Elbe. (The source for the data are listed in the Appendix.)

trends can be discerned. The first is that the major regional variations in the percentages of the bone fragments of the four domestic species seem to have been due primarily to differences in the natural environment; thus pigs are common at sites in forested regions, whereas sheep dominate at sites in open country. The relationship between animal husbandry and environment is further underlined in Figure 9.5 by the negative correlations between cattle and pig values from Danish rural sites of the Viking Age, and between cattle and sheep–goat values from sites of the early first millennium A.D. on the Dutch and Lower Saxony coasts, suggesting husbandry systems in which different species were competing for the same resources, with pigs and sheep favoured over cattle or vice versa. The second trend is a drop in cattle percentages and a rise in pig percentages on rural sites between the late first millennium B.C. and the beginning of the second millennium A.D., particularly after the first phase of agricultural expansion in the opening centuries of the first millennium A.D., when sheep were particularly common. This trend would again appear to reflect environmental adaptation, with a greater reliance on pigs developing as forest cover increased in the wetter and cooler oscillation during the central centuries of the first millennium. However, other factors have to be taken into account: The landscape was more open at the end of the millennium, but levels of cattle did not rise on the rural sites. Presumably, this was in part a result of the trade in beef to the towns, but a more significant factor was probably the restraint placed on cattle husbandry by expanding cereal production.

The levels of cattle, sheep, and pig diminished during the first millennium A.D., probably in response to poor nutrition (Møhl 1957), but the horse was becoming more common by approximately A.D. 1000. Before the introduction of horse-drawn ploughs, the horse was primarily kept for meat and as a status animal for riding, but by the late first millennium A.D. it was increasingly kept as a draught animal.

Plant Remains

The study of plant remains recovered from excavations in the study area is beset with the same problems of preservation, sampling, and analytical variability that were found with animal bones. Simple counts of species frequency have acknowledged sampling biases. For example, certain species may be more apt for storage and therefore more plentiful in archaeological contexts. Again, frequencies of impressions in pottery are particularly difficult to use, since it is not known if all species had the same chance of occurring in potters' workshops. However, as with animal bones, clear trends in species variability can be discerned in these data. This discussion concentrates on the five main cereals recorded (wheat, barley, rye, oats, and millet) but does not take account of material published in recent papers in *Zeitschrift für Archäologie* (1981, Vol. 15) nor does it consider the wild species that were certainly utilised, especially in the early periods.

Lange (1971) studied the plant remains from a number of first-millennium A.D. settlements in Germany, Poland, and Czechoslovakia, grouping his material on either side of A.D. 500. In Table 9.1, I have isolated the main species used for baking bread (rye and wheat) from the rest of Lange's data. In non-Roman Germany and in Czechoslovakia, the high barley percentages stand out; beer may have been an important asset to the diet. In the late period, however, the northern zones adopted the 'bread' cereals, especially rye, to the same extent as their neighbours. These observations correlate with pollen diagrams from the northern parts of the study area showing that the animal-based subsistence of the early period (marked by high values for ribwort plantain and low values for cereals) was supplanted by a mixed economy, with relatively modest values for plantain and substantial values for cereals (Lange 1971, 1976; Widgren 1977). Lange's data suggest that rye was probably introduced into the German and Scandinavian area from the east, and that Roman agriculture had hardly any impact. In Poland and Czechoslovakia, wheat remained more important than rye throughout the first millennium A.D.

Willerding (1979) summarises the botanical data for the Middle Ages (Lange's

Table 9.1

Percentages of Cereals Found on Sites in Central Europe[a]

	Roman empire	Germany	Czechoslovakia	Poland
Early period				
(0–A.D. 500)				
Barley	17	41	18	19
Millet	21	15	18	16
Oats	11	11	27	10
Rye	15	4	0	19
Wheat	36	30	36	36
Late period				
(A.D. 500–1000)				
Barley	0	17	17	21
Millet	0	23	20	26
Oats	0	3	10	13
Rye	0	33	22	19
Wheat	0	23	32	22
Total 'bread' cereals[b]				
Early period	51	34	36	55
Late period	0	56	54	41

[a]After Lange (1971).
[b]Rye and wheat.

Table 9.2

Frequencies (%) of Cereals in Terms of Site Occurrences in Different Regions of Northern Europe[a]

	Germany	Czechoslovakia	Poland	The Netherlands	Denmark
Barley	21	15	20	36	35
Millet	13	15	26	0	0
Oats	14	13	7	21	35
Rye	35	28	24	21	24
Wheat	17	29	23	21	6
Bread cereals[b]	52	57	47	42	30

[a] After Willerding (1979).
[b] Rye and wheat.

'late period' and after), but in a different form. The figures in Table 9.2 give the number of sites (in percentages) where cereals have been found. The sites are plentiful for Germany, Czechoslovakia, and Poland but rather few for Denmark and the Netherlands; these results should not be compared directly with Lange's data. The table clearly shows the potential for bread production of the eastern or Slav regions especially, and the poor suitability of the northern regions. The introduction of rye to the north was of crucial importance for the development of cereal-dominated farming there in the latter part of the first millennium A.D.

There is a sequence of cereal finds in the Netherlands from the Bronze Age to the early Middle Ages (roughly Lange's late period) (van Zeist 1968; van Zeist and Palfenier-Vegter 1979). The settlements of the Roman period are divided between imperial sites south of the Rhine and sites from northern Holland (Table 9.3). The figures in this table correspond well with the trends discerned in the

Table 9.3

Percentages of Cereals Found on Dutch Sites[a]

	Bronze age	Pre-Roman iron age	Roman imperial	Roman period, non-imperial	Early Middle Ages
Barley	57	76	29	94	33
Millet	+	+	0	0	0
Oats	0	0	+	0	5
Rye	0	0	+	0	59
Wheat	43	24	71	7	4
Bread cereals[b]	43	24	71	7	63

[a] After van Zeist (1968). +, slight occurrence.
[b] Rye and wheat.

preceding tables. In the Roman period, the differing frequencies of wheat (very high on Roman sites, very low on settlements beyond the limes) may indicate the export of wheat from northern Holland to the imperial markets, parallel to the meat trade discussed earlier. Wheat also seems to be rare on the coastal sites of Lower Saxony, but here the reason may be climatic (Behre 1970). At Feddersen Wierde, for example, wheat is extremely rare, but barley and oats are common, presumably correlating with the importance of horses at this site (Körber-Grohne 1967). Gold-of-pleasure (*Camelina sativa*) was very common at many marginal locations on the coast and was quite probably cultivated, as in parts of Denmark (Helbaek 1954).

For the Danish area, the study of grain impressions in pottery was an early source of knowledge of ancient agriculture, especially in Jutland (Hatt 1937). The main results from the Late Bronze Age onwards are summarised in Table 9.4. The dominance of barley (particularly naked barley) is striking. Barley also dominated in the Roman Iron Age in Denmark, whereas wheat and millet were more common at this time on the northern European plain (Table 9.1), probably because the latter were better adapted to the warmer climate there. The number of cereal impressions recorded on Viking ceramics is few, but they confirm the increasing importance of rye in Denmark. The same pattern is indicated by carbonised grains on settlement sites. At Aggersborg, for example, the cereal proportions were 60% barley, 31% rye, and 9% oats (Jessen 1954). For the crucial centuries in the middle of the first millennium A.D., the best data are from two settlements on the Danish island of Bornholm in the Baltic, where the carbonised cereals from Dalshøj (first century A.D.) can be compared with those of Sorte Muld (fifth century A.D.) (Helbaek 1957; Table 9.5); the increase in the role of oats and rye is clearly apparent. From the Swedish island of Gotland

Table 9.4

Percentages of Grain Impressions in Pottery from Denmark[a]

	Late Bronze Age 1000– 500 b.c.	Pre-Roman Iron Age 500–0 b.c.	Early Roman Iron Age A.D. 0–200	Late Roman Iron Age A.D. 200– 400	Viking Age A.D. 800– 1250
Barley	83	80	79	84	37
Millet	2	6	0	0	0
Oats	4	1	17	7	20
Rye	0	0	4	7	43
Wheat	10	13	1	2	0
Bread cereals[b]	10	13	5	9	43

[a]After Jessen 1951.
[b]Rye and wheat.

Table 9.5

Percentages of Carbonised Grain
from Two Settlements on Bornholm
Island, Denmark[a]

	Dalshøj	Sorte Muld
Barley	61	15
Oats	24	68
Rye	0	16
Wheat	15	1

[a]After Helbaek 1957.

further north in the Baltic, the site of Vallhagar (approximately contemporary with Sorte Muld) has yielded both carbonised grain and grain impressions in pottery (Helbaek 1955). Again, rye seems to have been rather common, with barley the dominant crop (Table 9.6). The same is true of Eketorp, a pre-Viking age settlement on the island of Öland (Helbaek 1967; Näsman and Wegraeus 1979).

The evidence of grain impressions in pottery has recently been summarised for Sweden by Hjelmquist (1979, 1981). The data are mainly from the southern province of Sweden (Skåne or Scania), as well as from the southeastern part of the mainland and the Baltic islands, with a chronological range from the Early Bronze Age to the Viking Age (Table 9.7). The sample is rather poor for the later periods, and the lack of rye in the first millennium A.D. (when it was increasingly common in adjacent regions) may be the result of sampling bias, or it might reflect the warmer climatic oscillation of the period, with wheat being preferred over rye to the north of Scania. The similarities in the crop ratios of the phase at approximately A.D. 0 with those of A.D. 600–800 are striking, particularly in

Table 9.6

Percentages of Cereal Remains From the
Pre-Viking Age Settlement of Vallhagar on
Gotland Island, Sweden[a]

	Carbonised grains	Pottery impressions
Barley	60	79
Oats	13	7
Rye	16	10
Wheat	10	3

[a]After Helbaek (1955).

Table 9.7

Percentages of Grain Impressions in Pottery from Sweden[a]

	Early Bronze Age 1800–1000 b.c.		Late Bronze Age 1000–500 b.c.		Pre-Roman Iron Age 500 b.c.–0		Roman Iron Age A.D. 0–400		Late Iron Age A.D. 400–600		Late Iron Age A.D. 600–800		Viking Age A.D. 800–1050	
	S	T	S	T	S	T	S	T	S	T	S	T	S	T
Barley	30	33	74	70	86	88	93	94	0	71	85	81	75	64
Millet	0	0	3	2	0	0	0	0	0	0	0	0	0	0
Oats	0	0	3	6	10	8	5	3	0	16	12	9	6	10
Rye	0	0	0	0	0	1	0	0	0	9	0	0	19	10
Wheat	70	67	20	22	4	3	2	2	0	4	3	11	0	16
Bread cereals	70	67	22	22	4	4	2	2	0	13	3	11	19	26

[a]After Hjelmquist (1979). S, Scania or Skåne province; T, total sample from Scania, the rest of the mainland, and the islands.

Scania, and it may be that rye was introduced in the first phase, abandoned in the warmer oscillation, and then reintroduced in the later phase.

The variability in the crop ratios across the study area as a whole indicates the same mixture of environmental and economic factors as was noted earlier in the discussion of the faunal remains. Some differences are at first sight economic but were ultimately responses to environmental and ecological changes, such as the distribution of millet. Others are clearly economic, such as the impact of the Roman markets on wheat production within the empire and in immediately adjacent regions outside the limes such as northern Holland, whereas Germany and Scandinavia were more or less unaffected. The single clear trend that links the whole area was the increased importance of bread species in the later first millennium A.D. (though rye was more important than wheat in the west, and wheat more important than rye in the east). The plant remains, like the pollen diagrams, show the development of arable-based farming side by side with the growth of population in this period.

Settlements

Settlement patterns in the first millennium A.D. are rather difficult to summarize in a simple fashion because the data are very unevenly distributed in time and space. Best known are the longhouse farmsteads from the Dutch-Lower Saxony-Holstein-Jutland zone bordering the North Sea (Müller-Wille 1977). The main building was both house and stable, often associated with adjacent outbuildings and fenced crofts. This type of farmstead was first established here in the Bronze Age and endured until the earlier Middle Ages. The sequence has survived best in northeastern Holland (Waterbolk 1979), but there is also excellent settlement information from elsewhere in Holland (Gasselte: Waterbolk 1979; Odoorn: Waterbolk 1973; Wijster: van Es 1965), northern Germany (Flögeln: Schmid and Zimmerman 1976; Zimmerman 1978; Sylt: Kossack et al. 1974; Kossack et al. 1980), and Denmark (Vorbasse: Hvass 1979, 1980). The most detailed data by far are from the Feddersen Wierde village in Lower Saxony, the occupation of which spans the entire first half of the first millennium A.D. (Haarnagel 1979). Vorbasse was also occupied for most of the first millennium A.D., except perhaps in the sixth and seventh centuries.

In general, the settlement record of eastern Denmark and southern Sweden is less well known, with notable exceptions such as Vallhagar on Gotland (Stenberger and Klindt-Jensen 1955) and Eketorp on Öland (Borg et al. 1976; Näsman and Wegraeus 1979). Germany east of the coastal zone is also poorly understood, but some longhouse farmsteads are known from the first half of the first millennium A.D. (Behm-Blancke 1956; Jankuhn 1977). It is clear that in the second half of the millennium there was a very different form of settlement here (and in adjacent parts of Poland and Czechoslovakia) from the western long-houses. Small log cabins, and in some areas well-built rectangular pit houses, seem to have been the normal type of habitation, with space for people and a little storage, but not for stock (Donat 1980; Figure 9.6). Log cabins are common on the lowlands of eastern Germany and Poland, whilst pit houses for habitation were a feature of upland areas such as the middle and upper Elbe.

The division between western and eastern settlement forms correlates approx-imately with the division between Germanic and Slavic Europe, respectively, although pit houses were also used in both areas as workshops and for storage. The Slav settlements are irregular in layout but are roughly the same size as the western longhouses. Whilst the western farmsteads are more amenable to analy-sis than the eastern sites (economic potential can be gauged from barn capacities, numbers of cattle stalls, and so on, and pens and fields are a guide to land control), social and cultural differences between the two areas seem very clear. These differences are all the more notable given the similar trends in subsistence described in the preceding sections.

In the first millennium b.c., most settlement was somewhat mobile, although within defined territorial units (Becker 1971; Randsborg 1982; Waterbolk 1979). Fields on less fertile soils were abandoned after some years of cultivation, and old fallow was returned to cultivation. The prehistoric field systems of Holland (Brongers 1976), Denmark (Hatt 1949), and—at a rather later date—of Gotland (Carlsson 1979) are identified with this kind of farming (Müller-Wille 1965). In the early centuries of the first millennium A.D., production was intensified, settlements were longer-lived, and settlement movements often involved only very short distances. The settlements up to this period tend to be rather irregular in plan; any fences were built around the whole complex or around the single small farmstead, with little 'private' space demarcated. In the third and fourth centuries A.D., however, a new type of settlement developed on the western coastal zone, with several buildings situated in a very large croft (Hvass 1980). The central structure was large, housing living quarters and stabling and storage facilities, often together with pit-house workshops that reflect the increased importance of crafts. Whereas most earlier settlements seem to have been family farms, the new settlements such as Wijster (van Es 1965) and Vorbasse (Hvass 1980) were much more extensive and regular in plan, with streets and open spaces between compounds (Figure 9.7). By the late first millennium A.D., some settlements consisted of very large compounds, with a central substantial house for the headman, and with stables housed in separate buildings. Major farms such as Warendorf in Lower Saxony (Winkelmann 1954) and Vorbasse in Jutland (Hvass 1980; Figure 9.8) reveal a degree of stratification (expressed in terms of the economic potential and the standard of living of the primary pro-ducers) not seen in earlier periods. The structure of at least some of these villages

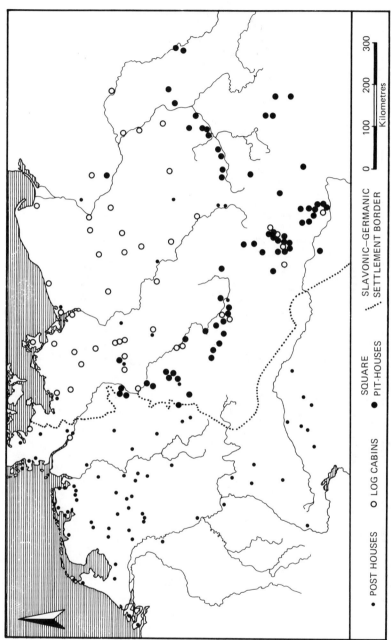

Figure 9.6 Types of dwellings in north central Europe in the latter part of the first millennium A.D. (After Donat, 1980.)

POST HOUSES   O LOG CABINS   SQUARE   ● PIT-HOUSES

SLAVONIC–GERMANIC SETTLEMENT BORDER

Kilometres

0   100   200   300

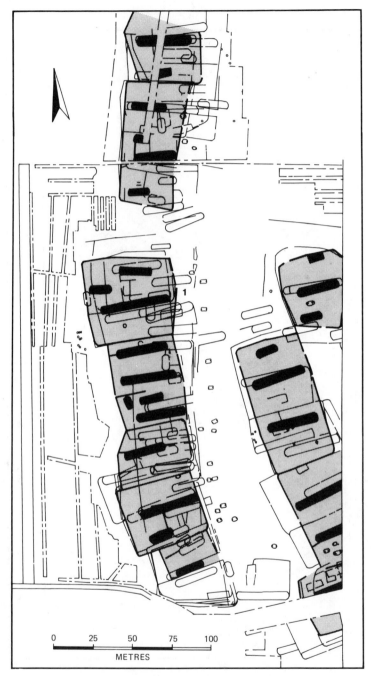

Figure 9.7 Part of the Vorbasse settlement in Jutland (fourth century A.D.), showing the street layout of the settlement and the division into separate fenced compounds. The compound marked 1 is the headman's compound shown in detail in Fig. 9.8.

Figure   9.8   The central compound of the Vorbasse settlement (fourth century A.D.), showing the headman's house and separate stables and stores. (After Hvass, 1980.)

clearly demonstrates the social differentiation among the early Germanic state societies.

The settlement record suggests that there was a real decline in population during the early first millennium A.D. (a trend that coincides with the pollen evidence for a decline in cultivation and an increase in woodland), followed by expansion in the latter part of the millennium. The agricultural contraction of the first half of the millennium is particularly clear at Feddersen Wierde (Haarnagel 1979; Figure 9.9). The early settlement here (at the beginning of the first millennium) consisted of a few rather undifferentiated holdings. The site was at its most extensive in the third century A.D. (in terms of square metres of total structures, or of cattle stalls), when there was a single large farm with accompanying workshops. In the final phase in the fifth century A.D. the settlement contracted, there was a marked decline in cattle keeping, and the number of workshops

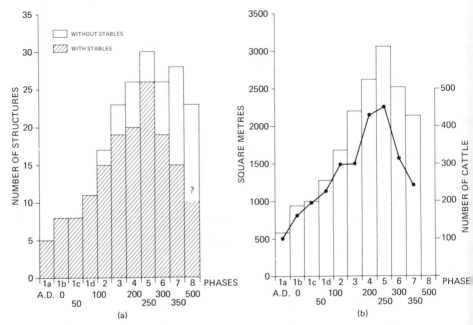

Figure 9.9 The settlement of Feddersen Wierde on the North Sea coast of Germany. (a) number of structures during the life of the settlement; (b) total size in square meters (bar histogram) of the structures, with estimated numbers of cattle (single line). (Based on Haarnagel, 1979.)

suggests that trade (presumably controlled by the headman) assumed much more importance in the economic life of the community; indeed, Roman imports cluster around the site. The length of occupation at Feddersen Wierde (5 centuries) is quite remarkable; it was finally abandoned when the rich marshlands of the locality were flooded in the climatic recession of the mid-first millennium. The same pattern of contraction, recession, and final abandonment occurred at Wijster (van Es 1965) and Vorbasse (Hvass 1979). A catastrophic collapse in settlement has often been postulated for this period and linked with contemporary migrations such as the Anglo-Saxon invasion of England. However, whilst there were undoubtedly site desertions and minor movements, it is likely that the 'catastrophic' model is exaggerated and at least partly a result of research biases.

Further insights into settlement trends in the study area have been provided by Janssen's (1977) study of the chronology of foundation and abandonment of 109 sites, principally in northern and western Germany but with outliers in southern Scandinavia, Holland, and Britain (Figure 9.10). The total chronological range is from the first century B.C. to the present day. The sample may be underrepresented in the early phases, as all the early sites span more than 1 century, and many contemporary short-lived settlements are not included. Nevertheless, when

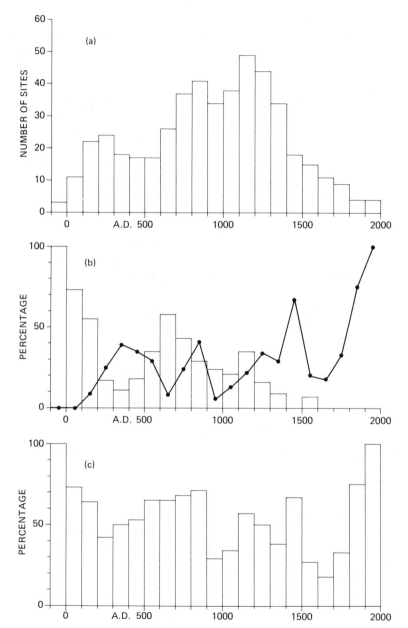

Figure 9.10 Settlement trends in northwestern Europe, using data from Janssen (1977). (a) number of sites per century; (b) numbers of foundations (bar histograms) and abandonments (single line), expressed as a percentage of the total number of sites for each century; (c) an instability index of settlement, the sum of the percentages of foundations and abandonments shown in (b).

settlements are 'constantly' moving, they may leave more archaeological traces, thus producing an exaggerated record of settlement numbers. There are other biases in the sample to take into account. For example, Danish settlements before A.D. 200 have many rubbish pits, which are relatively easy to find, whereas rubbish pits became much less common thereafter (making sites more difficult to find). Because longer-lived settlements had to be sustained by more intensive cultivation, household refuse was used as extra manuring for the fields.

According to the number of sites per century (Figure 9.10a), there was a recession in settlement in approximately A.D. 500, followed by an increasing number of sites per century, with some evidence for another recession in approximately A.D. 1000. However, the diminishing number of sites from the Late Middle Ages onwards is probably due to the decline in village abandonment the closer we get to the present. Also, modern Danish villages were founded in the Early Middle Ages, after approximately A.D. 1000 (Jeppesen, 1981). In spite of a true recession in the Late Middle Ages, overall population growth did not allow many villages to be abandoned (and so to enter the archaeological record). Settlement trends are clearer in Figure 9.10b, in which numbers of foundations and abandonments are expressed as a percentage of the total number of sites for each century. At the beginning of the sequence, of course, only foundations or continuations of existing sites are noted, with the first abandonments coming in the second century A.D. In the fourth century, almost 40% of all sites were abandoned and only 10% newly established. Three centuries later, the situation had more than reversed. In the short-lived recession of the ninth century, 40% of all sites were abandoned while 30% were newly established. This trend may reflect in part the general restructuring of settlement following state formation in northwestern Europe (a process that did not occur in Denmark until the eleventh century). However, very few Danish sites are included in Janssen's (1977) sample. The late medieval recession (especially that of the fifteenth century) stands out clearly.

The 'instability index' in Figure 9.10c is the sum of the percentages of foundations and abandonments in Janssen's data. For the third century A.D., the index is low because the sample is dominated by settlements founded in the second century or earlier, even though the third century witnessed the development of new, more extensive, and more stratified settlements (mainly on existing sites such as Feddersen Wierde). The amount of instability or change then rose steadily until approximately A.D. 900 (but with a peak at approximately A.D. 500), followed by two centuries with few foundations or abandonments. Later periods of change were the twelfth, thirteenth, and especially fifteenth centuries, with stability in the fourteenth, sixteenth, seventeenth, and eighteenth centuries (after which the sample size is too small for assessment).

It is noteworthy that periods characterised by many abandonments coincide with climatic recessions, which presumably put stress on subsistence systems and may have caused dietary and health problems for the population, and with the evidence in pollen diagrams for increased forest cover and reduced human activity. The recession of the fourth and fifth centuries A.D. was probably less dramatic than that of the fourteenth and fifteenth centuries, since the pollen record of the former has probably been exaggerated by the trend at that time to longer-lived settlements. The decline in the number of sites in Figure 9.10a though clear, is rather slight. Carlsson's (1979) study in Gotland also shows that the scale of the recession had been exaggerated by the abandonment of stone-based architecture. By contrast, the late medieval recession is probably exaggerated in Figure 9.10a, since the number of settlements being abandoned was generally declining through the second millennium A.D. Also, administrative and organisational changes, rather than climatic and environmental changes, were sometimes responsible for high levels of settlement abandonment.

Conclusions

In this chapter I have discussed questions of subsistence and settlement in the first millennium A.D. in north central Europe, employing data on climate and environment, the animals and plants exploited, and the settlements themselves. The area and the time period contain data of prime quality in many respects, yet the area has traditionally been regarded as marginal and beyond the mainstream development of European society. It bordered on the Roman Empire but was basically outside of it, and was also rather peripheral to the Carolingian empire of approximately A.D. 800. For these reasons, the long research tradition and high standards of analysis have received less acknowledgement than they deserve.

This synthesis hardly does justice to the enormous amount of painstaking work by others in the procurement and analysis of the data I have used. At the same time, however, there has been little attempt in the past to compare the various categories of data discussed here. For example, we are only beginning to understand the problems of estimating the impact of the Roman imperial economic system on the parts of Europe beyond the limes. In the area I have considered, there is evidence that the Roman component should be seen as part of general trends in subsistence that can be observed both inside and outside the Empire. Similarly, we can see synchronous developments in settlement layout and economy from northern Holland to Jutland. Less is understood about the impact of political factors on settlement, although the formation of the Germanic state societies would appear to be reflected in rearrangements of both villages and the field systems that supported them. Another clear trend is the increased reliance on cereals in the later first millennium A.D., as is the evidence for the exchange of foodstuffs between Germania Libera and the Roman Empire, and more generally between countryside and towns where the latter existed. In all these cases, we are studying the interactions between subsistence and the larger economic and social system.

More unequivocal is the basic information about the animals and plants raised. Husbandry was clearly controlled first and foremost by environment. In forested areas, for example, pigs were the main stock, whereas cattle and sheep were preferred in more open country. We can also see evidence for 'competition' between species in broadly similar environments (Figure 9.5), with cattle and sheep correlating negatively on the North Sea coast, and cattle and pig doing so in Denmark. The better organised systems of agriculture in the later first millennium A.D. were marked by a rise in the frequency of pigs (presumably the relationship between arable land, pasture, and forest was better regulated). Pigs were generally preferred in the centres of population such as towns and fortresses, whether Roman or later. The bread cereals, especially wheat, were common in the Roman Empire and in the adjacent parts of Europe east of the frontier, but the Germanic societies beyond them relied on stock and grew mainly barley, which was suitable for making porridge and beer.

In the latter part of the first millennium, the intensification in subsistence resulted in a general concentration on crops, with barley giving way to bread cereals (especially rye) in the north. Within this trend, however, there are interesting fluctuations, particularly the transformations in settlement and subsistence that led up to the climatic low of approximately A.D. 500, when the irregular (and rather egalitarian) farms of the early first millennium were replaced by large farms with individually fenced crofts. The latter were cultivated by more hands than those of the owner's own family (Randsborg 1982). The rise in cereal pollen at this time marks the establishment of a more productive and stable system of subsistence coinciding with the metamorphosis of the Germanic peoples into quasi-state societies. These events are typical of the agricultural trends observed in this chapter: Subsistence systems were fundamentally controlled by the constraints and opportunities of the local environment and had to respond to the important climatic pressures of the first millennium A.D. At the same time, however, they responded in varied ways to the complex interrelationships of demographic, economic, and political factors.

Acknowledgements

The present study was largely undertaken during the tenure of a visiting professorship at the Instituut voor Prae- en Proto-historie (IPP), Universiteit van Amsterdam, in 1980–81. Archaeologists here and elsewhere in Holland gave every help both in providing data and discussing the wider problems dealt with in this chapter. I am particularly grateful to the director of the archaeozoological laboratory at the IPP, Dr. L. H. van Wijngarden-Bakker, and to her assistant, Ms. Seeman, for permission to quote the results of unpublished faunal studies.

Appendix: Faunal Data Used in the Figures

FIGURE 9.2: THE NETHERLANDS

Middle to Late Bronze Age

1. Zwaagdijk (Ijzereef 1981);   2. Hoogkarspel 1968–69 (Ijzereef 1981);   3. Andijk (Ijzereef 1981);   4. Bovenkarspel early period (Ijzereef 1981);   5. Medemblik 1975 (Ijzereef 1981); 6. Hoogkarspel 1974–75 (Ijzereef 1981);   7. Medemblik 1967–69 (Ijzereef 1981);   8. Hoogkarspel 1964–67 (Ijzereef 1981);   9. Bovenkarspel late period (Ijzereef 1981);   10. Vogelenzang (Clason 1977);   11. Dodeward (Clason 1977);   12. Zijderveld (Clason 1977);   13. Velzen (PEN) (Clason 1977). Averages: C = 78.1%, P = 7.4%, S–G = 13.4%, H = 1.1%

Pre-Roman Iron Age

1. Sparjaardsbergje (Clason 1977);   2. Vlaardingen (Clason 1977);   3. Amsterdam Waterworks (Clason 1977);   4. Vlaardingen old people's home (Clason 1977);   5. Culemborg (Clason 1977);   6. Driel (84 fragments) (Clason 1977). Averages: C = 59.0%, P = 14.7%, S–G = 19.9%, H = 6.5%; without Driel: C = 64.8%, P = 10.0%, S–G = 20.5%, H = 4.7%

Roman period, north of the Rhine

1. Velzen (Clason 1977);   2. Sneek (Clason 1977);   3. Paddepoel (Clason 1977);   4. Schagen (IPP, unpublished);   5. Assendelft B (IPP, unpublished);   6. Assendelft C (IPP, unpublished);   7. Assendelft F (IPP, unpublished);   8. Achtoven, northern bank of Rhine (van Mensch 1975). Averages: C = 69.0%, P = 3.6%, S–G = 22.9%, H = 4.5%.

Rural Sites Within the Roman Empire

1. Heteren (Clason 1977);   2. Vlaardingen (Clason 1977);   3. Rijswijk II (Clason 1978);   4. Rijswijk III (Clason 1978). Averages: C = 63.3%, P = 4.3%, S–G = 17.5%, H = 14.9%.

Roman Period, Nonrural Sites Within the Roman Empire

1. Valkenburg fortress, period 1 (IPP, unpublished);   2. Valkenburg fortress, period 2 (IPP, unpublished);   3. Valkenburg fortress, period 3 (IPP, unpublished);   4. Valkenburg fortress, period 6 (IPP, unpublished); (Valkenburg fortress, all periods (Clason 1977);   5. Zwammerdam fortress (Clason 1977);   6. Nijmegen town and fortress (Clason 1977);   7. Elst temples (Clason 1977). Averages: C = 76.3%, P = 14.6%, S–G = 7.3%, H = 1.8%

Post-Roman Rural Sites

1. Rijnsburg village (Clason 1977);   2. Rijnsburg river site (Clason 1977);   3. Valkenburg (IPP, unpublished);   4. Kootwijk (IPP, unpublished);   5. Texel—deviating sites with very high s–g to 47% (IPP, unpublished);   6. Schagen (Prummel 1979). Averages: C = 6.4%, P = 9.8%, S–G = 22.6%, H = 3.7%; without Texel: C = 68.2%, P = 11.8%, S–G = 17.6%, H = 2.3%.

Post-Roman Nonrural Sites

1. Dorestad (Prummel 1978);   2. Medemblik, from outside the town (IPP, unpublished); 3. Al-

kmaar early period (Prummel 1979). Averages: C = 58.7%, P = 15.2%, S–G = 24.3%, H = 1.8%; Dorestad alone: C = 50.9%, P = 34.1%, S–G = 10.6%, H = 4.4%.

FIGURE 9.3: THE NORTH SEA COAST AND THE GERMAN–POLISH LOWLANDS

Late Pre-Roman and Roman Between the Ems and the Elbe

1. Betumersiel (Zawatka and Reichstein 1977); 2. Jegumkloster (Zawatka and Reichstein 1977); 3. Wulfshof (Nobis 1955); 4. Einswarden, early period (Nobis 1955); 5. Einswarden, middle period (Nobis 1955); 6. Einswarden, late period (Nobis 1955); 7. Feddersen Wierde (Reichstein 1972, 1973); 8. Barnkrug (Nobis 1955). Averages: C = 62.7%, P = 9.7%, S–G = 15.5%, H 12.0%; without Einswarden middle phase: C = 64.1%, P = 9.3%, S–G = 14.1%, H = 12.5%. From the early Middle Ages, Hessens (Nobis 1955) has C = 66%, P = 7%, S–G = 20%, H = 7%.

Roman Period North of the Elbe

1. Hodorf (Nobis 1955); 2. Tofting, early period (Nobis 1955); 3. Tofting, late period (Nobis 1955); 4. Dankirke (unpublished; see Randsborg 1980, Appendix VII E). Averages: C = 64.5%, P = 9.4%, S–G = 20.8%, H = 5.4%.

Late Bronze Age–Early Iron Age, Northern Germany

1. Berlin-Eichterfelde (Pohle 1964); 2. Kratzenburg (Teichert 1964); 3. Gühlen-Glienicke (Teichert 1964); 4. Rundstedt (Stork and Boessneck 1973); 5. Tangermünde (Clason 1977); 6. Wüste Kunersdorf (Teichert 1968). Averages: C = 69.1%, P = 13.4%, S–G = 10.8%, H = 6.7%.

Pre-Roman and Roman Period, Northern Germany and Poland

1. Nauen-Bärhorst (Gandert 1937–38); 2. Klein-Büddenstedt (Boessneck and Stork 1973); 3. Seinstedt (Boessneck and Ciliga 1966); 4. Am Kaiserstein (Enderle 1975); 5. Gielde (von den Driesch 1970); 6. Gedynia (Wielowiejski 1981); 7. Tornow, Lütjenberg (Müller 1973); 8. Sünninghausen (Nobis 1973); 9. Wüste Kunersdorf (Teichert 1968); 10. Kablow (Teichert 1971). Averages: C = 47.7%, P = 28.1%, S–G = 15.4%, H = 8.7%. From the Early Middle AGes in the same zone are Klein-Büddenstedt (Boessneck and Stork 1973) with C = 22%, P = 41%, S–G = 8%, H = 29%, and Gielde (von den Driesch 1970) with C = 46%, P = 33%, S–G = 11%, H = 10% (based on 70 fragments).

FIGURE 9.4: DENMARK AND THE BALTIC ISLANDS OF ÖLAND AND GOTLAND

Late Bronze Age, Denmark and Scania

1. Voldtofte (Winge 1919); 2. Hasmark (Winge 1919); 3. Hötofta (Lepiksaar

1969); 4. Kvarnby (Persson 1973–74). Averages: C = 54.9%, P = 13.7%, S–G = 15.5%, H = 15.9%.

Early Iron Age, Denmark and Holstein

1. Bruneborg (Jacobsen 1979); 2. Vejleby (Higham 1967); 3. Dalshøj (Helbaek 1957); 4. Sorte Muld (Helbaek 1957); 5. Dankirke (unpublished, see Randsborg 1980, Appendix VII E); 6. Barsbek (Clason 1977). Averages: C = 51.0%, P = 11.8%, S–G = 28.2%, H = 9.3%.

Viking Age, Denmark and Adjacent Parts of Germany and Sweden (rural sites)

1. Vallebergen, 2. Karstorp, 3. Löddeköpinge, 4. Rinkaby, 5. Viborg village, 6. Vejleby, 7. Karby, 8. Saedding, 9. Tofting, latest period, 10. Elisenhof, 11. Aggersborg, 12. Fosie, 13. Oxie (deviating sample). For all samples, see Randsborg 1980, Appendix VII A. Averages: C = 39.3%, P = 25.8%, S–G = 25.0%, H = 9.9%; without Oxie: C = 41.1%, P = 23.2%, S–G = 25.1%, H = 10.6%. For comparison, the Zealand village of Store Valby approximately A.D. 1700 has C = 31%, P = 24%, S–G = 29%, H = 16% (Hatting 1974).

Viking Age, Denmark and Adjacent Parts of Germany and Sweden (towns)

1. Hedeby, 2. Hedeby, 3. Århus, 4. Lund, 5. Ribe. For all samples, see Randsborg 1980, Appendix VII C. Averages: C = 48.3%, P = 32.9%, S–G = 17.5%, H = 1.2%. Also Traelleborg fortress (Randsborg 1980, Appendix VII B), with C = 35.4%, P = 35.4%, S–G = 15.0%, H = 14.2%.

Öland and Gotland, Mid-first Millennium A.D.

1. Eketorp 1 (Boessneck et al. 1979); 2. Eketorp II (Boessneck et al. 1979); 3. Ormöga (Sellstedt 1966); 4. Sörby-tall (very deviant, with S–G = 98%) (Sellstedt 1966); 5. Vallhagar (Gejvall 1955). Averages (excluding Sörby-tall): C = 42.4%, P = 9.1%, S–G = 42.0%, H = 6.5%.

References

Aaby, B.
    1976 Cyclic climatic variations in climate over the past 5,500 yr reflected in raised bogs. *Nature* 263:281–284.
Becker, C. J.
    1971 Früheisenzeitliche Dörfer bei Grøntoft, Westjütland. *Acta Archaeologica* 42:79–110.
Behm-Blancke, G.
    1956 Die germanischen Dörfer von Kablow bei Königs Wusterhausen. *Ausgrabungen und Funde* 1:161–167.
Behre, K.-E.
    1970 Die Entwicklungsgeschichte der natürlichen Vegetation im Gebiet der unteren Ems und ihre Abhängigkeit von den Bewegungen des Meeresspiegels. *Probleme der Küstenforschung im südlichen Nordseegebiet* 9:13–47.

Behre, K.-E.
1976 Pollenanalytische Untersuchungen zur Vegetations- und Siedlungsgeschichte bei Flögeln und im Ahlenmoor (Elb-Weser-Winkel). *Probleme der Küstenforschung im südlichen Nordseegebiet* 11:101–118.

Berglund, B. E.
1969 Vegetation und human influence in south Scandinavia during prehistoric times. *Oikos* 12:9–28.

Biraben, J.-N., and J. Le Goff
1975 The plague in the early Middle Ages. In *Biology of man in history*, edited by R. Forster and O. Ranum, pp. 48–80. Annales Economies Sociétés Civilisations, Baltimore.

Boessneck, J., and T. Ciliga
1966 Zu den Tierknochenfunden aus der römischen Kaiserzeit auf dem 'Erbbrink' bei Seinstedt, Kr. Wolfenbüttel. *Neue Ausgrabungen und Forschungen in Niedersachsen* 3:145–179.

Boessneck, J., and M. Stork
1973 Die Tierknochenfunde aus der Ausgrabungen 1959 auf der Wüstung Klein-Büddenstedt, Kr. Helmstedt. *Neue Ausgrabungen und Forschungen in Niedersachsen* 8:179–213.

Boessneck, J., A. von den Driesch, and L. Stenberger (editors)
1979 *Eketorp, Befestigung und Siedlung auf Öland/Schweden: die Fauna*. Stockholm.

Borg, K., U. Näsman, and E. Wegraeus (editors)
1976 *Eketorp, fortification and settlement on Öland/Sweden: the monument*. Stockholm.

Brongers, J. A.
1976 Air photography and Celtic field research in the Netherlands. *Nederlandse Oudheden* 6.

Carlsson, D.
1979 Kulturlandskapets utveckling på Gotland: en studie av jordbruks- och bebyggelseförandringar. *Kulturgeografiska Institutionen Meddelande* B 49 (Stockholm University).

Clason, A. T.
1967 Animal and man in Holland's past. *Palaeohistoria* 13A.

Clason, A. T.
1977 *Jacht en Veeteelt van Prehistorie tot Middeleeuwen*. Haarlem.

Clason, A. T.
1978 Animal husbandry and hunting at Rijswijk (Z.H.). In 'De Bult': eine Siedlung der Cananefaten I–III, edited by J. H. F. Bloemers. *Nederlandse Oudheden* 8:424–437.

Donat, P.
1980 Haus, Hof und Dorf in Mitteleuropa vom 7.–12. Jahrhundert. *Schriften zur Ur- und Frühgeschichte* 33.

Driesch, A. von den
1970 Tierknochenfunde aus Giele, Kr. Goslar: Rühes Hofgarten. *Neue Ausgrabungen und Forschungen in Niedersachsen* 9:244–252.

Enderle, K.
1975 Die Tierknochen der kaiserzietlichen Siedlung 'Am Kaiserstein' bei Gielde, Kr. Goslar. *Neue Ausgrabungen und Forschungen in Niedersachsen* 9:201–244.

Es, W. A. van
1965 Wijster, a native village beyond the imperial frontier 150–425 A.D. *Palaeohistoria* 11.

Gandert, O. F.
1937–38 Vorläufige Bemerkungen über die Tierreste aus der Siedlung bei Nauen-Bärhorst. *Prähistorische Zeitschrift* 28–29(3/4):335–337.

Gehl, O. C.
1981 Gross Raden, Haustiere und Jagdwild der slawischen Siedler. *Beiträge zur Ur- und Frühgeschichte der Bezirke Rostock, Schwerin und Neubrandenburg* 13.

Gejvall, N.-G.
    1955 The animal remains from Vallhagar. In *Vallhagar* (Vol. 2), edited by M. Stenberger and
        O. Klindt-Jensen, pp. 786–805. Copenhagen.
Groenman-van Waateringe, W.
    1980 Die verhängnisvolle Auswirkung der römischen Herrschaft auf die Wirtschaft an den
        Grenzen des Reiches. *Offa* 37:366–371.
Haarnagel, W.
    1979 Die Grabung Feddersen Wierde: Methode, Hausbau, Siedlungs und Wirtschaftformen
        sowie Sozialstruktur. In *Feddersen Wierde* (Vol. 2), edited by W. Haarnagel. Wiesbaden.
Hammer, C. U., H. B. Hammer, and W. Dansgaard
    1980 Greenland ice sheet evidence of post-glacial volcanism and its climatic impact. *Nature*
        288:230–235.
Hatt, G.
    1937 *Landbrug i Danmarks Oldtid.* Copenhagen.
Hatt, G.
    1949 Oldtidsagre: Det Kongelige Danske Videnskabernes Selskab. *Arkaeologisk-
        Kunsthistoriske Skrifter* 2.1.
Hatting, T.
    1974 Zoological remains. In *Store Valby 1–3,* edited by A. Steensberg and J. Ø. Christensen,
        pp. 405–407. Historisk-Filosofiske Skrifter udgivet af Det kgl. danske Videnskabernes
        Selskab 8(1).
Helbaek, H.
    1954 Prehistoric food plants and weeds in Denmark. *Danmarks Geologiske Undersøgelse*
        2(80):250–261.
Helbaek, H.
    1955 The botany of the Vallhagor iron age field. In *Vallhagar* (Vol. 2), edited by M. Stens-
        berger and O. Klindt-Jensen, pp. 653–699. Copenhagen.
Helbaek, H.
    1957 Bornholm plant economy in the first half of the first millennium A.D. In Bornholm i
        Folkevandringstiden, edited by O. Klindt-Jensen. *Nationalmuseets Skrifter, Større Beret-
        ninger* 2:259–277.
Helbaek, H.
    1967 Vendeltime farming products at Eketorp on Öland. *Acta Archaeologica* 38:216–221.
Higham, C. F. W.
    1967 The economy of iron age Vejleby (Denmark). *Acta Archaeologica* 38:222–241.
Hjelmquist, H.
    1979 Beiträge zur Kenntnis der prähistorischen Nutzpflanzen in Schweden. *Opera Botanica* 47.
Hjelmquist, H.
    1981 Grain impressions from Gårdlösa. In Gårdlösa: an iron age community in its natural and
        social setting, edited by B. Stjernquist. *Acta Regiae Societatis Humaniorum Litterarum
        Lundensis* 75:54–58.
Hvass, S.
    1979 Vorbasse: the Viking-age settlement at Vorbasse, central Jutland. *Acta Archaeologica*
        50:137–172.
Hvass, S.
    1980 Die Struktur einer Siedlung der Zeit von Christi Geburt bis ins 5. Jahrhundert nach
        Christus. *Studien zur Sachsenforschung* 2:161–180.
Ijzereef, G. F.
    1981 Bronze age animal bones from Bovenkarspel. *Nederlandse Oudheden* 10.

262   Klavs Randsborg

Iversen, J.
   1973 The development of Denmark's nature since the last glacial. *Danmarks Geologiske Under-*
        søgelse 5 (7-C).
Jacobsen, J. A.
   1979 Bruneborg: en tidlig førromersk boplads med jernudvinding. In Fra jernalder til mid-
        delalder, edited by H. Thrane. *Skrifter fra Historisk Institut, 27:*4–14.
Jankuhn, H.
   1977 Typen und Funktionen eisenzeitlicher Siedlungen im Ostseegebiet. In Das Dorf der
        Eisenzeit und des früben Mittelalters, edited by H. Jankuhn et al. *Abhandlungen der*
        Akademie der Wissenschaft in Göttingen, Philologisch-historische Klasse 101:219–252.
Janssen, W.
   1977 Dorf und Dorfformen des 7. bis 12. Jahrhunderts im Lichte neuer Ausgrabungen in Mittel-
        und Nordeuropa. In Das Dorf der Eisenzeit und das frühe Mittelalter, edited by H. Jankuhn
        et al. *Abhandlungen der Akademie der Wissenschaften in Göttingen, Philologisch-histo-*
        rische Klasse 101:285–356.
Jeppesen, T. G.
   1981 Middelalderlandsbyens opståen: kontinuitet og brud i den fynske agrarbebyggelse mellem
        yngre jernalder og tidlig middelalder. *Fynske studier* 11.
Jessen, K.
   1951 Oldtidens korndyrkning i Danmark. *Viking* 15:15–37.
Jessen, K.
   1954 Plantefund fra vikingetiden i Danmark. *Botanisk Tidsskrift* 50(2):125–139.
Körber-Grohne, U.
   1967 Geobotanische Untersuchungen auf der Feddersen Wierde. In *Feddersen Wierde* (Vol. 1),
        edited by W. Haarnagel. Wiesbaden.
Kossack, G., O. Harck, and J. Reichstein
   1974 Zehn Jahre Siedlungsforschung in Archsum auf Sylt. *Berichte der römisch-germanischen*
        Kommission 55:261–427.
Kossack, G., et al.
   1980 Archsum auf Sylt. *Römisch-germanische Forschungen* 39.
La Marche, V. C.
   1974 Paleoclimatic inferences from long tree-ring records. *Science* 183:1043–1048.
Lamb, H. H.
   1981 Climate from 1000 BC to 1000 AD. In *The environment of man: the Iron Age and the*
        Anglo-Saxon period, edited by M. Jones and G. Dimbleby, pp. 53–65. British Archae-
        ological Reports, British Series 87, Oxford, England.
Lange, E.
   1971 Botanische Beiträge zur mitteleuropäischen Siedlungsgeschichte. *Schriften zur Ur- und*
        Frühgeschichte 27.
Lange, E.
   1976 Grundlagen und Entwicklungstendenzen der frühgeschichtlichen Agrarproduktion aus
        botanischer Sicht. *Zeitschrift für Archäologie* 10:75–120.
Lepiksaar, J.
   1969 Knochenfunde aus den bronzezeitlichen Siedlungen von Hötofta (18⁴N). In Beiträge zum
        Studium von bronzezeitlichen Siedlungen, edited by B. Stjernquist. *Acta Archaeologica*
        Lundensia 8:174–207.
Mensch, P. J. A. van
   1975 Dieeresten uit de polder Achthoven. *Westerheem* 24:111–116.
Møhl, U.
   1957 Zoologisk gennemgang af knoglematerialet fra jernalderbopladserne Dalshøj og Sorte

Muld, Bornholm. In Bornholm i Folkevandringstiden, edited by O. Klindt-Jensen. *Nationalmuseets skrifter, Større beretninger* 2:279–318.

Müller, H.-H.
1973 Das Tierknochenmaterial. In Die germanischen und slawischen Siedlungen und das mittelalterliche Dorf von Tornow, Kr. Calau, edited by J. Herrmann. *Schriften zur Ur- und Frühgeschichte* 26:267–310.

Müller-Wille, M.
1965 Eisenzeitlichen Fluren in den festländischen Nordseegebieten. *Siedlung und Landschaft in Westfalen* 5.

Müller-Wille, M.
1977 Bäuerliche Siedlungen der Bronze- und Eisenzeit in den Nordseegebiten. In Das Dorf der Eisenzeit und des frühen Mittelalters, edited by H. Jankuhn et al. *Abhandlungen der Akademie der Wissenschafter in Göttingen, Philologisch-historische Klasse* 101:153–218.

Näsman, U., and E. Wegraeus (editors)
1979 *Eketorp: fortification and settlement on Öland/Sweden: the setting.* Stockholm.

Nobis, G.
1955 Die Haustiere von Tofting. In Tofting, edited by A. Bantelmann. *Offa Bücher* 12:114–134.

Nobis, G.
1973 Tierreste aus einer Siedlung der vorrömischen Eisenzeit bei Sünninghausen, Kr. Beckum. *Bodenaltertümer Westfalens* 13:143–164.

Persson, O.
1973–1974 Bestämning av benmaterial från Kvarnby. In En bronsåldersboplats vid Kvarnby, edited by D. Widholm. *Kring Malmöhus* 4:43–89.

Pohle, H.
1964 Die Tierknochen. In Die jungbronzezeitliche Siedlung von Berlin-Lichterfelde, edited by A. von Müller. *Berliner Beiträge zur Vor- und Frühgeschichte* 9:58–70.

Prummel, W.
1978 Vlees, gevogelte en vis. *Westerheem* 27:282–294.

Prummel, W.
1979 Environment and stock-raising in Dutch settlements: the Bronze Age and the Middle Ages. *Palaeohistoria* 21:91–107.

Randsborg, K.
1980 *The Viking Age in Denmark: the formation of a state.* Duckworth, London.

Randsborg, K.
1982 Rank, rights and resources: an archaeological perspective from Denmark. In *Ranking, resource and exchange,* edited by C. Renfrew and S. Shennan, pp. 132–139. Cambridge University Press, Cambridge, England.

Reece, R.
1980 Town and country: the end of Roman Britain. *World Archaeology* 12:77–92.

Reece, R.
1981 The third century: crisis or change? In *The Roman West in the third century: contributions from archaeology and history,* edited by A. King and M. Henig, pp. 27–38. British Archaeological Reports, International Series 109, Oxford, England.

Reichstein, H.
1972 Einige Bemerkungen zu den Haustierfunden auf der Feddersen Wierde und vergleichbarer Siedlungen in Nordwestdeutschland. *Die Kunde* 23:142–156.

Reichstein, H.
1973 Die Haustier-Knochenfunde der Feddersen Wierde. *Probleme der Küstenforschung im südlichen Nordseegebiet* 10:95–112.

Reichstein, H., K.-C. Taege, H.-P. Vogel, and D. Heinrich
1980 Untersuchungen an Tierknochen von der frühslawische Wehranlage Bischofswarder an Grossen Plönersee. In *Bosau: Untersuchung einer Siedlungskammer in Ostholstein* (Vol. 4), edited by H. Hinz, pp. 9–96. Neumünster.

Schmid, P., and W. H. Zimmerman
1976 Flögeln: zur Struktur einer Siedlung des 1. bis 5. Jhdts. N.Chr. im Küstengebiet der südlichen Nordsee. *Probleme der Küstenforschung im südlichen Nordseegebiet* 11:1–77.

Sellstedt, H.
1966 Djurbensmaterial fran järnåldersboplatserne vid Ormöga och Sörby-tall på Öland. *Forvännen* 61:1–13.

Stenberger, M., and O. Klindt-Jensen (editors)
1955 *Vallhagar*. Copenhagen.

Stork, M., and J. Boessneck
1973 Tierknochenfunde aus der vorgeschichtlichen Elzrandsiedlung in der Gemarkung Rundstedt, Kr. Helmstedt. *Neue Ausgrabungen und Forschungen in Niedersachsen* 8:171–178.

Teichert, M.
1964 Die Tierreste von den jungbronzezeitlichen Burgwällen Kratzenburg und Gühlen-Glienicke. *Prähistorische Zeitschrift* 42(102):107–142.

Teichert, M.
1968 Die Tierreste der germanischen Siedlung Wüste Kunersdorf, Kr. Seelow. *Veröffentlichungen des Museums für Ur- und Frühgeschichte Potsdam* 4:101–125.

Teichert, M.
1971 Die Tierreste aus einer germanischen Siedlung bei Kablow, Kr. Königs Wusterhausen. *Veröffentlichungen des Museums für Ur- und Frühgeschichte Potsdam* 6:151–161.

Tolonen, M.
1976 On the prehistoric agriculture in Sääksmäki, S. Finland. *Finsk Museum* 83:67–84.

Waterbolk, H. T.
1973 Odoorn im frühen Mittelalter: Bericht der Grabung 1966. *Neue Ausgrabungen und Funde in Niedersachsen* 8:25–89.

Waterbolk, H. T.
1979 Siedlungskontinuität im Küstengebiet der Nordsee zwischen Rhein und Elbe. *Probleme der Küstenforschung im südlichen Nordseegebiet* 13:1–21.

Waterbolk, H. T., and O. H. Harsema
1979 Medieval farmsteads in Gasselte. *Palaeohistoria* 21:227–265.

Widgren, M.
1977 Pollenanalys från sjön Flären, Östergötland, kulturlandskapsutveckling från brosålder till nutid. *Kvartärgeologiska avdelningen*, Uppsala Universitet 73.

Wielowiejski, J. (editor)
1981 Późny okres Latenski i okres Rzymski. In *Prahistoria ziem Polskich*, edited by W. Hensel and Z. Bukowski. Warsaw.

Willerding, U.
1977 Über Klima-Entwicklung und Vegetationsverhältnisse im Zeitraum Eisenzeit bis Mittelalter. In Das Dorf der Eisenzeit und das frühe Mittelalter, edited by H. Jankuhn et al. *Abhandlungen der Akademie der Wissenschaften in Göttingen, Philologisch-historische Klasse* 101:357–405.

Willerding, U.
1979 Botanische Beiträge zur Kenntnis von Vegetation und Ackerbau im Mittelalter. In Geschichtwissenschaft und Archäologie: Untersuchungen zur Siedlungs-, Wirtschafts-, und Kirchengeschichte, edited by H. Jankuhn and R. Wenskus. *Vorträge und Forschungen* 22:271–353.

Winge, H.
   1919 Dyreknogler fra Bronzealders Bopladser. *Aarbøger for Nordisk Oldkyndighed og Historie*
      :93–105.
Winkelmann, W.
   1954 Eine westfälische Siedlung des 8. Jahrhunderts bei Warendorf, Kr. Warendorf. *Germania*
      32:189–213.
Zawatka, D., and H. Reichstein
   1977 Untersuchungen an Tierknochenfunden von den römerzeitlichen Siedlungsplätzen Be-
      tumersiel und Jegumkloster an der unteren Ems/Ostfriesland. *Probleme der Küsten-*
      forschung im südlichen Nordseegebiet 12:85–115.
Zeist, W. van
   1968 Prehistoric and early historic food plants in the Netherlands. *Palaeohistoria* 14:41–173.
Zeist, W. van, and R. M. Palfenier-Vegter,
   1979 Agriculture in medieval Gasselte. *Palaeohistoria* 21:267–299.
Zimmerman, W. H. (editor)
   1978 Die Siedlung Flögeln bei Cuxhaven. In *Sachsen und Angelsachsen,* edited by F. Laux, pp.
      363–386. Hamburg.

Index

STUDIES IN ARCHAEOLOGY

Consulting Editor: Stuart Struever

Department of Anthropology
Northwestern University
Evanston, Illinois

Charles R. McGimsey III. **Public Archeology**

Lewis R. Binford. **An Archaeological Perspective**

Muriel Porter Weaver. **The Aztecs, Maya, and Their Predecessors: Archaeology of Mesoamerica**

Joseph W. Michels. **Dating Methods in Archaeology**

C. Garth Sampson. **The Stone Age Archaeology of Southern Africa**

Fred T. Plog. **The Study of Prehistoric Change**

Patty Jo Watson (Ed.). **Archaeology of the Mammoth Cave Area**

George C. Frison (Ed.). **The Casper Site: A Hell Gap Bison Kill on the High Plains**

W. Raymond Wood and R. Bruce McMillan (Eds.). **Prehistoric Man and His Environments: A Case Study in the Ozark Highland**

Kent V. Flannery (Ed.). **The Early Mesoamerican Village**

Charles E. Cleland (Ed.). **Cultural Change and Continuity: Essays in Honor of James Bennett Griffin**

Michael B. Schiffer. **Behavioral Archeology**

Fred Wendorf and Romuald Schild. **Prehistory of the Nile Valley**

Michael A. Jochim. **Hunter-Gatherer Subsistence and Settlement: A Predictive Model**

Stanley South. **Method and Theory in Historical Archeology**

Timothy K. Earle and Jonathon E. Ericson (Eds.). **Exchange System in Prehistory**

Stanley South (Ed.). **Research Strategies in Historical Archaeology**

John E. Yellen. **Archaeological Approaches to the Present: Models for Reconstructing the Past**

Lewis R. Binford (Ed.). **For Theory Building in Archaeology: Essays on Faunal Remains, Aquatic Resources, Spatial Analysis, and Systemic Modeling**

James N. Hill and Joel Gunn (Eds.). **The Individual in Prehistory: Studies of Variability in Style in Prehistoric Technologies**

Michael B. Schiffer and George J. Gumerman (Eds.). **Conservation Archaeology: A Guide for Cultural Resource Management Studies**

Thomas F. King, Patricia Parker Hickman, and Gary Berg. **Anthropology in Historic Preservation: Caring for Culture's Clutter**

Richard E. Blanton. **Monte Albán: Settlement Patterns at the Ancient Zapotec Capital**

R. E. Taylor and Clement W. Meighan. **Chronologies in New World Archaeology**

Bruce D. Smith. **Prehistoric Patterns of Human Behavior: A Case Study in the Mississippi Valley**

Barbara L. Stark and Barbara Voorhies (Eds.). **Prehistoric Coastal Adaptations: The Economy and Ecology of Maritime Middle America**

Charles L. Redman, Mary Jane Berman, Edward V. Curtin, William T. Langhorne, Nina M. Versaggi, and Jeffery C.Wanser (Eds.). **Social Archaeology: Beyond Subsistence and Dating**

Bruce D. Smith (Ed.). **Mississippian Settlement Patterns**

Lewis R. Binford. **Nunamiut Ethnoarchaeology**

J. Barto Arnold III and Robert Weddle. **The Nautical Archeology of Padre Island: The Spanish Shipwrecks of 1554**

Sarunas Milisauskas. **European Prehistory**

Brian Hayden (Ed.). **Lithic Use-Wear Analysis**

William T. Sanders, Jeffrey R. Parsons, and Robert S. Santley. **The Basin of Mexico: Ecological Processes in the Evolution of a Civilization**

David L. Clarke. **Analytical Archaeologist: Collected Papers of David L. Clarke. Edited and Introduced by His Colleagues**

Arthur E. Spiess. **Reindeer and Caribou Hunters: An Archaeological Study**

Elizabeth S. Wing and Antoinette B. Brown. **Paleonutrition: Method and Theory in Prehistoric Foodways**

John W. Rick. **Prehistoric Hunters of the High Andes**

Timothy K. Earle and Andrew L. Christenson (Eds.). **Modeling Change in Prehistoric Economics**

Thomas F. Lynch (Ed.). **Guitarrero Cave: Early Man in the Andes**

Fred Wendorf and Romuald Schild. **Prehistory of the Eastern Sahara**

Henri Laville, Jean-Philippe Rigaud, and James Sackett. **Rock Shelters of the Perigord: Stratigraphy and Archaeological Succession**

Duane C. Anderson and Holmes A. Semken, Jr. (Eds.). **The Cherokee Excavations: Holocene Ecology and Human Adaptations in Northwestern Iowa**

Anna Curtenius Roosevelt. **Parmana: Prehistoric Maize and Manioc Subsistence along the Amazon and Orinoco**

Fekri A. Hassan. **Demographic Archaeology**

G. Barker. **Landscape and Society: Prehistoric Central Italy**

Lewis R. Binford. **Bones: Ancient Men and Modern Myths**

Richard A. Gould and Michael B. Schiffer (Eds.). **Modern Material Culture: The Archaeology of Us**

Muriel Porter Weaver. **The Aztecs, Maya, and Their Predecessors: Archaeology of Mesoamerica, 2nd edition**

Arthur S. Keene. **Prehistoric Foraging in a Temperate Forest: A Linear Programming Model**

Ross H. Cordy. **A Study of Prehistoric Social Change: The Development of Complex Societies in the Hawaiian Islands**

C. Melvin Aikens and Takayasu Higuchi. **Prehistory of Japan**

Kent V. Flannery (Ed.). **Maya Subsistence: Studies in Memory of Dennis E. Puleston**

Dean R. Snow (Ed.). **Foundations of Northeast Archaeology**

Charles S. Spencer. **The Cuicatlán Cañada and Monte Albán: A Study of Primary State Formation**

Steadman Upham. **Polities and Power: An Economic and Political History of the Western Pueblo**

Carol Cramer. **Village Ethnoarchaeology: Rural Iran in Archaeological Perspective**

Michael J. O'Brien, Robert E. Warren, and Dennis E. Lewarch (Eds.). **The Cannon Reservoir Human Ecology Project: An Archaeological Study of Cultural Adaptations in the Southern Prairie Peninsula**

Jonathon E. Ericson and Timothy K. Earle (Eds.). **Contexts for Prehistoric Exchange**

Merrilee H. Salmon. **Philosophy and Archaeology**

Vincas P. Steponaitis. **Ceramics, Chronology, and Community Patterns: An Archaeological Study at Moundville**

George C. Frison and Dennis J. Stanford. **The Agate Basin Site: A Record of the Paleoindian Occupation of the Northwestern High Plains**

James A. Moore and Arthur S. Keene (Eds.). **Archaeological Hammers and Theories**

Lewis R. Binford. **Working at Archaeology**

William J. Folan, Ellen R. Kintz, and Laraine A. Fletcher. **Coba: A Classic Maya Metropolis**

David A. Friedel and Jeremy A. Sabloff. **Cozumel: Late Maya Settlement Patterns**

John M. O'Shea. **Mortuary Variability: An Archaeological Investigation**

Lewis R. Binford. **Faunal Remains From Klasies River Mouth**

John Hyslop. **The Inka Road System**